LEARNERS,
LEARNING AND ASSESSMENT

Companion Volumes

The companion volumes in this series are: *Curriculum in Context* edited by Bob Moon and Patricia Murphy, *Learning and Knowledge* edited by Robert McCormick and Carrie Paechter and *Learners and Pedagogy* edited by Jenny Leach and Bob Moon.

All of these Readers are part of a course, Learning, Curriculum and Assessment, that is itself part of the Open University MA Programme.

The Open University MA in Education

The Open University MA in Education is now firmly established as the most popular postgraduate degree for education professionals in Europe, with over 3,500 students registering each year. The MA in Education is designed particularly for those with experience of teaching, the advisory service, educational administration or allied fields.

Structure of the MA

The MA is a modular degree, and students are therefore free to select from a range of options the programme which best fits in with their interests and professional goals. Specialist lines in management and primary education are also available. Study in the Open University's Advanced Diploma and Certificate Programmes can also be counted towards the MA, and successful study in the MA programme entitles students to apply for entry into the Open University Doctorate in Education programme.

COURSES CURRENTLY AVAILABLE:
- Management
- Child Development
- Primary Education
- Learning, Curriculum and Assessment
- Inclusive Education
- Language and Literacy
- Mentoring
- Education, Training and Employment
- Gender in Education
- Educational Research
- Science Education
- Adult Learners
- Maths Education

OU supported open learning

The MA in Education programme provides great flexibility. Students study at their own pace, in their own time, anywhere in the European Union. They receive specially prepared study materials, supported by tutorials, thus offering the chance to work with other students.

The Doctorate in Education

The Doctorate in Education is a new part-time doctoral degree, combining taught courses, research methods and a dissertation designed to meet the needs of professionals in education and related areas who are seeking to extend and deepen their knowledge and understanding of contemporary educational issues. It should help them to:

- develop appropriate skills in educational research and enquiry

- carry out research in order to contribute to professional knowledge and practice.

The Doctorate in Education builds upon successful study within the Open University MA in Education programme.

How to apply

If you would like to register for this programme, or simply to find out more information, please write for the *Professional Development in Education* prospectus to the Course Reservations Centre, PO Box 724, The Open University, Walton Hall, Milton Keynes, MK7 6ZS, UK (Telephone 0[044] 1908 653231).

LEARNERS,
LEARNING AND ASSESSMENT

edited by
Patricia Murphy
at The Open University

P·C·P
Paul Chapman
Publishing Ltd

Paul Chapman Publishing

in association with

The Open University

Paul Chapman Publishing Ltd
A SAGE Publications Company
6 Bonhill Street
London EC2A 4PU

SAGE Publications Inc.
2455 Teller Road
Thousand Oaks, California 91320

SAGE Publications India Pvt Ltd
32, M-Block Market
Greater Kailash-I
New Delhi 110 048

British Library Cataloguing in Publication Data
A catalogue record for this book is available from the British Library.

ISBN 1 85396 425 5
ISBN 1 85396 424 7 (pbk)

Library of Congress catalog card number available

Typeset by Dorwyn Ltd, Rowlands Castle
Printed in Great Britain by The Cromwell Press, Trowbridge

A B C D E F G H   3 2 1 0 9

Contents

Series Introduction

Learning, curriculum and assessment are at the core of the educational process. In the politically charged and value laden context of curriculum reform, an understanding of well grounded evidence about learning theories, knowledge and teaching and assessment practice is essential. Policy development and educational practice in a number of countries is being built around new understandings about the nature of mind, an acknowledgement that knowledge has long outgrown the traditional discipline categorisations of schools and universities and a realisation that learning and assessment is an essentially social process.

This book is one of a series of four readers that gather together recent research and writing around a number of key issues and themes in curriculum. The books, therefore, act as sources from which a number of narratives can be deduced. The broader contexts of curriculum are considered in the first volume of the series, the remaining three books focus us on learning and assessment, knowledge and pedagogy. The selection is a resource for anyone seeking a deeper understanding of the way any curriculum, formal and informal, is constructed, enacted and experienced. The accompanying Open University course (E836 *Learning, Curriculum and Assessment*) sets out to show one interpretation of the relevance of these ideas to practice in schools, colleges and other educational settings.

Jenny Leach
Robert McCormick
Bob Moon
Patricia Murphy
The Open University, Milton Keynes

Acknowledgements

The editor and publishers wish to thank the following for permission to use copyright material: American Educational Research Association for P. Cobb, 'Where is the Mind? . . .', *Educational Researcher*, 23:7 (1994) pp. 13–20. Copyright © 1994 American Educational Research Association; and material from J. Hiebert, P.T. Carpenter, E. Fennema, K. Fuson, P. Human, H. Murray, A. Olivier and D. Wearne, 'Problem Solving as a Basis for Reform in Curriculum and Instruction : The Case of Mathematics', *Educational Researcher*, 25:4 (1996) pp. 12–20. Copyright © 1996 American Educational Research Association; Baywood Publishing Co., Inc for material from Sadhana Puntambekar and Benedict du Boulay, 'Design and Development of MIST – A System to Help Students Develop Meta-cognition', *Journal of Educational Computing Research*, 16:1 (1997) pp. 1–14, 30–1. Copyright © 1997 Baywood Publishing Co., Inc; Billett, S. and Rose, J. (1997) Securing conceptual development in workplaces, *Australian Journal of Adult and Community Education*, 37 (1), pp. 12–26; Blackwell Publications for material from B. Cooper and M. Dunne, 'Anyone for tennis? Social Class Differences in Children's Responses to National Curriculum Mathematics Testing', *Sociological Review*, 46 (1998) pp. 116–43. Copyright © Editorial Board of Sociological Review; The British Psychological Society for material from J.A. Sloboda, J.W. Davidson and M.J.A. Howe, 'Is everyone musical?', *The Psychologist*, August (1994) pp. 349–53; Cambridge University Press for material from J. Lave and E. Wenger, *Situated Learning: Legitimate Peripheral Participation* (1991) pp. 29–34; and R.P. McDermott, 'The acquisition of a child by a learning disability' in Chalklin and Lave, eds. *Understanding Practice Perspectives on Activity and Context* (1993) pp. 269–95; Carfax Publishing Ltd for material from Y. Bennett, 'The Validity and Reliability of Assessments and Self-assessment of Work-based Learning', *Assessment and Evaluation in Higher Education*, 18:2 (1993) pp. 83–92; Elsevier Science for D. Macdonald and R. Brooker, 'Assessment issues in a performance-based subject: A case study of physical education', *Studies in Educational Evaluation*, 23:1 (1997) pp. 83–102; and material from H. Gruber, L.C. Law, H. Mandl and A. Renkl, 'Situated Learning and Transfer' in P. Relman and N. Spade, eds., *Learning in Humans and Machines* (1995) pp. 168–78, 182–4; Lawrence Erlbaum Associates, Inc for material from E. Bredo, 'Reconstructing Educational Psychology', *Educational Psychologist*, 29:1 (1994) pp. 23–45; Kluwer Academic Publishers for material from H. Gardner, 'Assessment in Context: The Alternative to Standardized Testing' in B.R. Gifford and M.C. O'Connor, eds., *Changing Assessments: Alternative Views of Aptitude Achievement and Instruction* (1992) pp. 77–116; Oxford University Press, Inc for material from Barbara Rogoff, *Apprenticeship in Thinking: Cognitive Development in Social Context*, pp. 137–150. Copyright © 1990 by Barbara Rogoff; Routledge for material from M. Wallace, 'When is experiential learning not experiential learning?' in G. Claxton, T. Atkinson, M. Osborn and M. Wallace, eds., *Liberating the Learner* (1996) pp. 16–31; The Wylie Agency, Inc on behalf of the author for material from Oliver Sacks, 'Making up the Mind', *The New York Review*, April 8 (1993). Copyright © 1993 by Oliver Sacks.

Every effort has been made to trace the copyright holders but if any have been inadvertently overlooked the publishers will be pleased to make the necessary arrangement at the first opportunity.

Introduction

Patricia Murphy

The book explores some current and influential thinking about learning and assessment. Along with the other volumes in this series it provides theoretical tools for examining: the dynamic between curriculum, assessment and pedagogy; the implications of different theories of mind and of learning for the development of teaching and learning; and examples of aspects of these theories translated into practice for the different phases and settings in which formal education occurs. The contents of the book provide one important element of a framework for understanding and developing practice. Consequently, although pedagogy is not in the title it is fundamental to the book. McDermott (Chapter 1), for example, refers to learning as the other side of an institutionalized dance called teaching. The relationship between learning and teaching is explored in the book; and what lies behind understandings about this relationship, i.e. the views of mind and of knowledge that underpin educational practices.

For McDermott 'Learning is in the conditions that bring people together and organize a point of contact that allows for particular pieces of information to take on relevance . . . Learning does not belong to individual persons but to the various conversations of which they are part' (p. 292). Such views of how we learn are, however, contested. Theories of learning have always changed but currently the field is seen to be in a state of upheaval. Two approaches to mind have emerged in the last decade that are seen by many to represent a clash of cultures. These approaches have grown out of two theoretical traditions, *situated cognition* and *symbolic cognition*. That is not to suggest that these two are the only approaches that exist. However, the tension between these two 'families' of theories is giving rise to a great deal of productive thinking about learners, learning and assessment which this book is concerned with. The two approaches are typically characterized in a number of simple ways. For example symbolic processing is said to separate the learner from the environment. The focus in understanding learning in this approach is therefore the individual's internal mental processing and the symbolic representations of mind. In the situated approach human knowledge and interaction are seen as inseparable from the world. Thus in this approach to cognition the focus is on the structures of the world and how they constrain and guide human behaviour. Within either family of theories there is considerable differences in perspective, even contradictory ones. At the moment though they are often presented as precise and exclusive approaches – one necessarily right and one necessarily wrong.

In the contributions in the first part (Sections 1 and 2) of the book the differences between the approaches in their representations of the nature of knowledge, learning and learners are considered. These determine in part what we understand about what to teach and how to teach it; and, in turn, what to assess and how to assess it. This analysis provides essential insights into the curriculum dynamic. Curriculum is negotiated and defined at a number of levels in a variety of arenas. Examining curriculum at the various levels where it is defined and redefined enables us to better understand and so challenge practice, our own and others'. Looking across the three message systems – curriculum, assessment and pedagogy – through which formal educational knowledge is realized (Bernstein, 1971) to consider how learning and knowledge construction are viewed also allows the possibility of identifying contradictions, which in turn allow for a better understanding of the possibilities for change. If views of mind include views of the nature of knowledge and of learners then they have major implications for how we assess learning and, importantly, how we interpret and use the outcomes of any assessment process. Similarly, if assessment as Broadfoot (1996) suggests, is the key determinant of education systems it is necessary to understand the views of learning, learners and knowledge behind assessment policy and practice.

Cobb (Chapter 9) suggests that the tension between the two approaches to mind creates 'pedagogical dilemmas'. As Hendry and King (1994) observe for example, many educationalists practise 'a kind of double think' in which they believe that teaching is the transmission of knowledge and yet view learning as an active process where individuals create meaning rather than receive it.

Individual theorists in any one 'family' offer alternative views of knowledge and indeed what it might mean to know. Understanding how we come to know is central to pedagogy and assessment. Sections 3 and 4 of the book consider the implications of different theories for practice. The contributions in the sections address a range of questions: What do the theories inform us about the *settings* and *activities* that promote understanding? What do they suggest about *what understandings* people need to develop through formal education? Are the specific teaching and assessment practices currently in use in institutions consonant with the views of mind inherent in curriculum definitions? How do we move from theoretical insights to develop practices that realize these insights? In these sections of the book we move between examples of 'theory out to practice' and examples of 'practice back to theory' to address these questions.

The exploration of views of mind begins first with a look at how we think of 'learners' and the consequences of this for how we view curriculum and learning. McDermott (Chapter 1) provides a rich perspective on this through the story of a learner in a range of curriculum settings. With these insights we then explore different perspectives on mind in the next three chapters in Section 2. Bredo (Chapter 2) contrasts the two families, the situated and symbolic, through a number of dualisms, mind and body, language and reality, and individual and society. He also links current theorizing and its context to that of the educational theorist, Dewey, who published at the beginning of the century. Bredo argues that for future progress in education we need to bring together different approaches in part-whole harmony as Dewey advocated so many years ago. Chapter 3 (Sloboda *et al.*) looks at the issue of innate 'talent' and how views of innate abilities have dominated education and continue in the folklore of professional and educational communities. In the chapter the community considered is that of musicians. Sack's abridged review of Edelman's biological theory of mind (Chapter 4) provides a neuroscientific perspective against which to think about educational theories of mind and of knowing.

In Chapter 5 Rogoff, drawing on her own theorizing about young children's development and learning, looks at aspects of the learning process and how influential theorists in education, Piaget and Vygotsky, perceived the role of social interaction. She highlights the similarities of the two theories in emphasizing the importance of shared understanding in social interaction. She sees, however, an essential difference in the conception of intersubjectivity and describes this as the focus on the individual versus the social. For Vygotsky shared thinking provides the opportunity for participation in joint decision-making. For Piaget interaction is not about the construction of joint, but rather individual, understanding. Thus other people *provide* social information in Piaget's process whereas for Vygotsky the process takes place *between* people. These differences are highly significant in both determining how interactions in learning situations might be established and fostered and in the view of what constitutes an outcome and how to judge it.

Chapter 6 is an excerpt from Lave and Wenger's seminal book on *Situated Learning*. Their perspective based on their work with adults raises many challenges for how we view the process of learning, of teaching and of knowledge, and therefore its assessment. They argue that learning is about becoming a participant, knowing is therefore judged in terms of belonging and participation within a community. What constitutes knowledge is the practices, activities and discourse of the community. If learning is achieved and revealed by 'doing' then this has major implications for teaching and assessment practice.

The extract from Gardner's writing (Chapter 7) demonstrates how a situated view of mind challenges traditional views of intelligence and of testing. He provides two case studies of assessment strategies to show how views of learning and assessment practice can be integrated so that what is assessed and how it is assessed are consistent with current understanding about the nature of learners, learning and knowledge. The projects reported are based in early years, middle and high school settings.

In Chapter 8 Black continues this examination of assessment practice. He contrasts behaviourist psychology with social constructivist views of learning and the implications of these theories for assessment practice. This leads him to prioritize formative assessment and he reports on studies that demonstrate the learning gains achieved by this assessment, and strategies for developing it in school settings. Black argues that assessment like learning is a social process and warns of the danger for learning and curriculum of using practices based on outmoded theories of learning.

In the final chapter of this section Cobb (Chapter 9) offers another view of the similarities and differences between situated and symbolic perspectives and offers a way of co-ordinating these for use.

In the third section of the book we turn to examine some of the curriculum implications of views of learning and assessment. Hiebert *et al.* (Chapter 10) adopt a particular situated view of learning. On the basis of this they advocate curriculum and teaching reforms that allow students to *problematize* subjects. They describe an important distinction between the *acquisition* and *application* of knowledge and, through examples from mathematics classrooms, how the latter can be achieved. Their analysis, however, leaves important question marks about the goals of such a curriculum in terms of what knowledge is valued. Macdonald and Brooker (Chapter 11) address this by looking at a state-wide assessment reform in the performance-based subject of physical education. They describe a study involving Australian High School teachers and students which attempted to implement authentic process assessment and the successes and difficulties that were experienced. We continue with this exploration of assessment and learning by looking at trends in vocational assessment in the UK and more widely in Europe (Wolf, Chapter 12). This raises the issues of competencies and core skills, how these are defined and assessed, and the problems of developing authentic assessment practices that are viable in the workplace. The section ends by looking across different theories of learning and views of knowledge to examine the concept of transfer. Transfer is a highly contested notion between the two approaches to mind. Some theorists argue that the concept is '*seriously misconceived*' (Lave, 1988, p. 39). Many others claim that it is a *rare event*. Gruber *et al.* (Chapter 13) offer a number of current views about the nature of 'generalizable' understanding and its use. Wallace (Chapter 14) reflects on his own professional development experience and the problems he found with transfer across settings.

In the final section of the book the chapters look at key learning and assessment processes and how these have been implemented and understood in practice. These include how to foster collaboration between learners, and develop metacognition and the impact of gendered learning on this (Puntambekar and du Boulay, Chapter 15; Murphy, Chapter 16). Stredder (Chapter 18) explores bridging strategies for building between learners' knowledge and institutional learning. She looks at the important issue of authenticity in the sense that learning has to be personally meaningful to learners. Stredder demonstrates through case studies in primary schools how learners' engagement was fostered and maintained and the positive cognitive and affective gains that accrued as a consequence. Cooper and Dunne (Chapter 19) look at this aspect of authenticity as well but from a critical review of national assessment practice in England in primary and secondary schools. Like Black they highlight the social nature of the assessment process and are concerned about the differential access of sub-groups to the cultural resources that schools demand, and how this leads to the under-estimation of some students' achievements. The final chapters are concerned with workplace learning and assessment. Bennett (Chapter 17) looks at issues of authentic assessment in work-based learning environments and how assessment concepts such as validity and reliability are determined by views of learning and of knowledge; Billett and Rose (Chapter 20) report on strategies for developing conceptual understanding in the workplace which reflect learning as a constructive process and knowledge as socially mediated.

The book's aim to cover a range of learning and assessment issues and to provide a strong theoretical grounding means that difficult selections have had to be made. In so doing it is clear that situated approaches to learning are gaining ground in education but there continues to be a mismatch between curriculum and assessment rhetoric and teaching and assessment practice. The debates covered in the book and the examples provided reveal the difficulties of addressing this mismatch but provide ways of thinking about it and possibilities for addressing it. (Possibilities which are explored further in the other volumes in the series.) Furthermore, the contributions to the book argue against attempts to look for overarching single theories of education but rather to use theories as tools to advance rather than constrain our thinking and our practice.

References

Bernstein, B. (1971) On the classification and framing of educational knowledge, in Young, M. F. (ed.) *Knowledge and Control*, London, Collier-Macmillan.
Broadfoot, P. (1996) *Education, Assessment and Society*, Milton Keynes, Open University Press.
Hendry, G. D. and King, R. C. (1994) On theory of learning and knowledge: educational implications of advances in neuroscience, *Science Education*, 78 (3), pp. 223–253.
Lave, J. (1988) *Cognition in Practice*, Cambridge, Cambridge University Press.

SECTION 1
THINKING ABOUT LEARNING

1

On Becoming Labelled –
the Story of Adam[1]

R. P. McDermott

Conceived as a deficiency in capacity, feeblemindedness *isolates* the subject by virtue of that deficiency. In seeking a definite cause of feeblemindedness one is denying that it can have any *meaning* – that is, a history – or that it may correspond to a *situation*.

(Maud Mannoni, 1972, p. 44)

The interiority of pains, afterimages and spots before the eyes cannot impugn the overt, public character of cognitive skills, or the external aims of practical moral decisions. It is only when mental activity regains its place within everyday life, therefore that its outer directness becomes finally clear.

(Stephen Toulmin, 1985, p. 17)

The emergence of institutionalized education is accompanied by a crisis in diffuse education, which goes directly from practice to practice without passing through discourse. Excellence has ceased to exist once people start asking whether it can be taught, i.e., as soon as the objective confrontation of different styles of excellence makes it necessary to say what goes without saying, justify what is taken for granted, make an ought-to-be and an ought-to-do out of what had up to then been regarded as the only way to be and do.

(Pierre Bourdieu, 1977, p. 200)

Sometimes if you try harder and harder, it just gets worser and worser.

(Adam, 1977, third grade)

From 1976 to 1978, Michael Cole, Lois Hood, and I gathered a series of videotapes from one classroom of eight- and nine-year-old children in various settings. Our effort at the time was to locate the children 'thinking' aloud in the hope that we could identify naturally occurring examples of some mental activities that seemed so well defined in experimental settings. [. . .] If experimental psychology was to be useful in the description of individual learners, as different perhaps from the task of modeling how 'minds' might work, then a tighter and more systematic fit would have to be achieved between experimental tasks and the demands on people as they lived their lives and plied their learning.

This chapter has been edited.

Our suspicion, and ultimately our conclusion, was that little such fit could be expected. [. . .] The problem was that in everyday life persons and tasks never quite stand still; the gap between subject and object, between stimulus and response, could not be filled by positing models of what was happening inside the organism, for the reason that neither subject nor object, neither stimulus nor response, was available for analysis as it was sequenced in the experience of persons in the lived world. In everyday life, tasks could be ongoingly altered, reframed, and pushed aside in ways that made it impossible for an experimenter to anticipate or to take systematically into account. [. . .]

As an offshoot of our main concern, we became fascinated by how we might describe the learning biographies of different children. There was Nadine, who seemed to know most things and to learn quickly whatever she did not already know; there was Reggie, who seemed to know a great deal about everything but how to get along with his peers; there was Matt, who hid out for the year and seemingly never engaged in any official, school-learning task; and there was Adam, who suffered as an officially described Learning Disabled (LD) child, but who seemed always eager to try. It was this last child who most captured our focus. As soon as we went to tell his story of course, we were immersed once again in the problems of how to do an ecologically valid description. His head did not seem to work very well on isolated cognitive tasks, either on standardized tests given by the school reading specialist or on the more theoretically sensitive tasks we gave him. Did we really want to describe what went on in his head? Just what was the phenomenon under investigation anyway? Where is LD to be found? Is it to be 'found' at all? Is it anything more than a way of talking about some children and available for analysis only as a kind of rhetoric? Might it not best be described as a political label, a resource for keeping people in their place, a 'display board' for the contradictions of our school system? We tried to consider all the options (Cole and Traupmann, 1981; Hood, McDermott and Cole, 1980). The present chapter revives Adam's story in order to raise some questions about various approaches to the explanation of learning failures and to provide a focus for an account of notions of context and learning.

The Argument

[. . .] LD is usually assumed to be acquired by children due to some lapse in their development. By the normal line of reasoning, the child is the unit of analysis, and the disability is a mishap that scars a child's road to competence. This chapter suggests an alternative way of thinking about the problem. LD exists as a category in our culture, and it will acquire a certain proportion of our children as long as it is given life in the organization of tasks, skills, and evaluations in our schools. In the daily construction of settings called educative in American culture, moments are put aside for the discovery, description, and re-mediation of certain children who display particular traits [. . .] Mehan, Hertwick and Meihls, 1986; Sarason and Doris, 1979). Although the folk theory has it that the traits (an inability to pay attention, an occasional lapse in word access, trouble with phonics, etc.) belong to the child and are the source of both the disordered behavior and the subsequent label, it is possible to argue that it is the labels that precede any child's entry into the world and that these labels, well-established resting places in adult conversations, stand poised to take their share from each new generation. What Goffman (1979) claimed for gender identity is no less true for LD:

> What the human nature of males and females really consists of, then is a capacity to learn to provide and to read depictions of masculinity and femininity and a willingness to adhere to a schedule for presenting these pictures. . . . One might just as well say there is no gender identity. There is only a schedule for the portrayal of gender . . . . There is only evidence of the practice between the sexes of choreographing behaviorally a portrait of relationship. (p. 8)

We might just as well say there is no such thing as LD, only a social practice of displaying, noticing, documenting, remediating, and explaining it. This theoretical shift makes LD no less real to the participants of life in schools where occasions for displaying LD are so frequent, but it should at least make us wonder what we all do that makes LD so commonly sensible and ubiquitous in our experiences with institutionalized learning. *Notice that the claim here is not that we have no children who for whatever reason learn much slower or in different ways than others. It is only that without social arrangements for making something of differential rates of learning, there is no such thing as LD.* In America, we make something of differential rates of learning to the point that the rate of learning rather than the learning is the total measure of the learner. In another culture, or in our own if one is rich enough to receive an appropriately protective education, learning problems might slow a person down, but they do not have to destroy the learner. Not all cultures make a fuss over different ways of learning. We seem to be extreme in this regard. There are great constraints on how childhood can be constructed in any given culture (Belmonte, 1989; Chamboredon and Prevot, 1975; Poster, 1980; Ramirez, 1990; Wartofsky, 1983). In allowing schools to become the site of sorting for recruitment into the wider social structure, we may have gone too far for the collective good. We may have made it necessary to invent occasions – millions of them – to make learning disabilities institutionally and unnecessarily consequential.

The good sense of a social structural and cultural account of LD can emerge from questions about the institutional arrangements served by having so many children designated LD. By institutional arrangements, we must consider everything from the most local level of the classroom to the more inclusive level of inequities throughout the political economy (preferably from both ends of the continuum at the same time). After following Adam for 18 months, we gave up on specifying his traits as the explanation of his behavior and began talking instead about what happened around him daily that seemed to organize his moments as an LD person. Even at this most local level, we could find that many people were involved in Adam's problem. On any occasion of his looking inattentive, for example, it took Adam to look away at just the right time, but it took many others to construct the right time for Adam to look away; it took others to look away from his looking away, and still more to discover his looking away, to make something of it, to diagnose it, to document it, and to remediate it. Whatever was Adam's problem inside his head, we had forced on us the recognition that Adam had plenty of problems all around him, in every person on the scene, in most every scene called educative. Analytically, the inside of his head became less interesting to us. The work that the participants did around Adam's disability and the sequencing of that work with other conversations required of persons in education became the phenomena of interest. It is in this vein that we claimed that Adam's disability was not just visible in the sense that the world was a neutral medium for what he could not do, but that the world was precisely organized for making his disability apparent, that he was the negative achievement of a school system that insisted that everyone do better than everyone else (Hood, McDermott and Cole, 1980).

Context

To gain support for such an account, a description would have to focus less on the traits of the children labeled and more on the contexts for the interactional display and management of the traits at just the right moments for all to notice. Context becomes a key term, not just in the common sense of the named organizational 'thing' in which a 'disability' becomes visible, but in the more demanding sense of the analytic device by which members' activities are shown to be constitutive of both the named organizational setting and the disability in ways that make them a function of each other and subject to erasure as units of analysis at any moment in which they cannot be shown to be mutually constitutive (Byers, 1985; McDermott, Gospodinoff and Aron, 1978; Scheflen, 1973). This is a difficult notion, which has been given a nice image by Birdwhistell (in McDermott, 1980):

> I like to think of it as a rope. The fibers that make up the rope are discontinuous; when you twist them together, you don't make *them* continuous, you make the *thread* continuous . . . The thread has no fibers in it, but, if you break up the thread, you can find the fibers again. So that, even though it may look in a thread as though each of those particles is going all through it, that isn't the case. That's essentially the descriptive model. (p. 4)

In school, Adam is a fiber, or many fibers, if you like. So are those about him. Together, they make up a rope. The category LD can be one way to name the rope, and, at the level of the rope, it might make sense to talk of

Adam as disabled. If he spends his day arranging, with the help of his friends, not getting caught not knowing how to do some school task, he might well, however substantial his mind, finish school without having learned much in the way of received knowledge and having been made, in effect, for such tasks under such conditions, LD. But notice that the disability in this case does not belong to Adam. A fiber cannot make a rope, and the very existence of a rope arranges for the fibers to disappear as units of analysis. Adam is a fiber, which, when joined by other fibers, helps to make the rope, or in this case the category LD, into the unit of analysis. It is not so much that Adam is disabled as that he participates in a scene well organized for the institutional designation of someone as LD. In their concerted activities, people arrange LD as a context for the management of persons in situ. People mutually constitute contexts for each other by erasing themselves, by giving themselves over to a new level of organization, which, in turn, acquires them and keeps them informed of what they are doing together. It is in this sense that LD is a context that acquires children. [. . .]

Learning

The argument put forth about Adam's disability requires not just a shift away from our commonsense notion of context, but a disruption of our most cherished notions about learning. Again we can turn to Birdwhistell (in McDermott, 1980) for a formulation. Note that he uses the terms *teaching* and *learning* interchangeably.

> We've always assumed that teaching is a special activity which necessarily goes on in special contexts in which certain orders of learning also occur. In my opinion in organizing such as activity, you are dealing with a calibration in which the behavior is at least as parallel as it is complementary and in which there are acted out, patterned participations, systematic dances which take place.
> I've been concerned with the difference between that model of teaching which is seen to come out of a dyadic (the so-called teacher–student) relationship and that model of teaching which comes from a contextually well-defined relationship in which the critical issue is the maintenance of the appropriate contact at the appropriate level. What I am concerned with are the conditions that maintain the contact in which the information not yet stored in specific instructions moves into the system and becomes a part of it so that 'learning' can take place. (p. 16)

In order to describe Adam, or better, in order to figure out what we had described after we spent a year trying to describe Adam, we needed a theory of learning that could take into account that learning is not an individual possession. The term *learning* simply glosses that some persons have achieved a particular relationship with each other, and it is in terms of these relations that information necessary to everyone's participation gets made available in ways that give people enough time on task to get good at what they do. If that happens enough, it can be said that learning happens. It probably makes more sense to talk about how learning acquires people more than it makes sense to talk about how people acquire learning. Individually we may spend our time trying to learn things, but this phenomenon pales before the fact that, however hard we try, we can only learn what is around to be learned. If a particular kind of learning is not made socially available to us, there will be no learning to do. This is a primary fact that we have made little use of theoretically. If we can stop focusing on who learns more or less of particular, culturally well-defined fragments of knowledge, and ask questions instead about what is around to be learned, in what circumstances, and to what end, learning achievements would become statements about the points of contact available to persons in various social settings (Lave, 1988a, b). What could LD be in such a world?

[. . .]

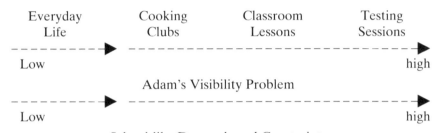

Figure 1.1   *The phenomenon*

Adam, Adam, Adam and Adam

Because we were interested in the social organization of learning and thinking, we followed the children in Adam's class across a number of settings. When the class went away to a farm for a few days, we went with them. We used school holidays to take individual children around the city. We videotaped all the children in their classrooms, in some one-to-one testing settings, and, most extensively, in afternoon activity clubs that we set up for them two days a week. We were often struck with how much some children varied across the different settings. Adam stood out as the child who varied the most, and we can use the order in that variation to organize our discussion.

There were four settings in which we knew Adam fairly well: Everyday Life, Cooking Club, Classroom Lessons, and Testing Sessions. We can roughly gloss them along a continuum displaying either Adam's visibility as a problem (from invisible to a source of constant embarrassment), or schoollike demands (from fairly loose to very constrained). Figure 1.1 tries to capture that Adam was least visible as a problem in Everyday Life situations. He appeared in every way competent, and, more than most of the children, he could be wonderfully charming, particularly if there was a good story to tell. In the Cooking Club, Adam was only a little more visible as a problem. When he worked with his friend Peter, he got his cake made without any trouble. When he had to work with someone else, there were often some arguments, some tears, and some taunting from others before he could get his work done. Classroom Lessons presented the same story, although troubles were more frequent, and the adults seemed to be drawn more obviously into his problem in the sense that they would try to reframe the task he was facing or they would chastise him for his misbehavior. Finally in the Testing Sessions, Adam stood out from his peers not just by his dismal performance but by the wild guesswork he tried to do.

As the settings differed in the degree to which Adam stood out as a problem, so they differed along a continuum to the extent that they were schoollike in their constraints and their demands. Our question about how to describe Adam turned into a question about how to describe the settings in which the different Adams could emerge. Our initial efforts focused on identifying how these different settings could call the different Adams forth. [. . .] Our effort in this chapter is to identify some of the approaches one could take to the description of the continuum, to point to some of the pretheoretical assumptions each makes about the nature of context and learning, and to extract what might be the most useful notions for our own purposes. The first approach focuses on the inadequacy in Adam's head, the second on the arbitrariness of the tasks Adam is asked to work on, and the third on the interactional dilemmas thrown in Adam's way as he moves through school.

The Continuum of Difficulty and Deficit

The approach most immediately available to common sense describes the continuum from Everyday Life to Testing Sessions in terms of difficulty. Everyday life is popularly understood to be the least demanding of the various settings we occupy during the course of our days. There is the argument from Bartlett (1958), rarely challenged, that in Everyday Life one can get away with all sorts of sloppy reasoning, forgetting, and losing track in a way that schools, and other institutional settings similarly con-strained (courtrooms, accounting offices, etc.), would never allow. By this way of theorizing, Testing Sessions stand at the opposite end of the con-tinuum from Everyday Life, because they demand so much precision in calculation and clarity in argument. There is no 'ya know' clause possible on a test; the reader cannot be expected to fill in the blank spaces or to make sense of what the test taker does not make clear. Testing Sessions are hard. Classroom Lessons only sometimes less so. Cooking Clubs generally less so. And Everyday Life generally undemanding. In comparison to tests, it takes fewer mental steps to get through our daily chores; we do not have to keep as much in mind. [. . .]

By our most popular line of folk reasoning, Adam becomes more visible as we move across the continuum because he is performing less well in the face of increasing demands. Under the loose constraints of Everyday Life,

Adam can blend into the crowd and do what he has to do without anyone worrying about the quality of his mind. In the Cooking Club, this is equally true when he can work with Peter, who can read the recipe and oversee the step-by-step planning of the cake. When he cannot work with Peter, he has to work hard to arrange for someone else's cooperation, and, if that is not forthcoming, he begins to stand out. In Classroom Lessons, the tasks can be even more demanding, and Adam appears even less adequate to meeting the challenge. A close inspection of the classroom tapes showed Adam acting out on those occasions when he could be called on to perform. For example, while the teacher was asking the class questions and calling on children for answers, Adam could be found crawling under his work table, giving the finger to a friend, and so on; when the teacher switched to the next part of the lesson and called the children forward to see a demonstration, Adam would join the crowd. When the going gets cognitively demanding, Adam stands out; otherwise, he is part of the crowd.

This approach has its attractions. It is coherent enough to support the bulk of professional interpretations of our children's learning troubles in and out of school. Adam had not been spared professional labels. His LD was well documented not just by the school, but by a university reading clinic that he attended for tutoring. As much as he seemed fine in Everyday Life, school work seemed terribly hard for him. Although Adam's case was extreme, this is an experience that we all recognize. That Everyday Life seems easier than Testing Sessions is a basic fact of life for us all, and tying it to cognitive difficulties makes great intuitive sense. In addition, once questions about children are framed in these terms, once our inquiry is narrowed down to the question of what is wrong with this or that child, support for a deficit theory can be found wherever one looks. If we go to our tapes of Adam and his friends, they constantly behaved as if they avoided tasks that were too difficult for them, and they worried about looking like they could have a deficit of some kind. If they did get caught not knowing something important, they offered excuses. In the Testing Sessions, Adam hardly seems to address the tasks at hand. Given that they are so hard, he simply uses what extratask information he can get to guess at the answer. If he has to choose between cup and spoon for the answer, he says, 'Cu- um-spoon' slowly enough to pick the answer that the tester seems to respond to; it is easier to use Everyday Life cues than to think out the questions. In the Cooking Club, if isolated from Peter and faced with thinking demands, he goes off to play with a friend; if there is no choice but to confront the task, he can feign crying or an allergy attack until someone comes to his aid. He can also be quite clear about his troubles; in a Classroom Lesson, he throws down his pencil and says that he can't do it – 'It's too hard.' Cognitive difficulties separate those who can from those who cannot and make the deficits obvious.

The deficit approach rests on a number of assumptions of questionable validity, however. Although it is true that Everyday Life *seems* easier than life in school, there is no reason to assume that the difference has only to do with increased cognitive demands. The tasks do not have to be cognitively more complex for us to experience them as harder. The trouble could lie along other dimensions; for example, school tasks could be harder simply because they are more arbitrarily constructed, or because an inadequate performance on school tasks could lead to a degradation ceremony. Experience is a good beginning place for an analysis, but we cannot risk the assumption that our experience can deliver the categories we need to complete an analysis. Apparent cognitive difficulty could be a cover for other realities, a fact that could make deficit and disability inappropriate words for describing Adam.

If we examine the notions of context and learning inherent in the deficit approach, we can gain a little more insight into what we are getting ourselves into when we describe someone as LD. In the deficit theory, as in all commonsense uses of the term, context refers to an empty slot, a container, into which other things are placed. It is the 'con' that contains the 'text', the bowl that contains the soup. As such, it shapes the contours of its contents; it has its effects only at the borders of the phenomenon under analysis. Notice how different this image is from Birdwhistell's image of the fibers and rope. In the static sense of context, the fibers remain fibers, each unto itself, no matter what their relations with the other fibers or how they are used in a rope. Adam is Adam, and, though different contexts might shape his behavior with different demands, he is what he is. Behind the moment-to-moment relations between things, there are the things, and it is the things that count. The soup does not shape the bowl, and the bowl most certainly does not alter the substance of the soup. Text and context, soup and bowl, fiber and rope, Adam and the various learning scenes, all can be analytically separated and studied on their own without doing violence to the complexity of their situation. A static sense of context delivers a stable world.

Accompanying this sense of context is a static theory of learning. By this account, knowledge and skill enter heads, where they wait passively for situations in which they might prove useful. School-derived knowledge and skill are supposed to generalize and to make children ready for a wide range of adaptive behaviors. The learner is a passive container, filled up by his efforts in school, slowly gathering up the skills purportedly essential to some jobs that will eventually have to be tackled. The problem with LD children is that they enter school without some rudimentary skills for paying attention and processing information. They are hard to fill. Some school situations are easier on them than some others, but in the long run their inability to keep pace with their peers forces them to stand out and fall even further behind. They are what they are; learner and environment are separable, and they do not greatly alter each other.

These static assumptions about context and learning are supported by static notions of both language and culture. The deficit theory assumes that language and culture are storehouses from which children acquire their competence. Some children get more and some get less. These are assertions about which we should be most uncomfortable. Language it seems is not available to the species just for purposes of expression, but for purposes of social alignment, for purposes of getting people into the necessary configurations for certain cultural jobs to get done (Bilmes, 1986; McDermott and Tylbor, 1986; Volosinov, 1929/1973; Wieder, 1974). When language is systematically unavailable to some, it is important that we not limit our explanation to the traits of the persons involved; it is equally essential that we take into account the interactional circumstances that position the people in the world with a differential access to the common tongue (McDermott, 1988). Similarly, it has become increasingly clear that any seeming lack of culture on the parts of some represents a systematic position within a cultural continuum of display only; that is, one way to be a perfectly normal member of a culture is to be a person who seemingly lacks what other members of the culture claim to have (Drummond, 1980; Varenne, 1983; Varenne and McDermott, 1986). Language and culture are not a gold-standard currency with only so much to go around; they are more like phonologies, in which each sound, each position in the mouth, is significant only as it is defined by the other sounds, and no sound is any more real, any more rich, or any more privileged than any other.

The social policy that flows from these static notions of context, learning, language, and culture are easily recognizable to us. Those who do not get enough knowledge from home or school need to be encouraged to get some more. They need to acquire more language and culture in order to be ready for more situations. They cannot afford to learn on the job; they cannot afford to assume that they will be shaped by new contexts, or that the language and culture that they need will be available to them in situ. They need to get more things in their heads to cut down their deficits in the face of difficult demands.

When we line up for consideration the assumptions about context, learning, language, and culture, we have to wonder whether we have available in the deficit theory a way of describing anything that is alive. Certainly, these static models have given us some predictive powers; for example, children called LD early in school generally continue to do badly. [. . .] In choosing an approach to Adam, we must be careful that we do not trust our common sense too much; if it were as sturdy a guide as we would like, why are we and many of our children in so much trouble. The same facts that we have suggested as support for a deficit approach to Adam's problem can be understood in other ways, and possibly with better results.

The Continuum of Arbitrary Demands and Left-out Participants

The second way of looking at the range in Adam's performances has us focusing less on Adam and more on the tasks he is asked to perform. In Everyday Life, Adam can use any resources to get a job done. If he has to remember a telephone number, he can memorize it, write it down, call information, or ask a friend. School tasks are different from this in that a person is often restricted in what he can make use of; procedure is of the essence. On tests, this trend is exaggerated. What else is a test but an occasion on which you cannot use any of the resources normally available for solving some problem; memory notes or helping friends are now called cheating. Is it possible that Adam is better understood as a child who is faced not by increasingly more difficult tasks, but increasingly more arbitrary tasks? We were quite sensitive to this possibility at the time when we first looked at Adam. At the very least, cross-cultural psychology had been extraordinarily clear in showing how various kinds of smartness could be reduced to apparent ignorance in the face of culturally arbitrary and cross-culturally foolish tasks (Cole and Means, 1981). We were interested in the possibility that the same problem existed in our own schools, most obviously for children from culturally and linguistically different minority groups, and more generally for us all at different times in our school career.

In Everyday Life, Adam found the resources at his disposal more than adequate. In the Cooking Club, he had an equivalent freedom if he was working with a friend. If, however, he was working with someone who was not willing to help, or if the people around him were trying to outdo him, then the task of cooking suddenly became more difficult. It is not just the case that Cooking Club can be made easy by someone helping Adam to do what he cannot; it is rather that, under the gentle circumstances of working with the friend to make a cake together, he can do what he cannot do if the task is both to make a cake and not to get caught not knowing how to read a recipe. In the Cooking Club, we quite by accident organized some confusing circumstances for children of this age: for example, a two-cup cup, teaspoon and tablespoon, baking soda and baking powder, ingredients on one side of the page and instructions on the other side. Adam's friend Peter is one of the children who could sort out these problems; when working with Peter, Adam not only followed the directions Peter reads to him, he sometimes reads the recipe himself. When working under less gentle circumstances, he will rarely look at the page. The task is obscured by the social work he must do to arrange not looking incompetent. In this way, reading 'teaspoon' for 'tablespoon' becomes more likely, not because Adam's head does not work, but because he barely looks at the page and ordinary resources for the solution to the problem are disallowed. In the Testing Session, Adam is so preoccupied with getting the answer that it is not clear he even hears many of the questions. He might be handling more mental steps avoiding the questions than he would have to handle if he addressed the questions. Arbitrary demands make him stand out. There may be more to LD than disability.

Understanding Adam by way of the arbitrariness of the demands placed on him represents an advance over the blind ascription of the deficit approach. It encourages, for example, a more careful look at the child and his circumstances and insists that we be more sensitive to what might be going on in the child's surround. However, to the extent that it leaves our commonsense assumptions of the relation between learner, task, and setting undisturbed, it quickly falls back into a deficit theory. Why is it, one could ask, that Peter can handle all the arbitrariness and Adam cannot? It is understandable why immigrants to the country run into these troubles for a few years, or even for a generation or two. But everyone should be able to adjust. Now consider that Peter is black and from a poor, tough neighborhood and Adam is from a wealthy, white family from the right part of town. It still comes down to one head against the world a few times a day, and Adam's head does not measure up. What are arbitrary demands anyway? What aren't arbitrary demands?

Upon careful examination, the continuum of arbitrariness leaves us with the same sense of context, learning, language, and culture as the deficit account. The conceptual assumptions remain the same. Contexts and their demands are still static, although there are more of them than allowed by the deficit approach. Adam is still Adam, and tests are tests. Contexts and their members are still separable. Learning still sits inside the student waiting to be called forth, although now in the form of specific sets of skills that must be used in situationally specific ways. Language and culture are still the sorts of things one can have more or less of, as if those who had less were not a systematic version of the culture everyone else had.

A Continuum of Degradation and Labeled Children

A third approach to Adam's behavior focuses on how much and on what grounds a person is liable to degradation in the different settings. What is at stake here is an appreciation of how much each setting organizes the search for and location of differential performances and how much that search further organizes the degradation of those found at the bottom of the pile. Garfinkel (1956; Pollner, 1978; see also Pollner and McDonald-Wikler, 1985, for a stunning reverse case) has shown how degradation is always a ceremony in which public agreement on what one can be degraded for is displayed and directed against the total identity of others. This means that it takes much work across persons to make an individual liable for some part of their behavior; a person must not only do the wrong thing, but exactly the wrong thing that everyone is looking for someone to do and then at just the right time.

By this line of reasoning, Adam is a problem in Everyday Life, primarily because everyday life is well organized for the systematic location of problems (Scott, 1985). Cooking Club is mostly about cooking, and only occasionally a source for a learning-related degradation ceremony. On one occasion, Adam and a friend made a green cranberry bread (a physical possibility, we are told, in an aluminum bowl with ingredients inserted in just the wrong order). When the others gathered around to see and laugh, he simply said, 'So I made a goddamn mistake, so what'. The issue passed. Other occasions for degradation do not move along so easily, no matter Adam's response. Classroom Lessons, for example, can be so well organized for putting the spotlight on those who are doing less well than the others that hiding becomes a sensible strategy for all of the kids some of the time and for some of the kids all the time. Adam seemed to suffer in the classroom, and this is in part how he became visible to us. During one small-group reading lesson, Adam was having a difficult time matching words with accompanying pictures. Reading 'fake' for 'face', he became tangled in a complex conversation with the teacher as she walked in and out of his group with occasional tips for the kids. It took us days of looking even to guess at the ways they seemed to be not understanding each other. What kept us curious was the attention paid to Adam's disability by the other children in his group. Adam's LD generally played to a packed house. Everyone knew how to look for, recognize, stimulate, make visible, and, depending upon the circumstances, keep quiet about or expose Adam's problem. Occasionally, they tried to explain it; 'cause it's hard for him', explained Peter to the other kids. Occasionally, they wondered aloud about it; while walking behind him on a day when things were not going well, René shook her whole body, stamped her foot, and yelled after him, 'Ohh. Why can't you read?' Testing Sessions, of course, exacerbate these problems, and Adam was at his least functional under these conditions.

There may be more to LD than disability. There may be many other people involved: certainly everyone in Adam's classroom, in various ways everyone in the school, everyone in the schooling business, all of us. This fact hit us hard the day Adam was asked to make banana bread in the Cooking Club. The adult showed them how to do it, and the pairs of children were then to do it on their own. Adam and Peter stayed close to each other as was their pattern when they entered the room. They then played ball on the side of the room as the adult did the demonstration bread. When they came to do it on their own, Peter announced he was allergic to bananas. Adam would have to go it alone or with someone else. Adam worked on getting others to help, but, to make a long and fascinating story unfortunately short, it came down to Adam against the recipe, his head against the world. The adult was annoyed with Adam for not watching the demonstration and was actively unhelpful. The other children were either making their own cakes or busy exposing Adam's not being able to work on his. In the first 10 minutes, from the time he first picked up the recipe, he asked for information from others 12 times, but each time came away unsure of what he needed to know. He looks at the recipe a few times, but it is not clear that he ever reads it; either way, it is perfectly clear that whatever he picks up from whatever source, he tries to double check it with those around him. After these 12 requests for information, he makes a crucial error. He is putting the ingredients into the bowl as they are listed in the ingredients section, and not in the order specified in the directions. This has him putting in yogurt second instead of fourth, and before the more efficient workers finish with their third entry, namely, bananas. Quite aside from using the list of ingredients as instructions, his error was in seemingly going faster than Nadine's group. Nadine liked to finish her cake first. Adam might be ahead of them, or he might be wrong. Either way, his disability might be a good way to focus on the problem. It might be time to spotlight Adam. It might be time for LD to make it into the room. For anyone needing to know who is doing what, how fast, and how well, the ascription of LD might offer an appropriate guide to perception. Let's listen to how a moment is organized for a conversational display of LD:

(The girls are screaming and Adam whimpering. The double vowels in Lucy's talk are chosen to show that she is reading to Adam as one would read to a child in a phonics lesson. The scene opens with Adam returning from the adult with the sense that he knows what to do next.)

Adam:	Finally!
	Where's the yogurt. Oh.
Nadine:	You're *up* to yogurt already.
Adam:	Yeah.
Nadine:	Where's the bananas?
Adam:	We, uhm, they didn't give us bananas yet.
Nadine:	Well, go get 'em.
Adult:	The bananas are here on the shelf.
Adam:	But this is our second page.
Lucy:	That is a teaspoon. That is a tablespoon.
Adam:	This is a teaspoon, and it says
Lucy:	It says tablespoon, twoo taablespoons.
Adam:	We're right here, Lawana. Lawana, we're right here.
Lucy:	That's
Nadine:	That's the ingredients, not the instructions.
Lucy:	That's baakiing powowder.
Adam:	What do you mean baking powder?
Nadine:	You go in this order.
Adam:	(Oh my God.) What do you mean, in what order?
Nadine:	Look! This is the instructions. That's what you need to do all this.
Adam:	Ai yai yai.
	One . . . Cup . . . Mashed . . . Fresh

(Everyone looks away, and Adam returns to the adult for more advice.)

When Adam takes the recipe back to his bowl, he holds the paper in front of his face, and offers a public, but mock reading (with the actual words from the ingredients list): 'One . . . Cup . . . Mashed . . . Fresh'. Then he is off to the adult for some questions and a little crying. Walking back into the group, he cries out, 'I was right stupid' to no one in particular and then calls his nominal partner, 'Ah, c'mon, Reggie. Wouldjya.' Reggie attends to the tears, 'Crying?' and, after a few seconds, says, 'Here, I'll help ya.'

How many people are involved in Adam's visibility? Reggie, Nadine, Lucy, the adult, of course. In addition to all the people in the room, did it make a difference that we set up the club to see what the kids could do with a minimum of help, or that we were all getting paid on government grants to figure out the nature of school failure? More of course. Could Adam be disabled on his own? Only if he could work on a task that was not culturally defined and had no consequences for his life with others; that not being a possibility, he can only be disabled through his interactions with others. Culture is a *sine qua non* of disability. Could he be disabled without LD being a part of the communicative resources available to the Cooking Club members in their dealings with each other? Why couldn't he be wrong just about how he was making the banana bread? There was something else in the air. There was the issue of his skill and how it measured up to the skills of others. Was he up to yogurt already? There are basic questions asked in all scenes called educative: [. . .] Who can do it? Who can't? Who is smart? Who is dumb? [. . .] For Adam, school scenes often result in everyone's recognition that he can't, that he has 'got it all wrong', that he may never be able, that he will always 'can't'. These questions acquire their answers, and in the process, with the help of tests, diagnoses, specialists, and government-sponsored budgets, LD acquires its share of the children.

The degradation account of Adam's behavior along the continuum of scenes relies on a different sense of context, learning, language, and culture than the previous approaches. If the assumptions of this approach are a little better tuned with our experiences, and possibly a little less lethal to our children, then we may have grounds to prefer a degradation approach to the others.

Context

Context is not a fixed entity to Adam, for it shifts with the interactional winds. Each new second produces new possibilities along with severe constraints on what is possible. So it is with the rest of the people in Adam's world. Everyday Life, Cooking Club, Classroom Lessons, and Testing Sessions all come stacked with limits on what can be accomplished together, while at the same time each scene is constantly on the verge of being something else. Generally, each scene turns out to have been approximately what it started out to be, but only because everyone worked to help each other to such an ending. Along the way, they followed each other's instructions and constructed a new day like the one before. In this sense, context is not so much something into which someone is put, but an order of behavior of which one is a part. In this same sense, fibers are not so much put into ropes as they participate in an organization of fibers that makes their every move relevant only to the extent that they play out the life of a rope. Similarly, Adam was a contributing member of various organizations that made his behavior relevant to the life of LD; this happened more often in Testing Sessions and Classroom Lessons than it did in Cooking Club or Everyday Life, and this was made possible by people, including Adam, organizing these scenes in ways that made LD differentially available in the different scenes.

Adam's LD is made available for all to see, because everyone was looking for it. In the Cooking Club, it is not so much the difficulty of the material as that Adam cannot address the material without worrying about whether he can get it straight or whether anyone will notice if he does not. This is not paranoia; everyone is often ready to notice, and, depending on the situation, ready also to look away or to make Adam's problem even more public. In the quoted transcript, Adam's LD is made public. Looking for Adam's LD has become something of a sport in Adam's class, a subset of the wider sport of finding each other not knowing things. In the Cooking Club, many kids get things wrong without too much worry; their wrong moves speak only to not knowing how to follow a badly organized recipe. The same mistakes are for Adam a source of degradation. They speak to his LD. Adam spends his day arranging not to get caught not having information that he could get from print. His every move is designed not to have LD again ascribed to him, and, as such, his every move confirms and recreates the possibility that the label of LD will be available in the classroom for anyone to ascribe to Adam. 'Where is the LD?' [. . .] It is all over the classroom as an interactional possibility. Everyone stands in some relation to it. Everyone is part of the choreography that produces moments for its public appearance. LD is distributed across persons, across the moment, as part of the contextual work members do in the different scenes. Neither Adam, nor his disability, can be separated from the contexts in which they emerge.

Learning

By taking such a radical stand on context, the degradation approach relies exclusively on the description of the *organization* of behavior for subject matter. Neither Adam nor his disability are analytically available as entities; they are only intelligible as relations, and then only moments in relations. What then of learning? Learning traditionally gets measured on the assumption that it is a possession of individuals that can be found inside their heads. By the degradation approach, learning is not in heads, but in the relations between people. Learning is in the conditions that bring people together and organize a point of contact that allows for particular pieces of information to take on relevance; without the points of contact, without the system of relevancies, there is no learning, and there is little memory. Learning does not belong to individual persons, but to the various conversations of which they are a part. What we call learning, warns Birdwhistell, is simply the other side of an institutionalized dance called teaching. [. . .]

When Adam works in the cooking club with Peter, he gets his cake made, and he reads the recipe. Conditions were ripe for new information to be made available to Adam, information that had him taking language from a printed page. When he has to work on his own, under the possibly degrading eyes of others, a quite different kind of information enters the system. Under these latter conditions, he gets no time to read, but he gets constant instruction on how to look LD. The instructions stored in the system are not simply about how to read. Reading to get the cake made is not Adam's only point of contact with the other members of the class. The instructions stored in the system are also about who is to finish first, with the best banana bread, with the recognition that they are the most competent. Given this more inclusive agenda, information about how to read can get lost easily, and Adam can get acquired by LD. It is the business of degradation and not education that seems to organize selected moments in the Cooking Club, even more moments in Classroom Lessons, and more still in the Testing Sessions.

Language and Culture

The language and culture that Adam encounters in his daily round may not be what most of us assume them to be. Language is easily understood as a neutral tool of expression that helps us to say and write what we like and to interpret what others have said and written for us. On these grounds, Adam needs more language. Like most children called LD, he loses his words at various important times, and reading and writing are pure torture for him. More language for sure. By the degradation stand, however, Adam's language may be quite complete. Language is not a neutral medium it comes to us loaded with social structure. It comes to us loaded with sensitivities to the circumstances under which it was born and maintained in previous encounters. It comes to us biased with the social agendas of a school system. [. . .] What is true of the contexts in which Adam finds himself called LD is no less true of the English language that we use in schools and in our interpretation of children in schools; they are well organized for the systematic creation of behavioral absences, which are carefully monitored by all in the system for use in their accounts of how the world works. [. . .] By this standard, Adam has exactly the language required of his position. Culturally, he is taking one of two perfectly normal pathways through school: He is failing. There is a language waiting in every classroom [. . .] for anyone who might take that road, and Adam has done his job well. He acquired and was acquired by a culturally recognized and mandated absence. He had achieved school failure. Adam had been acquired by the language of LD that was in place before he was born.

Languages help us to build the scales along which we calculate our pluses and minuses. So it is with culture. The poet John Montague grew up without a mother and was taunted by the members of his culture for not having what was prescribed for all children. Bad enough not to have a mother, but to be taunted for it as well is a double loss. 'There is an absence,' he warns, 'real as presence' (Montague, 1983, p. 29). Cultures do not just promise mothers; they require them, or worse, they require just one, your own. Nothing less than your own mother is acceptable, and nothing less than a perfectly normal cognitive development is acceptable either. To grow up unable to learn as fast as others is a loss in a school system that emphasizes and measures comparative development, and to be taunted for it is a double loss.

These are important distinctions. Mothers precede their children like languages precede their next generation of speakers. Cultures and languages fill the world before any given child's arrival, and they define what must be present and what must be noticed as absent. [. . .] Culture and language define what each of us needs, force us to attend to those of us who are left short, and ideally equip us to help them over their disabilities. Unfortunately, cultures are never so magnanimous, nor can they be. As a series of ideal types, *cultures are defined most essentially by the inability of all to live up to their directives.* Cultures offer only 'collective illusions', prescriptions that give us a way to talk about how we should live together in exchange for an inarticulateness about how we actually do live together (Murphy, 1971, 1987). Cultures cannot supply the resources members need in order to live in them without exposing the arbitrariness of their particular way of life. They exist by their promises, and they feed off each of us to the extent that we try to follow them and fail. [. . .]

Mothers acquire their children. Languages acquire their speakers. So disabilities acquire their learners. Who is there first? Long before Adam was born, we had LD – or an equivalent: strethosymbolia, for example, or just plain stupidity. It is an absence we know how to look for. American culture makes the absence of learning real as presence. Before any teachers of children enter the schools every September, failure is in every room. [. . .] There is never a question of whether everyone is going to succeed or fail, only of who is going to fail. Because everyone cannot do better than everyone else, failure is an absence real as presence, and it acquires its share of the children. Failure and success define each other into separate corners, and the children are evenly divided as if by a normal curve, into successful and failing. Among those who fail are those who fail in ways that the system knows how to identify with tests, and these children are called special names. LD acquires its share of the children.

The degradation approach alters considerably our commonsense resources for understanding our problems. Context and learning no longer have individual subjects as variables, but refer instead to the organizing devices people have available for dealing with each other. Similarly, language and culture are no longer scripts to be acquired, as much as they are conversations in which people can participate. The question of who is learning what and how much is essentially a question of what conversations they are a part of; and this question is a subset of the more powerful question of what conversations are around to be had in a given culture (Goodwin, 1991). To answer these questions, we must give up our preoccupation with individual performance and examine instead the structure of resources and disappointments made available to people in various institutions. To do this job, we may not need a theory of individual learning, and, given its use in our current educational system, we may not be able to afford one.

Note

[1] This edited version has reduced the specific references to American systems and does not include the Appendix.

References

Bartlett, F. (1958). *Thinking.* New York: Basic Books.
Bateson, G. (1972). *Steps to an ecology of mind* New York: Ballantine.
Beckett, F. (1938). *Murphy.* New York: Evergreen.
Belmonte, T. (1989). *Broken fountain* (2nd ed.). New York: Columbia University Press.
Bilmes, J. (1986). *Discourse and behavior.* New York: Plenum.
Birdwhistell, R. (1970). *Kinesics and context* Philadelphia: University of Pennsylvania Press.
Bourdieu, P. (1977). *Outline of a theory of practice* (R. Nice, Trans.). Cambridge: Cambridge University Press. (Original work published 1972.)
Byers, P. (1985). Conversation: A context for communication. *Nagoya Gakuin Daigaku, Gaikokugo Kyoiku Kiyo, 13*, pp. 26–40.
Chamboredon, J., and Prevot, J. (1975). Changes in the social definition of early childhood and the new forms of symbolic violence. *Theory and Society, 2*, pp. 331–350.
Cicourel, A. V. (1970). The acquisition of social structure: Toward a developmental sociology of language and meaning. In J. D. Douglas (Ed.), *Understanding everyday life* (pp. 136–168). Chicago: Aldine.
Cole, M., and Griffin, P. (1986). A sociohistorical approach to remediation. In S. deCastell, A. Luke, and K. Egan (Eds.), *Literacy, schooling, and society.* Cambridge: Cambridge University Press.
Cole, M., and Means, B. (1981). *Comparative studies of how people think.* Cambridge, MA: Harvard University Press.
Cole, M., and Traupmann, K. (1981). Comparative cognitive research: Learning from a learning disabled child. In W. A. Collins (Ed.), *Aspects of the development of competence* (Minnesota symposium on child psychology, Vol. 14, pp. 125–154). Hillsdale, NJ: Lawrence Erlbaum.
Drummond, L. (1980). The cultural continuum. *Man, 14*, pp. 352–374.
Engeström, Y. (1986). The zone of proximal development as the basic category of educational psychology. *Quarterly Newsletter of the Laboratory of Comparative Human Cognition, 8*(1), pp. 23–42.
Frake, C. (1980). *Language and cultural description.* Stanford, CA: Stanford University Press.
Garfinkel, H. (1956). Conditions for a successful degradation ceremony. *American Journal of Sociology, 61*, pp. 420–424.
Goffman, E. (1979). *Gender advertisements.* London: Macmillan.
Goodwin, M. (1991). *He-Said-She-Said.* Bloomington: Indiana University Press.
Hood, L., McDermott, R. P., and Cole, M. (1980). 'Let's try to make it a good day' – Some not so simple ways. *Discourse Processes, 3*, pp. 155–168.
Kendon, A. (1982). The organization of behavior in face to face interaction: Observations on the development of a methodology. In K. Scherer and P. Ekman

(Eds.), *Handbook of methods in nonverbal behavior research* (pp. 440–505). Cambridge: Cambridge University Press.

Kendon, A. (1990). *Conducting interaction.* Cambridge: Cambridge University Press.

Kohler, W. (1969). *The task of gestalt psychology.* Princeton: Princeton University Press.

Lave, J. (I988a). *Cognition in practice.* Cambridge: Cambridge University Press.

Lave, J. (1988b). *The culture of acquisition and the practice of understanding* (Report IRL88–0007). Palo Alto, CA: Institute for Research on Learning.

Lave, J., and Wenger, E. (1991). *Situated learning.: Legitimate peripheral participation* Cambridge: Cambridge University Press.

Lewin, K. (1935). A dynamic theory of the feeble-minded. In *Dynamic theory of personality*, (D. K. Adams and K. E. Zener, Trans.; pp. 194–238). New York: McGraw-Hill. (Original work published 1933.)

McDermott, R. P. (1980). Profile: Ray L. Birdwhistell. *Kinesis Report, 2*(3), pp. 1–4, 14–16.

McDermott, R. P. (1988). Inarticulateness. In D. Tannen (Ed.), *Linguistics in context* (pp. 37–68). Norwood, NJ: Ablex.

McDermott, R. P., Gospodinoff K., and Aron, J. (1978). Criteria for an ethnographically adequate description of the activities and their contexts. *Semiotica, 24*, pp. 245–275.

McDermott, R. P., and Tylbor, H. (1986). On the necessity of collusion in conversation. In S. Fisher and A. Todd (Eds.), *Discourse and institutional authority* (pp. 123–139). Norwood, NJ: Ablex.

Mannoni, M. (1972). *The backward child and his mother* (A. M. Sheridan, Trans.). New York: Random House. (Original work published 1964.)

Mehan, H., Hertweck, A., and Meihls, J. L. (1986). *Handicapping the handicapped.* Stanford, CA: Stanford University Press.

Minick, N. (1985). *L. S. Vygotsky and Soviet activity theory.* Unpublished doctoral dissertation, Northwestern University.

Montague, J. (1983). A flowering absence. *Irish Literary Supplement, 1*(3), p. 29.

Murphy, R. F. (1971). *Dialectics of social life.* New York: Basic Books.

Murphy, R. F. (1975). The quest for cultural reality: Adventures in Irish social anthropology. *Michigan Discussions in Anthropology, 1*, pp. 48–64.

Murphy, R. F. (1987). *The body silent.* New York: Holt.

Newman, D., Griffin, P., and Cole, M. (1989). *The construction zone.* Cambridge: Cambridge University Press.

Pollner, M. (1978). Constitutive and mundane versions of labeling theory. *Human Studies, 1*, pp. 269–288.

Pollner, M., and McDonald-Wikler, L. (1985). The social construction of unreality. *Family Process, 24*, pp. 241–257.

Poster, M. (1980). *Critical theory of the family.* New York: Continuum.

Ramirez, F. O. (1990). Reconstituting children: Extension of personhood and citizenship. In D. Kertzer and K. Schaie (Eds.), *Age structuring in comparative perspective* (pp. 143–165). Hillsdale, NJ: Lawrence Erlbaum.

Rawson, M. (1968). *Developmental language disabilities: Adult accomplishments of dyslexic boys.* Baltimore: Johns Hopkins Press.

Sankoff, G., and Laberge, S. (1973). On the acquisition of native speakers by a language. *Kivung, 6*, pp. 32–47.

Sarason, S., and Doris, J. (1979). *Educational handicap, public policy, and social change.* New York: Free Press.

Scheflen, A. E. (1973). *Communicational structure.* Bloomington: Indiana University Press.

Schegloff, E. (1984). On some questions and ambiguities in conversation. In J. M. Atkinson and J. Heritage (Eds.), *Structures of social action: Studies in conversation analysis* (pp. 28–52). Cambridge: Cambridge University Press.

Scott, J. (1985). *Weapons of the weak*. New Haven: Yale University Press.

Suchman, L. (1987). *Plans and situated actions*. Cambridge: Cambridge University Press.

Toulmin, S. (1985). *The inner life: The outer mind* (1984 Heinz Werner Lecture Series, Vol. 15). Worchester, MA: Clark University Press.

Varenne, H. (1983). *American school language*. New York: Irvington.

Varenne, H., and McDermott, R. P. (1986). 'Why' Sheila can read: Structure and indeterminacy in the reproduction of familial literacy. In B. B. Schieffelin and P. Gilmore (Eds.), *The acquisition of literacy: Ethnographic perspectives* (pp. 188–210). Norwood, NJ: Ablex.

Volosinov, V. N. (1973). *Marxism and the philosophy of language*. New York: Academic Press. (Original work published 1929.)

Vygotsky, L. S. (1978). *Mind in society: The development of higher psychological processes* (M. Cole, V. John-Steiner, S. Scribner, and E. Souberman, Eds.). Cambridge, MA: Harvard University Press.

Vygotsky, L. S. (1986). *Thought and language* (A. Kozulin, Ed. and Trans.). Cambridge, MA: MIT Press. (Original work published 1934.)

Wartofsky, M. (1983). The child's construction of the world and the world's construction of the child: From historical epistemology to historical psychology. In F. S. Kessel and A. V. Siegel (Eds.), *The child and other cultural inventions* (pp. 188–215). New York: Praeger.

Wieder, D. L. (1974). *Language and social reality*. The Hague: Mouton.

SECTION 2
VIEWS OF THE MIND: IMPLICATIONS FOR LEARNING AND ASSESSMENT

2

Reconstructing Educational Psychology

Eric Bredo

[. . .]

> . . . one of the weightiest problems with which the philosophy of education has to cope is the method of keeping a proper balance between the informal and the formal, the incidental and the intentional, modes of education. When the acquiring of information and of a technical intellectual skill do not influence the formation of a social disposition, ordinary vital experience fails to gain in meaning, while schooling, in so far, creates only 'sharps' in learning – that is, egoistic specialists. (Dewey, 1916, p. 9)

Recent interest in situated cognition has arisen in reaction to the currently dominant computational, or symbol-processing, view. The latter sees thinking and intelligence as akin to a computer performing formal operations on symbols. Although the symbol-processing view of intelligence has been quite successful in providing a relatively parsimonious and unified account of human thinking, knowing, learning, and development, a growing group of critics are nevertheless suggesting that the computer metaphor has been greatly oversold. They argue that 'we have gradually lost appreciation of the differences between today's computer models and the everyday capabilities of human beings' (Clancey, 1992, p. 3). We would do better, they suggest, by conceiving of cognition as it is involved in the practical doings of 'just plain folks' (Lave, 1988) rather than in the formal operations of computers.

An informal sense of the difference between these two approaches can be gained by considering the types of research that have been paradigmatic for each. Research in the symbol-processing (or computational) tradition has generally focused on the kinds of tasks familiar to academics or other professionals. Logical deduction, cryptarithmetic, chess playing, disease diagnosis, mechanical fault finding, and scientific discovery are examples.

This chapter has been edited.

Although work in this tradition has gradually progressed from 'toy' problems to more complex and important ones, the tasks remain recognizably those in which professional, schooled expertise is common. Recent work on situated cognition, on the other hand, has focused on methods of price comparison used by grocery shoppers, the ways in which dieters calculate their portions by physical manipulation, the way milkmen figure out their deliveries by using the constraints of the delivery boxes, the way Liberian tailors learn to sew through apprenticeship, and so on. The emphasis has been on problems arising in the performance of everyday activities, in which the problem is not defined aside from difficulties arising in the activity itself and social and physical interaction enter into both the definition of the problem and the construction of its solution.

The shift from a symbol-processing to a situated view of cognition involves much more than merely a move from computers to people or from formal operations to informal practices, however. It also involves a shift in philosophical orientation from a dualistic to a transactional perspective. In the symbol-processing view, mind is generally conceived to be inside the head. Symbols in the head then model objects in the external world. In a situated approach, however, mind is an aspect of person-environment interaction itself. In knowing something, for example, neither the object to be known nor its symbolic description is specified outside the process of inquiry and the conclusions that emerge from that process. I discuss this shift in perspective more fully and relate it to the analogous 'Copernican revolution' in psychology proposed by Dewey at the turn of the century (Dewey, 1900). I begin by briefly comparing the social and intellectual context of the present discussion with the context at Dewey's time. I discuss the symbol-processing view of cognition as a form of dualism and, then, a situated view of cognition as a form of pluralism (both of which contrast with behavioristic monism). I conclude by returning to the overall issue of the desirable relationship between the 'scientific' and 'everyday' or formal and informal approaches to cognition and education.

The Context Then and Now

When Dewey was writing, around the turn of the century, the United States was rapidly changing from a largely rural and agrarian society to a largely urban and industrial one. This involved significant moral and intellectual dislocation, with many people clinging to old beliefs despite changed conditions, while others focused on new possibilities that were inconsistent with older beliefs and mores. The result was a split between external and internal demands, between past and future, between habit and impulse, between 'one right way' and 'anything goes'. The most important philosophical tension in the United States at the time, which pitted Hegelian idealism against Spencerian naturalism (Miller, 1968, p. xxxii), embodied the same basic attitudes. The former suggested that everything was going according to a grand cosmic plan, however difficult to fathom: 'That history is reason and reason history, that the actual course of things has been rational, and that the rational is consequently the actual' (Miller, 1968, p. xvi). The latter suggested that the lack of an overall plan, as evidenced in unbridled competition and the survival of the fittest, was itself rational and in accord with natural law.

The educational expression of such tensions involved educational theories that also split outside from inside, and past from future; these were brilliantly analyzed in *Democracy and Education* (Dewey, 1916). For instance, some educational approaches emphasized the external demands of the curriculum, others the inner needs of the child; some thought schools should serve the interests of social efficiency, others that they should aid the natural development of the individual; some sought to use education to conserve the past, others as preparation for the future; some placed their emphasis on the content to be taught, others on the methods by which it was taught; some gave priority to the social world and the humanities, others gave it to the world of nature and the sciences. Dewey pointed out the 'evils' resulting from adopting any of these frozen, one-sided positions as a fixed orientation. Although a particular emphasis might make practical sense in a given situation, the division into fixed, unilateral positions and polarized either/or choices resulted in blindness with respect to other needs that might emerge as the situation changed. Each polarized response was an insecure attempt to make an answer the answer. Each represented a childish 'quest for certainty' in an uncertain world (Dewey, 1929). The result of adopting such impractical, one-sided theories was that they had to be supplemented by atheoretical ad hoc practices, at least after the conditions that made them originally relevant changed. Theory then became impractical and practice became atheoretical, impoverishing both.

Dewey's approach to these issues was not to seek a fixed synthesis of the opposing sides, for this would just be a new unilateral position that would become a new dogma. He sought, instead, to place theory within practice rather than outside of it. Rather than being split into inside and outside, with one side having to match one to the other, Dewey saw activity as involving a transaction between person and environment that changed both (Dewey and Bentley, 1949). Just as an evolutionary biologist might focus on the coevolution of horses and grasses, seeing how each changed the other in a series of interactional cycles (Bateson, 1972), so Dewey focused on 'doings and undergoings', which reciprocally change the character or structure of both person and environment, creating a joint history of development. When such transactions run into difficulties, their resolution depends on finding a way of approaching the situation that successfully defines it in a way that makes it solvable, allowing activity to proceed. Such a definition is a way of relating that allows activity to carry on (just as the coevolution of two species allows each to survive in new form) rather than a mirror of the way things are. In this way, Dewey sought to place reason in experience rather than outside of it, making mind immanent rather than transcendent. He saw this transactional approach as consistent with the latest science of his day, such as Darwinian evolutionary theory and Jamesian psychology, as well as with democratic practices of free inquiry and intelligent social reconstruction (Westbrook, 1991).

The end of the twentieth century seems to be similar to its beginning in its disjunction of old institutions and new conditions, to which people respond with rigid principles or unprincipled practices. There are also, however, some interesting differences. Today the impulse toward urban, industrial life is being questioned, as its undesirable side effects have become more evident (Schön, 1983). At least in some circles, belief in modernity seems to be on the downswing rather than the upswing, and science is not uncommonly viewed as oppressive rather than liberative. In a sense, science has taken over the ideological role of oppressor in which religion was sometimes placed at the turn of the century.

The present debate also takes place following the 'linguistic turn' in philosophy and other disciplines. As the philosopher Richard Rorty noted:

> Philosophers in the English-speaking world seem fated to end the century discussing the same topic – realism – which they were discussing in 1900. In that year the opposite of realism was still idealism. But by now language has replaced mind as that which, supposedly, stands over and against 'reality'. So discussion has shifted from whether material reality is 'mind-dependent' to questions about which sorts of true statements, if any, stand in representation relations to non-linguistic terms. (Rorty, 1991b, p. 2)

In this context, not only is science understood linguistically, and often equated with the linguistic formalism of the positivists, but so is whatever alternative there is to science. Literature is often viewed as the principal alternative, and thereby seen as a source of liberation from oppressive science. Discourse, texts, and hermeneutics now stand in opposition to propositions, nature, and science. The irony is that the current emphasis on local stories and cultures as a place of refuge from scientific and technical rationalism would, quite likely, have been seen as oppressive at the turn of the century, when our parents or grandparents were fleeing the country rather than the city. What ties these two periods together, however, despite their opposing attitudes toward modernity, is the fact that both have dealt with finding a proper relationship between the formal and informal, between science and everyday life. Both dealt with the same question of how to adapt to a changing world, whether by a more universalistic and scientific approach or a more particularistic and everyday one. This issue seems to form the broader background for the current debate.

Cognition as Symbol Processing

The symbol-processing approach to cognition can be conceived of as an evolving family of related approaches rather than a logically defined class.

Nevertheless, one assumption common to many members of the family is the assumption of a separately defined individual and environment, which must somehow match one another. Inside and outside, person and environment are viewed as separable, as independently definable, and then in need of being related. For instance, it is commonly assumed that an actor has symbolic statements 'in the head', which represent a separately defined set of objects in the external world. In Newell and Simon's (1972) influential model of problem solving, thinking consists of formal (i.e. syntactic) operations on symbols, which represent objects and their properties and relationships. In thinking or problem solving, one symbolic structure is transformed into another (using a set of rules or operators) until an initial state is changed into a goal state. The sequence of operations that successfully accomplishes this transformation is a plan of action that is itself a symbolic representation of the sequence of actions that will solve the problem in the real world. This approach has been summarized as follows:

Question 1: What is cognition? [. . .]
Answer: Information processing as symbolic computation – rule-based manipulation of symbols.
Question 2: How does it work? [. . .]
Answer: Through any device that can support and manipulate discrete functional elements – the symbols. The system interacts only with the form of the symbols (their physical attributes), not their meaning.
Question 3: How do I know when a cognitive system is functioning adequately? [. . .]
Answer: When the symbols appropriately represent some aspect of the real world, and the information processing leads to successful solution of the problem given to the system (Varela, Thompson and Rosch, 1991, p. 42–43).

Langley, Simon, Bradshaw and Zytkow's (1987, p. 8) more definitive description follows (note the emphasis on the brain as an isolated unit):

The human brain is an information-processing system whose memories hold interrelated symbol structures and whose sensory and motor connections receive encoded symbols from the outside via sensory organs and send encoded symbols to motor organs. It accomplishes its thinking by copying and reorganizing symbols in memory, receiving and outputting symbols, and comparing symbol structures for identity or difference.

The brain solves problems by creating a symbolic representation of the problem (called the *problem space*) that is capable of expressing initial, intermediate, and final problem situations . . . and using the *operators* that are contained in the definition of the problem space to modify the symbol structures that describe the problem situation (thereby conducting a mental *search* for a solution through the problem space).

The search for a problem solution is not carried on by random trial and error, but is selective. It is guided in the direction of a *goal situation* . . . by rules of thumb, called *heuristics*. Heuristics make use of information extracted from the problem definitions and the states already explored in the problem space to identify promising paths for search.

Because the same basic model is used in explaining human learning, development, and other processes, as well as forming the basis for many artificial systems, such as expert systems, intelligent tutoring systems, and robot planners, the potential target of criticism is quite broad. A similar symbol-processing model has, of course, also been popular in much educational research, such as research on student, teacher, and administrator problem-solving processes and knowledge representations and in expert-novice studies.

The subject/object dualism on which this approach is often based can be related to a number of more specific splits. Language and reality are often separated and treated as separate entities, for example, as are mind and body, and individual and society. The result is that mind is separated from its physical, biological, and social contexts. It is worthwhile to consider each of these dualisms in more detail, bearing in mind that this discussion can only briefly introduce the issues involved.

Language and Reality

In a symbol-processing approach, describing the world correctly is a matter of having the properties and relationships specified in a set of sentences match the properties and relationships present in the objects being described. In other words, this approach involves the tacit belief in *representationalism,* the belief that symbols mirror reality.

> At its simplest, the rationalistic [i.e. symbol-processing] view accepts the existence of an objective reality made up of things bearing properties and entering into relations. A cognitive being 'gathers information' about those things and builds up a 'mental model' which will be in some respects correct (a faithful representation of reality) and in other respects incorrect. Knowledge is a storehouse of representations, which can be called upon for use in reasoning and which can be translated into language. Thinking is a process of manipulating representations. (Winograd and Flores, 1986, p. 73)

The educational equivalent of this belief is the view that knowledge representing how the world really is must be transmitted to students. It is then presumed that when they have the same statements in their heads as the teacher has or as appear in the book they know something.

Beliefs about sentences mirroring reality have been thoroughly questioned in contemporary philosophy, which finds this position not so much false as incoherent (Rorty, 1979). The difficulty is that it is hard to understand what it would mean for there to be a language-independent reality against which a description could be compared, for any such reality must be something about which nothing can be said or expressed. As such, it represents a 'world well lost' in the eyes of many contemporary philosophers (Goodman, 1978). Even if one could specify a set of separate language-independent objects, it is unclear how one could know that a set of sentences corresponded with this 'reality'.

> How can we possibly know that our representations of the world are correct? The only answer seems to involve checking those representations against the

world to see if they in fact match, but, by assumption, the only epistemic contact we have with the world is via those representations themselves – any such check, therefore, is circular. . . . (Bickhard, 1992, p. 63)

As Rorty (1991b, p. 7) suggests, 'questions which we should have to climb out of our own minds to answer should not be asked'.

Not only is it being questioned that symbols mirror a separately given reality, so is the suggestion that computers represent anything to themselves. The difficulty is that a computer has, so to speak, no idea what the symbols or sentences it is operating on represent. It simply changes them from one form into another.

This separation of form from meaning was the masterstroke that created the cognitivist approach – indeed, it was the same one that had created modern logic. But this fundamental move also implies a weakness in addressing cognitive phenomena at a deeper level: How do the symbols acquire their meaning? (Varela, Thompson and Rosch, 1991, p. 99)

The problem is that representation is in the mind of the beholder. There is nothing in the design of the machine or the operation of the program that depends in any way on the fact that the symbol structures are viewed as representing anything at all. (Winograd and Flores, 1986, p. 86)

In effect, a symbol-processing approach to cognition, at least as often adopted, seems to confuse the standpoint of the observer for whom the symbols have meaning with that of the computer for whom they do not. Similar confusion often arises between an observer's description of a person's beliefs and what is thought to be in that person's head (Phillips, 1987, p. 87). That is, a theory used to describe a person's behavior is often confused with the concrete process by which the behavior is generated, as though those being observed had to hold the observer's theories to behave as they do.

in AI research we look at the structures of our models and we say, 'This is the knowledge; this program is an expert; this is what the student knows. . . .' In so doing, we have claimed an isomorphism. We have said that what is in the student's head and these representations are functionally identical. But if people literally followed such grammatical patterns or shuffled them about grammatically the way our learning programs do, they would not be very intelligent. We have confused our representations with the phenomenon we are modeling. The map is not the territory. (Clancey in Sandberg, 1991, p. 6)

An actor who followed a set of rules as blindly as symbol-processing theory seems to presuppose would be a 'judgmental dope' (Garfinkel, 1967). He or she would be like a mindless robot (or bureaucrat) who simply went by the rulebook without exercising judgment as to a rule's applicability or usefulness in the situation at hand.

Mind and Body

A second dualism involves the tacit separation of mind from body in symbol-processing approaches. Thinking is often conceived as something that goes on in the head without intimate physical interaction with the surroundings. Such physical contact and the mechanisms with which it comes about are viewed as parts of body rather than mind. The educational analog of this view is the belief that students can learn by passively sitting still and absorbing knowledge rather than by actively manipulating things and testing the results of their inquiries (Dewey, 1916).

Roboticist Rodney Brooks pointed out that such assumptions arose in work in artificial intelligence and robotics, in part, because these fields developed in a fragmented way (Brooks, 1991). Perception systems, representation and planning systems, and motor systems were all developed more or less separately. Current models of cognition (i.e. representation and planning systems) have thus been developed in isolation from perceptual and motor components, making it unsurprising that thinking is conceived of rather passively. When these separately developed components are stuck together to build a whole working system (what Brooks called a 'traditional academic robot'), the tendency has been to construct it in serial fashion with the perception system feeding into the planning and representing system, which then feeds into the motor system. Such a system first sees, then thinks, then acts. Its perception is passive and not tightly related to its activity. It has no direct feel for the situation or the consequences of its own actions, only cognitive descriptions of them. And it must always think before it acts because all action is driven by plans.

One of the practical difficulties with this architecture is that it takes an inordinately long time to act (Brooks, 1991, pp. 1227–8). Because every action has to be cleared through central control, planning can easily get bogged down. Another difficulty arises from the fact that the cognitive part of such systems uses a given vocabulary or set of primitives to describe the world. When its descriptions match the world, it can presumably maneuver successfully. Such a system, however, has no way of knowing whether its own descriptive language is a source of problems. Adoption of a certain vocabulary or set of primitives amounts to adoption of a certain theory or set of theories about the world. Any such theory, however, will be blind or limited in certain areas. Most notably, it will be blind to the side effects of adopting that theory or vocabulary in the first place, making these blind spots totally uncorrectable.

> Whenever we treat a situation as present-at-hand, analyzing it in terms of objects and their properties, we thereby create a blindness. Our view is limited to what can be expressed in the terms we have adopted . . . In writing a computer program, the programmer is responsible for characterizing the task domain as a collection of objects, properties, and operations, and for formulating the goals in terms of these . . . The program is forelimited to working within the world determined by the programmer's explicit articulation of possible objects, properties, and relations among them. It therefore embodies the blindness that goes with this articulation. . . . (Winograd and Flores, 1986)

The practical consequence of this problem is that most current systems are limited to carefully engineered and well-known environments for which they have been carefully preprogrammed with the appropriate descriptors. The practical consequence for cognitive science is that symbol-processing models have had remarkably little to say about psychopathology, which often involves just such dysfunctionally rigid patterns of description.

Individual and Society

A third dualism involves the tacit separation of individual and group. Thinking, learning, and development are often thought of as processes taking place inside the individual, with social influences coming from the outside.

> In psychological research on cognitive change and instruction there is a tendency to distinguish between the external stimulus consisting of what the teacher says and the internal process by which the organism incorporates these external events into existing mental structures. For example, in Piaget's work we find a distinction between 'cultural transmission' and 'equilibration'. . . . Cultural transmission becomes identified with the coercive social processes of direct instruction. . . . We find a similar tendency to dichotomize external and individual sources of cognitive change in more recent work in cognitive science which has developed detailed models of the process of skill acquisition by examining in-process transformations of individual problem-solving behavior . . . (Newman, Griffin and Cole, 1989, pp. 91–2)

One of the principal methods for separating individual and social influences is through the adoption of a standardized task. If researchers or teachers think they know what the task is, they can then compare the performance of different individuals on the task or compare changes in the performance of the same individual over repeated trials, and so on. Common views of intelligence, problem solving, learning, and development presuppose such stable and known tasks or sets of tasks. Learning, for instance, involves individual improvement in performance on the same task (Bateson, 1972). Without this assumption of task stability, it is not clear what we would mean by *learning*. If a subject has a different interpretation of a given task than the researcher, however, judgments based on performance on that task could be misleading because, the subject is organizing his or her activity on entirely different terms. This seemingly abstract point is of great practical importance, because laboratory subjects and school pupils are often judged to be stupid or not to have learned anything when they might equally well be seen as having been doing something different than was thought (Newman, Griffin and Cole, 1989).

The problem is that in fairly standardized situations, such as exist in the classroom or laboratory, evidence of differences in goals or task interpretation is often difficult to come by or easy to ignore. In everyday situations, however, such differences seem likely to be more common and harder to overlook.

> In everyday situations, people are not always presented with clearly stated goals. They often have to figure out what the problem is, what the constraints

are, as well as how to solve the problem once they have formulated it. In other words, in everyday situations, people are confronted with the 'whole' task. There is no experimenter responsible for doing the presentation part . . . the practical methods of maintaining control in the laboratory veil a crucial process: *formulating the task and forming the goal.* (Newman, Griffin and Cole, 1989, pp. 33–4)

When the task is seen as a matter of interpretation, it becomes impossible to cleanly separate individual task performance from the social process of defining and negotiating 'what is going on here'. As Newman, Griffin and Cole pointed out, the whole task includes the task of figuring out what the task is. Of course, one can construct situations in which differences in goals or interpretation are swept aside as illegitimate, or viewed as random error, but psychologists then put themselves in danger of building a theory of human thinking that is as limited to well-controlled social conditions as the prevailing theory of robot intelligence is limited to well-controlled physical conditions [. . .]. The practical implication is that when psychologists ascribe difficulty in solving a formally similar problem to individual failure to generalize, they may be in error, because such failure may equally well result from the fact that the same task was not socially organized in the setting (Lave, 1988; Newman, Griffin and Cole, 1989). The difficulty may not be any weakness on the part of the individual but an insensitivity on the part of the researcher. Needless to say, the same point applies in school, where children are often seen as failures: Their performance is not understood in light of potentially different socially organized interpretations of the situation.

These criticisms of a symbol-processing approach can be summarized by noting that each of these dualisms, such as the split between language and reality, mind and body, or individual and society, is the product of a privileged description. Language is matched against a reality that is already described in terms of a certain vocabulary. An active agent or robot is similarly assumed to work with a certain description of the environment that is fine-tuned to the problems that are likely to arise. Individuals are judged and compared in terms of an interpretation based on a fixed framework for describing what is going on. Each dualism is based on the assumption that the proper space in which things are to be described is known. Everything revolves around this particular center – the unquestioned framework of an external observer. The problem, however, is that we generally don't know what the problem is in everyday life. We don't know how best to describe things or which vocabulary or orientation will be most helpful. Presupposing a particular description, vocabulary, or set of programming primitives amounts to adopting a fixed and unquestioning orientation before inquiry even begins. Such a fixed orientation has blindnesses built in from the start. If the vocabulary or way of defining things can emerge from within the process of acting and inquiring, however, rather than being given from the outside, it may be changed and adapted as needed. Such considerations bring us to a situated view of cognition.

Cognition as Situated

Research emphasizing the situated aspects of cognition is also varied in character and can also be seen as comprising an evolving family of related approaches. Nevertheless, a common theme uniting many different contributions is a shift in the way the relationship between person and environment is conceived. Rather than viewing a person as being in an environment ('like a cherry in a bowl', as Dewey once put it), the activities of person and environment are viewed as parts of a mutually constructed whole. The inside-outside relationship between person and environment, which is generally presupposed in a symbol-processing view, is replaced by a part-whole relationship.

This shift in view is made more plausible by viewing person and environment in terms of their contributions to an activity rather than as separate entities. Viewed actively, the adaptation of person and environment involves dynamic mutual modification rather than static matching. Such an 'inter-activist' (Bickhard, 1992), 'relational' (Lave and Wenger, 1991), or 'dialectical' (Clancey, 1991) view seems to be as central to work on situated cognition as a 'transactional' view was to pragmatism (Dewey and Bentley, 1949). Work relating to this view can be seen to include that inspired by Vygotsky's socio-historical approach (Newman, Griffin and Cole, 1989; Rogoff and Lave, 1984; [. . .] Wertsch, 1991), Garfinkel's ethnomethodology and its successors in conversational analysis (Suchman, 1987), evolutionary epistemology and cybernetics (Bateson, 1972; Bickhard, 1992; Varela, Thompson and Rosch, 1991), neo-Marxist theories of practice (Lave, 1988; Lave and Wenger, 1991), philosophical situation theory (Barwise and Perry, 1983), and Deweyian pragmatism (Schön, 1983), not to mention others.

In fleshing out this view, it may help to think about a performance as the product of a history of relating, in which both person and environment change over the course of the transaction (Dewey, 1958; Varela, Thompson and Rosch, 1991). Drawing, for example, is a drawn out affair when viewed in this way: One draws, responds to what one has drawn, draws more, and so on. The goals for the drawing change as the drawing evolves and different effects become possible, making the whole development a mutual affair rather than a matter of one-way determinism. Writing can similarly be seen as a mutual matter of composition rather than simply the transfer of ideas from brain to paper. One writes, responds to what one has written, and so on, altering interpretation and aim in the process. The same may be said for conversing or for thinking itself. Each is the result of a dialogue, a way of relating or mutually modulating activity, in which person and environment (ideally) modify each other so as to create an integral performance. Seen in this way, a successful person acts with the environment, shaping it to modify himself or herself, in turn, and then to shape the environment, and so on, until some end is achieved. Acting with the environment in this way contrasts with acting on it, because this approach presupposes that the environment will turn around and alter the individual in return. There is no fixed fulcrum from which to move things. Given this view, the production of a well-coordinated performance involves a kind of dance between person and environment rather than the one-way action of one on the other. Such performances are quite naturally described in artistic terms that acknowledge interplay, such as 'concerted', 'orchestrated', or 'composed', (Erickson and Schultz, 1982).

Thinking or planning can be viewed as only one small part of the overall person-environment interaction when seen in this way, rather than as the operation of an unmoved mover. Planning is not unlike the governor of an engine whose behavior may become part of a larger problem of system-environment interaction (Bateson, 1972). For instance, if one focuses on the practical behavior of a system, including its governor, one must observe the interactive behavior of the whole system and environment over time. Seeing certain outcomes as direct products of a plan is a great simplification because it does not make clear how planning works, adaptively or not, within a whole system of activity (Suchman, 1987). Dewey (1916) made much the same point when he suggested that one consider the consequences of adopting a particular 'aim in view', as opposed to equating an aim with the thing aimed at. The focus is then shifted to the process of aiming, or of adopting differing aims as the situation changes, rather than merely on the attainment of a given aim.

Shifting the focus from individual *in* environment to individual *and* environment also alters other assumptions. Considered in this active way, the boundaries of a cognitive system are no longer limited to a person's brain, head, or body, but include aspects of the environment as well.

> Anyone who has closely observed the practices of cognition will have been struck by the fact that 'mind' rarely works alone. The intelligences revealed through practices are distributed – across mind, persons, and the symbolic and physical environments, both natural and artificial. (Pea, 1989, p. 1)

Individuals trying to solve a problem use the environment to affect themselves in useful ways, such as by making notes on a scratch pad, labeling objects as a reminder of how to treat them, discussing the issue with others, or asking for help. Causal responsibility for outcomes also alters from the person or the environment alone (or some linear combination of the two), to the particular history of person-environment interaction. As with interpersonal relationships, it is the history of a relationship that causes a particular outcome, not the actions of one or another party alone. Constraints that are relevant for interpreting and guiding the process are also reconceived in relational (rather than internal or external) terms, as signified by such concepts as *situation* or *context*. With this shift in viewpoint, all of the central concepts of educational psychology, such as thinking, knowing, learning, and development, are placed in need of revision, because all are commonly conceived in dualistic terms. All must be reconceived in more active and relational terms rather than in terms of static matching and fixed descriptive frameworks.

Language and Reality

Rather than viewing language as mirroring a separately given reality, a relational or situated view tends to see it as a means for social coordination and adaptation. It can then be seen as 'strings of marks and noises which organisms use as tools for getting what they want' (Rorty, 1991a, p. 4). If language is viewed as a means for social coordination and adaptation, then it makes no sense to think of linguistic utterances as given truths or falsehoods, depending on whether they mirror separately given objects, because knowledge is not a matter of mirroring reality. It is simply the endpoint or product of a particular line of inquiry and needs to be viewed in the context of that inquiry (Dewey and Bentley, 1949). Yet much educational practice assumes that knowledge has this sort of 'canned' status.

> Many methods of didactic education assume a separation between knowing and doing, treating knowledge as an integral, self-sufficient substance, theoretically independent of the situations in which it is learned and used. The primary concern of schools often seems to be the transfer of this substance, which comprises abstract, decontextualized formal concepts. The activity and context in which learning takes place are thus regarded as merely ancillary to learning – pedagogically useful, of course, but fundamentally distinct and even neutral with respect to what is learned . . . Recent investigations of learning, however, challenge this separating of what is learned from how it is learned and used. The activity in which knowledge is developed and deployed, it is now argued, is not separable from or ancillary to learning and cognition. (Brown, Collins and Duguid, 1989, p. 32)

Knowledge is thus (in a situated interpretation) inseparable from the occasions and activities of which it is the product.

Dewey placed a similar emphasis on the dependence of the meaning of linguistic expressions on practical social contexts. He argued that linguistic expressions must function in a joint social activity if they are to have any determinate meaning. In fact, such functioning is what gives them meaning in the first place.

> The sound h-a-t would remain as meaningless as a sound in Choctaw . . . if it were not uttered in connection with an action that is participated in by a number of people . . . the sound h-a-t gains meaning in precisely the same way that the thing 'hat' gains it, by being used in a given way. And they acquire the same meaning with the child which they have with the adult because they are used in a common experience by both . . . Understanding one another means that objects, including sounds, have the same value for both with respect to carrying on a common pursuit. . . . We conclude . . . that the use of language to convey and acquire ideas is an extension and refinement of the principle that things gain meaning by being used in a shared experience or joint action. . . . When words do not enter as factors into a shared situation, either overtly or imaginatively, they operate as pure physical stimuli, not as having a meaning or intellectual value. They set activity running in a given groove, but there is no accompanying conscious purpose or meaning. Thus, for example, the plus sign may be a stimulus to perform the act of writing one number under another and adding the numbers, but the person performing the act will operate much as an automaton would. . . . (Dewey, 1916, pp. 15–16)

The situation in which an expression is used not only helps disambiguate the expression, the use of an expression also helps construct the situation. An expressive act and the overall person-environment relation (i.e. the situation) are related as part and whole. In line with this, Dewey (1958) and Brown, Collins and Duguid (1989) suggest we think of concepts as tools.

> People who use tools actively rather than just acquire them build an increasingly rich implicit understanding of the world in which they use the tools and of the tools themselves. The understanding, both of the world and of the tool, continually changes as a result of their interaction. Learning and acting are interestingly indistinct, learning being a continuous, life-long process resulting from acting in situations. (Brown, Collins and Duguid, 1989, p. 33)

Conceiving of knowledge as a tool thus helps break down the dualism between knower and known. It makes clear that knowledge is the result of a transaction – the result of a process of inquiry, rather than a passive reflection of a separately given world. Given this approach, there is no question of a privileged representation of things as they really are, only a variety of descriptions useful for different purposes in differing situations. (It is important to note that this statement also applies to itself, a point to which I will return shortly.)

If language is a socially shared tool for signaling and coordinating activity, utterances and other expressions are no longer separate from social interaction; these acts make up part of the social context that disambiguates them. Viewed in this Darwinian way, linguistic statements and language itself are no longer separate from nature, but parts of it. As Dewey put this view:

> If . . . language . . . is recognized as the instrument of social cooperation and mutual participation, continuity is established between natural events (animal sound, cries, etc.) and the origin and development of meanings. Mind is seen to be a function of social interactions, and to be a genuine character of natural events when these attain the stage of widest and most complex interaction with one another. (Dewey, 1958, pp. xii-xiii)

Mind and Body

As pointed out earlier, the symbol-processing view of cognition often assumes that mind is in the head. The educational equivalent of this assumption is a passive 'spectator' approach to knowing, which views it as separable from doing. These assumptions separate mind from the full person-environment relationship. If one thinks of mind not as a thing, but as a verb or an adverb, however, such as *minding* or acting *mindfully,* it is clear that mind is a property of the interaction between individual and environment rather than something inside the individual or tucked away in the cranium. As Dewey suggested:

> psychological does not mean psychic, or refer to events going on exclusively within the head or 'subcutaneously.' To become aware of an object cognitively

. . . involves external physical movements and external physical appliances physically manipulated. (Dewey, 1958, pp. 379–380)

Dewey (1896) explicitly argued against the view that thinking was some sort of separate activity interposed between perception and action. Activity often involves direct sensor-motor cycles with little thinking at all, unlike the academic robots discussed previously, which had to first see, then think, then act. Perception is shaped by actively moving and manipulating things, just as action is controlled by properly coordinated perception. Each must co-construct the other. There is no separate 'thing out there' that is passively perceived or 'intention in here' that is actively applied. As Dewey suggested, a better way to view activity may be as the product of a mutually shaping cycle of interaction or 'coordination'. In much the same way, Brooks (1991, p. 1227) suggested that robot intelligence should be *embodied*, meaning that 'actions are part of a dynamic with the world, and the actions have immediate feedback on the robot's own sensations'. Clancey also makes much the same point:

> The claim of situated cognition (in my formulation) is that perception and action arise together, dialectically forming each other. Perceiving landmarks is not retrieving descriptions and matching against current categorizations . . . Simply put, the claim is that people navigate through familiar space without referring to representations; sensations are directly coupled to actions without intermediate *acts* of description . . . we can walk through a room *without referring to an internal map of where things are located*, by directly coordinating our behaviors through space and time in ways we have composed and sequenced them before . . . (Clancey, 1992, pp. 5–7)

In other words, physical interaction using existing habits often carries one through without the need for any central representation or thinking, unlike the traditional academic view discussed earlier. As Clancey summarized the point, ' "Situated" means coordination without deliberation'.

When conscious problem solving does arise, it does so within a blocked or puzzling cycle of activity. The situation in which the blockage occurs forms the practical context or background for present thinking, as opposed to a static set of relevancies. When a course of action is blocked, for instance, one inspects the actual site of blockage, looking around, touching, pulling, or testing to help determine the nature of the problem. Testing the proposed solution, then, involves practical action to see whether anticipated consequences occur rather than mere passive contemplation; without such testing, there is no telling whether the ideas are correct. Viewed in this way, there is no separation of mind and body, because the physical interaction involved in inquiry is simply a part of the process of acting mindfully.

The embodied view of mind offers a number of important implications. One is that a real difficulty is had and felt; the difficulty is tangible and precognitive. It is a tangle of conflicting habits and interrupted action, not just something 'in the head'. Active problem solving, then, begins with immediately present conditions, which may be interpreted in any number of ways, rather than with a problem space that is predefined. Possible solutions need to be actively tested to see whether they allow the activity to continue. Considered in this way, minding is a tangibly physical matter.

Individual and Society

As suggested earlier, presupposing a task whose interpretation is known is one of the principal ways in which an individual's contributions are separated from those of others. If everyone has his or her own task to perform, like good students doing independent work at school, the task furnishes a means of interpreting and assessing individual behavior. If children are working on qualitatively different tasks, however, it is not appropriate to compare them on the same scale or to single out differences among them as responsible for differences in outcomes, because they are doing quite different things. In particular, if there are different conceptions of the task among different participants, or if the definition of the task is changing and gaining new meaning as interaction proceeds, it is impossible to statically separate changing social relationships from changing individual tasks. The very division between individual and society as separately given entities breaks down.

As an example, imagine two people. When they engage in such mutually coordinated activity, they form a group or society, albeit a small and temporary one. Their patterned activity together, however, is not an external entity to which the dancers may be contrasted. Individual and group are simply different standpoints from which the interactive relationship or activity may be analyzed. One can choose to look at an individual's contribution to the whole or one can look at the whole formed by the coordinated contributions of the individuals, but neither is defined independently of the other. As Dewey pointed out, we only think that individual and society are different entities when interaction runs into recurrent difficulties. Then there is a tendency to contrast the natural individual with artificial social constraint, or the organic society with the unruly individual, and so on. The solution to such interactional difficulties, however, is not to 'free' the individual from social constraint or to impose a separately conceived form of social control on him or her. It is, rather, to find better ways of organizing activity together – for example, devising a better division of labor – thereby altering both individual and society.

The practical inseparability of individual task performance from social relationships is one of the central tenets of a situated approach. Any sequence of interaction can have multiple interpretations and be aligned to different goals, just as a given number series can be generated by any number of different rules. Different interpretations of a given part of the series can only be disambiguated by further moves, but these then become part of a new sequence for which multiple interpretations are possible.

> An object, such as a poem, a chart or a spoken concept may be understood very differently by the child and the teacher. But these differences need not cause

'trouble' for the teacher or the child or the social interaction; the participants can act *as if* their understandings are the same. At first, this systematic vagueness . . . may appear to make cognitive analysis impossible. However, it now appears that this looseness is just what is needed to allow change to happen when people with differing analyses interact. (Newman, Griffin and Cole, 1989, p. 62)

Behaving as if there were only one interpretation, one descriptive framework, is a possible way of interacting. It is a form of interaction, however, that is likely to make it painful or difficult for others who may have a different interpretation to join the 'dance'. It is continued openness to new interpretations that allows real relationships – those that are not dead or stultifying – to continue. As a scientific mode of analysis, the presumption that one interpretation is the correct one also throws out some of the most significant and revealing data, such as that which suggests how a task comes to be defined in a certain way (or ways) in the first place.

If individual and society are not separately defined insofar as social activity is concerned, individual change becomes inseparable from social change. Hanks summarizes Lave and Wegner's position in this regard as follows:

Learning is a process that takes place in a participation framework, not in an individual mind. This means, among other things, that it is mediated by the differences in perspective among the coparticipants. It is the community, or at least those participating in the learning context, who 'learn' under this definition. Learning is, as it were, distributed among coparticipants, not a one-person act. While the apprentice may be the one transformed most dramatically by increased participation in a productive process it is the wider process that is the crucial locus and precondition for this transformation. . . . The larger community of practitioners reproduces itself through the formation of apprentices, yet it would presumably be transformed as well. (Lave and Wenger, 1991, pp. 15–16)

On this conception, one cannot independently define individual learning as separate from change in one's social role or identity. Any meaningful social action – that is, any action that is other than autistic – becomes oriented to the actions of others. Changes in how one behaves have implications for one's relationship with others, just as these relationships have implications for one's behavior. Bateson (1976, p. 54) made much the same point when he noted that:

'socialization' (by definition) requires interaction, usually of two or more organisms. From this it follows that, whatever goes on below the surface, inside the organisms where we cannot see it, there must be a large part of that 'iceberg' showing above the surface. We, biologists, are lucky in that evolution is always a co-evolution and learning is always a co-learning. Moreover, this visible part of the process is no mere by-product. It is precisely that production, that set of appearances, to produce which is supposedly the 'goal' of all learning which we call 'socialization'.

As this statement makes plain, being properly taught to participate in an activity does not involve just performing one's own task in isolation. In a well-functioning division of labor, one's contribution is modulated and coordinated in terms of the whole activity it helps to construct, along with the contributions of others. This practical inseparability of individual and social change has led some to suggest that the term learning be jettisoned because of its inappropriately individualistic connotations (Suchman, 1992), whereas others have suggested it be replaced with a more neutral term, such as *cognitive change* (Newman, Griffin and Cole, 1989). For Dewey, such socially informed and meaningful change would simply be termed *education*.

To summarize, work on situated cognition has emphasized the inseparability of cognition and context. Knowledge is viewed as inseparable from the activities by which it is acquired and tested and from the practices of the community of fellow language users. Problem solving is seen as inseparable from the embodied activity in which consciousness arises and which successful conscious problem solving ultimately allows to proceed. Individual change, or learning, is considered to be inseparable from change in the social relationships in which people participate. In each case, one can make an analytical distinction between one or the other side of the dualism, but this does not imply an ontological distinction between two different things. Rather, they are two different phases or aspects of a larger process that they help compose, which is used, in turn, to define and interpret the parts. Thus conceived, a situated approach ends up being a species of pluralism (Dewey, 1958) rather than a monism (e.g. behaviorism) or a dualism (e.g. cognitivism). It is not pluralistic in the sense that there really are multiple realities – this would be just another attempt to climb outside our heads to see how things really are – but in the sense that different descriptions have varied uses and value in different situations.

Balancing the Formal and Informal

The debate between symbol-processing and situated approaches to cognition is clearly related to other tensions in society, education, and the social sciences. It relates to apparent tensions between science and everyday life, between formal schooling and life outside of school, and between approaches to cognitive research based on natural science and those based on a cultural, historical, or literary model (Cole and Scribner, 1976; Phillips, 1987, 1992). This debate embodies some of the same tensions between the formal and informal, or between universalism and particularism, evident in the society more broadly. A symbol-processing view can be seen as the more universalistic in this context. It has been based on the assumption that there are certain universal features of human cognition (e.g. limited short-term memory, memory as list-structure) that enable us to understand human thinking in general. More than this, it has assumed that human thinking is itself universalistic (i.e. that it basically involves logical deduction using context-free rules). On the other hand, a situated approach focuses precisely on the varied contexts in which any such process occurs. It assumes great context sensitivity – great contingency, because interpretation and meaning vary with context. In effect, the former view suggests that it is the same river every time one steps into it, and the latter suggests that one can never step into the same river twice. The question I address in concluding is: What are the respective roles for these two approaches to cognition? Is one right and the other wrong? (One true and the other false?) Or is there some other way we should think about their relationship?

A first approach to this issue is to assume that the more formalistic approach is the most correct – because it has been nailed down best – so the informal or everyday should emulate it. This seems to be what has happened with at least a runaway version of the symbol-processing approach. What began as an effort to use computers to simulate human thinking ended (all too often) by defining human cognition as computation. Of course, the power of a formalistic approach comes from the fact that there is no limit to what can be formalized. With enough rules, enough computational power, and clever enough programmers, more and more sophisticated activities can be modeled. The difficulty is that the more aspects of a practice become formalized, the more evident it is that formalization can go on forever and that there are different, competing formalisms. Trying to explicitly spell out all of the assumptions involved in a practical activity is an endless, bottomless task because things can break down in myriad ways (Garfinkel, 1967). One can specify how a well-behaved machine should work, for example, but virtually any part can break in unforeseen ways with unforeseen consequences, making it difficult to know which formalism will be relevant. Although there is nothing wrong with formal modeling using a given vocabulary, and it can, indeed, be very helpful in showing the complex consequences of a way of thinking, the attempt to reduce practice to theory involves side effects of its own, such as rigidity and the devaluation of everyday experience. For example, if abstract school knowledge comes to define all knowing, everyday practical experience is devalued. Similarly, if *intelligence* is tacitly defined as the ability to do well in school, as it has been in traditional IQ testing (Gould, 1981), many people who function extremely well outside of school will be labeled unintelligent, and much of the intelligence of those who do well in school will be overlooked. So conceived, social science and schooling lose the common touch.

A second approach is to assume that an informal or situated view is the only true or correct one. In the midst of enthusiasm for a new approach, it is understandable that some might want to claim that cognition is really or essentially situated. A possible example includes the following:

> I take it that there is a reality of human action, beyond either the cognitive scientist's models or my own accounts, to which both are trying to do justice. In that sense, I am not just examining the cognitive science model with the dispassion of the uncommitted anthropologist of science, I am examining it in light of an alternative account of human action to which I am committed. . . . (Suchman, 1987, p. x)

The point is that the claim that cognition is really or essentially situated, that this is how things are 'beyond the cognitive scientist's models', tacitly accepts the very dualism that this approach criticizes in others. Such self-contradiction is not uncommon. For example, the rather popular claim that there really are multiple, socially constructed realities is similarly self-contradictory, because it seems to involve appeal to a single, unconstructed way in which things really are. The suggestion that 'all generalization is impossible' because the conditions of any generalization are socially constructed is similarly self-defeating. Clearly, antidogmatists need to be careful if they are not to become like that which they oppose. If a situated approach were to be taken to be the really true or correct one, the proper practical conclusion would seem to be that we should seek to absorb the formal or theoretical into the informal or practical. At times, this seems to be what is being suggested by those favoring a situated approach – although usually only by way of polemical over-emphasis. Brooks (1991) attempts to build robots that act intelligently but have no central cognitive capabilities, for example, thereby reducing mind to body. Clancey's (1992) slogan, ' "Situated" means coordination without deliberation' can also be too easily understood as suggesting that a situated approach leaves no room for conscious deliberation – although this is clearly not what he wants to suggest. That Lave (1988) and Becker (1986) wrote on the virtues of apprenticeship as opposed to formal schooling could be taken to imply hostility towards all schooling – although both would surely deny this as their intent. Taking this to an extreme, one can imagine an approach that allowed little or no independent role for specialized scientific investigation, formal modeling, formal schooling, or conscious thought. All would be seen as too removed and formalistic and in need of being absorbed into, or driven by, unspecialized, unreflective social practice. The difficulty is that this reduces human intelligence to that of a nonlanguage-using animal or so hampers inquiry by tying it to immediate practical demands that only relatively local and unprogressive forms of social life would be possible. Practice without reflection looks as bad as reflection without practice.

The third possibility is to seek divorce rather than dominance. One could conceive of two different types of cognition – one theoretical and symbolic, the other practical and situated – requiring two different theories or approaches to deal with them. This would be like saying that formal schooling is entirely different from and irrelevant to life outside of school. Alternatively, it would be like saying that scientific understanding is one thing and everyday understanding another, and the two have nothing to do with one another because they apply to different objects. As a final example, one might say that no communication is possible between psychology and anthropology because they deal with essentially different entities. Current attempts to define social affairs as different in kind from natural ones, thereby requiring hermeneutic rather than naturalistic forms of research, are an example of this approach (Phillips, 1992). The difficulty with this strategy is that entanglements remain despite attempts at divorce. Theory and practice, schooling and life outside school, and science and everyday social life have fairly evident ways of affecting one another, making the presumption of their independence an unrealistic denial of the obvious. In any event, proponents of both symbol-processing and situated approaches deny that there are two different types of cognition requiring two different theories (Vera and Simon, 1993; Greeno and Moore, 1993). Both sides want their theories to be all-inclusive.

The fourth possibility (and obviously the one I advocate) is to seek a more collaborative relationship between the formal and informal, the theoretical and practical, the universalistic and the particularistic. We can seek a well-functioning division of labor between the two rather than the dominance by one or the other or their total divorce. This fourth possibility involves both respecting their differences and using these differences for common effect. For instance, formal schooling is often at odds with the everyday lives of children or adults outside of school. This typically leads reformers to want to make everyday life like school, with people having to pass IQ or other school-like tests for jobs for which such skills are largely irrelevant. It also leads to the attempt to make schools like everyday life, as in 'free' schools or home schools, which are alike in their attempt to bend schooling to particularistic interests. I suspect that most people would not see any of these alternatives as desirable, although they might want to nudge things in one direction or the other. They would rather have schools begin with everyday life, with all its differences and tensions and practical difficulties, and use these as starting points for generalization and theorizing and the development of broadened sympathies, which are, in turn, brought to bear to change the conduct of everyday life, altering and improving its course. Such a 'balance between formal and informal' was, of course, what Dewey sought to articulate at the turn of the century.

When this line of reasoning is applied to the relationship between the symbol-processing and situated views of cognition, it becomes evident that the principal source of conflict lies in absolutism and exaggerated self-importance. The symbol-processing view began as an attempt to model or simulate human intelligence. The qualitative modeling techniques that became available in the field of artificial intelligence were, in effect, ways of seeing how a theory would behave in practice. By helping to clarify the practical implications of a given system of thought, such formal models also made clearer what was omitted from that system. It is therefore natural that models become ladders to be thrown away after one has climbed them. [. . .] Somewhere along the line, however, this use of computer simulation – and the computer metaphor more generally – became confused with the way things really are. Rather than being usefully modeled by computers, human beings became computers. The informal was reduced to the formal. All of the dualisms criticized earlier [. . .] would not even arise if computer models had simply been taken as tools for understanding rather than mirrors of reality.

With its emphasis on the everyday and practical and socially contingent, a situated approach has its appeal precisely because of this exaggerated belief in the computer metaphor. Pointing out how the practical implications of any formal model depend on the contingent, particular, and historically constructed context is a good antidote to the former approach. It helps bring us back to ourselves, to the particular place and moment, and to the importance of the everyday and informal. As I suggested previously, however, a situated approach can become arrogant and absolutist as well. It may become a new dogma, a new 'the way the world is'. Such an assertion would be self-contradictory, because if all meaningful and relevant cognition is situated, situated cognition theory must be as well [. . .]. However, such considerations never seem to stop empire builders for long. What is needed, then, for a more cooperative relationship between systematizers and contextualizers is mostly greater humility. This would reflect Dewey's efforts at the turn of the century to define a kind of evolving part-whole harmony relating cognition and context, science and everyday life. [. . .] It seems clear that our theorizing about human cognition should both represent and express this open and evolving quality of mind.

References

Barwise, J., & Perry, J. (1983). *Situations and attitudes.* Cambridge, MA: MIT Press.

Bateson, G. (1972). *Steps to an ecology of mind.* New York: Ballantine.

Bateson, G. (1976). Some components of socialization for trance. In T. Schwartz *(Ed.), Socialization as cultural communication* (pp. 51-63). Berkeley, CA: University of California Press.

Becker, H. S. (1986). A school is a lousy place to learn anything in. In H. S. Becker (Ed.), *Doing things together: Selected papers* (pp. 173–190). Evanston, IL: Northwestern University Press.

Bickhard, M. H. (1992). How does the environment affect the person? In L. T. Winegar & J. Valsiner (Eds.), *Children's development in social context.* Hillsdale, NJ: Lawrence Erlbaum Associates, Inc.

Brooks, R. A. (1991). New approaches to robotics. *Science, 253*, pp. 1227–1232.

Brown, J. S., Collins, A., & Duguid, P. (1989). Situated cognition and the culture of learning. *Educational Researcher, 18*(1), pp. 32–42.

Clancey, W. J. (1991). A boy scout, Toto, and a bird: How situated cognition is different from situated robotics. In *NATO Workshop on Emergence, Situatedness, Subsumption, and Symbol Grounding.*

Clancey, W. J. (1992). *'Situated' means coordinating without deliberation.* Santa Fe, NM: McDonnel Foundation Conference.

Cole, M., & Scribner, S. (1976). Theorizing about socialization of cognition. In T. Schwartz (Ed.), *Socialization as cultural communication* (pp. 157–176). Berkeley, CA: University of California Press.

Dewey, J. (1896). The reflex arc concept in psychology. *The Psychological Review, 3*, pp. 356–370.

Dewey, J. (1900). *The school and society.* Chicago: University of Chicago Press.

Dewey, J. (1916). *Democracy and education.* New York: Macmillan.

Dewey, J. (1929). *Quest for certainty.* New York: Putnam.

Dewey, J. (1958). *Experience and nature.* New York: Dover.

Dewey, J. & Bentley, A. (1949). *Knowing and the known.* Boston: Beacon Press.

Erickson, F., & Schultz, J. (1982). *The counselor as gatekeeper: Social interaction in interviews.* New York: Academic.

Garfinkel, H. (1967). *Studies in ethnomethodology.* Englewood Cliffs, NJ: Prentice-Hall.

Goodman, N. (1978). *Ways of worldmaking.* Indianapolis: Hackett Publishing.
Gould, S. J. (1981). *The mismeasure of man.* New York: Norton.
Greeno, J. G., & Moore, J. L. (1993). Situativity and symbols: Response to Vera and Simon. *Cognitive Science, 17*(1), pp. 49–59.
Langley, P., Simon, H. A., Bradshaw, G. L., & Zytkow, J. M. (1987). *Scientific discovery: Computational explorations of the creative process.* Cambridge, MA: MIT Press.
Lave, J. (1988). *Cognition in practice.* Cambridge, England: Cambridge University Press.
Lave, J., & Wenger, E. (1991). *Situated learning: Legitimate peripheral participation.* Cambridge, England: Cambridge University Press.
Miller, P. (1 968). *American thought Civil War to World War I.* New York: Holt, Rinehart & Winston.
Newell, A., & Simon, H. A. (1972). *Human problem solving.* Englewood Cliffs, NJ: Prentice-Hall.
Newman, D., Griffin, P.,& Cole, M. (1989). *The construction zone: Working for cognitive change in schools.* Cambridge, England: Cambridge University Press.
Pea, R. D. (1989). *Distributed intelligence and education.* Unpublished manuscript, Institute for Research on Learning.
Phillips, D. C. (1987). *Philosophy, science, and social inquiry.* Elmsford, New York: Pergamon.
Phillips, D. C. (1992). *The social scientist's bestiary: A guide to fabled threats to, and defenses of naturalistic social science.* Oxford, England: Pergamon.
Rogoff, B., & Lave, J. (Eds.). (1984). *Everyday cognition: its development in social context.* Cambridge, MA: Harvard University Press.
Rorty, R. (1979). *Philosophy and the mirror of nature.* Princeton: Princeton University Press.
Rorty, R. (1991a). *Essays on Heidegger and others.* Cambridge, England: Cambridge University Press.
Rorty, R. (1991b). *Objectivity, relativism, and truth* Cambridge, England: Cambridge University Press.
Sandberg, J. (1991, March). Invited Speaker: Bill Clancey. AICOM, *4.*
Schön, D. A. (1983). *The reflective practitioner: How professionals think in action.* New York: Basic Books.
Suchman, L. A. (1987). *Plans and situated actions: The problem of human-machine communication.* Cambridge, England: Cambridge University Press.
Suchman, L. A. (1992, April). *Discussion.* Oral presentation at the annual meeting of the American Educational Research Association, San Francisco, CA.
Varela, A. H., Thompson, E., & Rosch, E. (1991). *The embodied mind: Cognitive science and human experience.* Cambridge, MA: MIT Press.
Vera, A. H., & Simon, H. A. (1993). Situated action: A symbolic interpretation. *Cognitive Science, 17*(1), pp. 7–48.
Wertsch, J. V. (1991). *Voices of the mind: A sociocultural approach to mediated action.* Cambridge, MA: Harvard University Press.
Westbrook, R. B. (1991). *John Dewey and American democracy.* Ithaca, NY: Cornell University Press.
Winograd, T., & Flores, F. (1986). *Understanding computers and cognition.* Reading, MA: Addison-Wesley.

3

Is Everyone Musical?

John A. Sloboda, Jane W. Davidson and Michael J. A. Howe

[. . .]

The Origins of Musicality: a Folk Psychology View

People vary enormously in their musical accomplishments, with some individuals finding it far easier than others to make progress. Parents often report that one child struggles in vain to master an instrument while a younger brother or sister moves ahead with seemingly little effort. To account for this, folk psychology assumes that differences between people in musical ability are directly caused by inherent biological variability. From birth, some individuals are supposed to have an in-born potential to be musical, or have a natural talent or gift for music, or an innate aptitude for it. Beliefs of this kind are widely held by musicians, music teachers and others, and are influential in helping to decide how limited teaching resources are to be allocated. As one young musician reported:

> When I was about six I started getting on; I'd done Grade 2 recorder the year before and my mum thought then that I'd got a gift of music. She wasn't quite sure. And then when I started, when I was a year older and I'd done lots, I did grades in piano and grades in violin. And then she knew I was musical . . . My mum thought [my sister] has a gift in music but she hasn't, she's got a gift in school work (Howe and Sloboda, 1991a: p. 46).

A person making a statement like this one would appear to believe that evidence of high achievement forms sufficient grounds for assuming that a gift is present, even though there is no independent evidence or logical justification for such a belief. In reality, all that has been established is that the child's ability to perform has reached a certain level. Nevertheless, a belief in the centrality of innate gifts or talents may seem innocent enough, even if a person's reasons for holding such a belief are inadequate by scientific standards. Self-beliefs exert powerful effects on persistence and mastery at a range of intellectual and artistic endeavours, and differences

---

This chapter has been edited.

between individuals in such beliefs can provide better predictors of future achievement than IQ differences (Dweck, 1986; Vispoel and Austin, 1993). In the above case, it could be argued that because the child has perceived herself as possessing some gift that others do not have, she has been encouraged to be confident of success in her field of expertise. However, there is a less benign corollary: self-fulfilling beliefs about the consequences of an innate gift being present are inevitably coupled with self-fulfilling beliefs about the outcome of a person lacking such a gift. The supposed absence of a specific gift or talent in certain young people may be used as a reason to justify failing to make musical opportunities available to them.

Is the Folk Psychology Account Correct?

If only because of its potential for damaging the lives of those young people who have not been identified as being gifted, it is necessary to ask whether, or to what extent, the folk psychology account of the causes of musical ability is actually correct. There are a number of reasons for questioning the view which attributes musical expertise to the presence of innate gifts or talents.

1. In some non-Western cultures musical achievements are much more widespread than in our own. [. . .] Messenger's (1958) account of the Anang Ibibo of Nigeria is representative:

> We were constantly amazed at the musical abilities displayed by these people, especially by the children who, before the age of five, can sing hundreds of songs, both individually and in choral groups and, in addition, are able to play several percussion instruments and have learned dozens of intricate dance movements calling for incredible muscular control. We searched in vain for the 'non-musical' person, finding it difficult to make enquiries about tone-deafness and its assumed effects because the Anang language possesses no comparable concept . . . They will not admit, as we tried so hard to get them to, that there are those that lack the requisite abilities. This same attitude applies to the other aesthetic areas. Some dancers, singers and weavers are considered more skilled than most, but everyone can dance and sing well (Messenger, 1958: pp. 20–22).

Cultural factors are clearly important. Western cultures may have unique features that are inimical to the widespread development of high musical achievement. However, even within western society there are sub-cultures in which musical expertise is especially prevalent. They can emerge quite quickly, often as a result of deliberate efforts. For instance, in eighteenth-century Venice, certain orphanages, notably the famous la Pieta, established a cultural ambience in which musical expertise was valued and encouraged. Ample opportunities for training were made available, thus creating environments in which a substantial proportion of the orphans became highly accomplished musicians (Howe, 1990; Kunkel, 1985). The fact that the distribution of musical expertise is so greatly affected by cultural factors is hard to reconcile with the proposal that the presence or absence of musical skills in an individual largely depends upon differences in inherent characteristics.

2. Even in our own culture, people normally classified as 'non-musical' do in fact possess many musical skills, with most children acquiring many of the basic skills needed for perceiving and performing music (Hargreaves, 1986). For instance, even without any prior musical instruction, most children are capable by the age of 10 of reaching the same level of performance as musically trained adults at judging which of two musical passages conforms to the rules of tonal harmony (Sloboda, 1985a) [. . .]. Receptive skills appear to emerge in the majority of members of a culture through casual exposure to the normal musical products of that culture. The existence of these skills may not be apparent to a casual observer unless the individual concerned has also developed recognizable performance skills.

3. Contrary to common belief, in early childhood the kinds of indicators of later ability that would be consistent with the notion of innate factors being important are conspicuous mainly by their absence. In an investigation of the early backgrounds of notably successful young musicians, Sloboda and Howe (1991) discovered that very few of the individuals displayed any overt signs of musical precocity. Sosniak (1985), who interviewed 24 American concert pianists in their early thirties, found that even after these individuals had been playing the piano for several years there were few signs to indicate that they would eventually have more success than hundreds of other young pianists.

4. Whilst it may be true that some people find it easier than others to gain musical skills, the common view that certain 'gifted' individuals are capable of effortless progress is contradicted by the evidence. For example, Hayes (1981) found that among 76 major composers whose careers he investigated, hardly any of them produced major works prior to their having had at least ten years of rigourous and intensive musical training. Ericsson, Krampe, and Tesch-Romer (1993) found that the best violinists at a conservatoire had accumulated over 10,000 hours of arduous formal practice by the age of 21, whereas the less able had accumulated only half that number of hours. Becoming a fine musician is not, of course, just a matter of investing in huge quantities of technical practice. The development of an understanding of musical structure and musical styles is also essential, but this too takes time and experience.

5. Although it appears to be the case that musical ability runs in families, inheritance of innate talent is not necessarily the most satisfactory explanation. There is firm evidence that when given opportunities and encouragement to learn, even children whose close relatives have no musical expertise often make good progress. For example, Sloboda and Howe (1991) found that 30 per cent of the pupils at a highly selective specialist music school came from families where neither parent had any musical interest or skill which went beyond simply listening. In the most outstanding pupils, the proportion of non-musician parents increased to 40 per cent.

It is clearly not necessary for a successful musician to have relatives who are serious musicians.

6. There is a growing body of evidence to suggest that early experience can have a significant influence on musical ability. Musical learning can even begin before a child is born. The fetal ear begins to pick up sounds five to six months before birth (Parncutt, 1993). Studies by Hepper (1991) revealed that specific pieces of music played to prenatal infants (via loudspeakers placed on the mother's stomach), were subsequently recognized by the infants when played to them after birth (as evidenced by changes in attentiveness to these pieces as compared with novel ones).

In studies of the early lives of high achieving young musicians Howe and Sloboda (1991a; Sloboda and Howe, 1991) found that many of the parents sang to their children (particularly at sleep time) every day from birth. Many also engaged in song games, encouraging children to dance and sing to music. Because these activities are seen by many parents as 'ordinary' ones, their importance as learning opportunities may be seriously underestimated (Papousek, 1982).

Although there is a lack of research into the long-term effects of early musical stimulation, there is good evidence for the effectiveness of language stimulation (e.g. Fowler, 1990) [. . .], and there are reasons for believing that musical development is subject to broadly similar influences. Our current research is beginning to indicate higher levels of such early musical stimulation in families whose children make the most subsequent progress with music. Taken together, these observations suggest that early differences, possibly incidental and unintended, in exposure to music can lead to substantial variability in children's ability to take advantage of later formal learning opportunities such as instrumental lessons.

7. Folk psychology assumes that there exists some definite set of underlying qualities which differentiates between the innately talented and the untalented. The reality is that musical achievements draw on different combinations of a large number of distinct skills and sub-skills, and correlations between people's performance level at different skills are often low. For example, one musician may be able to pick up a musical score and play it at sight, yet not be able to hear a melody, reproduce and then extemporize around it. In contrast, another musician may have extemporization skills, but be unable to read a score.

One accomplishment, 'perfect pitch', is often assumed to be a special sign of innate musical talent, despite the fact that it is not necessary for reaching the highest levels of musical accomplishment. Perfect pitch is a skill limited to a relatively small proportion of musicians and seems to depend on a particularly systematic exposure to musical stimuli in early childhood (Sergeant, 1969). There is evidence to suggest that with a sufficiently persistent approach, the skill can be learned by any determined person (Cuddy, 1970; Brady, 1970). Levitin (1994) has argued that most measures of perfect pitch in fact draw on two independent abilities, pitch memory and pitch labelling (the ability to name a remembered pitch).

When Levitin measured pitch memory in a task where pitch labelling was not required (singing well-known popular songs from memory), over two-thirds of an unselected sample of college students demonstrated some evidence of perfect pitch.

These seven factors present a cogent challenge to the prevailing folk view. Despite the widespread acceptance of the idea that only certain people are born to be musical, the notion that everyone is musical is probably closer to the true situation. Taking into account the significance of the specific environmental and cultural factors mentioned above, it is clear that the development of musical ability is determined to a greater extent by experience than folk psychology would have us believe.

Whilst we are critical of the notion of innate musical gifts, we are not proposing that individual differences can necessarily be accounted for entirely by differences in experience, learning, motivation or practice. Nor are we denying that inherent biological differences between people may make a contribution to differences in their eventual musical capabilities. It is essential to extend our understanding of the mechanisms and processes by which inherent biological differences exert effects that may eventually influence musical achievements. New approaches to the study of behavioural genetics (e.g. Plomin and Thompson, 1993) offer the promise of more precise identification of genes contributing to psychological differences between individuals. However it is very likely that the links between biology and musical competence, when fully understood, will turn out to be complicated, indirect, not all-or-none, and in no way corresponding to the notion of a unitary 'blueprint for music' that is implied by the notion of innate talents or gifts.

Why is the Folk Psychology View so Widely Accepted?

One reason for the prevalence of the folk psychology account is that the music profession is dominated by it. In other areas of expertise, lay accounts and beliefs are systematically challenged at many points by more scientifically based explanations. For instance, in folk medicine, the common cold is often believed to be something that can be caught from sitting in a draught. Research demonstrates, however, that colds are caused by viruses, and although viruses are airborne, colds are not caused by cold air currents as such. Virology explains why the folk view has developed (viruses are carried in air), but also highlights the partial and potentially misleading nature of the folk explanation.

In the musical world there is no widespread acceptance of a comparable account, based on scientific research, which could provide an alternative view of how musical ability emerges. Therefore the folk view prevails.

Kingsbury's (1988) ethnographic study of an American music conservatory offers insights into the way in which the rhetoric of gifts and talents is given a central place in institutional philosophy and practice. In particular, this rhetoric underpins the assessment of musical performance, which is based almost entirely on the subjective judgements of the instrumental teachers of the conservatory. Their own credentials for making such judgements are ultimately grounded in their own training and performance pedigree, since other professionals, in their turn, have made positive subjective assessments of them. Although there are clearly some objective technical standards below which no aspiring musician can fall, final decisions are not generally open to objective verification in the way that the subjective judgements of, say, tennis experts can be publicly verified by anyone through seeing games being won or lost. Public music competitions are unlike tennis championships in this respect, because it still requires a professional panel of judges to determine the 'winners', and there is ample evidence that such judges can be extremely unreliable. Manturszewska (1970) reports a study in which the panel of a major international piano competition rated a set of performances of the same piece. Without the judges realizing it, the set contained repetitions of the same performance. Not only was the overall inter-judge agreement low, but some judges gave the repeated piece quite different ratings on the two hearings.

The essential subjectivity of musical assessments within the conservatory would not in itself ensure the dominance of the folk psychology of talent unless it was generally coupled with a reverence for the superior knowledge and wisdom of master musicians. There is a ritual quality to many of the central social acts, such as recitals, in which the music takes on an almost sacred character. According to Kingsbury, the music professors then become 'high priests' of the musical offering, being attributed with the capability to discern the quality of performances, in a way which is not easily challenged even by experts of another instrument or period. From the safety of this professional mystique assessors can, and often do, issue firm pronouncements about the musicality of their students. As Kingsbury puts it:

> A person whose playing is said to sound 'mechanical', or 'contrived' . . . will to that extent be considered unmusical or not talented. A person whose performance is 'expressive' or 'from the heart' and 'with feeling' will conversely be considered to be talented. A person will be judged 'musical' as distinguished from 'accomplished' to the extent that performance was not, or could not have been, determined by self-conscious preparation, such as systematic rehearsing, formal lessons, and technical drills (Kingsbury, 1988: 70–1).

Apart from doubts about whether such qualities of performances are reliably discernible by experts, there is the further problem of attribution error. Kingsbury cites the example of a student who gave a performance which, by her own admission was 'detached' because of high levels of performance anxiety. Instead of judging the performance to be 'unmusical' for situational reasons, the assessors instead judged the student to be an 'unmusical' person, thus reversing a previous decision made only a year before, with devastating impact on the student's self-image and self-confidence. According to Kingsbury, music professors routinely tell each other and their students that musicality is a fixed attribute – 'you either have it or you don't, and there really isn't anything to be done to change things'.

A second possible factor contributing to the prevalence of the folk account is the way in which the school music curriculum is organized in many Western countries. This has undoubtedly been informed by the professional ethos described above. In many countries classroom teachers of children under 12 are expected (and trained) to teach most subjects. Music is an exception, and is usually taught by a specialist, if at all. Although minimum standards of attainment are usually set in subjects such as language or mathematics, with remedial tuition for those falling behind, there have been no such standards for music. Instrumental tuition has usually been reserved for those who express an interest or are identified by a professional as being talented. The basic music provision that is available to all children can involve little more than supervised listening. It is interesting that in sport, the other area often taught by a specialist teacher rather than the generalist classroom teacher, the notion that some children might be simply spectators has little credence. Everyone is usually encouraged to attain some level of competence as a performer.

A study by S. O'Neill (1994) is providing intriguing preliminary evidence that the message implicit in these curricular arrangements begins to be communicated to children at an early age. When 6–10 year olds were asked whether they believed musical and other performance abilities were fixed or could be developed, many children reported a belief that musical ability could not be altered, whereas the vast majority of the same children believed that abilities to play games or sports could be improved with practice.

A third reason for the dominance of the folk psychology of talent may be that the processes by which children begin to differ from one another in musical ability may not be obvious or easily observable ones. Earlier, we pointed out how many foundational musical skills are receptive skills, acquired through exposure to music rather than through overt practice. The rate of learning will depend, not only on the amount of exposure, but also on the degree of attention that the individual pays to the material. This in turn may be affected by a range of motivational variables which are linked to music only by a long chain of intermediate factors. It is not difficult to see how two siblings who, from their parents' point of view, have had similar levels of musical exposure, could in fact demonstrate quite different levels of ability when presented with an overt task (such as instrumental performance) for the first time.

A fourth and final reason for the survival of the folk account is that by promoting a positive self-concept in a person identified as talented, it provides that individual with sources of motivation which are prerequisites to the investment in long hours of practice required to develop musical skills. in other words the folk attribution gives the musician a *raison d'être*. Because of the rarity of this supposed gift, the possessor of it is set apart as one of the chosen few. Many musicians talk about the gift as something (analogous to the poet's 'muse') of which they may at times be a reluctant recipient, but which imposes on them a duty to develop it, regardless of their transient personal inclinations. [. . .]

An Alternative Explanation for Differences in 'Musicality'

Our challenge to the folk explanation assumes that there are many routes to success or failure, not just one – talent or its absence. Nonetheless we would like to conclude by describing in some detail just one important route which several studies have strongly suggested.

Few people seem to doubt that technical expertise is, at root, just a matter of hard work; and it is not difficult to see how many of the differences between individuals in such expertise may be accounted for by differences in experience, motivation, and practice. However, as Kingsbury's observations of conservatory culture demonstrate, it is not these technical differences which are normally held to underlie differences in talent. Rather, talented musicians are those who are believed to have superior abilities in the more 'intangible' features of expressive performance (identified by some as 'playing from the heart'). When it comes to such features (the small variations in timing, loudness, pitch and tone quality which transform a piece of music from a merely technical reproduction to an individually distinctive product), there is an implicit assumption that 'gifts', not just hard work, are required

However, a number of research studies (e.g. Clarke, 1988; Gabrielsson, 1988; Shaffer, 1981; Sloboda, 1983) have shown that expressive 'microvariations' are, in fact, highly systematic, both within the same performer and across different performers within a musical culture. Many of these variations have the effect of making important structural features of the music more prominent to the listener, and the nature of such variations can be broadly predicted from general principles of perceptual grouping and organization. These microvariations display essential characteristics of acquired skills: they become more systematic with experience, they can be elicited in situations of unprepared performance (sight-reading), and their application by skilled practitioners is largely automatic. Differences between performers occur not so much because the fundamental principles of expression are different, but because performers have options concerning the distribution and intensity of different expressive devices. Such differences can be characterized as differences in expressive 'style' (Sloboda, 1985b).

Evidently then, despite justifiable doubt about the reliability of professional judgements of 'musicality', there is an objectively measurable continuum of expressive ability, at one end of which are situated musicians who consistently provide appropriate expressive performance in a wide variety of performance situations, and at the other end of which are those who tend to provide unexpressive 'routine' performances. We wish to argue that an individual's position on this continuum is just as likely to be determined by experience as is their technical expertise.

In particular it appears that the development of expressive skill may be significantly influenced by emotional and motivational circumstances accompanying early engagement with music. There is a considerable body of evidence that there are two types of motivation to engage with music, as with any other activity in which creativity may be displayed (Amabile, 1983; Persson, Pratt and Robson, 1992). One motivation is 'intrinsic'. It develops from intense pleasurable experiences with music (of a sensual, aesthetic or emotional kind) and contributes to the development of a personal commitment to music in and of itself. The other motivation is 'extrinsic', and is concerned with achievement. Here, the focus is not so much on the music itself as on achieving certain goals such as the approval of parents, identification with role models, and winning competitions. Clearly any one individual will have a mixture of both types of motivation. There is evidence, however, that a too early emphasis on achievement can inhibit intrinsic motivation. Children become so concerned about what others may be thinking of their performance, that they have little attention left for the potential of the music to engage their aesthetic and emotional sensibilities.

This conclusion is supported by a study of autobiographical memories (Sloboda, 1990). In this study, adult musicians and non-musicians were asked to recall events from the first ten years of life that had any connection at all with music. They were given a number of questions to stimulate recall concerning, for instance, where the event took place, what event the music was part of, who they were with, and what significance the experience had for them. Many of the musicians reported deeply felt and intensely positive early experiences to the 'internal' aspect of musical events, which seemed to lift them outside the normal state of awareness. For instance, one young woman reminisced as follows:

> I was seven years old, and sitting in morning assembly in school. The music formed part of the assembly service. I was with my friends Karen, Amelia, Jenny, Allan. The music was a clarinet duet, classical, probably by Mozart. I was astounded at the beauty of the sound. It was liquid, resonant, vibrant. It seemed to send tingles through me. I felt as if it was a significant moment. Listening to this music led to me learning to play first the recorder and then to achieve my ambition of playing the clarinet. Playing the clarinet has altered my life; going on a paper round and saving up to buy my own clarinet; meeting friends in the county band . . . Whenever I hear clarinets being played I remember the impact of this first experience (Sloboda, 1990: p. 37).

Others, more often the non-musicians, recalled events in which the music itself was not remembered as significant in itself, but rather its context, which was often one of anxiety, humiliation, or embarrassment. Being made to perform in front of others, being criticised, being laughed at, were common experiences.

Frequency analyses of the subcomponents of the recalls showed three factors which were statistically associated with positive internal experiences. First, the event occurred at home, in church, or at a concert hall, rather than at school. Second, the event occurred while the child was listening rather than performing. Third, the child was on her own, with family or friends rather than with a teacher. In each case, these conditions seem to be connected with a relaxed, non-threatening environment where nothing is being asked of the child. It seems that such an environment is necessary for music to work its strongest emotional effects on individuals.

These positive 'peak' childhood experiences seem important for the development of musical ability for two reasons. First, these experiences are so pleasurable that children often increase their engagement with music in the hope of repeating them, thus providing motivation for the very large amounts of practice required to attain high levels of performance skill. Second, these experiences seem to be intimately connected to the person's understanding of the musical structures which are crucial to expressive performance. Sloboda (1991) has shown that adult music listeners identify many of their moments of most intense emotional response with quite specific musical events such as sudden shifts in the musical harmony (for example, enharmonic changes). These events are ones which manipulate listener's expectancies in some way. Unless one has experienced the 'delicious' surprise of an enharmonic change through listening, it is hard to see how one could effectively add the appropriate performance expression to such a change to heighten its effect for listeners. Such expression might arguably be a slight slowing which delays and emphasizes the onset of the unexpected chord. Emotional experience must precede performance. Children who are focusing emotional attention on their performance and other extrinsic factors rather than on the music itself may not be able to build the structure-emotion links that are the necessary foundations of spontaneous expressive playing.

Thus, the musician who plays with technical competence but 'unmusically' may often be the person who has developed an extrinsic rather than an intrinsic focus for musical activity. The absence of an intrinsic focus has nothing to do with absence of 'talent' but the absence of opportunities to learn, by experience, how musical structures affect the emotions.

Conclusion

The above account demonstrates just one of the many possible routes by which the differing experiences of individuals may have lasting and significant effects on their musical ability. To understand fully the origins of musical ability will require a great deal more research into the lives of developing musicians. However, we hope that we have sketched enough of a picture to show that a preoccupation with simplistic notions of innate gifts and talents can only serve to inhibit efforts to gain a proper scientific understanding of this complex phenomenon.

References

Amabile, T. M. (1983) *The Social Psychology of Creativity.* New York: Springer Verlag.

Brady, P. T. (1970) Fixed-scale mechanism of absolute pitch. *Journal of the Acoustical Society of America*, 48, pp. 883–7.

Clarke, E. F. (1988) Generative principles in music performance. In J. A. Sloboda (Ed.) *Generative processes in music: the psychology of performance, improvisation, and composition.* London: Oxford University Press.

Cuddy, L. L. (1970) Training the absolute identification of pitch. *Perception and Psychophysics*, 8, pp. 265–9.

Dweck, C. S. (1986) Motivational processes affecting learning. *American Psychologist*, 41, pp. 1040–1048.

Ericsson K. A., Krampe, R. T., and Tesch-Romer, C. (1993) The role of deliberate practice in the acquisition of expert performance. *Psychological Review*, 100, pp. 363–406.

Fowler, W. (1990) Early stimulation and the development of verbal talents. In M. J. A. Howe (Ed.) *Encouraging the Development of Exceptional Skills and Talents.* Leicester: BPS Books.

Gabrielsson, A. (1988) Timing in music performance and its relations to music experience. In J. A. Sloboda (Ed.) *Generative processes in music: the psychology of performance, improvisation, and composition.* London: Oxford University Press.

Hargreaves D. J. (1986) *The Developmental Psychology of Music.* Cambridge: Cambridge University Press.

Hayes, J. R. (1981) The *Complete Problem Solver.* Philadelphia: Franklin Institute Press.

Hepper, P. G. (1991) An examination of fetal learning before and after birth. *Irish Journal of Psychology*, 12, pp. 95–107.

Howe, M. J. A. (1990) The *Origins of Exceptional Abilities.* Oxford: Blackwell.

Howe, M. J. A. and Sloboda, J. A. (1991a) Young musicians' accounts of significant influences in their early lives: 1. the family and the musical background. *British Journal of Music Education*, 8, pp. 39–52.

Howe, M. J. A. and Sloboda, J. A. (1991b) Problems experience by young musicians as a result of the failure of other children to value musical accomplishments. *Gifted Education*, 8, pp. 102–111.

Kingsbury, H. (1988) *Music, Talent, and Performance: a Conservatory Cultural System.* Philadelphia: Temple University Press.

Kunkel, J. H. (1985) Vivaldi in Venice: an historical test of psychological propositions. *Psychological Record*, 35, pp. 445–457.

Levitin, D. (1994) Absolute representation in auditory memory: evidence from the production of learned melodies. *Perception and Psychophysics.*

Manturszewska, M. (1970) Rzetelnose ocen wykonowslwa muzycznego, wydawanych przez ekspertow muzycznych (Reliability of evaluation of musical performances given by musical experts) *Ruch Muzyczny*, 21, pp. 3–8.

Messenger, J. (1958) Esthetic talent. *Basic College Quarterly*, 4, pp. 20–24.

O'Neill, S. A. (1994) Children's conceptions of ability: a comparison of major domains. Internal research report, Department of Psychology, Keele University.

Papousek, M. (1982) The 'mother tongue method' of music education: psycho-biological roots in oroverbal parent-infant communication. In J. Dobbs (Ed.), *International Music Education.* ISME Year-book 1982.

Parncutt, R. (1993) Prenatal experience and the origins of music. In T. Blum (Ed.) *Prenatal perception, learning and bonding.* Berlin: Leonardo.

Persson, R. S., Pratt, G., and Robson, C. (1992) Motivational and influential components of musical performance: a qualitative analysis. *European Journal for High Ability*, 3, pp. 206–217.

Plomin, R, and Thompson, L. A. (1993) Genetics and high cognitive ability. In K. Ackrill (Ed.) *The Origins and Development of High Ability: Proceedings of Ciba symposium 178.* London: Wiley.

Sergeant, D. (1969) Experimental investigation of absolute pitch. *Journal of Research in Music Education*, 17, pp. 135–43.

Shaffer, L. H. (1981) Performances of Chopin, Bach, and Bartok: studies in motor programming. *Cognitive Psychology*, 13, pp. 326–376.

Sloboda, J. A. (1983) The communication of musical metre in piano performance. *Quarterly Journal of Experimental Psychology*, 35A, pp. 377–396.

Sloboda, J. A. (1985a) *The Musical Mind: the Cognitive Psychology of Music.* London: Oxford University Press.

Sloboda, J. A. (1985b) Expressive skill in two pianists: style and effectiveness in music performance. *Canadian Journal of Psychology*, 39, pp. 273–293.

Sloboda, J. A. (1990) Music as a language. In F. Wilson and F. Roehmann (Eds.) *Music and child development.* St. Louis, Miss.: MMB Inc.

Sloboda, J. A. (1991) Music structure and emotional response: some empirical findings. *Psychology of Music*, 19, pp. 110–120.

Sloboda, J. A. and Howe, M. J. A. (1991) Biographical precursors of musical excellence: an interview study. *Psychology of Music*, 19, pp. 3–21.

Sosniak, L. A. (1985) Learning to be a concert pianist. In B. S. Bloom (Ed.)*Young People.* New York: Ballantine.

Vispoel, W. P. and Austin, J. R. (1993) Constructive response to failure in music: the role of attribution feedback and classroom goal structure. *British Journal of Educational Psychology*, 63, pp. 110–129.

4

Making up the Mind

Oliver Sacks

Five years ago the concepts of 'mind' and 'consciousness' were virtually excluded from scientific discourse. Now they have come back, and every week we see the publication of new books on the subject.

[. . .]

If we are to have a model or theory of mind as this actually occurs in living creatures in the world, it may have to be radically different from anything like a computational one. It will have to be grounded in biological reality, in the anatomical and developmental and functional details of the nervous system; and also in the inner life or mental life of the living creature, the play of its sensations and feelings and drives and intentions, its perception of objects and people and situations, and, in higher creatures at least, the ability to think abstractly and to share through language and culture the consciousness of others.

Above all such a theory must account for the development and adaptation peculiar to living systems. Living organisms are born into a world of challenge and novelty, a world of significances, to which they must adapt or die. Living organisms grow, learn, develop, organize knowledge, and use memory in a way that has no analogue in the nonliving. Memory itself is characteristic of life. And memory brings about a change in the organism, so that it is better adapted, better fitted, to meet environmental challenges. The very 'self' of the organism is enlarged by memory.

Such a notion of organic change as taking place with experience and learning, and as being an essential change in the structure and 'being' of the organism, had no place in the classical theories of memory, which tended to portray it as a thing-in-itself, something *deposited* in the brain and mind – an impression, a trace, a replica of the original experience, like a photograph. (For Socrates, the brain was soft wax, imprinted with impressions as with a seal or signet ring.) This was certainly the case with Locke and the empiricists, and has its counterpart in many of the current models of memory, which see it as having a definite location in the brain, something like the memory core of a computer.

This chapter has been edited.

The neural basis of memory, and of learning generally, the Canadian neuroscientist Donald Hebb hypothesized, lay in a selective strengthening or inhibition of the synapses between nerve cells and the development of groups of cells or 'cell-assemblies' embodying the remembered experience. This change, for Hebb, was only a local one, not a change in the brain (or the self) as a whole. At the opposite extreme, his teacher Karl Lashley, who trained rats to do complex tasks after removing various parts of their brains, came to feel that it was impossible to localize memory or learning; that, with remembering and learning, changes took place throughout the entire brain. Thus, for Lashley, memory, and indeed identity, did not have discrete locations in the brain.[1] There seemed no possible meeting point between these two views: an atomistic or mosaic view of the brain as parceling memory and perception into small, discrete areas, and a global or 'gestalt' view, which saw them as being somehow spread out across the entire brain.

These disparate views of memory and brain function were only part of a more general chaos, a flourishing of many fields and many theories, independently and in isolation, a fragmentation of our approaches to, and views about, the brain. [. . .]

A comprehensive theory of brain function that could make sense of the diverse observations of a dozen different disciplines has been missing, and the enormous but fragmented growth of neuroscience in the last two decades has made the need for such a general theory more and more pressing. [. . .]

The needed theory [. . .] must account for (or at least be compatible with) all the facts of evolution and neural development and neurophysiology that we know, on the one hand, and on the other all the facts of neurology and psychology, of mental life, that we know. It must be a theory of self-organization and emergent order at every level and scale, from the scurrying of molecules and their micropatterns in a million synaptic clefts to the grand macro-patterns of an actual lived life. [. . .]

[. . .] Just such a theory has been imagined, and with great force and originality, by Gerald Edelman, who, with his colleagues at the Neurosciences Institute at Rockefeller University over the past fifteen years, has been developing a biological theory of mind, which he calls Neural Darwinism, or the Theory of Neuronal Group Selection (TNGS).

[. . .] He now presents the theory more informally, but within a richer historical and philosophical discussion, in his new book *Bright Air, Brilliant Fire*.

Edelman's early work dealt not with the nervous system, but with the immune system, by which all vertebrates defend themselves against invading bacteria and viruses. It was previously accepted that the immune system 'learned', or was 'instructed', by means of a single type of antibody which molded itself around the foreign body, or antigen, to produce an appropriate, 'tailored' antibody. These molds then multiplied and entered the bloodstream and destroyed the alien organisms. But Edelman showed that a radically different mechanism was at work; that we possess not one basic kind of antibody, but millions of them, an enormous repertoire of antibodies, from which the invading antigen 'selects' one that fits. It is such a selection, rather than a direct shaping or instruction, that leads to the multiplication of the appropriate antibody and the destruction of the invader. Such a mechanism, which he called a 'clonal selection', was suggested in 1959 by MacFarlane Burnet, but Edelman was the first to demonstrate that such a 'Darwinian' mechanism actually occurs, and for this he shared a Nobel Prize in 1972.

Edelman then began to study the nervous system, to see whether this too was a selective system, and whether its workings could be understood as evolving, or emerging, by a similar process of selection. Both the immune system and the nervous system can be seen as systems for recognition. The immune system has to recognize all foreign intruders, to categorize them, reliably, as 'self' or 'not self'. The task of the nervous system is roughly analogous, but far more demanding: it has to classify, to categorize, the whole sensory experience of life, to build from the first categorizations, by degrees, an adequate model of the world; and in the absence of any specific programming or instruction to discover or create its own way of doing this. How does an animal come to recognize and deal with the novel situations it confronts? How is such individual development possible?

The answer, Edelman proposes, is that an evolutionary process takes place – not one that selects organisms and takes millions of years, but one that occurs within each particular organism and during its lifetime, by competition among cells, or selection of cells (or, rather, cell groups) in the brain. This for Edelman is 'somatic selection'.

Edelman and his colleagues have been concerned not only to propose a principle of selection but to explore the mechanisms by which it may take place. Thus they have tried to answer three kinds of questions: Which units in the nervous system select and give different emphasis to sensory experience? How does selection occur? What is the relation of the selecting mechanisms to such functions of brain and mind as perception, categorization, and, finally, consciousness?

Edelman discusses two kinds of selection in the evolution of the nervous system – 'developmental' and 'experiential'. The first takes place largely before birth. The genetic instructions in each organism provide general constraints for neural development, but they cannot specify the exact destination of each developing nerve cell – for these grow and die, migrate in great numbers and in entirely unpredictable ways: all of them are 'gypsies', as Edelman likes to say. The vicissitudes of fetal development themselves produce in every brain unique patterns of neurons and neuronal groups. Even identical twins with identical genes will not have identical brains at birth: the fine details of cortical circuitry will be quite different. Such variability, Edelman points out, would be a catastrophe in virtually any mechanical or computational system, where exactness and reproducibility are of the essence. But in a system in which selection is central, the consequences are entirely different; here variation and diversity are themselves of the essence.

Now, already possessing a unique and individual pattern of neuronal groups through developmental selection, the creature is born, thrown into the world, there to be exposed to a new form of selection which forms the basis of experience. What is the world of a newborn infant (or chimp) like? Is it a sudden incomprehensible (perhaps terrifying) explosion of electro-magnetic radiations, sound waves, and chemical stimuli which make the infant cry and sneeze? Or an ordered, intelligible world, in which the infant discerns people, objects, meanings, and smiles? We know that the world encountered is not one of complete meaninglessness and pandemonium, for the infant shows selective attention and preferences from the start.

Clearly there are some innate biases or dispositions at work; otherwise the infant would have no tendencies whatever, would not be moved to do anything, seek anything, to stay alive. These basic biases Edelman calls 'values'. Such values are essential for adaptation and survival; some have been developed through eons of evolution; and some are acquired through exploration and experience. Thus if the infant instinctively values food, warmth, and contact with other people (for example), this will direct its first movements and strivings. These 'values' – drives, instincts, inten-tionalities – serve to differentially weight experience, to orient the organ-ism toward survival and adaptation, to allow what Edelman calls 'categorization *on* value', e.g. to form categories such as 'edible' and 'non-edible' as part of the process of getting food. It needs to be stressed that 'values' are experienced, internally, as *feelings* – without feeling there can be no animal life. 'Thus', in the words of the late philosopher Hans Jonas, 'the capacity for feeling, which arose in all organisms, is the mother-value of all'.

At a more elementary physiological level, there are various sensory and motor 'givens', from the reflexes that automatically occur (for example, in response to pain) to innate mechanisms in the brain, as, for example, the feature detectors in the visual cortex which, as soon as they are activated, detect verticals, horizontals, boundaries, angles, etc., in the visual world.

Thus we have a certain amount of basic equipment; but, in Edelman's view, very little else is programmed or built in. It is up to the infant animal, given its elementary physiological capacities, and given its inborn values, to create its own categories and to use them to make sense of, to *construct*, a world – and it is not just a world that the infant constructs, but its *own* world, a world constituted from the first by personal meaning and reference.

Such a neuro-evolutionary view is highly consistent with some of the conclusions of psychoanalysis and developmental psychology – in particu-lar, the psychoanalyst Daniel Stern's description of 'an emergent self'. 'In-fants seek sensory stimulation', writes Stern. 'They have distinct biases or preferences with regard to the sensations they seek . . . These are innate. From birth on, there appears to be a central tendency to form and test hypotheses about what is occurring in the world . . . [to] categorize . . . into conforming and contrasting patterns, events, sets, and experiences'.[2] Stern emphasizes how crucial are the active processes of connecting, correlating, and categorizing information, and how with these a distinctive organization emerges, which is experienced by the infant as the sense of a self.

It is precisely such processes that Edelman is concerned with. He sees them as grounded in a process of selection acting upon the primary neuronal units with which each of us is equipped. These units are not individual nerve cells or neurons, but groups ranging in size from about fifty to ten thousand neurons; there are perhaps a hundred million such groups in the entire brain. During the development of the fetus, a unique neuronal pattern of connections is created, and then in the infant experience acts upon this pattern, modifying it by selectively strengthening or weakening connections between neuronal groups, or creating entirely new connections.

Thus experience itself is not passive, a matter of 'impressions' or 'sense-data', but active, and constructed by the organism from the start. Active experience 'selects', or carves out, a new, more complexly connected pattern of neuronal groups, a neuronal reflection of the individual experience of the child, of the procedures by which it has come to categorize reality.

But these neuronal circuits are still at a low level – how do they connect with the inner life, the mind, the behavior of the creature? It is at this point that Edelman introduces the most radical of his concepts – the concepts of 'maps' and 'reentrant signaling'. A 'map', as he uses the term, is not a representation in the ordinary sense, but an interconnected series of neuronal groups that responds selectively to certain elemental categories – for example, to movements or colors in the visual world. The creation of maps, Edelman postulates, involves the synchronization of hundreds of neuronal groups. Some mappings, some categorizations, take place in discrete and anatomically fixed (or 'prededicated') parts of the cerebral cortex – thus color is 'constructed' in an area called V4. The visual system alone, for example, has over thirty different maps for representing color, movement, shape, etc.

But where perception of *objects* is concerned, the world, Edelman likes to say, is not 'labeled', it does not come 'already parsed into objects'. We must *make* them, in effect, through our own categorizations: 'Perception makes', Emerson said. 'Every perception', says Edelman, echoing Emerson, 'is an act of creation'. Thus, our sense organs, as we move about, take samplings of the world, creating maps in the brain. Then a sort of neurological 'survival of the fittest' occurs, a selective strengthening of those mappings which correspond to 'successful' perceptions – successful in that they prove the most useful and powerful for the building of 'reality'.

In this view, there are no innate mechanisms for complex 'personal' recognition, such as the 'grandmother cell' postulated by researchers in the 1970s to correspond to one's perception of one's grandmother.[3] Nor is there any 'master area', or 'final common path', whereby all perceptions relating (say) to one's grandmother converge in one single place. There is no such place in the brain where a final image is synthesized, nor any miniature person or homunculus to view this image. Such images or representations do not exist in Edelman's theory, nor do any such homunculi. (Classical theory, with its concept of 'images' or 'representations' in the brain, demanded a sort of dualism – for there had to be a miniature 'someone in the brain' to view the images; and then another, still smaller, someone in the brain of that someone; and so on, in an infinite regress. There is no way of escaping from this regress, except by eliminating the very concept of images and viewers, and replacing it by a dynamic concept of process or interaction.)

Rather, the perception of a grandmother or, say, of a chair depends on the synchronization of a number of scattered mappings throughout the visual cortex – mappings relating to many different perceptual aspects of the chair (its size, its shape, its color, its 'leggedness', its relation to other sorts of chairs – armchairs, kneeling chairs, baby chairs, etc.). In this way the brain, the creature, achieves a rich and flexible percept of 'chairhood', which allows the recognition of innumerable sorts of chairs *as* chairs (computers, by contrast, with their need for unambiguous definitions and criteria, are quite unable to achieve this). This perceptual generalization is dynamic and not static, and depends on the active and incessant orchestration of countless details. Such a correlation is possible because of the very rich connections between the brain's maps – connections which are reciprocal, and may contain millions of fibers.

These extensive connections allow what Edelman calls 'reentrant signaling', a continuous 'communication' *between* the active maps themselves, which enables a coherent construct such as 'chair' to be made. This construct arises from the interaction of many sources. Stimuli from, say, touching a chair may affect one set of maps, stimuli from seeing it may affect another set. Reentrant signaling takes place between the two sets of maps – and between many other maps as well – as part of the process of perceiving a chair.

This construct, it must be emphasized once again, is not comparable to a single image or representation – it is, rather, comparable to a giant and continually modulating equation, as the outputs of innumerable maps, connected by reentry, not only complement one another at a perceptual level but are built up to higher and higher levels. For the brain, in Edelman's vision, makes maps of its own maps, or 'categorizes its own categorizations', and does so by a process which can ascend indefinitely to yield ever more generalized pictures of the world.

This reentrant signaling is different from the process of 'feedback', which merely corrects errors.[4] Simple feedback loops are not only common in the technological world (as thermostats, governors, cruise controls, etc.) but are crucial in the nervous system, where they are used for control of all the body's automatic functions, from temperature to blood pressure to the fine control of movement. (This concept of feedback is at the heart of both Wiener's cybernetics and Claude Bernard's concept of homeostasis.) But at higher levels, where flexibility and individuality are all-important, and where new powers and new functions are needed and created, one requires a mechanism that can construct, not just control or correct.

The process of reentrant signaling, with its scores – perhaps hundreds – of reciprocal connections within and between maps, may be likened to a sort of neural United Nations, in which dozens of voices are talking together, while including in their conversation a variety of constantly inflowing reports from the outside world, and giving them coherence, bringing them together into a larger picture as new information is correlated and new insights emerge. There is, to continue the metaphor, no secretary general in the brain; the activity of reentrant signaling itself achieves the synthesis. How is this possible?

Edelman, who himself once planned to be a concert violinist, uses musical metaphors here. 'Think', he said in a recent BBC radio broadcast,

> if you had a hundred thousand wires randomly connecting four string quartet players and that, even though they weren't speaking words, signals were going back and forth in all kinds of hidden ways [as you usually get them by the subtle nonverbal interactions between the players] that make the whole set of sounds a unified ensemble. That's how the maps of the brain work by re-entry.

The players are connected. Each player, interpreting the music individually, constantly modulates and is modulated by the others. There is no final or 'master' interpretation – the music is *collectively* created. This, then, is Edelman's picture of the brain, an orchestra, an ensemble – but without a conductor, an orchestra which makes its own music.

The construction of perceptual categorizations and maps, the capacity for generalization made possible by reentrant signaling, is the beginning of psychic development, and far precedes the development of consciousness or mind, or of attention or concept formation – yet it is a prerequisite for all of these; it is the beginning of an enormous upward path, and it can achieve remarkable power. [. . .] Perceptual categorization, whether of colors, movements, or shapes, is the first step, and it is crucial for learning, but it is not something fixed, something that occurs once and for all. On the contrary – and this is central to the dynamic picture presented by Edelman – there is then a continual *re*categorization, and this itself constitutes memory.

'In computers', Edelman writes, 'memory depends on the specification and storage of bits of coded information'. This is *not* the case in the nervous system. Memory in living organisms by contrast take's place through activity and continual recategorization.

> By its nature, memory . . . involves continual motor activity . . . in different contexts. Because of the new associations arising in these contexts, because of changing inputs and stimuli, and because different combinations of neuronal groups can give rise to a similar output, a given categorical response in memory may be achieved in several ways. Unlike computer-based memory, brain-based memory is inexact, but it is also capable of great degrees of generalization.

In the extended Theory of Neuronal Group Selection, which he has developed since 1987, Edelman has been able, in a very economical way, to accommodate all the 'higher' aspects of mind – concept formation, language, consciousness itself – without bringing in any additional considerations. Edelman's most ambitious project, indeed, is to try to delineate a possible biological basis for consciousness. He distinguishes, first, 'primary' from 'higher-order' consciousness:

> Primary consciousness is the state of being mentally aware of things in the world – of having mental images in the present. But it is not accompanied by any sense of [being] a person with a past and a future . . . In contrast, higher-order consciousness involves the recognition by a thinking subject of his or her own acts and affections. It embodies a model of the personal, and, of the past and future as well as the present . . . It is what we as humans have in addition to primary consciousness.

The essential achievement of primary consciousness, as Edelman sees it, is to bring together the many categorizations involved in perception into a *scene*. The advantage of this is that 'events that may have had significance to an animal's past learning can be related to new events'. The relation established will not be a causal one, one necessarily related to anything in the outside world; it will be an *individual* (or 'subjective') one, based on what has had 'value' or 'meaning' for the animal in the past.

Edelman proposed that the ability to create scenes in the mind depends upon the emergence of a new neuronal circuit during evolution, a circuit allowing for continual reentrant signaling between, on the one hand, the parts of the brain where memory of such value categories as warmth, food, and light takes place and, on the other, the ongoing global mappings that categorize perceptions as they actually take place. This 'bootstrapping process' (as Edelman calls it) goes on in all the senses, thus allowing for the construction of a complex scene. The 'scene', one must stress, is not an image, not a picture (any more than a 'map' is), but a correlation between different kinds of categorization.

[. . .]

Only in ourselves – and to some extent in apes – does a higher-order consciousness emerge. Higher-order consciousness arises from primary consciousness – it supplements it, it does not replace it. It is dependent on the evolutionary development of language, along with the evolution of symbols, of cultural exchange; and with all this brings an unprecedented power of detachment, generalization, and reflection, so that finally self-consciousness is achieved, the consciousness of being a self in the world, with human experience and imagination to call upon.

Higher-order consciousness releases us from the thrall of the here and now, allowing us to reflect, to introspect, to draw upon culture and history, and to achieve by these means a new order of development and mind. The most difficult and tantalizing portions of *Bright Air, Brilliant Fire* are about how this higher-order consciousness is achieved and how it emerges from the primary consciousness. No other theorist I know of has even attempted a biological understanding of this step. To become conscious of being conscious, Edelman stresses, systems of memory must be related to representation of a self. This is not possible unless the contents, the 'scenes', of primary consciousness are subjected to a further process and are themselves recategorized.

Though language, in Edelman's view, is not crucial for the development of higher-order consciousness – there is some evidence of higher order consciousness and self-consciousness in apes – it immensely facilitates and expands this by making possible previously unattainable conceptual and symbolic powers. Thus two steps, two reentrant processes are envisaged here: first the linking of primary (or 'value-category') memory with current perception – a perceptual 'bootstrapping', which creates primary consciousness; second, a linking between symbolic memory and conceptual centers – the 'semantic boot-strapping' necessary for higher consciousness. The effects of this are momentous: 'The acquisition of a new kind of memory', Edelman writes, '. . . leads to a conceptual explosion. As a result, concepts of the self, the past, and the future can be connected to primary consciousness. "Consciousness of consciousness" becomes possible'.

At this point Edelman makes explicit what is implicit throughout his work – the interaction of 'neural Darwinism' with classical Darwinism. What occurs 'explosively' in individual development must have been equally critical in evolutionary development. Thus 'at some transcendent moment in evolution', Edelman writes, there emerged 'a variant with a reentrant circuit linking value-category memory' to current perception. 'At that moment', Edelman continues, 'memory became the substrate and servant of consciousness'. And then, at another transcendent moment, by another, higher turn of reentry, higher-order consciousness arose.

[. . .]

Esther Thelen and her colleagues at the University of Indiana in Bloomington, [. . .] have for some years been making a minute analysis of the development of motor skills – walking, reaching for objects – in infants. 'For the developmental theorist', Thelen writes, 'individual differences pose an enormous challenge . . . Developmental theory has not met this challenge with much success'. And this is, in part, because individual differences are seen as extraneous, whereas Thelen argues that it is precisely such differences, the huge variation between individuals, that allow the evolution of unique motor patterns.

Thelen found that the development of such skills, as Edelman's theory would suggest, follows no single programmed or prescribed pattern. Indeed there is great variability among infants at first, with many patterns of reaching for objects; but there then occurs, over the course of several months, a competition among these patterns, a discovery or selection of workable patterns, or workable motor solutions. These solutions, though roughly similar (for there are a limited number of ways in which an infant can reach), are always different and individual, adapted to the particular dynamics of each child, and they emerge by degrees, through exploration and trial. Each child, Thelen showed, explores a rich range of possible ways to reach for an object and selects its own path, without the benefit of any blueprint or program. The child is forced to be original, to create its own solutions. Such an adventurous course carries its own risks – the child may evolve a *bad* motor solution – but sooner or later such bad solutions tend to destabilize, break down, and make way for further exploration, and better solutions.

When Thelen tries to envisage the neural basis of such learning, she uses terms very similar to Edelman's: she sees a 'population' of movements being selected or 'pruned' by experience. She writes of infants 're-mapping' the neuronal groups that are correlated with their movements, and 'selectively strengthening particular neuronal groups'. She has, of course, no direct evidence for this, and such evidence cannot be obtained until we have a way of visualizing vast numbers of neuronal groups simultaneously in a conscious subject, and following their interactions for months on end. No such visualization is possible at the present time, but it will perhaps become possible by the end of the decade. Meanwhile, the close correspondence between Thelen's observations and the kind of behavior that would be expected from Edelman's theory is striking.

[. . .]

Others too – cognitive psychologists and linguists – have become intensely interested in Edelman's ideas, in particular by the implication of the extended Theory of Neuronal Group Selection which suggests that the exploring child, the exploring organism, seeks (or imposes) meaning at all times, that its mappings are mappings of meaning, that its world and (if higher consciousness is present) its symbolic systems are *constructed* of 'meanings'. When Jerome Bruner and others launched the 'cognitive revolution' in the mid-1950s; this was in part a reaction to behaviorism and other 'isms' which denied the existence and structure of the mind. The cognitive revolution was designed 'to replace the mind in nature', to see the seeking of meaning as central to the organism. In a recent book, *Acts of Meaning,* Bruner describes how this original impetus was subverted, and replaced by notions of computation, information processing, etc. [. . .]

But, as Edelman writes, it is increasingly clear, from studying the natural acquisition of language in the child, and, equally, from the persistent failure of computers to 'understand' language, its rich ambiguity and polysemy, that syntax cannot be separated from semantics. It is precisely through the medium of 'meanings' that natural language and natural intelligence are built up. [. . .]

Neural Darwinism [. . .] coincides with our sense of 'flow', that feeling we have when we are functioning optimally, of a swift, effortless, complex, ever-changing, but integrated and orchestrated stream of consciousness; it coincides with the sense that this consciousness is ours, and that all we experience and do and say is, implicitly, a form of self-expression, and that we are destined, whether we wish it or not, to a life of particularity and self-development; it coincides, finally, with our sense that life is a journey –

unpredictable, full of risk and uncertainty, but, equally, full of novelty and adventure, and characterized (if not sabotaged by external constraints or pathology) by constant advance, an ever deeper exploration and understanding of the world.

Edelman's theory proposes a way of grounding all this in known facts about the nervous system and testable hypotheses about its operations. Any theory, even a wrong theory, is better than no theory; and this theory – the first truly global theory of mind and consciousness, the first biological theory of individuality and autonomy – should at least stimulate a storm of experiment and discussion.

[. . .]

Notes

Abridged from *The New York Review*, 8 April 1993.
1   Lashley expressed this in a famous paper, 'In Search of the Engram', published shortly before his death; London: *Symposia of the Society for Experimental Biology*, Vol. 4, 1950.
2   *The Interpersonal World of the Infant: A View from Psychoanalysis and Developmental. Psychology* (Basic Books, 1985).
3   There may however be built-in mechanisms for certain generic recognitions – such as the ability, which we share with all primates, to recognize the category of 'snakes', even if we have never seen a snake before; or infants' ability to recognize the generic category of 'faces' long before they recognize particular ones. There is now evidence for 'face-detecting' cells, in the cerebral cortex.
4   Confusingly, the very term 'reentrant' has occasionally been used in the past to denote such feedback loops. Edelman gives the term 'reentry' a radically new meaning.

5

Cognitive Development Through Social Interaction: Vygotsky and Piaget

Barbara Rogoff

When I discuss and I sincerely seek to understand someone else, I become engaged, not just in avoiding contradicting myself, in avoiding playing on words, etc., but also in entering into an indefinite series of viewpoints other than my own . . . . It is a moving equilibrium . . . . The engagements . . . that I make by nature of cooperation lead me I don't know where. (Piaget, *Logique genetique et sociologie*)

Under conditions of cooperation, an activity that is initially shared by those participating in it emerges as an original and fundamental foundation for the development of *individual* activity. (Rubtsov, *The Role of Cooperation in the Development of Intelligence*)

[. . .] What do children gain from social interaction, and under what circumstances? What aspects of social interaction contribute to children's advances? What is the significance of variations in social interaction, such as whether partners are adults or peers, the extent of their expertise, their authority or equality relative to the children, and the extent to which partners share in decision making? Are there differences in the role of social interaction depending on the age of the child?

These questions were addressed by Vygotsky and by Piaget, and they came to rather different conclusions. In this chapter, I describe the similarities and differences in mechanisms of social interactional influence on cognitive development posited by these two theorists, focusing on the importance of expertise versus equal status and the related question of the role of adults versus peers. I also address the differences in Vygotsky's and Piaget's assumptions about when in childhood social interaction can affect individual development. [. . .]

I have suggested that the day-to-day engagement of children and adults in shared activities contributes to the rapid progress of children in becoming skilled participants in the intellectual and social lives of their society. With Vygotsky, I have argued for the influential role of children's engagement with more skilled partners. But such suggestions and evidence of the structure and tuning of adult-child interaction and arrangements do not necessarily demonstrate that adult-child involvement fosters children's individual learning and development. Features of adult-child interaction and

This chapter has been edited.

arrangements may have little relation to children's learning. It is important to examine explicitly the influence of expertise of partners, of equality of status, of shared problem solving, of the structuring of children's efforts, and of the transfer of responsibility to children over the course of development.

As we do so, however, it is important to recognize that we are examining a very limited part of the question of the role of the social world in cognitive development. [. . .] The social context includes much more than social interaction between partners. A primary aspect of the social context is at the level of society – the institutions, technologies, norms, and practices developed by and appropriated from previous generations.

In addition, children's social partners, especially their caregivers, make arrangements for children's daily routine, tasks, circumstances, and partners. Much of this is accomplished independently of social interaction between children and their partners. Consider the time spent by middle-class parents in choosing day care, schools, or summer camp; interviewing and scheduling baby sitters; arranging for playmates to visit; selecting and preparing children's food, clothing, toys, and furniture; and ferrying them to after-school activities. In other cultures, parents may arrange children's activities by assigning them to the care of a sibling, holding them responsible for certain tasks, or restricting or requiring their presence at certain events. Such arrangements for children have an impact on children's activities, but may not involve social interaction in the decisions or the work of arrangement.

Thus it is obvious and necessary to acknowledge the role of guided participation in learning and development. So much of what children are able to do requires their being embedded in their culture. They would certainly not learn English without exposure to that language, nor would they develop scripts for the events involved in eating in restaurants, playing Peekaboo, or reading books without involvement as observers or participants. Most of the skills studied in cognitive research are tied closely to the technology – the books, number system, language, logic – of the culture in which children develop and that children learn to master with the assistance of more skilled partners.

Like genes, social interaction and social arrangements are an essential aspect of child development, without which it would be impossible to conceive of a child developing. (Even the process of conception is inherently social!) The impact of social partners and of social conventions is a logical necessity that is not addressed by the bounded variables and interventions examined in correlational and experimental studies of the effects of social interaction.

Most research on the effects of a particular variable requires that other variables be held constant, but with questions of the impact of sociocultural experience, it is impossible to exert such control over the phenomenon without destroying it. As I have argued earlier, the particular actions and skills of an individual cannot be understood out of the context of the immediate practical goals being sought and the enveloping sociocultural goals into which they fit.

What of processes that appear to be very stable across wide variations in the human condition? Should they be considered as not having sociocultural involvement? No. It is a fallacy to think that sociocultural processes lead to variation and biological processes lead to universals. For example, it is obvious that variations in hair color and height have genetic bases. And it is clear that universal features of human activities and skills are founded on commonalities in the social environment that go with being human.

It is easier for us to recognize the role of sociocultural variation than that of sociocultural universals, which we tend to take for granted. Human problems and some of the constraints on their solution are held in common in all human situations. It is those that *vary* that capture our attention. For example, different groups vary in their solution to the problem of communicating (e.g., using English, Spanish, or sign language) or of calculating (e.g., on abacuses, calculators, or fingers). The relation to specific social experience is obvious in these differences; it is necessary to be surrounded by English speakers to learn English. It may be necessary to be exposed to some sort of language to learn the rudiments of grammar, even those aspects that may be common across languages. But, consistent with Trevarthen's idea of innate intersubjectivity, the basics of the potential for social communication, such as turn taking and attention to others' intentions, may be inborn features of being human.

Even panhuman processes are likely to rely on the support of the social world, however. There are similarities among human babies around the world, because of both our species similarities and the panhuman social environment in which babies are nurtured. Although variations in cognitive processes and in development make the role of variations in social context obvious, universals of cognition and development are based on universals of human cultural as well as biological heritage, which cannot be dissociated. They have evolved together over the history of our species.

The role of societal institutions and intellectual technologies is central to Vygotsky's theory, but barely appears in Piaget's theory (i.e., his statement that the hypothetico-deductive thought of formal operations is based on social convention). Thus the context of the discussion of specific forms of social interaction and their impact on cognitive development differs in the two theories.

Mechanisms of Social Influence

The theories of Piaget and Vygotsky differ in the mechanisms proposed to underlie social influence, the phase of childhood seen as being open to social influence, and the ideal partner and role relations. It is to these differences that we now turn; further discussion of points of similarity and contrast is available in Tudge and Rogoff (1989). I speculate that the differences between the theories relate to differences in the phenomena the two theorists attempted to explain.

The two theories are based on different perspectives; Vygotsky focuses on the social basis of mind, while Piaget focuses on the individual as starting point. To understand cognition in social context, I believe that Vygotsky's perspective is essential; it cannot be reached by simply adding social context onto Piaget's individualist approach.

Both theories emphasize the importance of a common frame of reference, or intersubjectivity, in social interaction. However, consistent with the difference in centrality of the social and the individual in the two theories are differences in the locus of intersubjectivity. In Vygotsky's perspective, joint problem solving occurs *between* partners, whereas in Piaget's view, individuals work with independence and equality on each other's ideas.

In Vygotsky's theory, consistent with his emphasis on development as a process of learning to use the intellectual tools provided through social history, social interaction is expected to promote development through the guidance provided by interaction with people who have achieved some skill in the use of those intellectual tools. The model of most effective social interaction is thus joint problem solving with guidance by a person who is more skilled.

In Piaget's theory, children are seen as revising their ways of thinking to provide a better fit with reality when faced with discrepancies between their own ways of viewing the world and new information. Vygotsky (1987) characterized Piaget's theory as follows: 'Development is reduced to a continual *conflict between antagonistic forms of thinking;* it is reduced to the establishment of a unique compromise between these two forms of thinking at each stage in the developmental process' (p. 176). For the most part, this conflict was considered solitary, but Piaget (1926) also speculated that social interaction could bring about cognitive conflict, resulting in efforts to reestablish equilibrium. According to Piaget, social influence fosters change through the induction of cognitive conflict and the logical operations carried out by children attempting to reconcile their differing views to achieve equilibrium in their understanding. The Piagetian model of most effective social interaction is thus cooperation between equals who attempt to understand each others' views through reciprocal consideration of their alternative views.

Piaget emphasized cooperation as the ideal form of social interaction promoting development because he believed that the social relations involved in cooperation are the same as the logical relations that children construct in regard to the physical world. He considered cooperation to be a parallel form of logic in which children discuss propositions that provoke cognitive conflict and its logical resolution, yielding equilibrium:

> Cooperation itself constitutes a system of co-operations: putting in correspondence (which is an operation) the operations of one partner with those of the others, uniting (which is another operation) the acquisition of one partner with that of others, etc.; and in case of conflicts, raising the contradictions (which presupposes an operational process) or above all differentiating the different

points of view and introducing between them a reciprocity (which is an operational transformation). (Piaget, 1963/1977, p. 347)

Piaget (1977, pp. 160–2) laid out three conditions under which equilibrium is achieved in intellectual exchange. The first is that the partners have a common scale of intellectual values, allowing them to understand terms in the same sense. This involves a language and a system of ideas in which they converge, providing a key that allows each to translate into common terms the differing conceptions. The second condition is that the partners recognize a conservation of their propositions in which one does not contradict oneself, and in which the partners search for agreement on propositions or find facts that justify their difference in points of view. The third condition for equilibrium is that there is a reciprocity between partners such that the propositions of each are treated interchangeably. Piaget emphasized cognitive conflict as the working out of differences of opinion by coming to understand the other's perspective and by logically comparing the value of the two perspectives.

Vygotsky's model for the mechanism through which social interaction facilitates cognitive development resembles apprenticeship, in which a novice works closely with an expert in joint problem solving in the zone of proximal development. The novice is thereby able to participate in skills beyond those that he or she is independently capable of handling. Development builds on the internalization by the novice of the shared cognitive processes, appropriating what was carried out in collaboration to extend existing knowledge and skills.

Differences between the two theories in the model of social influence relate to important differences in the aspects of cognitive development that the theorists sought to explain. Piaget's emphasis was on children's qualitative shifts in perspective on logico-mathematical problems, whereas Vygotsky was interested in children's development of skills and information useful for the application of culturally developed tools for thinking. The resolution of cognitive conflict may be necessary for a child to discard an existing belief to consider one that is qualitatively different, to achieve a Piagetian shift in perspective, as when children realize that the quantity of water does not change when it is poured into a container of another shape. And interaction with an expert may be necessary to provide practice in skills and access to information required to become proficient with culturally developed tools for thinking.

Variation in Social Processes May Relate to What is Developing

The nature of guided participation may differ according to whether a situation involves children's development of understanding and skill or of a shift in perspective. For present purposes, I refer to the development of understanding and skills as the integration and organization of information and component acts into plans for action under relevant circumstances (e.g., learning to tie shoes; to associate items to remember them, or to read). Shifts of perspective, for present purposes, involve giving up an understanding of a phenomenon to take another view contrasting with the original perspective. The problems that Piaget posed to children about whether quantities change when their shape is transformed are examples of shifts in perspective for children who make the transformation from non-conservation (the quantity of water changes when it is poured into a glass of a different shape) to conservation (the quantity of water does not change despite the change in its shape).

The purpose of making these distinctions is to facilitate discussion of different interactional processes that may contribute to the development of understanding and skills or shifts in perspective. The development of understanding and skills may occur with the aid of simple explanation or demonstration, but may involve fine-tuning of communication, when describing a skill out of context or providing a simple demonstration is insufficient. For example, simply telling a child how to tie a shoe is unlikely to be helpful, but helping the child hold the loops and suggesting a mnemonic for the sequence of events ('the bunny circles around and then goes down the hole') may provide the support, over a number of sessions, to assist the child in learning the skill. Similar examples could be drawn from other domains, such as mnemonic strategies, subtraction skills, and reading skills.

For social influences to enhance changes of perspective, however, it may be necessary to have greater shared communication. To see a problem from a qualitatively different vantage point requires a person to become aware that there is another perspective and that it may offer some advantages. For development of understanding and skills, individuals may more easily realize that there is information they do not know or tactics they could learn. But changes of perspective require dissatisfaction with one's current understanding of a problem. Social interaction may contribute to making the person aware that there are alternatives – for example, through the sort of cognitive conflict that Piaget posited to occur between peers who have different answers to the same question. Social interaction may then contribute to directing the individual to accept another view, through presentation of the alternatives and consideration of the merits of each.

But for such social effects to occur, some conditions must be satisfied: individuals must become aware of and interested in exploring alternatives to their own perspective, and there must be intersubjectivity between partners to explore the existence and value of the alternatives. True, interest is needed to develop understanding and skills, but there is no need to give up current understandings to achieve 'conversion' – a process that may require inter-subjectivity. Understanding and skills may develop through observing or eavesdropping on actions and statements that are not intended to communicate to the observer, but mutual engagement in the exploration of possibilities may be more necessary for changes in perspective to result from social interaction.

Intersubjectivity in problem solving may also be important in fostering the development of 'inaccessible' cognitive processes that are difficult to observe or explain – as with shifts in perspective as well as some kinds of understanding and skill. Communication of such processes may require skillful explanation and analysis. It is relevant to this argument that many technologies of education are designed to make opaque processes more transparent, and that many intellectual tools serve the purpose of communicating about abstract ideas or past, future, or imaginary events. For example, blueprints and time-management charts facilitate planning by individuals, but their necessity may arise in social situations, to enable people to communicate concretely about abstract ideas and to coordinate their actions. Conventions used in diagramming, gesturing, and speaking are ways of facilitating mutual understanding by making events and ideas more concrete. Hence, learning to handle 'inaccessible' problems involving nontransparent cognitive processes may rely on social conventions necessary for shared problem solving and on learning through joint participation in a process of osmosis, rather than on explanation or demonstration.

The difficulty of communicating some ideas or of negotiating mental responsibility in social groups may lead individuals to prefer to work alone. This preference may be based on expectations of greater effectiveness of individual effort, but it may also involve concern about the effort or risk of collaborative work – even though the collaboration may be more effective than individual work. Bos (1937) describes a pair of 12-year-olds who said that it is more difficult to work together than on their own 'because it is not so easy to grasp the other's point of view' (p. 362). From discussion of these feelings, however, each realized that the other had the same concerns, and this understanding led to an intensive and harmonious collaboration.

> It is indeed easier quietly to pursue ones [*sic*] own thoughts than to formulate them convincingly, express them verbally and moreover assimilate proposals and ideas of the partner. This love of facility probably contributes to the opposition of people to endeavour with their mental power in active co-operation to arrive at a better achievement. (Bos, 1937, p. 362)

Through collaboration, partners may develop ways to communicate about difficult problems that advance the definition or solution of the problems.

Consideration of the different tactics one might employ in assisting a child to develop understanding and skills or shifts in perspective may clarify age differences in the impact of social guidance as well as differences between adult and peer partners – issues on which Piaget and Vygotsky differed.

What Phase of Childhood Is Sensitive to Social Influence?

Piaget and Vygotsky appear to be almost in opposition on the question of the age at which social influence contributes to cognitive development. For

Piaget, development moves from the individual to the social, and for Vygotsky, development moves from the social to the individual.

According to Piaget, the young child is largely impervious to social influence because egocentricity blocks the establishment of reciprocity and cooperation in considering differing points of view. Thus, according to Piaget, it is not until middle childhood that children's intellect benefits from social interaction, when logical argument between children with varying points of view becomes possible. Young children would generally find it so difficult to consider the logic of another's point of view that they would either continue to see things from their own perspective or switch to the other person's perspective without understanding the rationale and hence without actually advancing developmentally.

The three conditions that Piaget (1977) set out for the achievement of equilibrium are not possible with egocentrism. First, there is not a common scale of reference in terms of language and ideas to allow a durable exchange of ideas. Second, there is not sufficient conservation of propositions (commitment to sticking to what you have said before) to oblige children to take account of what they have said or agreed to in order to apply these propositions in subsequent propositions. And third, there is not reciprocity between the partners to allow coordination of propositions.

Piaget (1977) specified that at the stage of concrete operations (from about 7 to 11 or 12 years), children become able to cooperate and to coordinate points of view. 'Thus the child becomes capable of discussion – and from this internalized discussion, and that conducted with oneself, which is reflection – of collaboration, of arguments that are orderly and understandable by another' (p. 157). Piaget suggests that cooperation provides an impetus to order thought in logical operations that involve a system of propositions that are free from contradiction and are reversible: 'Thinking in common promotes non-contradiction: It is much easier to contradict oneself, when one thinks for oneself (egocentrism) than when some partners are there to remember what one has said before and the propositions that one has agreed to admit' (Piaget, 1977, p. 157).

The importance of social interaction and the role of society becomes more obvious in the next stage, formal operations: 'Things are even clearer in the formal stage, which begins after 11–12 years, since hypothetico-deductive thought is above all thought supported by a language (common or mathematical) and is thus collective thought' (Piaget, 1977, pp. 158).

Vygotsky's approach contrasts with Piaget's in its assumption that from the beginning the child is a social being, involved in social exchanges that guide the development of higher cognitive processes:

> The child's rich and complex social contact leads to an early development of means of social connection. It has been clearly demonstrated that simple though unique reactions to the human voice are present in the third week of life (i.e., the presocial reactions) and that the first social reactions appear by the second month . . . . Laughter, babbling, pointing, and gesture emerge as means of social contact in the first months of the child's life . . . . However, the most important event in

the development of the child's thinking and speech occur at approximately two years of age . . . .This critical moment, the moment when speech becomes intellectual and thinking verbal, is marked by two clear and objective symptoms. . . . First, the child who has attained this level of development begins to *actively expand his vocabulary* by asking the name of each new thing he encounters. Second, these efforts result in an extremely rapid increase in the child's vocabulary. (Vygotsky, 1987, pp. 110–111)

In contrast with Piaget, Vygotsky assumes that social guidance aids children in learning to communicate and to plan and remember deliberately from the first years of life. This guidance provides children with the opportunity to participate beyond their own abilities and to internalize activities practiced socially, thus advancing their capabilities for independently managing problem solving.

Newson and Newson (1975) cite Vygotsky's perspective in their argument that from earliest infancy, children are guided in development by social interaction.

Knowledge itself originates within an interaction process (highly active on the part of the infant) between the infant himself and other, more mature, human individuals who already possess shared understandings with other communicating beings. Furthermore, these shared understandings are embedded in a uniquely human way of conceptualizing the world in spatial and temporal terms. In short, the child only achieves a fully articulated knowledge of his world, in a cognitive sense, as he becomes involved in social transactions with other communicating human beings. (p. 438)

Through such dialogues-of-action, the infant becomes thoroughly familiar with the role of a skilled communicator, participating in forms of communication long before he is able to understand the full content of what is being communicated. (p. 445)

Vygotsky argued that rather than deriving explanations of psychological activity from the individual's characteristics plus secondary social influences, the unit of analysis should be social activity, in which individual functioning develops (Wertsch, 1985). Piaget's approach was the reverse – to focus on the individual as the unit of analysis, with social influence overlaid on the individual's activity, after the child becomes able to take another person's perspective. These differences in the timing and centrality of social influence may relate to Vygotsky's focus on development of understanding and skills in using cultural tools and Piaget's focus on qualitative shifts in perspective.

Peers Versus Adults: Equal Status Versus Expertise

The two theorists attributed varying degrees of importance to the roles of adults and peers. Piaget (1926) emphasized peer interaction, with its exploration of cognitive conflict between companions of equal status. An example is provided by two 5-year-olds quarreling over drinks of soda that had been poured into glasses of different shapes (an everyday situation resembling Piaget's conservation task). An adult had attempted to pour equal quantities for the two children, but since Valerie's glass was tall and thin, and David's was wide and flaring at the top, the quantities were not obviously equal. Valerie attempted to convince David of the fairness of the distribution:

> 'Yours is fatter and mine is thinner, that's why it looks like I have more. See, I have to squeeze my hand to get it into my cup, but not into yours. [She squeezes her fingers together and puts them into the opening of each cup to demonstrate.] It's just that mine is thinner so it looks like it has more.'

The children proceeded to quench their thirst. It is such interaction between peers, Piaget argued, that can lead children to reconsider their ideas.

In contrast, Piaget felt that children's discussions with adults are unlikely to lead to cognitive restructuring because of the unequal power relations between adults and children. Only when children are able to discuss problems as equals are they likely to take into account new ways of thinking. Interaction with an adult, Piaget held, is essentially unequal; it is an asymmetric interaction in which the adult has the power, and this disrupts the condition of reciprocity for achieving equilibrium in thinking (Piaget, 1977, p. 165). 'The child's socialization with his fellows is greater than, or at least different to, his socialization with adults alone. Where the superiority of the adult prevents discussion and co-operation, the playfellow provides the opportunity for such social conduct as will determine the true socialization of the intelligence' (Piaget, 1926 [3rd ed., 1959], p. 258). When peers have different perspectives, no such asymmetry exists: 'Criticism is born of discussion, and discussion is only possible among equals: cooperation alone will therefore accomplish what intellectual constraint [caused by unquestioning belief in the adult's omniscience] failed to bring about' (Piaget, 1952, p. 409).

According to Piaget, the effect of lessons from adults is for young children to abandon their own ideas for those presented, since their ideas are poorly formulated and exist only as an 'orientation of the spirit' that cannot compete with the views of adults. But in such cases, children agree without examining the idea, and they do not learn to verify for themselves. Not until adolescence do children learn to discuss as equals with their teachers, when they have 'conquered their internal liberty' (Piaget, 1928/1977, p. 230).

Although Piaget argued that children's interaction with adults does not promote their cognitive development, his focus was on the use of adult authority. He allowed for the possibility that adults may be able to interact with children in a cooperative fashion that permits the sort of reciprocity required for children to advance to a new level of equilibrium:

> It is despite adult authority, and not because of it, that the child learns. And also it is to the extent that the intelligent teacher has known to efface him or herself, to become an equal and not a superior, to discuss and to examine, rather

than to agree and constrain morally, that the traditional school has been able to render service. (Piaget, 1928/1977, p. 231)

For Vygotsky, ideal partners are not equal, but the inequality is in skills and understanding rather than in power. For this reason, interaction with either adults or peers can bring about cognitive growth. But for cognitive development to occur in the course of interacting with a peer, the partner should be 'more capable' (Vygotsky, 1978).

Vygotsky's emphasis on interaction with more skilled partners is necessary to his theory, since such interaction is conceived as the means by which children begin to use the intellectual tools of their society. Thus the partner must be someone who knows more about the tools than does the child. By the same token, Piaget focused on changes in perspective, from one view of a problem to another, based on his interest in understanding qualitative transitions in the philosophy of science and logic.

The contrast I made earlier between developing understanding and skill and shifting perspective thus seem to relate to the status and relative expertise desirable for children's partners. A similar perspective is offered by Damon (1984) and Subbotskii (personal communication, 1988), who suggest that different types of learning may be differentially facilitated by equal or by more expert partners. Focusing on the relative advantages of interaction with more expert peers (in tutoring) and equal peers (in collaboration), Damon (1984) suggests that

> peer tutoring may be used whenever students need to acquire information or skills that do not extend beyond their conceptual reach. Learning historical facts, practicing word attack skills, becoming adept at multiplication tables, even figuring out how to make use of a computer . . . draw upon features of basic understanding that the child has already developed. . . .
>
> Peer collaboration, on the other hand, . . . is an ideal technique for encouraging children to wrestle with intellectual challenges in difficult new principles. Learning to communicate accurately through written and spoken language, grasping the logic behind scientific formulas, and realizing the political rationale underlying a societal governance system can all be fostered in a collaborative peer interaction context. Such intellectual accomplishments stretch the boundaries of children's mental abilities. Consequently, they flourish best under conditions of highly motivated discovery, the free exchange of ideas, and reciprocal feedback between mutually respected equals. These are precisely the characteristics of collaborative interchanges between children. (p. 340)

Intersubjectivity: Theoretical Convergence and Differences

The theories of Piaget and Vygotsky share an emphasis on the importance of partners' understanding of each other. For Piaget, the partners must have a common language and system of ideas, and must grant reciprocity in attempting to examine and adjust for differences in their opinions. Piaget emphasized logical consideration of alternative perspectives provided by coming to understand another person's point of view.

For Vygotsky, the child is assumed to be interested in gaining from the more expert partner, who is seen as responsible for adjusting the dialogue to fit within the child's zone of proximal development, where understanding is achieved with a stretch leading to growth. Both perspectives are similar in stressing the importance of a match between partners involving shared thinking, and the importance of the child's understanding as the point of departure.

The role of shared thinking has received attention in the Vygotskian tradition in Wertsch's (1984) writings on 'intersubjectivity', building on the work of Rommetveit (1985). It also appears in the work of Perret-Clermont and Schubauer-Leoni (1981) in the Piagetian tradition. The notion of intersubjectivity seems inherent in Piaget's view of social influences, but has been overlooked by some Piagetian scholars who focus on cognitive conflict as quarreling. Both theories and, increasingly, the literature on social influences focus on the role of intersubjectivity in social interaction (Forman and Kraker, 1985; Rogoff, 1986; Tudge and Rogoff, 1989; Youniss, 1987).

Despite the agreement between the two theories on the importance of sharing perspectives or thinking together, there is an essential difference in their conception of intersubjectivity. It relates to the contrast between them in the centrality of their focus on the social versus the individual. For Vygotsky, shared thinking provides the opportunity to participate in a joint decision-making process from which children may appropriate what they contribute for later use. For Piaget, the meeting of minds involves two separate individuals, each operating on the other's ideas, using the back-and-forth of discussion for each to advance his or her own development. This discussion is the product of two individuals considering alternatives provided socially, rather than the construction of a joint understanding between partners.

Forman (1987) discusses this distinction in collaborative problem solving in Piaget's and Vygotsky's theories. In Piaget's theory, collaborative problem solving is explained by deriving both cognitive and social processes from the same central intrapsychological process, whereas in Vygotsky's theory, the correspondence between cognitive and social processes is due to the derivation of individual cognitive processes from joint cognitive processes in social contexts.

These differing interpretations are accompanied by differences in the proposed mechanisms of cooperation. Forman (1987) contrasts intersubjectivity as a process that takes place between people from the Vygotskian perspective, with perspective taking or decentering as individual processes working on socially provided information from the Piagetian perspective.

A similar distinction also appears in the work of Rubtsov (1981), who observed that children's difficulties with the class-inclusion problem are sometimes resolved while collaborating with agemates, and these advances persist after the interaction. Rubtsov appears to agree with Piaget in focusing on parallels between the organization of joint activity and the organization of thought, but emphasizes the facilitation provided by the social arrangements and shared activity: 'The relations determining the logic of an intellectual structure consist of compact condensed forms of mutual relationships among the participants in cooperation' (p. 59).

Thus although both theories – and the research deriving from them – emphasize cooperation in cognitive activity, they differ in the extent to which the process of cognitive development is seen as occurring in this cooperative interaction. For Piaget, the cooperation provides information for the individual to use in becoming aware of differing perspectives and in resolving the differences between them. In the Vygotskian perspective, in contrast, the individual makes use of the joint decision-making process itself to expand understanding and skill. Cognitive development from a Piagetian view is a product of the individual, perhaps sparked by having to account for differences in perspective with others, whereas cognitive development from a Vygotskian point of view involves the individual's appropriation or internalization of the social process as it is carried out externally in joint problem solving.

Piaget's view is thus a limited version of social impact on the individual's cognitive development; in taking the individual as the basic unit, it does not reach a collective perspective on the social context of cognitive development. It is important, as far as it goes, but does not make the necessary shift in perspective to encompass the social construction of meaning. To understand how individuals are embedded in the social world, it is necessary to grant that meaning is more than a construction by individuals. [. . .]

References

Bos, M. C. (1937) 'Experimental study of productive collaboration', *Acta Psychologica*, **3**, pp. 315–426.

Damon, W. (1984) 'Peer education: The untapped potential', *Journal of Applied Developmental Psychology*, **5**, pp. 331–343.

Forman, E. A. (1987) 'Learning through peer interaction: A Vygotskian perspective', *Genetic Epistemologist*, **15**, pp. 6–15.

Forman, E. A., and Kraker, M. J. (1985) 'The social origins of logic: The contributions of Piaget and Vygotsky' in M. W. Berkowitz (ed.) *Peer conflict and psychological growth*, San Francisco, Jossey-Bass.

Newson, J. and Newson, E. (1975) 'Intersubjectivity and the transmission of culture: On the social origins of symbolic functioning', *Bulletin of the British Psychological Society*, **28**, pp. 437–446.

Perret-Clermont, A.N. and Schubauer-Leoni, M. L. (1981) 'Conflict and cooperation as opportunities for learning', in P. Robinson (ed.) *Communication in development*, London, Academic Press.

Piaget, J. (1926) *The language and thought of the child*, New York, Harcourt, Brace.

Piaget, J. (1952) *The origins of intelligence in children.* New York, Norton.

Piaget, J. (1977) 'Logique genetique et sociologie', in *Etudes sociologiques*, Geneva, Librairie Droz. (Reprinted from *Revue Philosophique de la France et de l'Etranger*, 1928, **53**, pp. 161–205).

Piaget, J. (1977) 'Les operations logiques et la vie sociale', in *Etudes sociologiques*, Geneva, Librairie Droz.

Piaget, J. (1977) 'Problèmes de la psycho-sociologie de l'enfance', in *Etudes sociologiques*, Geneva, Librarie Droz.

Rogoff, B. (1986) 'Adult assistance of children's learning', in T. E. Raphael (ed.) *The contexts of school based literacy*, New York, Random House.

Rommetveit, R. (1985) 'Language acquisition as increasing linguistics structuring of experience and symbolic behaviour control', in J. V. Wertsch (ed.) *Culture, communication, and cognition: Vygotskian perspectives*, Cambridge, Cambridge University Press.

Rubstov, V. V. (1981) 'The role of cooperation in the development of intelligence', *Soviet Psychology*, **19**, pp. 41–62.

Subbotskii, E. V. (1988) 'Communicative style and the genesis of personality in preschoolers', *Soviet Psychology*, **25**, pp. 38–58.

Tudge, J. R. H. and Rogoff, B. (1989) 'Peer influences on cognitive development: Piagetian and Vygotskian persopectives', in M. Bornstein and J. Bruner (eds.) *Interaction in human development*, Hillsdale, NJ, Erlbaum.

Vygotsky, L. S. (1978) *Mind in society: The development of higher psychological processes*, Cambridge, MA, Harvard University Press.

Vygotsky, L. S. (1987) *Thinking and speech*, in R. W. Rieber and A. S. Carton (eds.) *The collected works of L. S. Vygotsky*, (N. Minick, Trans.), New York, Plenum Press.

Wertsch, J. V. (1984) 'The zone of proximal development: Some conceptual issues', in B. Rogoff and J. V. Wertsch (eds.) *Children's learning in the 'zone of proximal development'*, San Francisco, Jossey-Bass.

Wertsch, J. V. (1985) *Vygotsky and the social formation of mind*, Cambridge, MA, Harvard University Press.

Youniss, J. (1987) 'Social construction and moral development: Update and expansion of an idea', in W. M. Kurtines and J. L. Gewirtz (eds.), *Moral development through social interation*, New York, Wiley.

6

Legitimate Peripheral Participation

Jean Lave and Etienne Wenger

Learning viewed as situated activity has as its central defining characteristic a process that we call *legitimate peripheral participation*. By this we mean to draw attention to the point that learners inevitably participate in communities of practitioners and that the mastery of knowledge and skill requires newcomers to move toward full participation in the sociocultural practices of a community. 'Legitimate peripheral participation' provides a way to speak about the relations between newcomers and old-timers, and about activities, identities, artifacts, and communities of knowledge and practice. It concerns the process by which newcomers become part of a community of practice. A person's intentions to learn are engaged and the meaning of learning is configured through the process of becoming a full participant in a sociocultural practice. This social process includes, indeed it subsumes, the learning of knowledgeable skills.

In order to explain our interest in the concept of legitimate peripheral participation, we will try to convey a sense of the perspectives that it opens and the kinds of questions that it raises. A good way to start is to outline the history of the concept as it has become increasingly central to our thinking about issues of learning. Our initial intention in writing [. . .] was to rescue the idea of *apprenticeship*. In 1988, notions about apprenticeship were flying around the halls of the Institute for Research on Learning, acting as a token of solidarity and as a focus for discussions on the nature of learning. We and our colleagues had begun to talk about learners as apprentices, about teachers and computers as masters, and about cognitive apprenticeship, apprenticeship learning, and even life as apprenticeship. It was evident that no one was certain what the term meant. Furthermore, it was understood to be a synonym for *situated learning*, about which we were equally uncertain. Resort to one did not clarify the other. Apprenticeship had become yet another panacea for a broad spectrum of learning-research problems, and it was in danger of becoming meaningless.

Other considerations motivated this work as well. Our own earlier work on craft apprenticeship in West Africa, on intelligent tutoring systems, and on the cultural transparency of technology seemed relevant and at the same time insufficient for the development of an adequate theory of learning, giving us an urgent sense that we needed such a theory. Indeed, our central

---

This chapter has been edited.

ideas took shape as we came to see that the most interesting features both of apprenticeship and of 'glass-box' approaches to the development and understanding of technology could be characterized – and analyzed – as legitimate peripheral participation in communities of practice.

The notion that learning through apprenticeship was a matter of legitimate peripheral participation arose first in research on craft apprenticeship among Vai and Gola tailors in Liberia [. . .]. In that context it was simply an observation about the tailors' apprentices within an analysis addressing questions of how apprentices might engage in a common, structured pattern of learning experiences without being taught, examined, or reduced to mechanical copiers of everyday tailoring tasks, and of how they become, with remarkably few exceptions, skilled and respected master tailors. It was difficult, however, to separate the historically and culturally specific circumstances that made Vai and Gola apprenticeship both effective and benign as a form of education from the critique of schooling and school practices that this inevitably suggested, or from a more general theory of situated learning.

[. . .]

Over the past two years we have attempted to clarify the confusion. Two moments in that process were especially important. To begin with, the uses of 'apprenticeship' in cognitive and educational research were largely metaphorical even though apprenticeship as an actual educational form clearly had a long and varied train of historically and culturally specific realizations. We gradually became convinced that we needed to reexamine the relationship between the 'apprenticeship' of speculation and historical forms of apprenticeship. This led us to insist on the distinction between our theoretical framework for analyzing educational forms and specific historical instances of apprenticeship. This in turn led us to explore learning as 'situated learning'.

Second, this conception of situated learning clearly was more encompassing in intent than conventional notions of 'learning *in situ*' or 'learning by doing' for which it was used as a rough equivalent. But, to articulate this intuition usefully, we needed a better characterization of 'situatedness' as a theoretical perspective. The attempt to clarify the concept of situated learning led to critical concerns about the theory and to further revisions that resulted in the move to our present view that learning is an integral and inseparable aspect of social practice. We have tried to capture this new view under the rubric of legitimate peripheral participation.

Discussing each shift in turn may help to clarify our reasons for coming to characterize learning as legitimate peripheral participation in communities of practice.

From Apprenticeship to Situated Learning

Fashioning a firm distinction between historical *forms* of apprenticeship and situated learning as a historical-cultural *theory* required that we stop trying to use empirical cases of apprenticeship as a lens through which to view all forms of learning. On these grounds we started to reconsider the forms of apprenticeship with which we were most familiar as models of effective learning in the context of a broader theoretical goal. Nevertheless, specific cases of apprenticeship were of vital interest in the process of developing and exemplifying a theory of situated learning and we thus continued to use some of these studies as resources in working out our ideas. We might equally have turned to studies of socialization; children are, after all, quintessentially legitimate peripheral participants in adult social worlds. But various forms of apprenticeship seemed to capture very well our interest in learning in situated ways – in the transformative possibilities of being and becoming complex, full cultural-historical participants in the world – and it would be difficult to think of a more apt range of social practices for this purpose.

The distinction between historical cases of apprenticeship and a theory of situated learning was strengthened as we developed a more comprehensive view of different approaches to situatedness. Existing confusion over the meaning of situated learning and, more generally, situated activity resulted from differing interpretations of the concept. On some occasions 'situated' seemed to mean merely that some of people's thoughts and actions were located in space and time. On other occasions, it seemed to mean that thought and action were social only in the narrow sense that they involved other people, or that they were immediately dependent for meaning on the social setting that occasioned them. These types of interpretations, akin to naive views of indexicality, usually took some activities to be situated and some not.

In the concept of situated activity we were developing, however, the situatedness of activity appeared to be anything but a simple empirical attribute of everyday activity or a corrective to conventional pessimism about informal, experience-based learning. Instead, it took on the proportions of a general theoretical perspective, the basis of claims about the relational character of knowledge and learning, about the negotiated character of meaning, and about the concerned (engaged, dilemma-driven) nature of learning activity for the people involved. That perspective meant that there is no activity that is not situated. It implied emphasis on comprehensive understanding involving the whole person rather than 'receiving' a body of factual knowledge about the world; on activity in and with the world; and on the view that agent, activity, and the world mutually constitute each other.

We have discovered that this last conception of situated activity and situated learning, which has gradually emerged in our understanding, frequently generates resistance, for it seems to carry with it connotations of parochialism, particularity, and the limitations of a given time and task. This misinterpretation of situated learning requires comment. The first point to consider is that even so-called general knowledge only has power in specific circumstances. Generality is often associated with abstract representations, with decontextualization. But abstract representations are meaningless unless they can be made specific to the situation at hand. Moreover, the formation or acquisition of an abstract principle is itself a specific event in specific circumstances. Knowing a general rule by itself in no way assures that any generality it may carry is enabled in the specific circumstances in which it is relevant. In this sense, any 'power of abstraction' is thoroughly situated, in the lives of persons and in the culture that makes it possible. On the other hand, the world carries its own structure so that specificity always implies generality (and in this sense generality is not to be assimilated to abstractness): That is why stories can be so powerful in conveying ideas, often more so than an articulation of the idea itself. What is called general knowledge is not privileged with respect to other 'kinds' of knowledge. It too can be gained only in specific circumstances. And it too must be brought into play in specific circumstances. The generality of any form of knowledge always lies in the power to renegotiate the meaning of the past and future in constructing the meaning of present circumstances.

From Situated Learning to Legitimate Peripheral Participation

This brings us to the second shift in perspective that led us to explore learning as legitimate peripheral participation. The notion of situated learning now appears to be a transitory concept, a bridge, between a view according to which cognitive processes (and thus learning) are primary and a view according to which social practice is the primary, generative phenomenon, and learning is one of its characteristics. There is a significant contrast between a theory of learning in which practice (in a narrow, replicative sense) is subsumed within processes of learning and one in which learning is taken to be an integral aspect of practice (in a historical, generative sense). In our view, learning is not merely situated in practice – as if it were some independently reifiable process that just happened to be located somewhere; learning is an integral part of generative social practice in the lived-in world. [. . .] Legitimate peripheral participation is proposed as a descriptor of engagement in social practice that entails learning as an integral constituent.

    [. . .] The composite character of legitimate peripheral participation and the fact that it is not difficult to propose a contrary for each of its components, may be misleading. It seems all too natural to decompose it into a set of three contrasting pairs: legitimate versus illegitimate, peripheral versus central, participation versus nonparticipation. But we intend for the concept to be taken as a whole. Each of its aspects is indispensable in defining the others and cannot be considered in isolation. Its constituents contribute inseparable aspects whose combinations create a landscape – shapes, degrees, textures – of community membership.

Thus, in the terms proposed here there may very well be no such thing as an 'illegitimate peripheral participant'. The form that the legitimacy of participation takes is a defining characteristic of ways of belonging, and is therefore not only a crucial condition for learning, but a constitutive element of its content. Similarly, with regard to 'peripherality' there may well be no such simple thing as 'central participation' in a community of practice. Peripherality suggests that there are multiple, varied, more- or less-engaged and -inclusive ways of being located in the fields of participation defined by a community. Peripheral participation is about being located in the social world. *Changing* locations and perspectives are part of actors' learning trajectories, developing identities, and forms of membership.

Furthermore, legitimate peripherality is a complex notion, implicated in social structures involving relations of power. As a place in which one moves toward more-intensive participation, peripherality is an empowering position. As a place in which one is kept from participating more fully – often legitimately, from the broader perspective of society at large – it is a disempowering position. Beyond that, legitimate peripherality can be a position at the articulation of related communities. In this sense, it can itself be a source of power or powerlessness, in affording or preventing articulation and interchange among communities of practice. The ambiguous potentialities of legitimate peripherality reflect the concept's pivotal role in providing access to a nexus of relations otherwise not perceived as connected.

Given the complex, differentiated nature of communities, it seems important not to reduce the end point of centripetal participation in a community of practice to a uniform or univocal 'center', or to a linear notion of skill acquisition. There is no place in a community of practice designated 'the periphery', and, most emphatically, it has no single core or center. *Central participation* would imply that there is a center (physical, political, or metaphorical) to a community with respect to an individual's 'place' in it. *Complete participation* would suggest a closed domain of knowledge or collective practice for which there might be measurable degrees of 'acquisition' by newcomers. We have chosen to call that to which peripheral participation leads, *full participation.* Full participation is intended to do justice to the diversity of relations involved in varying forms of community membership.

Full participation, however, stands in contrast to only one aspect of the concept of peripherality as we see it: It places the emphasis on what partial participation is not, or not yet. In our usage, *peripherality* is also a *positive* term, whose most salient conceptual antonyms are *unrelatedness* or *irrelevance* to ongoing activity. The partial participation of newcomers is by no means 'disconnected' from the practice of interest. Furthermore, it is also a dynamic concept. In this sense, peripherality, when it is enabled, suggests an opening, a way of gaining access to sources for understanding through growing involvement. The ambiguity inherent in peripheral participation must then be connected to issues of legitimacy, of the social organization of and control over resources, if it is to gain its full analytical potential.

An Analytic Perspective on Learning

[. . .] Coming to see that a theory of situated activity challenges the very meaning of abstraction and/or generalization has led us to reject conventional readings of the generalizability and/or abstraction of 'knowledge'. Arguing in favor of a shift away from a theory of situated activity in which learning is reified as one kind of activity, and toward a theory of social practice in which learning is viewed as an aspect of all activity, has led us to consider how we are to think about our own practice. And this has revealed a dilemma: How can we purport to be working out a *theoretical conception* of learning without, in fact, engaging in just the project of abstraction rejected above?

There are several classical dualist oppositions that in many contexts are treated as synonymous, or nearly so: abstract-concrete; general-particular; theory about the world, and the world so described. Theory is assumed to be general and abstract, the world, concrete and particular. But in the Marxist historical tradition that underpins social practice theory these terms take on different relations with each other and different meanings. They do so as part of a general method of social analysis. This method does not deny that there is a concrete world, which is ordinarily perceived as some collection of particularities, just as it is possible to invent simple, thin, abstract theoretical propositions about it. But these two possibilities are not considered as the two poles of interest. Instead, both of them offer points of departure for starting to explore and produce an understanding of multiply determined, diversely unified – that is, complexly concrete – historical processes, of which particularities (including initial theories) are the result (Marx, 1857; Hall, 1973; Ilyenkov, 1977). The theorist is trying to recapture those relations in an analytic way that turns the apparently 'natural' categories and forms of social life into challenges to our understanding of how they are (historically and culturally) produced and reproduced. The goal, in Marx's memorable phrase, is to 'ascend (from both the particular and the abstract) to the concrete'.

It may now be clearer why it is not appropriate to treat legitimate peripheral participation as a mere distillation of apprenticeship, an abstracting process of generalizing from examples of apprenticeship. (Indeed, turned onto apprenticeship, the concept should provide the same analytical leverage as it would for any other educational form.) Our theorizing about legitimate peripheral participation thus is not intended as abstraction, but as an attempt to explore its concrete relations. To think about a concept like legitimate peripheral participation in this way is to argue that its theoretical significance derives from the richness of its interconnections: in historical terms, through time and across cultures. It may convey better what we mean by a historically, culturally concrete 'concept' to describe legitimate peripheral participation as an 'analytical perspective'.

With Legitimate Peripheral Participation

[. . .] The organization of schooling as an educational form is predicated on claims that knowledge can be decontextualized, and yet schools themselves as social institutions and as places of learning constitute very specific contexts. Thus, analysis of school learning as situated requires a multilayered view of how knowing and learning are part of social practice – a major project in its own right. Last, but not least, pervasive claims concerning the sources of the effectiveness of schooling [. . .] stand in contradiction with the situated perspective we have adopted. All this has meant that our discussions of schooling were often contrastive, even oppositional. But we did not want to define our thinking and build our theory primarily by contrast to the claims of any educational form, including schooling. We wanted to develop a view of learning that would stand on its own, reserving the analysis of schooling and other specific educational forms for the future.

We should emphasize, therefore, that legitimate peripheral participation is not itself an educational form, much less a pedagogical strategy or a teaching technique. It is an analytical viewpoint on learning, a way of understanding learning. [. . .] Learning through legitimate peripheral participation takes place no matter which educational form provides a context for learning, or whether there is any intentional educational form at all. Indeed, this viewpoint makes a fundamental distinction between learning and intentional instruction. Such decoupling does not deny that learning can take place where there is teaching, but does not take intentional instruction to be in itself the source or cause of learning, and thus does not blunt the claim that what gets learned is problematic with respect to what is taught. [. . .]

Note

This is an excerpt from Chapter 1 of *Situated Learning: Legitimate Peripheral Participation*, New York, Cambridge University Press.

References

Hall, S. 1973. A 'reading' of Marx's 1857 'Introduction to the Grundrisse.' General Series: Stencilled Occasional Paper No. 1. Center for Contemporary Cultural Studies. University of Birmingham, U.K.

Ilyenkov, E. V. 1977. *Dialectical logic: Essays on its history and theory*. Moscow: Progress Publishers.

Marx, K. 1857. Introduction to a critique of political economy. Version of the introduction to the Grundrisse published as supplementary text in C. J. Arthur (ed.), *The German Ideology*, 1988, New York: International Publishers.

7

Assessment in Context

Howard Gardner

Contrasting Models of Assessment

A familiar scene almost anywhere in the United States today: Several hundred students file into a large examination hall. They sit nervously, waiting for sealed packets to be handed out. At the appointed hour, booklets are distributed, brief instructions are issued and formal testing begins. The hall is still as students at each desk bear down on number two pencils and fill in the bubbles which punctuate the answer sheets. A few hours later, the testing ends and the booklets are collected; several weeks later, a sheet bearing a set of scores arrives at each student's home and at the colleges to which the students have directed their scores. The results of a morning's testing become a powerful factor in decisions about the future of each student.

An equally familiar scene in most pre-industrial societies over the centuries: A youth of ten or eleven moves into the home of a man who has mastered a trade. Initially, the lad is asked to carry out menial tasks as he helps the master to prepare for his work or to clean up the shop at the end of the day. During this initial phase, the lad has the opportunity to watch the master at work, while the master monitors the youth to discover his special talents or serious flaws. Over the months the apprentice slowly enters into the practice of the trade. After initially aiding in the more peripheral aspects of the trade, he eventually gains familiarity with the full gamut of skilled work. Directed by tradition, but also guided by the youth's particular skills and motivation, the master guides his charge through the various steps from novice to journeyman. Finally, after several years of supervised training, the youth is ready to practice the craft on his own.

While both of these scenes are idealized, they should be readily recognizable to anyone concerned with the assessment and training of young people. Indeed, they may be said to represent two extremes. The first 'formal testing' model is conceived of as an objective, decontextualized form of assessment which can be adopted and implemented widely, with some assurance that similar results will be obtained. The second 'apprenticeship' model is implemented almost entirely within a naturally occurring

---

This chapter has been edited.

context in which the particularities of a craft are embedded. The assessment is based upon a prior analysis of the skills involved in a particular craft, but it may also be influenced by subjective factors, including the master's personal views about his apprentice, his relationship with other masters, or his need for other kinds of services.

It should he evident that these two forms of assessment were designed to meet different needs. Apprenticeships made sense when the practice of various crafts was the major form of employment for non-rural youths. Formal testing is a contemporary means of comparing the performance of thousands of students who are being educated in schools. Yet these forms of assessment are not limited to the two prototypical contexts described above. Despite the overwhelmingly agrarian nature of Chinese society, formal tests have been used there for over two thousand years in selecting government officials. And, by the same token, in many art forms, athletic practices, and areas of scientific research Polanyi (1958), apprenticeships and the concomitant ongoing, context-determined forms of assessment continue to be used in our highly industrialized society.

Thus, the choice of 'formal testing' as opposed to 'apprenticeship' is not dictated solely by the historical era or the primary means of production in the society. It would be possible in our society to utilize the apprenticeship method to a much greater extent than we do. [. . .]

Following an account of the origins of standardized testing and the one-dimensional view of mentation often implied by such testing methods, I review several lines of evidence from the cognitive, neural, and developmental sciences which point to a far more capacious view of the human mind and of human learning than that which informed earlier conceptions.

Our task here is to envision forms of education and modes of assessment which have a firm rooting in current scientific understanding and which contribute to enlightened educational goals. [. . .]

Binet, the Testing Society, and the 'Uniform' View of Schooling

The widespread use of formal testing can be traced to the work on intelligence testing carried out in Paris at the turn of the century by Alfred Binet and his colleagues. Binet was asked by city educational leaders to assist in determining which students would succeed, and which would likely fail, in elementary school (Binet and Simon 1905; Block and Dworkin 1976). He hit upon the inspired idea of administering a large set of items to young school children and identifying which of the items proved most discriminating in light of his particular goal. The work carried out by the Binet team ultimately led to the first intelligence tests, and the construct of intelligence quotient, or IQ. So great was the appeal of the Binet method that it soon became a dominant feature of the [. . .] educational and assessment landscape. [. . .]

There is within the testing profession considerable belief in 'raw', possibly genetically based potential (Eysenck 1967; Jensen 1980). The most highly valued tests, such as IQ tests and the SATs, are thought to measure ability or potential performance. There is no necessary reason why a test cannot assess skills which have been learned, and many 'achievement' tests purport to do this. Yet, for tests that purport to measure raw ability or potential, it is important that performance cannot be readily improved by instruction; otherwise, the test would not be a valid indicator of ability. Most authorities on testing believe that performance on ability and achievement tests reflects inherent capacities.

Adherents of testing also tend to embrace a view of human development which assumes that a young organism contains less knowledge and exhibits less skill than a more mature organism, but that no qualitative changes occur over time in human mind or behavior (Bijou and Baer 1965). Making such assumptions enables the testmaker to use the same kinds of instruments for individuals of all ages; and he or she can legitimately claim that descriptions of data at a certain point in development can be extended to later ages, because one is dealing with the same kind of scale and the same property of mind or behavior. [. . .]

Reflecting general American technological pressures, as well as the desire for elegance and economy, most testmakers and buyers place a premium on instruments which are efficient, brief, and can be readily administered. In the early days of testing, assessment sometimes took hours and was individually administered; now, group-administered instruments are desired. Virtually every widely used test has spawned a 'brief' version. Indeed, some of the staunchest supporters of formal intelligence tests hope to strip them down even further: Arthur Jensen (1987) has embraced 'reaction time' measures, Michael Anderson (1987) looks to sensory discrimination, and Hans Eysenck (1979) has called for the examination of patterns of brain waves.

Accompanying a fealty to formal testing is a view of education which I have termed the 'uniform view of schooling'. This view does not necessarily entail the wearing of uniforms, but it does call for homogenized education in other respects. According to the uniform view, as much as possible students should study the same subject matter. [. . .]. Moreover, as much as possible that subject matter ought to be conveyed in the same way to all students.

In the uniform view, progress in school ought to be assessed by frequent formal tests. These tests should be administered under uniform conditions, and students, teachers, and parents should receive quantitative scores which detail the student's progress or lack thereof. These tests should be nationally normed instruments, so that the maximum comparability is possible. The most important subject matters are those which lend themselves readily to such assessment, such as mathematics and science. In other subjects, value is assigned to the aspects which can be efficiently assessed (grammar rather than 'voice' in writing; facts rather than interpretation in history). Those disciplines which prove most refractory to formal testing, such as the arts, are least valued in the uniform school.

In putting forth this picture of Binet, the testing society, and the uniform view of schooling, I am aware that I am overemphasizing certain tendencies and lumping together views and attitudes in a way which is not entirely fair to those who are closely associated with formal testing. Some individuals intimately involved with testing have voiced the same concerns (Cronbach 1984; Messick 1988). Indeed, had I put this picture forth fifteen or twenty years ago it might have seemed an outrageous caricature. However, the trends within American education since the early 1980s bear a strong resemblance to the views I have just sketched. At the very least, these views serve as a necessary 'contrast case' to the picture of contextualized and individualized assessment and schooling which I present later in the chapter; they should be taken in that contrastive spirit.

Sources for an Alternative Approach to Assessment

While the testing society has responded more to pragmatic needs than to scientific dictates, it does reflect a certain view of human nature. The scientific ideas on which the testing society has been based derive from an earlier era in which behaviorist, learning theoretical, and associationist views of cognition and development were regnant (see Gardner 1985 for a summary). According to these views, it made sense to believe in 'inborn' human abilities, in a smooth, probably linear curve of learning from infancy to old age, in a hierarchy of disciplines, and in the desirability of assessing potential and achievement under carefully controlled and maximally decontextualized conditions.

Over the past few decades, however, the various assumptions on which this testing edifice was based have been gradually undermined by work in developmental, cognitive, and educational studies, and a quite different view has emerged. [. . .] Because my alternative picture of assessment builds on the newly emerging picture of human development, it is important to highlight the principal features of this perspective and to indicate where it may clash with standard views of testing.

The Necessity for a Developmental Perspective

Owing to the pioneering work of Jean Piaget (1983), it is widely recognized that children are not simply miniature versions of adults. The infant or the toddler conceives of the world in a way which is internally consistent but which deviates in important particulars from a more mature conception. Here are some of the most familiar instances from the Piagetian canon: the infant does not appreciate that an object continues to exist when it has been removed from view; the toddler does not understand that material remains constant in quantity, even when its physical configuration has been altered (for example, squashing a ball of clay); the young school child is unable to reason solely from the implications of one proposition to another but instead proceeds on the basis of knowledge of concrete instances and perceived empirical regularities.

According to Piaget's view, children pass through a number of qualitatively different stages called sensori-motor, pre-operational, concrete operational, and formal operational. A child at one stage in one area of knowledge will necessarily be at the same stage in other domains of experience. Few investigators hold any longer to a literal version of this 'structured-stage' perspective; there have been too many findings which do not support it (Brainerd 1978; Gelman 1978). But most developmental psychologists continue to subscribe to the point of view that the world of the infant or toddler has its own peculiar structures [. . .].

Another feature of this approach is its assumption that development is neither smooth, nor unilinear, nor free of perturbations. While details differ among theorists, most researchers believe that there may be critical or sensitive periods during which it is especially easy – or especially difficult – to master certain kinds of materials. Similarly, while youngsters tend to improve in most areas with age, there will be periods of more rapid growth and periods of stasis. And a minority of researchers believes that in some domains there may actually be regressions or 'U-shapes', with younger children performing in a more sophisticated or integrated fashion than students in middle childhood (Strauss 1982).

[. . .]

The Emergence of a Symbol-system Perspective

[. . .]

Over the past few decades, there has been increasing recognition of the importance in human cognition of the capacity to use various kinds of symbols and symbol systems (Gardner, Howard, and Perkins 1974; Goodman 1976; Langer 1942). Humans are deemed the creatures par excellence of communication, who garner meanings through words, pictures, gestures, numbers, musical patterns, and a whole host of other symbolic forms. The manifestations of these symbols are public: all can observe written language, number systems, drawings, charts, gestural languages, and the like. However, the mental processes needed to manipulate such symbols must be inferred from the performances of individuals on various kinds of tasks. Unexpectedly potent support for the belief in internal symbol-manipulation has come from the invention and widespread use of computers; if these human-made machines engage in operations of symbol use and transformation, it seems ludicrous to withhold the same kinds of capacities from the humans who invented them (Newell and Simon 1972).

Considerable effort has been expended in the relevant sciences to investigate the development of the human capacity for symbol use. It is widely (though not universally) agreed that infants do not use symbols or exhibit internal symbolic manipulation and that the emergence of symbol use during the second year of life is a major hallmark of human cognition. Thereafter, human beings rapidly acquire skill in the use of those symbols and symbol systems which are featured in their culture. By the age of five or six most children have acquired a 'first draft' knowledge of how to create and understand stories, works of music, drawings, and simple scientific explanations (Gardner 1982).

In literate cultures, however, there is a second level of symbol use. Children must learn to utilize the *invented symbol* (or *notational*) systems of their culture, such as writing and numbers. With few exceptions, this assignment is restricted to school settings, which are relatively decontextualized. Mastering notational systems can be difficult for many students in our society, including students whose mastery of 'practical knowledge' and 'first-order symbol systems' has been unproblematic. Even those students who prove facile at acquiring notational systems face a non-trivial challenge: they must mesh their newly acquired 'second-order' symbolic knowledge with the earlier forms of 'practical' and 'first-order' symbolic knowledge they brought with them to school (Bamberger 1982; Gardner 1986; Resnick 1987).

Nearly all formal tests presuppose that their users will be literate in the second-level symbol systems of the culture. These tests thus pose special difficulties for individuals who, for whatever reason, have had difficulty in attaining second-level symbol knowledge or cannot map that knowledge onto earlier forms of mental representation. Moreover, it is my belief that individuals with well-developed second-level symbolic skills can often 'psyche out' such tests, scoring well even when their knowledge of the subject matter which is ostensibly being assessed is modest (Gardner 1983). At any rate, what the exact relations are which exist among 'practical', 'first-order', and 'second-order' symbolic knowledge and the best way to assess these remain difficult issues to resolve.

Evidence for the Existence of Multiple Faculties or 'Intelligences'

When intelligence tests were first assembled, there was little attention paid to the underlying theory of intelligence. But soon the idea gained currency that the different abilities being tapped all fed into or reflected a single 'general intelligence'. This perspective has remained the view-of-choice among most students of intelligence, though a minority has been open to the idea of different 'vectors of mind' or different 'products, content, and operations' of intellect (Guilford 1967; Thurstone 1938). This minority has based its conclusions on the results of factor analyses of test results;

however, it has been shown that one can arrive at either unitary or pluralistic views of intellect, depending upon which assumptions guide factor analytic procedures (Gould 1981).

In recent years, there has been a resurgence of interest in the idea of a multiplicity of intelligences. Mental phenomena have been discovered that some researchers construe as evidence for mental *modules* – fast-operating, reflex-like, information-processing devices which seem impervious to the influence of other modules. The discovery of these modules has given rise to the view that there may be separate analytic devices involved in tasks like syntactic parsing, tonal recognition, or facial perception (Fodor 1983).

A second source of evidence for a multiplicity of intelligences has been the fine-grained analysis of the mental operations involved in the solution of items used in intelligence tests (Sternberg 1977, 1985). These analyses have suggested the existence of different components which contribute to success on any standard intellectual assessment. Individuals may differ from one another in the facility with which the different components operate, and different tasks may call upon a differential use of the various components, meta-components, and sub-components.

My proposal for a set of 'multiple intelligences' (Gardner 1983, 1987) has been prompted by a different set of considerations. Initially I was impressed in my research by two lines of findings: (1) normal children can distinguish themselves in one or two areas of performance with no predictive value about how they will perform in other areas and (2) brain-damaged individuals may lose capacities in one or two areas but otherwise appear to be as competent as before (Gardner 1975).

I subsequently surveyed research on the development of different capacities in normal children; the breakdown of these capacities under different varieties of brain damage; the existence in special populations of highly jagged cognitive profiles (prodigies, idiot savants, autistic children, individuals with learning disabilities); the sets of abilities found in individuals from different cultures; the evolution of cognition over the millenia in humans and in infra-human species; and two kinds of psychological evidence – correlations among psychometric tests and the results of studies of transfer and generalization of skills.

Pulling together the results of this massive survey, I isolated the existence of seven different mental faculties or intelligences. As outlined in *Frames of Mind: The Theory of Multiple Intelligences* (Gardner 1983), humans have evolved as a species to carry out at least seven kinds of computations or analyses: those involving language (linguistic intelligence, as exemplified by a poet); logical-mathematical analysis (in a scientist, mathematician, or logician); spatial representation (for instance, the painter, sculptor, architect, sailor, geometer, or engineer); musical analysis; bodily-kinesthetic thinking (for example, the dancer, athlete, mime, actor, surgeon, craftsman); and two forms of personal understanding – interpersonal knowledge (of other persons, as in a salesman, teacher, therapist, leader) and intrapersonal knowledge (the ability to know one's own desires, fears, and competences and to act productively on the basis of that knowledge).

According to my analysis, most formal testing – whatever the area that is allegedly being tested – engages primarily the linguistic and logical-mathematical faculties. If one has high linguistic and logical-mathematical intelligences, one is likely to do well in school and in formal testing. Poor endowment or learning in one or both of these intelligences is likely to result in poor standardized scores.

If life consisted solely of schooling, most formal tests would serve their purpose well – though last year's grades would fulfill the same predictive purposes equally well. Schooling, however, is supposed to be a preparation for life, and there is ample evidence that formal testing alone is an indifferent predictor for success once a student has left school (Jencks 1972).

I therefore call for assessment which is 'intelligence-fair' – which looks *directly* at an individual's skills in areas such as music, spatial knowledge, or interpersonal understanding, rather than looking through the 'window' of linguistic and/or logical-mathematical prowess. It is the desire for modes of assessment that can detect capacities in the other intelligences, even in the face of indifferent linguistic or logical-mathematical capacities, which animates much of the applied research program described below.

[. . .]

Recognition of Vast Individual Differences

A consequence of the 'multiple intelligence' perspective is the recognition that instead of a single dimension called intellect, on which individuals can be rank-ordered, there are vast differences among individuals in their intellectual strengths and weaknesses and also in their styles of attack in cognitive pursuits (Kagan and Kogan 1970). Our own evidence suggests that these differences may be evident even before the years of formal schooling.

The literature on different individual strengths, as well as the findings on diverse cognitive styles, has crucial educational implications. To begin with, it is important to identify strengths and weaknesses at an early point so that they can become part of educational planning. Striking differences among individuals also call into question whether individuals ought to all be taking the same curriculum and whether, to the extent that there is a uniform curriculum, it needs to be presented in the same fashion to all individuals.

Formal tests can be an ally to the recognition of different cognitive features, but only if the tests are designed to elicit – rather than mask – these differences (Cronbach and Snow 1977). It is particularly important that instruments used in 'gatekeeping' niches (like college admissions) be designed to allow students to show their strengths and to perform optimally. Until now, little effort has been made in this regard and tests are more frequently used to point up weaknesses than to designate strengths.

A Search for Human Creative Capacities

[. . .] In the post-Sputnik era, when scientific ingenuity was suddenly at a premium, American educators became convinced of the importance of imaginativeness, inventiveness, and creativity. They called for the devising of instruments which would assess creativity or creative potential (Guilford 1950). Regrettably (from my perspective), in their search for creativity measures they repeated most of the mistakes that had been made throughout the history of intelligence testing. That is, they tried to devise short-answer, timed measures of the abilities they thought central to creativity – the capacity to come up with a variety of answers to a question (divergent thinking) or to issue as many unusual associations as possible to a stimulus (ideational fluency).

While the field of intelligence testing is currently filled with controversy, there is consensus that creativity tests have not fulfilled their potential (Wallach 1971, 1985). These instruments are reliable, and they do measure something other than psychometric intelligence, but they cannot predict which individuals will be judged as creative on the basis of their productions within a domain. Rather than attempting to devise more and better 'creativity tests', researchers have instead begun to examine more closely what actually happens when individuals are engaged in problem-solving or problem-finding activities (Gruber 1981; Sternberg 1988).

These recent studies have yielded two major findings. On the one hand, creative individuals do not seem to have at their disposal mental operations which are theirs alone; creative individuals make use of the same cognitive processes as do other persons, but they use them in a more efficient and flexible way and in the service of goals which are ambitious and often quite risky (Perkins 1981). On the other hand, highly creative individuals do seem to lead their lives in a way different from most others. They are fully engaged in and passionate about their work; they exhibit a need to do something new and have a strong sense of their purpose and ultimate goals; they are extremely reflective about their activities, their use of time, and the quality of their products (Gruber 1985).

[. . .]

The Desirability of Assessing Learning in Context

When standardized tests and paradigmatic experimental designs were first introduced into non-Western cultural contexts, they led to a single result: preliterate individuals and others from non-Western societies appeared to be much less skilled and much less intelligent than Western control groups. An interesting phenomenon was then discovered. Simple alterations of materials, test setting, or instructions frequently elicited dramatic improvements in performance. The 'performance gap' between the subjects from another culture and the subjects from our own culture narrowed or even disappeared when familiar materials were used, when knowledgeable and linguistically fluent examiners were employed, when revised instructions were given, or when the 'same' cognitive capacities were tapped in a form which made more sense within the non-Western context (Laboratory of Comparative Human Cognition 1982).

Now a huge body of experimental evidence exists to indicate that assessment materials designed for one target audience cannot be transported directly to another cultural setting; there are no purely culture-fair or culture-blind materials. Every instrument reflects its origins. Formal tests that make some sense in a Western context do so because students are accustomed to learn about materials at a site removed from the habitual application of such materials; however, in unschooled or lightly schooled environments, most instruction takes place in situ, and so it only makes sense to administer assessments which are similarly in context.

Building upon this cross-cultural research, there is also an accumulation of findings about the cognitive abilities of various kinds of experts. It has been shown that experts often fail on 'formal' measures of their calculating or reasoning capacities but can be shown to exhibit precisely those same skills in the course of their ordinary work – such as tailoring clothes, shopping in a supermarket, loading dairy cases onto a truck, or defending one's rights in a dispute (Lave 1980; Rogoff 1982; Scribner 1986). In such cases, it is not the person who has failed but rather the measurement instrument which purported to document the person's level of competence.

Locating Competence and Skill Outside the Head of the Individual

The research just reviewed has yielded another novel conceptualization. In many cases it is erroneous to conclude that the knowledge required to execute a task resides completely in the mind of a single individual. This knowledge can be 'distributed': that is, successful performance of a task may depend upon a team of individuals, no single one of whom possesses all of the necessary expertise but all of whom, working together, are able to accomplish the task in a reliable way (Scribner 1986). Relatedly, it is too simple to say that an individual either 'has' or 'does not have' the requisite knowledge; that knowledge may show up reliably in the presence of the appropriate human and physical 'triggers' but might be otherwise invisible to probing (Squire 1986).

It makes sense to think of human cognitive competence as an emerging capacity, one likely to be manifest at the intersection of three different constituents: the 'individual', with his or her skills, knowledge, and aims; the structure of a 'domain of knowledge', within which these skills can be aroused; and a set of institutions and roles – a surrounding 'field' – which judges when a particular performance is acceptable and when it fails to meet specifications (Csikszentmihalyi 1988; Csikszentmihalyi and Robinson 1986; Gardner and Wolf 1988). The acquisition and transmission of knowledge depends upon a dynamic which sustains itself among these three components. Particularly beyond the years of early childhood, human accomplishment presupposes an awareness of the different domains of knowledge in one's culture and the various 'field forces' which affect opportunity, progress, and recognition. By focusing on the knowledge that resides within a single mind at a single moment, formal testing may distort, magnify, or grossly underestimate the contributions which an individual can make within a larger social setting.

The foregoing research findings point to a differentiated and nuanced view of assessment, one which, in at least certain ways, might more closely resemble traditional apprenticeship measures than formal testing. An assessment initiative being planned today, in light of these findings, should be sensitive to developmental stages and trajectories. Such an initiative should investigate human symbolic capacities in an appropriate fashion in the years following infancy and investigate the relationship between practical knowledge and first- and second-level symbolic skills. It should recognize the existence of different intelligences and of diverse cognitive and stylistic profiles, and it should incorporate an awareness of these variations into assessments; it should possess an understanding of those features which characterize creative individuals in different domains. Finally, a new assessment initiative should acknowledge the effects of context on performance and provide the most appropriate contexts in which to assess competences, including ones which extend outside the skin of the individual being assessed.
[. . .]

General Features of a New Approach to Assessment

[. . .]

Assessment as Simple, Natural, and Occurring on a Reliable Schedule

Rather than being imposed 'externally' at odd times during the year, assessment ought to become part of the natural learning environment. As much as possible it should occur 'on the fly', as part of an individual's natural engagement in a learning situation. Initially, the assessment would probably have to be introduced explicitly; but after a while, much assessment would occur naturally on the part of student and teacher, with little need for explicit recognition or labeling on anyone's part.

The model of the assessment of the cognitive abilities of the expert is relevant here. On the one hand, it is rarely necessary for the expert to be assessed by others unless engaged in competition. It is assumed that experts will go about their business with little external monitoring. However, it is also true that the expert is constantly in the process of assessing; such assessment occurs naturally, almost without conscious reflection, in the course of working. When I first began to write, I was highly dependent upon the detailed criticism of teachers and editors; now most of the needed assessment occurs at a preconscious level as I sit at my desk scribbling, or typing a first draft, or editing an earlier version of the material.

As assessment gradually becomes part of the landscape, it no longer needs to be set off from the rest of classroom activity. As in a good apprenticeship, the teachers and the students are always assessing. There is also no need to 'teach for the assessment' because the assessment is ubiquitous; indeed, the need for formal tests might atrophy altogether.

Ecological Validity

A problem for most formal tests is their validity, that is, their correlation with some criterion (Messick 1988). As noted, creativity tests are no longer used much because their validity has never been adequately established. The predictive validity of intelligence tests and scholastic aptitude tests is often questioned in view of their limited usefulness in predicting performance beyond the next year of schooling.

Returning to our example of the apprenticeship it would make little sense to question the validity of the judgments by the master. He is so intimately associated with his novice that he can probably predict his behaviors with a high degree of accuracy. When such prediction does not occur reliably, trouble lies ahead. I believe that current assessments have moved too far away from the territory that they are supposed to cover. When individuals are assessed in situations which more closely resemble 'actual working conditions', it is possible to make much better predictions about their ultimate performance. [. . .]

Instruments Which Are 'Intelligence-fair'

As already noted, most testing instruments are biased heavily in favor of two varieties of intelligence – linguistic and logical-mathematical. Individuals blessed with this particular combination are likely to do well on most kinds of formal tests, even if they are not particularly adept in the domain actually under investigation. By the same token, individuals with problems in either or both linguistic and logical-mathematical intelligence may fail at measures of other domains, just because they cannot master the particular format of most standard instruments.

The solution – easier to describe than to realize – is to devise instruments which are 'intelligence-fair', which peer directly at the intelligence-in-operation rather than proceed via the detour of language and logical faculties. Spatial intelligence can be assessed by having an individual navigate around an unfamiliar territory; bodily intelligence by seeing how a person learns and remembers a new dance or physical exercise; interpersonal intelligence by watching an individual handle a dispute with a sales clerk or navigate a way through a difficult committee meeting. These homely instances indicate that 'intelligence-fairer' measures could be devised, though they cannot necessarily be implemented in the psychological laboratory or the testing hall.

Uses of Multiple Measures

Few practices are more nefarious in education than the drawing of widespread educational implications from the composite score of a single test – like the Wechsler Intelligence Scale for Children. Even intelligence tests contain subtests and, at the very least, recommendations ought to take into account the 'scatter' on these tests and the strategies for approaching particular items (Kaplan 1983).

Attention to a range of measures designed specifically to tap different facets of the capacity in question is even more desirable. [. . .]

Sensitivity to Individual Differences, Developmental Levels, and Forms of Expertise

Assessment programs which fail to take into account the vast differences among individuals, developmental levels, and varieties of expertise are increasingly anachronistic. Formal testing could, in principle, be adjusted to take these documented variations into account. But it would require a suspension of some of the key assumptions of standardized testing, such as uniformity of individuals in key respects and the penchant for cost-efficient instruments.

Individual differences should also be highlighted when educating teachers and assessors. Those charged with the responsibility of assessing youngsters need to be introduced formally to such distinctions; one cannot expect teachers to arrive at empirically valid taxonomies of individual differences on their own. Such an introduction should occur in education courses or during teaching apprenticeships. Once introduced to these distinctions, and given the opportunity to observe and to work with children who exhibit different profiles, these distinctions come to life for teachers.

It then becomes possible to take these differences into account in a tacit way. Good teachers – whether they teach second grade, piano to toddlers, or research design to graduate students – have always realized that different approaches will be effective with different kinds of students. Such sensitivities to individual differences can become part of the teacher's competence and can be drawn upon in the course of regular instruction as well as during assessment. It is also possible – and perhaps optimal – for teachers to season their own intuitive sense of individual differences with judicious occasions of assessment, crafted with the particular domain of practice in mind.

Use of Intrinsically Interesting and Motivating Materials

[. . .] A good assessment instrument can be a learning experience. But more to the point, it is extremely desirable to have assessment occur in the context of students working on problems, projects, or products which genuinely engage them, which hold their interest and motivate them to do well. Such exercises may not be as easy to design as the standard multiple-choice entry; but they are far more likely to elicit a student's full repertoire of skills and to yield information that is useful for subsequent advice and placement.

Application of Assessment for the Student's Benefit

[. . .] In my own view, psychologists spend far too much time ranking individuals and not nearly enough time helping them. All assessment should be undertaken primarily to aid students. It is incumbent upon the assessor to provide feedback to the student that will be helpful at the present time – identifying areas of strength as well as weakness, giving suggestions of what to study or work on, pointing out which habits are productive and which are not, indicating what can be expected in the way of future assessments, and the like. It is especially important that some of the feedback take the form of concrete suggestions and indicate relative strengths to build upon, independent of rank within a comparable group of students.

Armed with findings about human cognition and development, and in light of these desiderata for a new approach to assessment, it should be possible to begin to design programs which are more adequate than those which exist today. Without having any grand design to create a 'new alternative to formal testing', my colleagues and I at Harvard Project Zero have become engaged in a number of projects over the last several years which feature new approaches to assessment. In the following sections of this chapter, I describe our two principal efforts at the present time. [. . .]

Project Spectrum: Assessment at the Preschool Level

Project Spectrum is a collaborative project undertaken by several researchers at Harvard Project Zero in conjunction with our colleague David Feldman at Tufts University and the staff and students of the Eliot-Pearson

Children's School in Medford, Massachusetts. The project was originally designed to assess the different intellectual strengths or 'intelligences' in a representative group of three- and four-year-old children. As I will indicate, however, it has evolved over its four-year history into a preschool curriculum, with assessment aspects folded in at various points (see Hatch and Gardner 1986; Malkus, Feldman, and Gardner 1988 for further details).

When we first undertook Project Spectrum, we were interested in whether the cognitive profiles of children three or four years old could be distinguished from one another. Stated differently, we were searching for early indices of the seven intelligences identified in *Frames of Mind*. It soon became apparent, however, that far more than seven intellectual capacities wanted examination; moreover, it was also clear, at least for that age group, that it is important to examine cognitive or working styles (such as attention, planfulness, ability to reflect upon a task) as well as 'sheer' cognitive strengths. Thus, at the present time, we monitor in our population approximately fifteen different cognitive strengths as well as a dozen stylistic features (see Table 7.1).

Even as we had to broaden the ensemble of skills at which we were looking, we also came to reconceptualize the nature of our assessment project. Like many others in the assessment field, we had initially assumed that one could assess 'potential' or 'gifts' directly, without the need for involvement in curriculum or teaching. We have come to believe, however, that this assumption is flawed. There is no 'pure potential' apart from some experience in working with a domain or symbol system. As soon as one assesses, one is assessing some form of prior learning, whether or not it has been deemed relevant to the particular target domain. And so, if one wants any assurance that one is assessing the domain of interest, it is advisable to present individuals with an ample set of experiences in that domain.

Let me use an example. Suppose that one is interested in assessing talent at chess. One could see how quickly the person can respond to a light bulb, or one might examine the size of the person's vocabulary. It is conceivable that these two measures might correlate with chess talent, though I would not be surprised if neither did. One could also try to break down chess into its components and assess an individual's spatial imagery or logical reasoning skills or interpersonal skill in outwitting an opponent. Conceivably one or more of these measures might foretell chess wit or wisdom.

What is clear is that, in both of these examples, one is assessing something, whether or not it turns out to be related to facility in chess. One could simply give a chess board to children and see how well they play; but in the absence of knowing the rules of chess, the children are as likely to play chess as the proverbial monkeys are likely to pen the plays of Shakespeare.

This presentation of the chessboard does, however, point to the path that I would endorse. If you want to assess chess potential, you should teach your subjects the rules of the game and let them play chess with one another over a period of months. I have little doubt that the students would

Table 7.1   *Dimensions examined in Project Spectrum*

Activities which sample different cognitive strengths:

Music	Production Measures:	Happy Birthday
		New Songs – Up in the Air
		– Animal Song
	Perception Measures:	Montessori Bells
		Incidental Music Task
Language	Narrative Measure:	Storytelling Board
	Descriptive Measure:	Reporter Task
Numbers	Counting Measure:	Dinosaur Game
	Calculating Measure:	Bus Game
Science	Hypothesis-Testing Measure:	Water Table Activity
	Logical Inference Measure:	Treasure Hunt Game
	Mechanical Measure:	Assembly Task
	Naturalist Measure:	Discovery Area
Visual Arts	Drawing Measures:	Art Portfolios
		Farm animal, person, imaginary animal
	3-D Measure:	(Clay Activity)
Movement	Creative Movement Measure:	Biweekly Movement Curriculum
	Athletics Measure:	Obstacle Course
Social	Social Analysis Measure:	Classroom Model
	Social Roles Measure:	Observations of children's interactive styles

Measures of Working Style:

Child is	easily engaged/reluctant to engage in activity
	confident/tentative
	playful/serious
	focused/distractible
	persistent/frustrated by task
	reflects on own work/impulsive
	apt to work slowly/apt to work quickly
	conversational/quiet
Child	responds to visual/auditory/kinesthetic cues
	demonstrates planful approach
	brings personal agenda/strength to task
	finds humor in content area
	uses materials in unexpected ways
	shows pride in accomplishment
	shows attention to detail/is observant
	is curious about materials
	shows concern over 'correct' answer
	focuses on interaction with adult
	transforms task/material

sort themselves quite reliably in terms of 'chess aptitude' and that the distribution of chess talent in this population would emerge after thirty or forty games.

My colleagues and I have followed this line of thinking in surveying a variety of intellectual domains, including those which utilize linguistic, musical, and/or bodily intelligences. In each case our approach has been to expose students to experiences in the particular domain of interest and to observe the way in which they become engaged in that domain. The ensuing record provides a powerful indication of how much talent or potential the students exhibit in the domain of interest.

Having said a bit about the general philosophy and approach of Project Spectrum, let me indicate how it operates in practice. A Spectrum classroom is equipped with a rich set of materials. There are musical instruments, a fantasy play area, puzzles and games which stimulate numerical and logical thinking, a naturalist area in which students can examine different kinds of biological preparations, and the like, all of which are designed to engage the interest of students and to encourage them to play with these materials. There are also regular activities – like 'Weekend News' – which give observers the opportunity to observe the child's oral language skills. A careful observer, watching children interact with these materials and participate in the activities over a semester or a year, gains considerable information about the profile of interests of each child and should also be able to perceive the degree of sophistication with which the materials have been plumbed.

Complementing these enriched classroom materials and activities is a set of tasks and measures which we have designed to look specifically at different intellectual spheres. These tasks are engaging to children and can be introduced in the course of a natural classroom interchange. In the area of number, for example, we feature two games. The dinosaur game pits the child against the experimenter in a race to escape from the dinosaur's mouth to his tail. The number and direction of moves is determined by two dice: one bearing numbers, the second featuring plus and minus signs. The players shake their dice and, at times, the child is allowed to 'fix' his or her own or the experimenter's dice. The child's success at this game can be fully quantified, and the score provides a 'user-friendly' index of the child's numerical sophistication.

For children who 'ceiling' on the dinosaur game, there is the bus task. In this game the child plays the role of busdriver while the experimenter is 'the boss'. The bus proceeds on its route and, at each stop, some children and adults mount the bus and some depart. Every once in a while 'the boss' telephones and asks the driver for a count of how many adults and children are currently on the bus. Tokens are available to aid in the counting. Children of this age do not ordinarily have written numbers or other tally systems at their disposal, but sheer involvement in this game stimulates the most able among them to develop 'on-line' a system whereby they are better able to keep track of the comings and goings on the bus.

In other areas analogous games and exercises have been devised (see Table 7.1). Some of these exercises feature a fully quantifiable scoring system; others include more holistic and subjective scoring, as appropriate. In certain areas, it is not necessary to devise special exercises: for example, we evaluate talent in the visual arts by rating a collection of 'spontaneous' drawings made by the child; and we evaluate social strengths through a checklist which probes how children respond to certain 'charged' situations which arise in the ordinary course of events (for example, a new child coming to school, a fight breaking out, a bossy child throwing his weight around). While we wish for our scoring systems to be as precise and reliable as possible, we recognize that rough-and-ready measures can be useful as well.

The school year is divided into biweekly intervals during which a particular set of measures is taken on the children. When the classroom is an experimental one, the exercises are administered and assessed by the experimenter; in an ordinary classroom each teacher decides how to approach the targeted assessments. It is our expectation that most teachers will not wish to administer most tasks formally, nor will they generally assess them using our score sheets. Instead, they will monitor children's activities in an informal way, using our tests and sheets chiefly in instances where there is uncertainty about the child's competence. (I believe that the same philosophy should be followed in the case of standardized instruments, such as intelligence tests, which can be helpful when children appear to be 'at-risk'.)

By the end of the year, the teachers or experimenters will have amassed a great deal of information about the intellectual strengths and working styles of all the children in the classroom. This material becomes the basis of Spectrum Reports, brief essays which describe the particular pattern exhibited by the child: strengths, weaknesses, stylistic features, and the like. This information is presented relativistically; that is, each child's strengths are described with reference to the child's other strengths and weaknesses. In the less frequent case in which the child stands out in comparison to the entire population of pre-schoolers, an 'absolute' strength or weakness is indicated.

As important as the trajectory of strengths illustrated in the Spectrum Report is the list of recommendations which are offered. Consistent with our belief that psychologists should help rather than rank students, we include in the report concrete suggestions about what might be done at home, in school, and/or in the community, in light of a particular profile of competences and proclivities.

With its detailed assessments and its year-end reports, Project Spectrum raises a number of questions, including the advisability of such an undertaking. Is such detailed assessment really necessary and might it in some way be injurious? Recall that our initial goal was to find out whether individual differences do exist and can be documented at this early age. However, we posed this question not only out of curiosity but because of our belief that such information can be educationally beneficial. The mind of the preschooler is both flexible and trainable; thus, if difficulties can be identified at an early age, they are much more likely to be remediable. By the same token, if our scales identify unusual strengths that have somehow been missed before, the parents or teachers gain the option of seeking special help or training.

However, there is a clear risk to the early labeling by Spectrum, particularly in view of our current practice of describing child abilities in terms of readily recognizable adult 'end-states' (for example, dancer, naturalist, mediator). The danger is of premature billeting, by which an early attempt at description ends up by engendering a self-fulfilling prophecy. This risk is best mitigated by two procedures. The first is to stress to consumers of Spectrum Reports that these are descriptions at a particular historical moment; especially when children are young and active, the profile of abilities and disabilities can change dramatically from one year to the next. The second is to maintain Spectrum-like procedures each year. So long as students continue to be exposed to a variety of inviting materials and exercises, and so long as assessment is not a one-shot affair, there is every reason to believe that the cognitive profile will evolve – not remain static – and that subsequent reports will capture the new profile accurately.

Another question concerns the ultimate purpose of Project Spectrum. Is it simply an assessment program, or can it fulfill a broader and more integrative function? [. . .] Spectrum can constitute a valuable intervention even apart from any formal assessment. That is, the range of exercises provided and the number of intellectual spheres touched upon compare favorably with offerings in most preschool programs. Even if teachers were to decide that they were not primarily interested in the Spectrum assessment materials but simply in the games, or if they used the assessment tools only in cases of children with special problems, these materials could still fulfill an important educational goal.

Indeed, this potential for curricular as well as assessment use is consistent with our belief that the line between curriculum and assessment ought ordinarily to be blurred, particularly at the younger age levels. Moreover, it is our expectation that teachers who regularly use the Spectrum materials would develop that 'sixth sense' of individual differences which would allow them to make on-line assessments without necessarily having to use our formal procedures. Thus the Spectrum materials can be seen as potentially shaping teacher understandings and consequently affecting teacher practices in ways that we hope will foster the development of individual potential.

[. . .]

ARTS PROPEL: Assessment at the Middle and High School Levels

Like Project Spectrum, ARTS PROPEL is a collaborative project. The partners are Harvard Project Zero, the Educational Testing Service, and the Pittsburgh public school system. As with Project Spectrum, the original aim was to develop new means of assessing intellectual competences, particularly in the arts; over the years there has been a gradual evolution toward curriculum, so that the line between assessment and curriculum has become almost invisible (see Gardner 1989; Zessoules, Wolf, and Gardner 1988 for further details).

The initial impetus that brought the partners together was the desire to identify youngsters who possessed intellectual strengths which are not detected by standard scholastic aptitude tests. Because the arts are an area of intellect not usually or readily tapped through standard instruments, they were selected as the arena for the collaboration.

Traditionally, arts education in our country has focused almost exclusively on artistic production. When students are assessed at all, the assessment takes place as a holistic, and often subjective, judgment about the merits of student work. Occasional objective tests sample knowledge of art history or criticism, but these are unusual.

Our desire to keep production central in arts education but to tie it more closely to other forms of artistic knowledge has colored our approach to this project. The name ARTS PROPEL captures the thinking which underlies our approach. Artistic education ought to feature at least three activities: *Artistic Production* – the creation of art objects and the gaining of facility in 'thinking in' particular artistic symbol systems; *Artistic Perception* – the ability to make fine and appropriate discriminations in one's own art works and in art works produced by others, including artistic masters; and *Artistic Reflection* – the capacity to step back from works of art, to think about their purpose, the extent to which and the manner in which they have been achieved, and to clarify the nature of one's own productions and perceptions.

In embracing this trio of goals, our ARTS PROPEL team is possibly at odds with the approach called Discipline-Based-Arts Education (DBAE). The DBAE perspective, developed by the Getty Center for Education in the Arts, calls for a kindergarten through twelfth grade sequential curriculum in art history, art production, art criticism, and aesthetics (Eisner 1987; Getty Center 1985). While we share the Getty belief that arts education should not be limited to artistic production, we believe that artistic production ought to remain central in arts education at the pre-collegiate level. In effective arts education, perceptual and reflective activities ought to be ubiquitous; but they should grow naturally out of one's own productions, particularly during the early years of formal education. Historical, critical, and analytic work ought to be directly tied to one's own art work and should not ordinarily be presented as separate disciplines.

As in Project Spectrum, we initially hoped to devise a battery of assessment instruments which would bring to the fore those students possessing talents or potentials in a number of art forms – specifically, creative writing, graphic arts, and musical performance. We wanted these instruments to be useful for all students in an ordinary school system, not just for those who were members of an elite school population or had special training in the arts.

We soon discovered, however, that the likelihood of assessing potential, in the absence of previous training, is as remote in high school art programs as in the preschool classes in which we are working. And so we found ourselves working directly in the region of curriculum development – not in the sense of developing a full-scale curriculum, but rather becoming deeply involved in the curricular concerns which daily preoccupy teachers. Also, our desire to pick out 'stars' gave way gradually to a wish to develop means of assessing growth and learning in all students.

Our approach in the curricular area is worth chronicling. We develop our materials through an extensive and intensive collaboration among a large number of individuals: skilled artists, dedicated classroom teachers, researchers in developmental psychology, experts in testing and assessment, and arts supervisors and students. Each of our exercises and concepts is reviewed by these various individuals; those which cannot be justified are revised or dropped. At the end of this extensive collaborative process, we expect to have materials that satisfy each of the partners in our project.

The core of our program is the devising of two kinds of instruments, both of which span the region between curriculum and assessment in a way that makes sense to us.

Domain-projects are sets of exercises designed to present an idea, concept, or practice which is central within a particular artistic domain. Thus, a specimen domain-project in the visual arts presents the notion of graphic composition, while such a project in imaginative writing deals with character and dialogue in the crafting of a play, and a sample project in music involves the learning which accrues from rehearsing a section of a piece. Each domain-project can be carried out in a few sessions. It is deliberately designed to be flexible: flexible in that it can be fit into different junctures of the standard curriculum and flexible in that teachers can substitute their own examples or questions for those in our specimen projects. We speak of the domain-projects as being curriculum-compatible – capable of being slipped into a variety of standardized (or tailor-made) curricula in a number of ways. The domain-projects each feature several assessment components, some to be used by the students themselves, some by teachers or others charged with assessing student learning.

As an example, let me describe in more detail the current version of the aforementioned domain-project in graphic composition in the visual arts. In an initial session, each student is given a piece of white paper and ten oddly shaped black cutouts. The opening assignment is to drop these cutouts randomly on the background paper and then glue them on – a so-called random composition. Next, the students are given identical sets of the same materials, but this time they are asked to put together a composition to their liking – a deliberate composition. Then they are given work sheets on which they compare the properties of the two compositions. It should be noted that this domain-project, like most others, begins with production but contains ample opportunities for perception (comparing the two compositions) and reflection (articulating the reasons for the differing impact of the two compositions). In a second session most likely to occur the following week, students are introduced to sets of paintings executed by well-regarded artists. They are asked to describe in their own words the different compositional patterns which they see – balanced, lopsided, symmetrical, dynamic, and so on. Literal as well as metaphoric descriptions are welcome. The teachers are provided with a discussion of compositional facets of these paintings prepared by an artist consultant. The teachers can make as much use as they like of this accessory material, adapting it to introduce ways of discussing composition, balance, and harmony.

At the conclusion of the session, students are shown some additional pairs of slides and asked to contrast them using the concepts and vocabulary which have been introduced. They are also asked to be on the lookout during the next week for examples of interesting compositions – instances in art work which come to their attention as well as instances in their natural environment which they may have to 'crop' on their own. These observations can become the basis for future discussions and can be included in the students' notebooks or portfolios (see below).

In the third session, attempts are made to build upon and integrate the lessons of the first two sessions. There is discussion of what students have collected during the previous week. Then students are asked to plan a second *deliberate composition* and to anticipate what it will look like. They are asked to make the composition which they planned and are allowed to move the cutouts around. Their final assignment is to evaluate their new deliberate composition along the same lines as the earlier compositions but also in light of their newly acquired vocabulary and conceptual understanding. The teacher then fills out score sheets; these evaluate the different compositions produced by the students as well as any enhancement of the students' perceptual and reflective capacities over the course of the exercise.

It is our goal to produce a set of domain-projects for each of the artistic areas in which we are working. Taken together, an ensemble of domain-projects should survey important concepts (for example, style, composition, expressiveness), techniques, procedures, and background knowledge. These allow students to appreciate the full context of a work. The domain-projects are so devised that they can be used more than once a year and also carried over from one year to the next. And of course teachers are encouraged to alter them in whatever way makes sense to them.

Student performance can also be assessed in a developmental scheme. That is, for each domain-project we are defining levels which span the range of performances from novice to student-expert. All teachers will be exposed, during the period of their training, to this full gamut of possible responses and conceptualizations. Scoring then places the students somewhere along this continuum on as many dimensions as are being assessed. Some of the scoring focuses on explicit dimensions which are readily quantified (for example, correct notes in a performance), while some of the scoring calls on more holistic or subjective judgments (the quality of the interpretation in a performance).

Special attention is paid in the assessments to individuating features of students' productions. Thus in domain-projects of poetry writing, it is possible to secure measures of each student's command of imagery, figurative language, rhythmic sensitivity, thematic development, and other aspects of poetic skill. By the same token, in musical performance, the scales which accompany domain-projects are sensitive to technical mastery, fingering, pitch control, rhythmic expertise, interpretive skills, and so on. In reviewing the assessment with students, the teachers can assess more than overall improvement in developmental level; in addition, both students and teachers can discuss the students' progress with reference to particular features of the artistic medium.

The second curriculum-cum-assessment device with which we have been working is called a *portfolio* (or, perhaps more accurately, a *process-folio*). Portfolios are familiar in the arts as repositories of the best works fashioned by a student. Portfolios are the basis of decisions made regarding admission to art school, prizes in a competition, or display in an art gallery.

Our process-folios, however, are instruments of learning rather than showpieces of final accomplishment. A PROPEL process-folio contains full process-tracing records of a student's involvement in one or more art works. A typical process-folio contains initial plans, drafts, early self-evaluations, feedback on the part of peers, teachers, and other experts, collections of works which students like or dislike, together with comments on the reasons for the reaction, a record of the final work, together with any relevant comments, and plans for subsequent projects, whether or not these are ever carried out.

Process-folios can fulfill several purposes. They serve as convenient means of collecting information which may be relevant to the growth of individual students over a significant period of time. Process-folios can document the biography of a specific work or domain-project but can also span much longer periods of time and document growth over a year or more. Process-folios focus on students' artistic productions, where they are free to go in a direction which has meaning to them; these stand in contrast to classroom assignments, which may (however unintentionally) be confining.

Process-folios can be extremely valuable to present as well as future teachers, for they serve as complete records of the students' growth. Teachers can assess process-folios on a variety of dimensions: number of entries, richness of entry, degree of reflection shown, improvement in technical skill, achievement of one's goals, interplay of production, perception, and reflection, use of art-historical and art-critical materials, responsiveness to internal and external feedback, development of themes, and the like. [. . .]

But, in my view, the process-folio is most important as an aid and even 'silent mentor' to the students. Productive individuals in any domain must go through – at least tacitly – a process of self-monitoring: observing their skills, reassessing their missions, noting their growth or regression. Ultimately, these processes can take place implicitly, but in early education it is advisable to assemble a tangible record in a notebook or some other convenient format. By asking students to keep and review process-folios regularly, we hope to involve them in constant reflection on their activities and to allow them the opportunity to monitor and to learn from their own growth and even their own setbacks. [. . .]

In my view, process-folios have a special role to play in the educational environment of today. At the time of apprenticeships in artistic ateliers, a portfolio or process-folio was perhaps less necessary; after all, the involvement of the master in his own work was completely evident, and students soon became at least accessories to the master's current project. But in the contemporary educational environment, where so much attention is directed toward the inculcation and the testing of particulate knowledge, students may have a pressing (though often unrealized) need: to become involved in significant, long-term projects, where they can reflect upon their development and use their skills in productive ways. [. . .]

As currently devised, PROPEL is a pilot project in the area of artistic education for children from ages eleven to seventeen. The required assessment tools are still in the stage of development and formative evaluation; we cannot yet say how successful they will be. It is our belief, however, that our orientation might prove valuable beyond the particular bounds of our current assignment. The completion of domain-projects and the keeping of process-folios could be extended both to younger pupils and to students who are already in college. By the same token, while these procedures have been developed for use in the arts, they may well prove adaptable and welcome in other areas of the curriculum. Some of the critiques which have been leveled at standard teaching and assessment in the arts can be extended to other areas of the curriculum as well, ranging from science and social studies to mathematics.

[. . .]

As should be evident, our assessment experiments are designed largely as a means of improving the quality of education. [. . .] The use of these instruments for purposes of selection has been a secondary consideration. In principle, of course, the materials developed for Spectrum and for ARTS PROPEL could be employed by elementary or high school teachers for placement purposes, and in the case of PROPEL process-folios, for college admissions. I am comfortable with such usages because I think that these forms of information could usefully supplement – and perhaps even replace – the more common standardized testing instruments. In addition, and not incidentally, the assessment techniques on which we are working can provide useful feedback to students, independent of their selection or non-selection. They have valuable educational purpose in themselves. [. . .]

Toward the Assessing Society

This chapter has been an extended essay in favor of regular assessment occurring in a natural fashion throughout the educational system and across the trajectory of life-long learning. I have reviewed a sizeable body of theoretical innovations and experimental evidence, which, by and large, point up problems with standard formal testing as an exclusive mode of assessment. Many of these findings suggest that it would be more fruitful to create environments in which assessments occur naturally and to devise curricular entities, like domain-projects and process-folios, which lend themselves to assessment within the context of their production. It would be an exaggeration to say that I have called for a reintroduction of the apprentice method. Yet I do claim that we have moved too far from that mode of assessment; contemporary assessment might well be informed by some of the concepts and assumptions associated with traditional apprenticeships.

[. . .]

Some objections to the perspective introduced here can be anticipated. One is the claim that formal testing is, as advertised, objective and that I am calling for a regression to subjective forms of evaluation. I reject this characterization for two reasons. First of all, there is no reason in principle to regard the assessment of domain-projects, process-folios, or Spectrum-style measures as intrinsically less objective than other forms. Reliability can be achieved in these domains as well. The establishment of reliability has not been a focus of these projects; however, the conceptual and psycho-metric tools exist to investigate reliability in these cases. Moreover, these assessment measures are more likely to possess 'ecological' validity.

A second retort to this characterization has to do with the alleged objectivity or non-bias of standard formal tests. In a technical sense, it is true that the best of these instruments avoid the dangers of subjectivity and statistical bias. However, any kind of instrument is necessarily skewed toward one kind (or a few kinds) of individual and one (or a few) intellectual and cognitive styles. Formal tests are especially friendly to those individuals who possess a certain blend of linguistic and logical intelligences and who are comfortable in being assessed in a decontextualized setting under timed and impersonal conditions. Correlatively, such tests are biased against individuals who do not exhibit that blend of intelligences, those whose strengths show up better in sustained projects or when they are examined in situ.

I believe that, especially when resources are scarce, every individual ought to have the opportunity to show her or his strength. [. . .]

There are those who might be in sympathy with the line of analysis pursued here and yet would reject its implications because of considerations of cost or efficiency. According to this argument, it is simply too inefficient or expensive to mobilize the country around more sustained forms of assessment; and so, even if formal testing is imperfect, we will have to settle for it and simply try to improve it as much as possible.

This line of argument has a surface plausibility, but I reject it as well. To be sure, formal testing is now cost-effective, but it has taken millions, perhaps billions of dollars expended over many decades to bring it to its current far-from-perfect state. Nor do I think that more money spent on current testing would improve it more than marginally. [. . .]

Our current pilot projects, while dependent on research funds, are modest by any standard. In each instance we believe that the main points of the approach can be taught readily to teachers and made available to interested schools or school districts. [. . .]

The major obstacle I see to assessment-in-context is not availability of resources but rather lack of will. There is in the country today an enormous desire to make education uniform, to treat all students in the same way, and to apply the same kinds of one-dimensional metrics to all. This trend is inappropriate on scientific grounds and distasteful on ethical grounds. The current sentiment is based in part on an understandable disaffection with some of the excesses of earlier educational experiments but, to a disturbing degree, it is also based on a general hostility to students, teachers, and the learning process. In other countries, where the educational process is held in higher regard, it has proved possible to have higher-quality education without subscribing to some of the worst features of one-dimensional educational thinking and assessment.

[. . .]

To my way of thinking, the ultimate policy debate is – or at least should be – centered on competing concepts of the purposes and aims of education. As I have intimated above, the 'formal standard testing' view harbors a concept of education as a collection of individual elements of information which are to be mastered and then spewed back in a decontextualized setting. On this 'bucket view' it is expected that individuals who acquire a sufficient amount of such knowledge will be effective members of the society.

The 'assessment view' values the development of productive and reflective skills, cultivated in long-term projects. The animating impulse seeks to bridge the gap between school activities and activities after school, with the thought that the same habits of mind and discipline can he useful in both kinds of undertakings. Especial attention is paid to individual strengths. On this view, assessment should occur as unobtrusively as possible during the course of daily activities, and the information obtained should be furnished to gatekeepers in useful and economical form.

[. . .]

In the end, whatever the forms and the incidence of 'official assessments', the actual daily learning in schools, as well as the learning stimulated long after 'formal' school has been completed, should be its own reward.

Note

This abridged chapter focuses on models of assessment and descriptions of assessment projects. The full chapter includes discussion of the individual-centred school which is dealt with in a volume of this series.

References

Anderson, M. 1987. Inspection time and the development of intelligence. Paper delivered to British Psychological Society Conference, Sussex University.

Bamberger. J. 1982. Revisiting children's drawings of simple rhythms: A function for reflection-in-action. In *U-shaped behavioral growth.* ed. S. Strauss. New York: Academic Press.

Bijou. S., and D. Baer. 1965. *Child development.* New York: Appleton Century Crofts.

Binet, A., and T. Simon. 1905. Methodes nouvelles pour le diagnostique du niveau intellectuel des anormaux. *L'annee psychologique* II:245–336.

Block, N., and G. Dworkin. 1976. *The IQ controversy.* New York: Pantheon.

Brainerd, C. 1978. The stage question in cognitive-developmental theory. *The Behavioral and Brain Sciences* 2:173–213.

Cronbach, L. 1984. *Essentials of psychological testing.* New York: Harper and Row.

Cronbach, L., and R. Snow. 1977. *Aptitudes and instructional methods.* New York: Irvington.

Csikszentmihalyi, M. 1988. Society, culture, and persons: A systems view of creativity. In *The nature of creativity,* ed. R. Sternberg. New York: Cambridge University Press.

Csikszentmihalyi, M., and R. Robinson. 1986. Culture, time, and the development of talent. In *Conceptions of giftedness,* ed. R. Sternberg and J. Davidson. New York: Cambridge University Press.

Eisner, E. 1987. Structure and magic in discipline-based arts education. In *Proceedings of a National Invitational Conference,* Los Angeles: The Getty Center for Education in the Arts.

Eysenck, H. J. 1967. Intelligence assessment: A theoretical and experimental approach. *British Journal of Educational Psychology* 37:81–98.

Eysenck, H. J. 1979. *The nature and measurement of intelligence.* New York: Springer-Verlag.

Fodor, J. 1983. *The modularity of mind.* Cambridge: MIT Press.

Gardner, H. 1975. *The shattered mind.* New York: Knopf.

Gardner, H. 1982. *Art, mind, and brain.* New York: Basic Books.

Gardner, H. 1983. *Frames of mind.* New York: Basic Books.

Gardner, H. 1985. *The mind's new science.* New York: Basic Books.

Gardner, H. 1986. The development of symbolic literacy. In *Toward a greater understanding of literacy,* ed. M. Wrolstad and D. Fisher. New York: Praeger.

Gardner, H. 1987. Developing the spectrum of human intelligence. *Harvard Education Review* 57:187–93.

Gardner, H. 1989. Zero-based arts education: An introduction to ARTS PROPEL. *Studies in Art Education* 30 (2): 71–83.

Gardner, H., and C. Wolf. 1988. The fruits of asynchrony: Creativity from a psychological point of view. *Adolescent psychiatry* 15:106–23.

Gardner, H., V. Howard, and D. Perkins. 1974. Symbol systems: A philosophical, psychological and educational investigation. In *Media and symbols,* ed. D. Olson. Chicago: University of Chicago Press.

Gelman, R. 1978. Cognitive development. *Annual Review of Psychology* 29:297–332.

Getty Center for Education in the Arts. 1985. *Beyond creating: The Place for art in American schools.* Los Angeles: J. Paul Getty Trust.

Goodman, N. 1976. *Languages of art.* Indianapolis: Hackett.

Gould, S. J. 1981. *The mismeasure of man.* New York: Norton.

Gruber, H. 1981. *Darwin on man.* 2d ed. Chicago: University of Chicago Press.

Gruber, H. 1985. Giftedness and moral responsibility: Creative thinking and human survival. In *The gifted and talented: developmental perspectives,* ed. F. Horowitz and M. O'Brien. Washington: American Psychological Association.

Guilford, J. P. 1950. Creativity. *American Psychologist* 5:444–54.

Guilford, J. P. 1967. *The nature of human intelligence.* New York: McGraw Hill.

Hatch, T., and H. Gardner. 1986. From testing intelligence to assessing competences: A pluralistic view of intellect. *The Roeper Review* 8:147–50.

Jencks, C. 1972. *Inequality.* New York: Basic Books.

Jensen, A. R. 1980. *Bias in mental testing.* New York: Free Press.

Jensen, A. R. 1987. Individual differences in the Hick paradigm. In *Speed of information processing and intelligence*, ed. P. Vernon. Norwood, NJ: Ablex.

Kagan, J., and N. Kogan. 1970. Individual variation in cognitive processing. In *Handbook of child psychology*, ed. P. Mussen. New York: Wiley.

Kaplan, E. 1983. Process and achievement revisited. In *Toward a holistic developmental psychology*, ed. S. Wapner and B. Kaplan. Hillsdale, NJ: Lawrence Erlbaum.

Laboratory of Comparative Human Cognition. 1982. Culture and intelligence. In *Handbook of human intelligence.* ed. R. J. Sternberg. New York: Cambridge University Press.

Langer, S. K. 1942. *Philosophy in a new key.* Cambridge: Harvard University Press.

Lave, J. 1980. What's special about experiments as contexts for thinking? *Quarterly Newsletter of the Laboratory of Comparative Human Cognition* 2:86–91.

Malkus, U., D. Feldman, and H. Gardner. 1988. Dimensions of mind in early childhood. In *The psychological bases of early childhood*, ed. A. D. Pelligrini. Chichester, U.K.: Wiley.

Messick, S. 1988. Validity. In *Educational measurement.* 3d ed., ed. R. Linn. New York: Macmillan.

Newell, A., and H. A. Simon. 1972. *Human problem-solving.* Englewood Cliffs, NJ: Prentice-Hall.

Perkins, D. 1981. *The mind's best work.* Cambridge: Harvard University Press.

Piaget, J. 1983. Piaget's theory. In *Manual of child psychology*, ed. P. Mussen. New York: Wiley.

Polanyi, M. 1958. *Personal knowledge.* Chicago: University of Chicago Press.

Resnick, L. 1987. The 1987 presidential address: Learning in school and out. *Educational Researcher* 16 (9): 13–20.

Rogoff, B. 1982. Integrating context and cognitive development. In *Advances in developmental psychology.* vol. 2, ed. M. Lamb and A. Brown. Hillsdale, NJ: Lawrence Erlbaum.

Scribner, S. 1986. Thinking in action: Some characteristics of practical thought. In *Practical Intelligence*, ed. R. Sternberg and R. K. Wagner. New York: Cambridge University Press.

Squire, L. 1986. Mechanisms of memory. *Science* 232:1612–19.

Sternberg, R. 1977. *Intelligence, information processing, and analogical reasoning.* Hillsdale, NJ: Lawrence Erlbaum.

Sternberg, R. 1985. *Beyond IQ.* New York: Cambridge University Press.

Sternberg, R., ed. 1988. *The nature of creativity.* New York: Cambridge University Press.

Strauss, S. 1982. *U-shaped behavioral growth.* New York: Academic Press.

Thurstone, L. 1938. *Primary mental abilities.* Chicago: University of Chicago Press.

Wallach, M. 1971. The *intelligence/creativity distinction.* Morristown, NJ: General Learning Press.

Wallach, M. 1985. Creativity testing and giftedness. In *The gifted and talented: Developmental perspectives.* ed. F. Horowitz and M. O'Brien. Washington, DC: American Psychological Association.

Wexler-Sherman, C., H. Gardner, and D. H. Feldman. 1988. A pluralistic view of early assessment: The Project Spectrum approach. *Theory into Practice* 27 (1): 77–83.

Zessoules, R., D. Wolf, and H. Gardner. 1988. A better balance: ARTS PROPEL as an alternative to discipline-based art education. In *Beyond discipline-based art education*, ed. J. Burton, A. Lederman, and P. London. North Dartmouth, MA: University Council on Art Education.

8

Assessment, Learning Theories and Testing Systems

Paul Black

Introduction: Formative and Summative

The purposes of testing and assessment can be considered in two broad categories – the summative and the formative.

Summative assessment serves to inform an overall judgement of achievement, which may be needed for reporting and review, perhaps on transfer between years in a school or on transfer between schools, perhaps for providing certificates at the end of schooling. Such test results may also be used for judging the achievements of individual teachers or of schools as a whole. **Formative assessment** is concerned with the short term collection and use of evidence for the guidance of learning, mainly in day to day classroom practice.

It is clear from this distinction that the function of assessment that is directly concerned with learning is the formative function, and it is also evident that this aspect is being neglected, both in public policy and in everyday practice. So this chapter concentrates on formative assessment, starting with a brief outline of the current state of practice in Section 1. Then Section 2 surveys those features of theories of learning which are concerned with cognitive development. This survey serves as a basis for a discussion of current theories and research findings on formative assessment in Section 3. In exploring these, this section also introduces motivational and social aspects of learning theory.

Whilst the practices of summative assessment have less direct effects on learning, these effects can nevertheless be powerful. The issues involved here are discussed in Section 4. Finally, Section 5, looks briefly at the problems of formulating national policies in relation to the interactions between formative and summative functions.

1   Surveying Formative Practice

Whilst all teachers look at the work pupils do in class, set and mark written homework, ask questions in class and so on, the quality of this work is very variable. There is a wealth of research evidence that the everyday practice of assessment in classrooms, in the UK but also elsewhere, is beset with problems and short-comings (Black and Wiliam, 1998).

The most important difficulties may be briefly summarized in three groups. The first is concerned with *effective learning*:

- Teachers' tests encourage rote and superficial learning.
- The questions and other methods used are not shared between teachers, and they are not critically reviewed in relation to what they actually assess.
- There is a tendency to emphasize quantity of work and to neglect its quality in relation to learning.

The second group is concerned with *negative impact*:

- The giving of marks and the grading functions are over-emphasized, while the giving of advice and the learning function are under-emphasized.
- Pupils are compared with one another, which highlights competition rather than personal improvement. Such feedback teaches pupils with low attainments that they lack 'ability', and that they are not able to learn.

The third group focuses on *the managerial role* of assessments:

- Teachers' feedback to pupils often seems to serve social and managerial functions rather than learning.
- The collection of marks to fill up records is given greater priority than the analysis of pupils' work to discern learning needs; yet some teachers pay no attention to the assessment records of previous teachers of their pupils.

Given this picture, one can ask why things have worked out this way. The answer must be a multiple and complex one. It is clear that the culture and history of a country's education help fashion what may be taken for granted in its current practices (Chapter 2 of Black, 1998; Broadfoot, 1996). This chapter will focus mainly on one feature only of this complex – namely assumptions about the nature of learning. Such assumptions may be explicit, or implicit and unacknowledged, but they are always powerful in determining practice.

2   Theories of Learning – the Cognitive Perspective

Two common assumptions about learning are that a complex skill can be taught by breaking it up and teaching and testing the pieces separately; and that an idea which is common to action in many contexts can be taught most economically by presenting it in abstract isolation so that it can then be deployed in many situations.

These assumptions are consistent with behaviourist psychology, which lays emphasis on stimulus-response theory. The test item is the stimulus, the answer the response, and a learner has to be 'conditioned' to produce the appropriate response to any given stimulus. Because the response is the only observable, attention is not paid to any model of the thinking process of the pupil which might intervene between stimulus and response. It follows that distinctions between rote learning and learning with understanding are not considered – what is needed is to deliver appropriate stimuli, teach by repetition and then reward the appropriate responses. A test composed of many short, 'atomized', out-of-context questions, and 'teaching to the test', are both consistent with this approach.

Contemporary understanding of the ways that children learn look at the process quite differently (Wood, 1998). A first important lesson is illustrated by the following quotation:

> even comprehension of simple texts requires a process of inferring and thinking about what the text means. Children who are drilled in number facts, algorithms, decoding skills or vocabulary lists without developing a basic conceptual model or seeing the meaning of what they are doing have a very difficult time retaining information (because all the bits are disconnected) and are unable to apply what they have memorised (because it makes no sense).
>
> (Shepard, 1992, p. 303)

Numerous studies have exposed the debilitating consequences of rule bound traditional learning. Recent examples are the studies of Nuthall and Alton-Lee (1995) on the methods pupils use to answer tests, showing that long-term retention depends on the capacity to understand and so re-construct procedures, and of Boaler (1997) who, by comparing the effects of traditional and more open methods on pupils' attitudes and performance, showed that only those taught by open methods could see the applications of their mathematics in their daily lives. A consequence for both formative and summative assessment is that capacity to apply cannot be inferred from tests which call only for recall of the 'pure' knowledge and understanding.

In rejecting behaviourism, current 'constructivist' theories focus attention on the need for models of the mental processes involved when anyone responds to new information or to new problems. The learner is taken to be active in analysing and transforming any new information or question. Piaget stressed that such transformation depends on the mind's capacity to learn from experience by projecting beyond it and to engage in abstract thought. He proposed that this capacity developed through distinct stages rather than by a steady progression. Some have used this view to propose that we should match the stages at which learners are likely to have reached at various ages, to the sophistication of the ideas, for learning and assessment, that are proposed in the curricula for these ages.

However, current theories take a more complex view of learning. Piaget's focus on thought in terms of logical structures is now seen to deal only with the logical mode of thinking, whereas there are many other modes, each of which might develop in different ways and at different rates from one person to another. On this view, it makes no sense to talk of an individual's general capacity for abstract thought – such capacity may be exhibited in (say) family relationships but quite absent in (say) physics concepts. However, one of Piaget's principles that still commands acceptance is that we learn by actions, by self-directed problem-solving aimed at trying to control the world, and that abstract thought evolves from concrete action. Wood spells out the consequence of this view:

> teaching that teaches children only how to manipulate abstract procedures (e.g. learning how to solve equations) without first establishing the deep connections between such procedures and the activities involved in the solution of practical concrete problems (which the procedures serve to represent at a more abstract level) is bound to fail.
>
> (Wood, 1998, p. 9)

It is also evident that transformations of incoming ideas can only be achieved in the light of what the learner already knows and understands, so the reception of new knowledge depends on existing knowledge and understanding. It follows that formative assessment must first seek to clarify this existing knowledge and understanding and must then explore using both abstract tasks and practical concrete ones.

It is not easy to change learners' schemes of understanding. Research in the learning of science for example has shown that many pupils resist changing their everyday and naive views on how the natural world works, despite being able to play back the 'correct' science explanations in formal tests. So teaching must start by exploring existing ideas and encouraging expression and defence of them in argument, for unless the learners' thinking is made explicit, to themselves as well as to their teachers, they cannot be fully aware of the need for conceptual modification, and reconstruction cannot be monitored. A second step is to find ways to challenge ideas, usually through providing examples and experiences which are new to pupils and with which their ideas cannot cope without modification. It follows that formative assessment must be skilfully directed to reveal important aspects of understanding, and then be developed, within contexts that challenge pupils' ideas, in order to explore response to such challenge (Fensham *et al.*, 1994). Such strategies receive strong support from research which shows that those who progress better in learning turn out to have better self-awareness and better strategies for self-regulation than their slower learning peers (Brown and Ferrara, 1985). One consequence here, that self-assessment may be an important aspect of formative assessment, will be taken up later.

The directions of desirable change are to be chosen in the light of the learning aims of each subject. Thus both pedagogy and assessment have to be fashioned in the light of assumptions, both about how learning is best achieved and about the epistemology of the subject under consideration. Progress in learning physics (say) may be quite different from progress in learning history. The idea of 'progress' implies that any teaching plan must be founded on some notion of what constitutes progress towards the learning goals of the subject taught. A model of progress would serve to guide the construction of formative assessment procedures and of items of helpful diagnostic quality, and could set criteria for grading summative assessments. This idea lay behind the – controversial – level system (originally 10-level, now 8) for the national curriculum in England and Wales (Black, 1997).

The role of the teacher as supporter rather than director of learning was given prominence by Vygotsky (1962), who has had an important impact on education because he started from a view that learning proceeds by an interaction between the teacher and the learner. His approach can be linked to another concept introduced by Wood *et al.* (1976) expressed by the the metaphor of 'scaffolding' – the teacher provides the scaffold for the building, but the building itself can only be constructed by the learner. In this supportive role, the teacher has to discern the potential of the learner to advance in understanding, so that new challenges are neither too trivial nor too demanding. Thus there is an area of appropriate and productive challenge which Vygotsky called the 'zone of proximal development'. This is the gap between what the learner can do on his own and what he can do with the help of others. One function of assessment would then be to help to identify this zone accurately and to explore progress within it.

For Vygotsky, intelligence is the capacity to learn through instruction. It has been commonly believed that a suitable form of (content-free) IQ test would serve as a good predictor of academic potential. However, it is arguable whether any test can really be 'content-free' – in particular, it is very hard to escape dependence on the language capacity of the pupil. Some would oppose all such approaches arguing that people have a variety of modes of 'intelligence', that it is a mistake to view it as a unitary concept (Gardner, 1992), and that 'intelligence', far from being fixed, is a collection of thinking skills that can be taught. Related objections are that such tests only assess closed forms of thinking, whilst neglecting more open, holistic forms. It follows that the claim that future performance can be predicted using conventional IQ tests, or other content-free standardized tests, must be suspect.

Emphasis on learning as an interaction has important practical consequences. Brown and Ferrara (1985) highlight one facet of low achievement, by showing that low-achieving students lack self-regulation skills, and that when these are taught to them, they progress rapidly. In such teaching, low-achieving students can be seen to start with a wide zone of proximal development, the gap between their initial achievement and their potential being wide because of the lack of self-regulation.

A second feature is that low achievement may arise because of a breakdown in communication, a gap in mutual understanding between the learner and those who possess the expertise being taught, rather than from some defect inside the learner. All theorists after Piaget give emphasis, albeit to different extents and within different theoretical frameworks, to the importance of language in learning. Interaction takes place through language discourse, which is learnt and understood in particular social contexts. Vygotsky's emphasis on interaction arose from his interests in the historical and cultural origins of our thought and action. The terms and conventions of discourse are socially determined, and it would follow that the nature of our learning depends on the particular character of this discourse, and its effectiveness on the extent to which its terms and conventions are shared.

Since a learner's response will be sensitive to the language and social context of any communication, it follows that assessments have to be very carefully framed, both in their language and context of presentation, if they are to avoid bias i.e. unfair effects on those from particular gender, social, ethnic or linguistic groups. The importance of context is a far-reaching issue. Two well researched examples are that tests set about use of mathematics in the street might be failed by a student who can use the same mathematics in a familiar school context, and tests on paper about designing an experiment produce quite different results when the same task is presented with real equipment in a laboratory.

The account in this section has been limited to the cognitive aspect of links between assessment and student response. Other important elements will be explored in the course of the next section.

3   Assessment and Learning in Practice

The importance of formative assessment, and some of the key features which characterize its effects, will be explored in this section. The section starts with an account of two research studies which illustrate the various issues.

Examples of Success

The *first* example is of research reported by Schunk (1996), in which 44 students in one USA elementary school, all nine or ten years of age, worked over seven days on seven packages of instructional materials on fractions under the instructions of graduate students. Students worked in four separate groups subject to different treatments – for two groups the instructors stressed *learning goals* (learn how to solve problems) whilst for the other two they stressed *performance goals* (merely solve them). For each set of goals, one group had to evaluate their problem solving capabilities at the end of each of the first sessions, whereas the others were asked instead to complete an attitude questionnaire about the work. Outcome measures of skill, motivation and self-efficacy showed that the group given *performance goals* without self-evaluation came out lower than the other three on all measures. The interpretation of this result suggested that the effect of the frequent self-evaluation had out-weighed the differential effect of the two types of goal. This was confirmed in a second study in which all students undertook the self-evaluation, but on only one occasion near the end rather than after all of the first six sessions. There were two groups who differed only in the types of goal that were emphasized – the aim being to allow the goal effects to show without the possible overwhelming effect of the frequent self-evaluation. The *learning goal* orientation led to higher motivation and achievement outcomes than did the *performance goal*.

The *second* example is a meta-analysis of 21 different studies, of children ranging from pre-school to grade 12, which between them yielded 96 different measures of learning gains (Fuchs and Fuchs, 1986). The studies were carefully selected – all involved the use of formative feedback by teachers, comparison between experimental and control groups, and assessment activities with frequencies of between two and five times per week. The mean effect size obtained was 0.70 (this means that the size difference in mean scores between the experimental and control groups was about 70 per cent of the standard deviation estimated from the spread in the scores of either group). Studies for children without handicap gave a mean effect size of 0.63 over 22 sets of results, whilst those for handicapped children gave a mean of 0.73 for the handicapped groups over 74 sets. In about half of the studies teachers worked to set rules about reviews of the data and actions to follow, whereas in the others actions were left to teachers' judgements. The former produced a mean effect size of 0.92 compared with 0.42 for the latter.

One feature of this last example is of particular interest here. The authors compare the striking success of the formative approach with the unsatisfactory outcomes of programmes which had attempted to work from *a priori* prescriptions for individualized learning programmes for children, based on particular learning theories and diagnostic pre-tests. Such programmes embodied a deductive approach in contrast with the inductive approach of formative feedback programmes.

The work involved in both of these studies was based on quantitative comparisons of learning gains, using pre- and post-tests, and comparisons of experimental with control groups. Comparable results have been obtained in a wide and diverse range of studies, and the consistent feature across the variety of examples is that they all show that attention to formative assessment can lead to significant learning gains. Furthermore, many of the studies show that the greatest learning gains are secured for pupils initially classified as low achievers. A possible reason is that such pupils have previously suffered from lack of clear guidance, rather than from lack of 'ability'. Underlying the various approaches are assumptions about the psychology of learning, as in the emphasis on self-evaluation in Schunk's work.

Analysis of the research literature, from which the above three studies were selected, suggests that the general lessons about formative assessment can be considered under four main headings, namely pupils' reception, teachers' practices, the theory of feedback and the social setting of the classroom. These four will now be considered in turn.

Pupils' Reception

In his analysis of formative assessment by teachers in France, Perrenoud comments that

> A number of pupils do not aspire to learn as much as possible, but are content to 'get by', . . . Every teacher who wants to practise formative assessment *must reconstruct the teaching contracts so as to counteract the habits acquired by his pupils*. Moreover, some of the children and adolescents with whom he is dealing are imprisoned in the identity of a bad pupil and an opponent.
>
> (author's italics – Perrenoud, 1991, p. 92)

The reluctance of pupils described here does not simply arise from laziness. Other relevant factors are fear, failure to see feedback as a positive signal, and negative attitudes towards learning. Thus, the effectiveness of formative work depends not only on the content of the feedback and associated learning opportunities, but also on the broader context of assumptions about the motivations and self-perceptions of students within which it occurs. In particular, feedback which is directed to the objective needs revealed, with the assumption that each student can and will succeed (Schunk's *learning goals*), has a very different effect from that feedback which is subjective in mentioning comparison with peers (*performance goals*). This type of distinction is reflected in many other studies. Feedback which focuses on performance has been described as 'ego-involving'. By being comparative, it draws attention to the pupil's self-esteem (Butler and Neuman, 1995). Where this is done, pupils tend to attribute any failure to their lack of ability and tend to avoid seeking help in order to hide their incapacity. Even the giving of praise can be harmful if it is not linked to objective feedback.

Whilst extrinsic rewards, such as marks, gold stars, merit awards, can be counter productive because they focus on 'ability' rather than on the belief that one's efforts can produce success, feedback which is associated with goal criteria has different effects. Comparative studies by several authors show that such feedback enhances performance, but also enhances attitudes to work and self-esteem mainly through its effect on pupils' beliefs about their own capacity to learn. Combining extrinsic rewards with explicit guidance is as ineffective as giving these rewards on their own – the extrinsic seems to dominate. For effective learning, it makes a difference if pupils believe that effort is more important than ability, that mistakes are an inevitable part of learning, and that they have control over their own learning.

The overall message here is that the way in which formative information is conveyed to a student, and the context of classroom culture and beliefs about ability and effort within which feedback is interpreted by the individual recipient, can affect pupils' beliefs about themselves – for good or ill. Thus the direct effect of particular feedback on a pupil's learning can be enhanced by the indirect effect on the pupil's attitudes, self-concept and motivation.

Several innovators have introduced self-assessment by students – some because of a belief that a teacher in a typical class cannot individually assess every pupil, others because of a belief that self-assessment is essential if pupils are to be helped to take responsibility for their own learning (Arthur, 1995; Parkin and Richards, 1995). Most of these innovations have encountered one initial difficulty – pupils have to understand the goals of their learning so that they can judge their own progress against them, and such grasp by pupils of the overall purposes and direction of learning work is unusual and hard to convey. However, on a constructivist view, it is essential to grasp the goals of one's work and compare them with one's present understanding if learning is to be meaningful and permanent. On this view, self-assessment is essential to learning, and this is reinforced by the work quoted in Section 2 on the importance of self-regulation.

Many studies have shown that training in self-monitoring produces significant learning gains (Fontana and Fernandes, 1994; Frederiksen and White, 1997). A main conclusion of one of these was that students did better because they started by reflecting on a problem and considered the possibilities of using different strategies before proceeding. Others stress that an emphasis on independent learning requires and promotes reflection on one's learning (Bonniol, 1991). Such reflection, leading to a strategic approach to one's work guided by a clear view of its goals, is summed up in the term 'meta-cognition' (Brown, 1987). This seems a grand term, but work to achieve it can take several specific and mundane directions. Examples shown to be effective are asking pupils to score one another's work and discuss their conclusions, and asking them to invent questions appropriate for the assessment of their work rather than answer other people's questions. Many such activities involve work in groups and this is often linked to peer assessment. Whilst such assessment is also productive, discussion of peer group work raises issues about collaborative learning which are outside the scope of this article (Slavin, 1991; Wood and O'Malley, 1996).

Developing reflective habits of mind is an essential condition for learning (Zessoules and Gardner, 1991) – assessment has to be seen as a moment of learning which students can use to learn if they have an understanding of what it means to get better. The task of developing students' self-assessment capabilities may be approached as a task of providing them with appropriate models of better ways of working. Hattie *et al.* (1996) argue that direct teaching of study skills to students without attention to reflective, meta-cognitive, development may well be pointless. One reason for the need to look for radical change is that students bring to their work models of learning which may be an obstacle to their own learning.

Teachers' Strategies

There are several aspects of classroom strategies which require analysis. The first is the choice of tasks. These have to be selected and designed to evoke those aspects of understanding which are seen to be important for achieved learning, and to be necessary for progress. This is a difficult enterprise, and surveys have shown that many teachers do not succeed well with it. Tasks have to be attuned to be challenging to pupils without being daunting, and their construction has to be informed also by beliefs about learning and about the ways in which students make progress in it (Ames, 1992).

Testing at regular intervals (i.e. up to once a week) can enhance learning. However, for such assessment to be formative the feedback information has to be used – which means that a significant aspect of any approach will be the differential treatments which are incorporated in response to the feedback. Here assumptions about learning, and about the structure and nature of learning tasks which will provide the best challenges for improved learning, will be significant, and the criteria will be specific to each particular area of study. Frequent tests given without feedback are not formative, and if they are too frequent can cause a decline in performance. Tan (1992) reports a situation in which frequent summative testing was seen to damage learning by establishing a 'hidden curriculum' of low-level skills.

Questions used in classroom dialogue raise different issues. One survey (Stiggins *et al.*, 1989) found that two thirds of such questions were tests of recall only, and less than 20 per cent required deductive or inferential reasoning. This often happens because teachers want a quick response to questions addressed to a whole class – silence of more than a few seconds is regarded as embarrassing (Rowe, 1986). So students have no time to think, whilst in order to maintain the dialogue the questions are simplified until they reach the level at which they can be answered without time for thought. It also follows that only a few pupils give answers, most give up trying because they cannot respond quickly and fear to appear foolish. So the class dialogue is maintained, but with superficial feedback from a few and none at all from the majority.

Clarke (1988) has shown that post-test achievement in a sample of science classrooms was strongly associated with the quality of the discourse. This 'quality' can be analysed at several different levels. One way, illustrated above, is to look at the questions in isolation. Another way is to look at the dialogue in which they occur as part of a continuing exchange. Some analyses of such dialogue – with primary school children – have shown that a teacher can, quite unconsciously, ignore any original thoughts of the pupil, giving encouragement only to responses which fit the teacher's plan for progress. This seems to be done or to ensure that the discussion gets to the intended point in limited time. The effect, however, is to teach the pupil that the purpose is to guess what the teacher is thinking, not to come up with novel thoughts of your own. This point is further explored in the discussion below on the *Social setting*.

It is hard to see how any innovation in formative assessment can be treated as a marginal change in classroom work. All such work involves some degree of feedback between those taught and the teacher, and this is entailed in the quality of their interactions which is at the heart of pedagogy. The nature of these interactions between teachers and students, and of students with one another, will be key determinants for the outcomes of any changes. In particular, feedback, whether on written work or in dialogue, should be against learning criteria and should avoid comparative, ego-involving, discourse. However, it is difficult to obtain data about these qualities from many of the published reports.

Towards a Theory

The term feedback is inevitably introduced into discussions of formative assessment. In this context, the term implies that the system has reference points or goals, a means of measuring its present state and so estimating the gap between this state and the goals, and a means for closing this gap (Sadler, 1989). Such analysis is readily applied, and has been used above in the discussion about self-assessment. An underlying problem here is to specify how clear a concept of the goal has to be grasped by a learner in order to move from an imperfect to a less imperfect understanding of it.

The detailed quality of assessment tasks and the effectiveness of the advice given as feedback has been explored in the analysis of Tittle (1994) who proposed a framework with three dimensions. The first, the epistemology and theories involved, can relate both to positions held in relation to learning in general, and to the particular epistemology relevant to the subject matter concerned. The second dimension focuses on the details of the assessment instruments used and the cognitive level and style of teachers' oral and written comments. The third dimension brings in the interpreter and user. The teacher's beliefs, about the subject matter, about learning, and about the students and the class, must also be important components in any model, if only because it is on the basis of these that appraisals of Sadler's 'gap' must be formulated. Here the teacher's underlying values are at issue and Tittle stresses the value-laden nature of assessment processes.

The Social Setting of the Classroom

Emphasis on the ethical and moral aspects of assessment is a feature of the perspective outlined by Aikenhead (1997) who proposes that consideration of assessment can fall within three paradigms that are commonly encountered in the social sciences. One, the empirical-analytic, clearly links to the psychometric emphasis in standardized testing. The second, the interpretative paradigm, has to be adopted in formative assessment, and this link brings out the importance of understanding a learner's response in relation to that learner's expectations and assumptions about the classroom process, together with his or her interpretation of the task demand and of the criteria for success. In the third, the critical-theoretic paradigm, one would seek a critique of the wider purposes being pursued, notably the empowerment of the learner, and the choice between either selecting an elite or achieving excellence for all. This paradigm also calls into play the need for a critique of the learning goals which should ask whose interests these goals are designed to serve.

This analysis brings out the point that all the assessment processes are, at heart, social processes, taking place in social settings, conducted by, on and for social actors. Here, the ideas introduced near the end of Section 2 can be taken further. Brousseau (1984) has used the term 'didactical contract' to describe the network of (largely implicit) expectations and agreements that evolves between students and teachers. A particular feature of such contracts is that they serve to delimit 'legitimate' activity by the teacher. For example, in a classroom where the teacher's questioning has always been restricted to 'lower-order' skills, such as the production of correct procedures, students may well see questions about 'understanding' or 'application' as unfair, illegitimate or even meaningless.

The actions of teachers and students are also influenced by the structures of schools and society. Spaces in schools are designated for specified activities, and given the importance attached to 'orderliness' in most classrooms, teachers' actions are as often concerned with establishing routines, order and student satisfaction as they are with developing the students' capabilities (Pryor and Torrance, 1996). A review by Rismark (1996) shows that students are frequently marginalized and their work undervalued if they use frames of reference from their personal experiences outside school. Filer (1993) found that children learning handwriting and spelling in English primary school classrooms were constrained by the teacher to develop these skills in standard contexts, so that their own personal experiences were 'blocked out'. In this way, formal, purportedly 'objective' assessments made by teachers may be little more than the result of successive sedimentation of previous 'informal' assessments – in extreme cases the self-fulfilling prophecy of teachers' labelling of students (Filer, 1995).

It is clear therefore that a full theory of classroom has to reflect and inter-relate several different perspectives, notably the epistemological-cognitive, a theory of feedback, a theory of learning, and a theory of social discourse. The practical implication is that improvements in classroom practice need more than superficial changes. However, attention has also to be given to the wider context in which the teacher operates within a classroom. The closing section will pay some attention to this feature.

4   Summative Assessments

Because a summative test is designed to give an overall picture of performance, it has to aggregate several pieces of evidence. An example is an A-level physics examination, taken by pupils who have specialized in studying about three subjects in school between ages 16 and 18. In this examination, pupils do written tests, one on multiple choice, one on short problems, one on comprehension of an unseen passage, and one on analysis of data, together with two pieces of teacher assessed work, one an open experimental project and one essay requiring library research, both on individually chosen topics (Morland, 1994). The variety here serves both to reflect a range of aims of the learning in authentic ways, and to reduce bias which can arise because different candidates respond better to some kinds of contexts and challenges than to others.

However, this examination is costly, both in time of students and teachers and in the finance to pay examiners and administrators. By contrast, national tests taken by all pupils in England and Wales at age 14 (the end of what is termed Key Stage 3 in the national curriculum) cover three years' study of science in a two hour test, with the time devoted entirely to a variety of structured short answer questions. Teachers under pressure to produce good test results here will engage their pupils in the narrow range of learning activities that are reflected in such questions – and there is evidence that Key Stage tests have narrowed the range of teaching activities (Hacker and Rowe, 1997). The effect is to change teaching from a constructivist back to a behaviourist style – to the detriment of sound learning.

Summative examinations include components of teacher assessment because it is not possible to make valid assessment of some learning aims by short external written examinations. An example is pupils' ability to plan, carry out, analyse and report experimental investigations of their own. In the A-level example, there are detailed procedures to ensure the consistency and fairness of the teachers' results (i.e. moderation); their marks are then added in to the final aggregate. In the Key Stage assessment, the same problem has been 'resolved' by having teachers' assessments reported separately, with no arrangements for moderation. The result of this is that this aspect of pupils' assessments has low status, and teachers are tempted to concentrate on teaching to the tests.

These scenarios illustrate the inevitable tensions between the formative function of assessment and the summative and accountability functions. One possible response to such problems is to argue that the two functions are so different that different instruments and procedures are needed for them and that teachers should play no part in the summative because this is not compatible with their formative role. Others argue both that there is an overlap between the instruments and procedures needed for both purposes and that the difference may lie in the interpretation of test results rather than in their generation (Black, 1993; Wiliam and Black, 1996). Teachers cannot avoid a summative role, for example in annual end-of-year reports to parents, and if they cannot play such a role then some work that serves important educational aims will not have the value, in students' eyes, of generating recognized rewards.

These difficulties have been attacked in a number of ways. At one extreme, external testing is not used, as in some *lander* in Germany (Chapter 9 in Black, 1997); and in Queensland (Butler, 1995), Australia where teachers work in regional clusters to exchange marked work and achieve peer agreement. The tradition in post-16 vocational assessment in the UK has been to use inspection procedures to license colleges as assessment centres and give them the responsibility of determining test results, sometimes with some national standardized test to serve as calibration check. At the other extreme, standardized, supposedly 'content-independent' tests, set and marked externally, are the main instruments for accountability, as in many states in the USA. The damaging effects of such tests on learning has provoked new work to establish reliability and feasibility of more open forms of assessment.

One approach is to use portfolios, in which students select and assemble samples of their work throughout (say) a year and propose them for assessment – usually by their own teachers (see Calfee and Perfumo, 1996; Broadfoot, 1992). Where pupils have to make a selection themselves and write an overview to explain how their selections meet criteria, the assessment includes an assessment of their overview of their learning.

Other approaches resemble the portfolio approach in extending over time the production of assessment evidence. Systems for graded assessments, built up in the 1980s and early 1990s, similarly opened up the opportunities for pupils to accumulate credit over a long period rather than depend on a short final examination. Modular forms of course can work in this way, using summative assessment at the end of each module. Here, our government, worried about reliability, has called for short external tests to be added for calibration, and some also judge that a single terminal exam is a more valid indicator of learning than a series of module-by-module assessments. This concern does not appear to be based on any evidence.

A significant feature here is that some schemes depended on large banks of assessment items, each item categorized according to the specific aims and to the level of a scheme of progression for which it was relevant. Flexibility is protected by allowing teachers to select items, within overall constraints, which reflect their own teaching. This type of approach is used for national assessment in Scotland (Harlen and Malcolm, 1996). Given the difficulty of composing valid assessment instruments to cover a range of learning aims, there is a need both for teacher collaboration and for outside support in encouraging provision and sharing of banks of items in this way. Indeed, external summative tests can be helpful, provided that they are based on a sound model of learning and do not enhance concentration on only a narrow, possibly counter productive, set of learning aims.

5   Systems of Assessment and Testing

National policies on assessment must resolve many tensions, for example, between accountability and learning priorities, between formative and summative purposes, between teachers' assessments and external assessments, between frequent testing and end-of-course testing, and between the competing requirements of reliability and validity. It would be hard enough for teachers and other education professionals to agree on an optimum system. However, national debates also involve politicians, and many interested pressure groups, who have their own assumptions and priorities, some ill-informed, some legitimate, often driven by interests quite outside the sphere of the education profession.

The story of the development in the UK, from the founding of GCSE in the 1980s through the erratic trajectory of national assessment is a good example (Black, 1997). What is evident in this story is that three main influences were important. One was concern about the social effects of structural changes in education, notably the abandonment of selective secondary education. A second was suspicion and fear about the ideology and motives of educational reformers. A third was the beliefs about learning that were reflected in beliefs about the value of different approaches to assessment. The following comment by a US expert, albeit written about her country rather than the UK, is an appropriate summary:

> If they are unaware of new research findings about how children learn, policy makers are apt to rely on their own implicit theories which most probably were shaped by the theories that were current when they themselves attended school . . . Some things that psychologists can prove today even contradict the popular wisdom of several decades ago. Therefore, if policy makers proceed to implement outmoded theories or tests based on old theories, they might actually subvert their intended goal – of providing a rigorous and high quality education for all students.
>
> (Shepard, 1992, p. 301)

References

Three sources have been used extensively for this article and a fuller discussion, with further reference to the literature, can be found in these. They are as follows:
For theories of learning: Wood, D. (1998) *How Children Think and Learn: The Social Contexts of Cognitive Development (2nd edition)*. Oxford: Blackwell.
For the study of formative assessment: Black, P. and Wiliam, D. (1998) Assessment and classroom learning. *Assessment in Education*, 5(1), pp. 7–75.
For a general overview on formative and summative assessment: Black, P. (1998) *Testing: Friend or Foe? Theory and Practice of Assessment and Testing*. London: Falmer Press.

Other references cited in this chapter are as follows:
Aikenhead, G. (1997) A framework for reflecting on assessment and evaluation, in: *Globalization of Science Education – papers for the Seoul International Conference*, pp. 195–9. Seoul, Korea: Korean Educational Development Institute.
Ames, C. (1992) Classrooms: goals, structures, and student motivation. *Journal of Educational Psychology*, 84(3), pp. 261–71.

Arthur, H. (1995) Student self-evaluations – how useful – how valid. *International Journal Of Nursing Studies*, 32(3), pp. 271–6.

Black, P. J. (1993) Assessment policy and public confidence: Comments on the BERA Policy Task Group's article 'Assessment and the improvement of education'. *The Curriculum Journal*, 4(3), pp. 421–7.

Black, P. J. (1997) Whatever Happened to TGAT? in Cullingford, C. (ed.) *Assessment vs. Evaluation* pp. 24–50, London: Cassell.

Boaler, J. (1997) *Experiencing School Mathematics: Teaching Styles, Sex and Setting*. Buckingham, UK: Open University Press.

Bonniol, J. J. (1991) The mechanisms regulating the learning process of pupils: contribution to a theory of formative assessment, in: P. Weston (ed.) *Assessment of Pupils Achievement: Motivation and School Success*, pp. 119–37. Amsterdam: Swets and Zeitlinger.

Broadfoot, P. (1992) Multilateral evaluation: a case study of the national evaluation of records of achievement (PRAISE) project. *British Educational Research Journal*, 18(3), pp. 245–60.

Broadfoot, P. M. (1996) *Education, Assessment and Society. A Sociological Analysis*, Buckingham, Open University Press.

Brousseau, G. (1984) The crucial role of the didactical contract in the analysis and construction of situations in teaching and learning mathematics, in: H-G. Steiner (ed.) *Theory of Mathematics Education: ICME 5 topic area and miniconference*, pp. 110–119. Bielefeld, Germany: Institut für Didaktik der Mathematik der Universität Bielefeld.

Brown, A. (1987) Metacognition, executive control, self-regulation and other mysterious mechanisms, in Weinert, F. E and Kluwe, R. H. (eds.) *Metacognition, Motivation, and Understanding*, pp. 65–116, Hillsdale, New Jersey: Lawrence Erlbaum.

Brown, A. L. and Ferrara, R. A. (1985) Diagnosing zones of proximal development in culture, communication and cognition, in Wersch, J. V. (ed.) *Vygotskian perspectives*. Cambridge: Cambridge University Press.

Butler, J. (1995) Teachers judging standards in senior science subjects: fifteen years of the Queensland experiment. *Studies in Science Education*, 26, pp. 135–57.

Butler, R. and Neuman, O. (1995) Effects of task and ego-achievement goals on help-seeking behaviours and attitudes. *Journal of Educational Psychology*, 87 (2), pp. 261–71.

Calfee, R. and Perfumo. P. (eds.) (1996) *Writing Portfolios in the Classroom*; Mahwah, N. J.: Lawrence Erlbaum.

Clarke, J. (1988) Classroom dialogue and science achievement. *Research in Science Education*, 18, pp. 83–94.

Fensham, P. J., Gunstone, R. F. and White, R. T. (1994) *The Content of Science: A Constructivist Approach to its Teaching and Learning*. London: Falmer Press.

Filer, A. (1993) Contexts of assessment in a primary classroom. *British Educational Research Journal*, 19(1), pp. 95–107.

Filer, A. (1995) Teacher assessment: social process and social product. *Assessment in Education*, 2(1), 23–38.

Fontana, D. and Fernandes, M. (1994) Improvements in mathematics performance as a consequence of self-assessment in Portuguese primary school pupils. *British Journal of Educational Psychology*, 64, pp. 407–17.

Frederiksen, J. R. and White, B. J. (1997) Reflective assessment of students' research within an inquiry-based middle school science curriculum. Paper presented at the Annual Meeting of the AERA Chicago 1997.

Fuchs, L. S. and Fuchs, D. (1986) Effects of systematic formative evaluation: a meta-analysis. *Exceptional Children*, 53(3), pp. 199–208.

Gardner, H. Assessment in Context: The Alternative to Standardized Testing, in Gifford, B. R. and O'Connor, M. C. (eds.) (1992) *Changing Assessments: Alternative Views of Aptitude, Achievement and Instruction*, pp. 77–117. Boston and Dordrecht, Kluwer.

Hacker, R. J. and Rowe, M. J. (1997) The impact of a National Curriculum development on teaching and learning behaviours. *International Journal of Science Education*, 19(9) pp. 997–1004.

Harlen, W. and Malcolm, H. (1996) Assessment and testing in Scottish primary schools. *The Curriculum Journal*, 7(2), pp. 247–57.

Hattie, J., Biggs, J. and Purdie, N. (1996) Effects of learning skills interventions on student learning: a meta-analysis. *Review of Educational Research*, 66(2), pp. 99–136.

Morland, D. (1994) *Physics: Examinations and Assessment. Nuffield Advanced Science*, Harlow, Longman.

Nuthall, G. and Alton-Lee, A. (1995) Assessing classroom learning; how students use their knowledge and experience to answer classroom achievement test questions in science and social studies, *American Educational Research Journal*, 32(1), pp. 185–223.

Parkin, C. and Richards, N. (1995) Introducing formative assessment at KS3: an attempt using pupils' self-assessment, in Fairbrother, R., Black, P. J., and Gill, P. (eds.) *Teachers Assessing Pupils: Lessons from Science Classrooms*, pp. 13–28. Hatfield, UK: Association for Science Education.

Perrenoud, P. (1991) Towards a pragmatic approach to formative evaluation, in: P. Weston (ed.) *Assessment of Pupils' Achievement: Motivation and School Success*, pp. 79–101. Amsterdam: Swets and Zeitlinger.

Pryor, J. and Torrance, H. (1996) Teacher-pupil interaction in formative assessment: assessing the work or protecting the child? *The Curriculum Journal*, 7(2), pp. 205–26.

Rismark, M. (1996) The likelihood of success during classroom discourse. *Scandinavian Journal of Educational Research*, 40(1), pp. 57–68.

Rowe, M. B. (1986) Wait time: slowing down may be a way of speeding up. *Journal of Teacher Education*, 37(1), pp. 43–50.

Sadler, R. (1989) Formative assessment and the design of instructional systems. *Instructional Science*, 18, pp. 119–44.

Schunk, D. H. (1996) Goal and self-evaluative influences during children's cognitive skill learning. *American Educational Research Journal*, 33(2), pp. 359–82.

Shepard, L. A. (1992) Commentary: what policy makers who mandate tests should know about the new psychology of intellectual ability and learning, in Gifford, B. R. and O'Connor, M. C. (eds.) *Changing Assessments: Alternative Views of Aptitude, Achievement and Instruction*, pp. 301–28. Boston and Dordrecht, Kluwer.

Slavin, R. E. (1991) Synthesis of research of co-operative learning. *Educational Leadership*, 48(5), pp. 71–82.

Stiggins, R. J., Griswold, M. M. and Wikelund, K. R. (1989) Measuring thinking skills through classroom assessment. *Journal of Educational Measurement*, 26(3), pp. 233–46.

Tan, C. M. (1992) An evaluation of the use of continuous assessment in the teaching of physiology. *Higher Education*, 23(3), pp. 255–72.

Tittle, C. K. (1994) Toward an educational-psychology of assessment for teaching and learning – theories, contexts, and validation arguments. *Educational Psychologist*, 29(3), pp. 149–62.

Vygotsky, L. S. (1962) *Thought and language.* Wiley: New York.

Wiliam, D. and Black, P. J. (1996) Meanings and consequences: a basis for distinguishing formative and summative functions of assessment. *British Educational Research Journal*, 22(5), pp. 537–48.

Wood, D., Bruner, J. S. and Ross, G. (1976) The role of tutoring in problem solving. *Journal of Child Psychology and Psychiatry*, 17, pp. 89–100.

Wood, D. and O'Malley, C. (1996) Collaborative learning between peers: an overview. *Educational Psychology in Practice*, 11(4), pp. 4–9.

Zessoules, R. and Gardner, H. (1991) Authentic assessment: beyond the buzzword and into the classroom, in Perrone, V. (ed.) *Expanding Student Assessment*, pp. 47–71. Alexandria, Virginia, USA: Association for Supervision and Curriculum Development.

9

Where Is the Mind?

Paul Cobb

[. . .]

Two major trends can be identified in mathematics education research during the past decade. The first is the generally accepted view that students actively construct their mathematical ways of knowing as they strive to be effective by restoring coherence to the worlds of their personal experience. The theoretical arguments that underpin this position are primarily epistemological and have been advanced by von Glasersfeld (1984, 1987, 1989a). Empirical support is provided by numerous studies that document that there are significant qualitative differences in the understandings that students develop in instructional situations, and that these understandings are frequently very different from those that the teacher intends (Confrey, 1990; Hiebert and Carpenter, 1992). The acceptance of constructivism can be contrasted with a second trend that emphasizes the socially and culturally situated nature of mathematical activity. At least in the United States, this attempt to go beyond purely cognitive analyses reflects a growing disillusionment with the individualistic focus of mainstream psychology (Brown, Collins and Duguid, 1989; Greeno, 1991; Schoenfeld, 1987). The theoretical basis for this position is inspired in large measure by the work of Vygotsky and that of activity theorists such as Davydov, Leont'ev and Galperin (Nunes, 1992). Empirical support comes from paradigmatic studies such as those of Carraher, Carraher and Schliemann (1985), Lave (1988), Saxe (1991), and Scribner (1984), which demonstrate that an individual's arithmetical activity is profoundly influenced by his or her participation in encompassing cultural practices such as completing worksheets in school, shopping in a supermarket, selling candy on the street, and packing crates in a dairy.

These constructivist and sociocultural perspectives at times appear to be in direct conflict, with adherents to each claiming hegemony for their view of what it means to know and learn mathematics (Steffe, 1996; Voigt, 1992). Thus, there is currently a dispute over both whether the mind is located in the head or in the individual-in-social-action, and whether mathematical learning is primarily a process of active cognitive reorganization or a process of enculturation into a community of practice (Minick, 1989). Similarly, the issue of whether social and cultural processes have primacy over individual processes, or vice versa, is the subject of intense debate (van Oers, 1990). Further, adherents to the two positions differ on the role that signs and symbols play in psychological development. Constructivists tend to characterize them as a means by which students express and communicate their mathematical thinking, whereas sociocultural theorists typically treat them as carriers of either established mathematical meanings or of a practice's intellectual heritage. In general, the attempts of the two groups of theorists to understand the other's position are confounded by their differing usage of a variety of terms, including *activity*, *setting*, *context*, *task*, *problem*, *goal*, *negotiation*, and *meaning*.

The central focus of this article will be on the assumptions that give rise to an apparent forced choice between the two perspectives. In particular, I will argue that mathematical learning should be viewed as both a process of active individual construction and a process of enculturation into the mathematical practices of wider society. The central issue is then not that of adjudicating a dispute between opposing perspectives. Instead, it is to explore ways of coordinating constructivist and sociocultural perspectives in mathematics education. The particular perspective that comes to the fore at any point in an empirical analysis can then be seen to be relative to the problems and issues at hand.

It should be noted that the apparent conflict between constructivist and sociocultural perspectives is not merely a matter of theoretical contemplation. Instead, it finds expression in tensions endemic to the act of teaching. For example, Ball (1993) observes that 'current proposals for educational improvement are replete with notions of "understanding" and "community" – about building bridges between the experiences of the child and the knowledge of the expert' (p. 374). She then inquires:

> *How* do I create experiences for my students that connect with what they now know and care about but that also transcend the present? *How* do I value their interests and also connect them to ideas and traditions growing out of centuries of mathematical exploration and invention? (p. 375)

Ball's references to students' experiences and to valuing their interests imply a focus on their qualitatively distinct interpretations and on the personal goals that they pursue in the classroom. This, in my terms, implies a view of mathematical learning as active construction. In contrast, her reference to students' mathematical heritage suggests a view of mathematical learning as enculturation. Ball goes on to discuss three dilemmas that arise in the course of her practice as a mathematics teacher. She clarifies that these dilemmas of content, discourse, and community 'arise reasonably from competing and worthwhile aims and from the uncertainties inherent in striving to attain them' (p. 373). It would therefore seem that the aims of which she speaks and thus the pedagogical dilemmas reflect the tension between mathematical learning viewed as enculturation and as individual construction.

Comparisons and Contrasts

Sociocultural and constructivist theorists both highlight the crucial role that activity plays in mathematical learning and development. However, sociocultural theorists typically link activity to participation in culturally organized practices, whereas constructivists give priority to individual students' sensory-motor and conceptual activity. Further, sociocultural theorists tend to assume from the outset that cognitive processes are subsumed by social and cultural processes. In doing so, they adhere to Vygotsky's (1979) contention that 'the social dimension of consciousness is primary in fact and time. The individual dimension of consciousness is derivative and secondary' (p. 30). From this, it follows that 'thought (cognition) must not be reduced to a subjectively psychological process' (Davydov 1988, p. 16). Instead, thought should be viewed as

> something essentially 'on the surface', as something located . . . on the borderline between the organism and the outside world. For thought . . . has a life only in an environment of socially constituted meanings. (Bakhurst, 1988, p. 38)

Consequently, whereas constructivists analyze thought in terms of conceptual processes located in the individual, sociocultural theorists take the individual-in-social-action as their unit of analysis (Minick, 1989). From this latter perspective, the primary issue is that of explaining how participation in social interactions and culturally organized activities influences psychological development.

Sociocultural theorists formulate this issue in a variety of different ways. For example, Vygotsky (1978) emphasized the importance of social interaction with more knowledgeable others in the zone of proximal development and the role of culturally developed sign systems as psychological tools for thinking. In contrast, Leont'ev (1981) argued that thought develops from practical, object-oriented activity or labor. Several American theorists have elaborated constructs developed by Vygotsky and his students, and speak of cognitive apprenticeship (Brown, Collins and Duguid, 1989; Rogoff, 1990), legitimate peripheral participation (Forman, 1992; Lave and Wenger, 1991), or the negotiation of meaning in the construction zone (Newman, Griffin and Cole, 1989). In contrast to the constructivist's concern with individual students' conceptual reorganizations, each of these contemporary accounts locates learning in coparticipation in cultural practices. As a consequence, educational implications usually focus on the kinds of social engagements that increasingly enable students to participate in the activities of the expert rather than on the cognitive processes and conceptual structures involved (Hanks, 1991).

In contrast to sociocultural theorists' frequent references to the works of Vygotsky, Leont'ev, and Luria, constructivists usually trace their intellectual lineage to Piaget's genetic epistemology (1970, 1980), to ethnomethodology (Mehan and Wood, 1975), or to symbolic interactionism (Blumer, 1969). As this set of references indicates, it is possible to distinguish between what might be called psychological and interactionist variants of constructivism. Von Glasersfeld's development of the epistemological basis of the psychological variant incorporates both the Piagetian notions of assimilation and accommodation, and the cybernetic concept of viability. Thus, he uses the term *knowledge* in 'Piaget's *adaptational* sense to refer to those sensory-motor and conceptual operations that have proved viable in the knower's experience' (1992, p. 380). Further, traditional correspondence theories of truth are dispensed with in favor of an account that relates truth to the effective or viable organization of activity: 'Truths are replaced by viable models – and viability is always relative to a chosen goal' (1992, p. 384). In this model, perturbations that the cognizing subject generates relative to a purpose or goal are posited as the driving force of development. As a consequence, learning is characterized as a process of self-organization in which the subject reorganizes his or her activity to eliminate perturbations (von Glasersfeld, 1989b). As von Glasersfeld notes, his instrumentalist approach to knowledge is generally consistent with the views of contemporary neopragmatist philosophers such as Bernstein (1983), Putnam (1987), and Rorty (1978).

Although von Glasersfeld defines learning as self-organization, he acknowledges that this constructive activity occurs as the cognizing individual interacts with other members of a community. Thus, he elaborates that *knowledge* refers to 'conceptual structures that epistemic agents, given the range of present experience within their tradition of thought and language, consider *viable*' (1992, p. 381). Further, he contends that 'the most frequent source of perturbations for the developing cognitive subject is interaction with others' (1989b, p. 136). Bauersfeld's interactionist version of constructivism complements von Glasersfeld's psychological focus in that both view communication as a process of mutual adaptation wherein individuals negotiate meanings by continually modifying their interpretations (Bauersfeld, 1980; Bauersfeld, Krummheuer and Voigt, 1988). However, whereas von Glasersfeld tends to focus on individuals' construction of their ways of knowing, Bauersfeld emphasizes that 'learning is characterized by the subjective reconstruction of societal means and models through negotiation of meaning in social interaction' (1988, p. 39). In accounting for this process of subjective reconstruction, he focuses on the teacher's and students' interactive constitution of the classroom microculture. Thus, he argues that

> participating in the processes of a mathematics classroom is participating in a culture of mathematizing. The many skills, which an observer can identify and will take as the main performance of the culture, form the procedural surface only. These are the bricks of the building, but the design of the house of mathematizing is processed on another level. As it is with culture, the core of what is learned through participation is *when* to do what and *how* to do it. . . . The core part of school mathematics enculturation comes into effect on the meta-level and is 'learned' indirectly. (1995)

Bauersfeld's reference to indirect learning clarifies that the occurrence of perturbations is not limited to those occasions when participants in an interaction believe that communication has broken down and *explicitly negotiate* meanings. Instead, for him, communication is a process of often *implicit negotiations* in which subtle shifts and slides of meaning occur outside the participants' awareness [. . .]. In taking this approach, Bauersfeld uses an interactionist metaphor and characterizes negotiation as a process of mutual adaptation in the course of which the teacher and students establish expectations for others' activity and obligations for their own activity (cf. Cobb and Bauersfeld, 1995; Voigt, 1985). By way of contrast, Newman *et al.* (1989), speaking from the sociocultural perspective, define negotiation as a process of mutual appropriation in which the teacher and students continually coopt or use each others' contributions. Here, in line with Leont'ev's (1981) sociohistorical metaphor of appropriation, the teacher's role is characterized as that of mediating between students' personal meanings and culturally established mathematical meanings of wider society. From this point of view one of the teacher's primary responsibilities when negotiating mathematical meaning with students is to appropriate their actions into this wider system of mathematical practices. Bauersfeld, however, takes the local classroom microculture rather than the mathematical practices institutionalized by wider society as his primary point of reference when he speaks of negotiation. This focus reflects his concern with the process by which the teacher and students constitute social norms and mathematical practices in the course of their classroom interactions. Further, whereas sociocultural theorists give priority to social and cultural process, analyses compatible with Bauersfeld's perspective propose that individual students' mathematical activity and the classroom microculture are reflexively related (Cobb, 1989; Voigt, 1992). In this view, individual students are seen as actively contributing to the development of classroom mathematical practices, and these both enable and constrain their individual mathematical activities. Consequently, it is argued that neither an individual student's mathematical activity nor the classroom microculture can be adequately accounted for without considering the other.

It is apparent from this brief summary of the two perspectives that they address different problems and issues. A sociocultural analysis of a classroom episode might both locate it within a broader activity system that takes account of the function of schooling as a social institution and attend to the immediate interactions between the teacher and students (Axel, 1992). This dual focus is explicit in Lave and Wenger's (1991) claim that their 'concept of legitimate peripheral participation provides a framework for bringing together theories of situated activity and theories about the production and reproduction of the social order' (p. 47). In general, sociocultural accounts of psychological development use the individual's participation in culturally organized practices and face-to-face interactions as primary explanatory constructs. A basic tenet underpinning this work is that it is inappropriate to single out qualitative differences in individual thinking apart from their sociocultural situation because differences in students' interpretations of school tasks reflect qualitative differences in the communities in which they participate (Bredo and McDermott, 1992).

In contrast, constructivists are typically concerned with the quality of individual interpretative activity, with the development of ways of knowing at a more micro-level, and with the participants' interactive constitution of classroom social norms and mathematical practices. The burden of explanation in constructivist accounts of development falls on models of individual students' cognitive self-organization and on analyses of the processes by which these actively cognizing individuals constitute the local social situation of their development (Cobb, Wood and Yackel, 1993) Thus, whereas a sociocultural theorist might view classroom interactions as an instantiation of the culturally organized practices of schooling, a constructivist would see an evolving microculture that does not exist apart from the teacher's and students' attempts to coordinate their individual activities. Further, whereas a sociocultural theorist might see a student appropriating the teacher's contributions, a constructivist would see a student adapting to the actions of others in the course of ongoing negotiations. In making these differing interpretations, sociocultural theorists would tend to invoke sociohistorical metaphors such as *appropriation,* whereas constructivists would typically employ interactionist metaphors such as *accommodation* and *mutual adaptation.* Further, whereas sociocultural theorists typically stress the homogeneity of members of established communities and eschew analyses of qualitative differences in individual thinking, constructivists tend to stress heterogeneity and to eschew analyses that single out pregiven social and cultural practices. From one perspective, the focus is on the social and cultural basis of personal experience. From the other perspective, it is on the constitution of social and cultural processes by actively interpreting individuals

Construction in Social Practice

Against the background of these contrasts between the two perspectives, I now consider possible coordinations between them. In this section, I explore possible complementarities between Rogoff's (1990) analysis of internalization and von Glasersfeld's (1996) discussion of empirical and reflective abstraction. In a subsequent section, I elaborate my argument by focusing on potential relationships between Saxe's (1991) sociocultural analysis and Steffe, Cobb, and von Glasersfeld's (1988) constructivist analysis. My general strategy in both cases is to tease out aspects of one position that are implicit in the other.

One of the central notions in Vygotsky's account of development is internalization. For example, in his frequently cited general genetic law of cultural development, Vygotsky argued that

> any higher mental function was external and social before it was internal. It was once a social relationship between two people . . . We can formulate the general genetic law of cultural development in the following way. Any function appears twice or on two planes . . . It appears first between people as an intermental category, and then within the child as an intramental category. (1960, pp. 197–198)

From the constructivist perspective, this account of internalization from the social realm to the internal cognitive realm leads to difficulties because the interpersonal relations that are to be internalized are located outside the child. Researchers can indeed identify patterns of interaction, collective schemes, and so forth when they analyze videorecordings or transcripts. However, a constructivist might follow Blumer (1969) in arguing that people respond to things in terms of the meaning they have for them rather than to constructs that researchers project into their worlds. From this point of view, the problem of explaining how relations that are real for the detached observer get into the experiential world of the child appears intractable.

Rogoff (1990), who is in many ways a follower of Vygotsky, discusses this difficulty in reference to research on social learning and socialization. She notes that, in this research, children are considered to learn by observing or participating with others. 'The underlying assumption is that the external lesson [to be learned] is brought across a barrier into the mind of the child. How this is done is not specified, and remains a deep problem for these approaches' (p. 195). In proposing a solution, Rogoff elaborates Vygotsky's notion of internalization by arguing that children are already engaged in a social activity when they actively observe and participate with others. If children are viewed as being in the social activity in this way

> with the interpersonal aspects of *their* functioning integral to the individual aspects, then what is practiced in social interaction is never on the outside of a barrier, and there is no need for a separate process of internalization. (p. 195, italics added)

Here, Rogoff circumvents the need for an internalization process by proposing that the researcher change his or her perspective and focus on what children's interpersonal activity might mean to them. In constructivist terms, this involves a shift in focus to the mathematical meanings and practices that the child considers are shared with others.

Rogoff's point that children are already active participants in the social practice implies that they engage in and contribute to the development of classroom mathematical practices from the outset. Further,

> in the process of participation in social activity, the individual already functions with shared understanding. The individual's use of this shared understanding is not the same as what was constructed jointly; it is an appropriation of the shared understanding by each individual that reflects the individual's understanding of and involvement in the activity. (1990, p. 195)

Rogoff's distinction between the individual's use of a shared understanding and the shared understanding that is constructed jointly is closely related to the distinction that a constructivist might make between an individual child's understanding and the taken-as-shared meanings established by the group (Schutz, 1962). It therefore seems reasonable to conclude from Rogoff's treatment of internalization that mathematical learning is a process of active construction that occurs when children engage in classroom mathematical practices, frequently while interacting with others.

Significantly, a similar conclusion can be reached when considering von Glasersfeld's (1996) elaboration of Piaget's developmental theory.

Von Glasersfeld develops his view of learning as self-organization by clarifying the distinction that Piaget made between two types of cognitive reorganization, empirical abstraction and reflective abstraction. In doing so, he emphasizes that an empirical abstraction results in the construction of a property of a physical object, whereas the process of constructing mathematical and scientific concepts involves reflective abstraction. He illustrates the notion of empirical abstraction by describing a situation in which someone wants to drive a nail into a wall, but does not have a hammer. After looking around, the person finds a wooden mallet and begins to use this, only to find that the nail goes into the mallet instead of into the wall. Von Glasersfeld argues that, in this scenario, the person assimilates the mallet to her hammering scheme, but then makes an accommodation when things do not go as expected, and a perturbation is experienced. This accommodation involves an empirical abstraction in that it results in the construction of a novel property for the mallet – it is not the sort of thing that can be used to hammer nails into walls.

The interesting feature of this example for my purposes is that hammering is a cultural practice that involves acting with particular cultural artifacts, hammers and nails. The person's hammering scheme can be viewed as the product of active constructions she made in the course of her initiation into this practice. In other words, hammers, nails, and mallets are, for her, cultural tools that she can use for certain purposes. It is against the background of her engagement in this practice of hammering that she makes the empirical abstraction described by von Glasersfeld. This being the case, it seems reasonable to extend the definition of empirical abstraction by emphasizing both that it results in the emergence of novel physical properties and that it occurs as the individual participates in a cultural practice, often while interacting with others. This formulation involves the coordination of perspectives in that the first part, referring as it does to an experienced novelty, is said from the 'inside', whereas the second part is said from the 'outside' and locates the individual in a cultural practice.

The assumption that individual activity is culturally situated is also implicit in von Glasersfeld's discussion of the construction of mathematical concepts. Here, the notion of reflective abstraction is used to account for the process by which actions are reified and become mental mathematical objects that can themselves be acted upon (cf. Sfard, 1991; Thompson, 1994). For von Glasersfeld, it is by means of reflective abstraction that students reorganize their initially informal mathematical activity. Consider, for example, a situation in which the teacher introduces conventional written fraction symbols to record the results of students' attempts to partition objects such as pizzas fairly. Von Glasersfeld stresses that the students can only interpret the teacher's actions within the context of their ongoing activity. Further, the process by which the symbols come to signify the composition and decomposition of fractional units of some type for at least some of the students is accounted for in terms of the reification of partitioning activity via reflective abstraction. As with the example of the mallet, it can be observed that these conceptual reorganizations occur as the students participate in cultural practices. In this case, these are the mathematical practices that the students help to establish in the classroom. The mathematical concepts they each individually construct are relative to and are constrained by their participation in these practices. It can also be noted that the activities from which the students abstract include their interpretations of others' activity and of joint activities (Voigt, 1992). These considerations suggest that in defining reflective abstraction, we should emphasize both that it involves the reification of sensory-motor and conceptual activity and that it occurs while engaging in cultural practices, frequently while interacting with others. As was the case with the characterization of empirical abstraction, this formulation involves the coordination of perspectives.

In comparing Rogoff's and von Glasersfeld's work, it can be noted that Rogoff's view of learning as acculturation via guided participation implicitly assumes an actively constructing child. Conversely, von Glasersfeld's view of learning as cognitive self-organization implicitly assumes that the child is participating in cultural practices. In effect, active individual construction constitutes the background against which guided participation in cultural practices comes to the fore for Rogoff, and this participation is the background against which self-organization comes to the fore for von Glasersfeld.

Coordinating Perspectives

The complementarity between the sociocultural and constructivist perspectives can be further clarified by considering the analyses of arithmetical activity offered by Saxe (1991) and Steffe *et al.* (1988). In contrast to the majority of sociocultural theorists, Saxe takes an explicitly developmental perspective that focuses on individuals' understandings while simultaneously emphasizing the influence of cultural practices and the use of sign forms and cultural artifacts. He illustrates his theoretical approach by analyzing the body-parts counting system developed by the Oksapmin people of Papua New Guinea.

Saxe explains that 'to count as Oksapmin do, one begins with the thumb on one hand, and follows a trajectory around the upper periphery of the body down to the little finger of the opposite hand' (1991, p. 16). With Western contact and the introduction of tradestores, the Oksapmin had to use this indigenous counting system to solve arithmetical problems that did not emerge in traditional life, such as those of adding and subtracting values. In the course of his analysis of the interplay between the Oksapmin's participation in tradestore activities and their construction of mathematical understandings, Saxe identifies four developmental levels in the evolution of the body-parts counting system. At the least sophisticated level, individuals do not recognize the need to keep track of the second addend when they attempt to add, say, seven and nine coins. As a consequence, they frequently produce an incorrect sum. In contrast, the most sophisticated of the four levels involves the use of a 'halved-body strategy' that incorporates a base-10 system linked to the currency. Here, in adding seven and nine coins,

> individuals use the shoulder (10) as a privileged value. In their computation, they may represent the 9 on one side of the body as biceps (9) and 7 on the other side of the body as forearm (7). To accomplish the problem, a tradestore owner might simply 'remove' the forearm from the second side . . . and transfer it to the first side where it becomes the shoulder (the 10th). He then 'reads' the answer as 10 + 6 or 16. (p. 21)

In sociocultural terms, the Oksapmin's increasingly sophisticated computational strategies can be viewed as cultural forms. An account of development made from this perspective might focus on the extent to which individual Oksapmin participate in the new practice of economic exchange. Such an account would stress that typically only tradestore owners, who have the most experience with economic transactions, use the sophisticated halved-body strategy. In contrast to this view that social and cultural practices drive development, a constructivist analysis might treat the Oksapmin's computational strategies as cognitive forms created by self-organizing individuals. An account of this latter type might focus on the processes by which individual Oksapmin reflectively abstract from and thus reorganize their enumerating activity, thereby creating increasingly sophisticated arithmetical units. Interestingly, it is possible to develop such an account by using the cognitive models of American children's arithmetical development proposed by Steffe as a source of analogies (Steffe *et al.*, 1988).

We have seen that Oksapmin at the least sophisticated level do not recognize the need to keep track of counting. In contrast, Oksapmin at the next level consciously attempt to keep track This suggests that these Oksapmin view their counting acts as entities that can themselves be counted. In Steffe *et al.*'s (1988) terms, these acts carry the significance of counting abstract units. This analysis, which is made from the 'inside' rather than the 'outside', explains why Oksapmin at the initial level do not recognize the need to keep track of counting. They are yet to reify their counting acts, and, as a consequence, body-parts counting as they currently understand it is simply not the kind of activity that can be kept track of.

This analysis can be extended to account for the development of more sophisticated strategies. For example, when the halved-body strategy is used, a body part such as the biceps (9) appears to symbolize not a single unit but the composite of nine abstract units that would be created by counting to the biceps. In Piagetian terminology, counting has been reified via reflective abstraction, and the biceps symbolizes nine experienced as an arithmetical object that can be conceptually manipulated.

Each of the two perspectives, the sociocultural and the constructivist, tells half of a good story, and each can be used to complement the other. For example, consider a situation in which a young Oksapmin works in a tradestore and eventually learns the halved-body strategy used by the store owner. A sociocultural explanation might talk of the novice appropriating or internalizing a cultural form. As we have seen, an account of this type has difficulty in explaining how a cultural form that is external to the novice is brought across the barrier and becomes a cognitive form. The constructivist analysis circumvents this difficulty by stressing that rather than internalizing a cultural form that appears to be pregiven, the novice reorganizes his or her own activity. Thus, to paraphrase Rogoff (1990), there is nothing to bring across the barrier and, consequently, no need to posit a process of internalization from the sociocultural to the cognitive realm.

By the same token, the sociocultural perspective complements the constructivist perspective by emphasizing that the novice trader reorganizes his or her counting activity while attempting to achieve goals that emerge in the course of his or her participation in the practice of economic exchange (Saxe, 1991). From this point of view, it is readily apparent that both what counts as a problem and what counts as a legitimate solution are highly normative (cf. Solomon, 1989). Thus, both the process of individual construction and its products, increasingly sophisticated conceptual units, are social through and through. Conversely, it can be argued that the various strategies, viewed as cultural forms, are cognitive through and through in that they result from individual Oksapmin's constructive activities. As was the case with the discussion of Rogoff's and von Glasersfeld's analyses, this coordination of perspectives leads to the view that learning is a process of both self-organization and a process of enculturation that occurs while participating in cultural practices, frequently while interacting with others.

Theoretical Pragmatism

The discussion of Rogoff's, von Glasersfeld's, Saxe's, and Steffe's work indicates that sociocultural analyses involve implicit cognitive commitments, and vice versa. It is as if one perspective constitutes the background against which the other comes to the fore. This contention concerning the relationship between the perspectives can be contrasted with the claims made by adherents to each perspective that mind is either in the head or in the individual-in-social-action. Claims of this type reflect essentialist assumptions. In effect, adherents of both positions claim that they have got the mind right – this is what the mind really is, always was, and always will be, independent of history and culture. A perusal of Geertz's (1983) discussion of Western, Arabic, and Indic visions of the self and of community might lead proponents of a particular perspective to question whether theirs is the God's-eye view.

Following Fish (1989), it can be argued that theorizing is itself a form of practice rather than an activity that stands in opposition to practice. The discussion thus far suggests that if we want our practice of theorizing to be reflexively consistent with the theories we develop as we engage in that practice, we have to give up essentialist claims and take a more pragmatic approach. In this regard, Rorty (1983), who uses the metaphor of wielding vocabulary rather than taking a perspective, argues that

> the idea that only a certain vocabulary is suited to human beings or human societies, that only that vocabulary permits them to be 'understood', is the seventeenth-century myth of 'nature's own vocabulary' all over again. (p. 163)

For Rorty, the various vocabularies we use or the particular perspectives we take are instruments for coping with things rather than ways of representing their intrinsic nature. Here, Rorty follows Dewey and Kuhn in arguing that we should 'give up the notion of science traveling towards an end called "corresponding with reality" and instead say merely that a given vocabulary works better than another for a given purpose' (p. 157). Thus, 'to say something is better understood in one vocabulary than another is always an ellipsis for the claim that a description in the preferred vocabulary is most useful for a certain purpose' (p. 162).

The implication of this pragmatic approach for mathematics education, and for education more generally, is to consider what various perspectives might have to offer relative to the problems or issues at hand. In this regard, I suggest that the sociocultural perspective gives rise to theories of the conditions for the possibility of learning (Krummheuer, 1992), whereas theories developed from the constructivist perspective focus on both what students learn and the processes by which they do so. For example, Lave and Wenger (1991), who take a relatively radical position by attempting to avoid any reference to mind in the head, say that 'a learning curriculum unfolds in *opportunities for engagement* in practice' (p. 93, italics added). Consistent with this formulation, they note that their analysis of various examples of apprenticeship in terms of legitimate peripheral participation accounts for the occurrence of learning or failure to learn (p. 63). In contrast, a constructivist analysis would typically focus on the ways in which students reorganize their activity as they participate in a learning curriculum, and on the processes by which the curriculum is interactively constituted in the local situation of development. In my view, both these perspectives are of value in the current era of educational reform that stresses both students' meaningful mathematical learning and the restructuring of the school while simultaneously taking issues of diversity seriously. Constructivists might argue that sociocultural theories do not adequately account for the process of learning, and sociocultural theorists might retort that constructivist theories fail to account for the production and reproduction of the practices of schooling and the social order. The challenge of relating actively constructing students, the local microculture, and the established practices of the broader community requires that adherents to each perspective acknowledge the potential positive contributions of the other perspective. In doing so, constructivists would accept the relevance of work that addresses the broader sociopolitical setting of reform. Conversely, sociocultural theorists would acknowledge the pedagogical dilemmas articulated by Ball (1993) when she spoke of attending to both students' interests and understandings, and to their mathematical heritage.

In dispensing with essentialist claims, this pragmatic approach to theorizing instead proposes that the adoption of one perspective or another should be justified in terms of its potential to address issues whose resolution might contribute to the improvement of students' education. Voigt (1992) offered a justification of this type when he stated that

> personally the author takes the emphasis on the [individual] subject as the starting-point in order to understand the negotiation of meaning and the learning of mathematics in classrooms . . . The main reason is that concepts like 'socialization', 'internalization', 'initiation into a social tradition', etc. do not (directly) explain what I think is the most important objective of mathematics education . . . The prominent objective of mathematics education is not that students produce correct solutions to mathematical problems but that they do it insightfully and by reasonable thinking. What on the behavioral level does in fact not make a difference should be an important subjective difference. (p. 10)

Justification of this type are, of course, open to challenge. For example, a critic might argue that, in certain circumstances, it is more important that students produce correct answers than that they develop insight. This counterargument does not claim that Voigt's chosen perspective fails to capture the essence of mathematical development. Instead, it questions assumptions about educational objectives and, ultimately, about what counts as improvement in students' mathematics education. In general, claims about what counts as improvement reflect beliefs and values about what it ought to mean to know and do mathematics (or science or social studies) in school. These beliefs and values are themselves open to challenge and criticism, thus bringing to the fore the moral and ethical aspects of educational research and theorizing (Nicholls, 1989).

The central claim of this chapter, that the sociocultural and constructivist perspectives each constitute the background for the other, implies that justifications should explicitly bring the researcher into the picture by acknowledging his or her interpretive activity. Essentialist claims involve a denial of responsibility – it is social reality that dictates the correct theoretical perspective. In contrast, pragmatic justifications reflect the researcher's awareness that he or she has adopted a particular position for particular reasons. From the sociocultural perspective, a justification of this type would explain why it is not necessary to focus on the actively cognizing student for the purposes at hand. Conversely, constructivists would be obliged to explain why it is not necessary to go beyond the box of the classroom for their purposes, while acknowledging that it is appropriate to take a perspective that locates classroom events within a wider sociopolitical setting for other purposes.

This pragmatic approach to theorizing also contends that ways of coordinating perspectives should be developed while addressing specific problems and issues. In addition, the suggestion acknowledges that Ball and other teachers have something interesting to say when they suggest that the tension in teaching between individual construction and enculturation cannot be resolved once and for all. Teachers instead have to act with wisdom and judgment by continually developing ways to cope with dilemmas in particular situations. A similar modus operandi would appear to be appropriate for researchers as we engage in our practice. In place of attempts to subjugate research to a single, overarching theoretical scheme that is posited a priori, we might follow Ball in reflecting on and documenting our attempts to coordinate perspectives as we attempt to cope with our specific problems. In doing so, we would give up the quest for an acontextual, one-size-fits-all perspective. Instead, we would acknowledge that we, like teachers, cast around for ways of making sense of things as we address the situated problems of our practice.

[. . .]

References

Axel, E. (1992). One developmental line in European activity theories. *Quarterly Newsletter of the Laboratory of Comparative Human Cognition, 14*(1), 8–17.

Bakhurst, D. (1988). Activity, consciousness, and communication. *Quarterly Newsletter of the Laboratory of Comparative Human Cognition, 10*, 31–39.

Ball, D. L. (1993). With an eye on the mathematical horizon: Dilemmas of teaching elementary school mathematics. *Elementary School Journal, 93*, 373–397.

Bauersfeld, H. (1980). Hidden dimensions in the so-called reality of a mathematics classroom. *Educational Studies in Mathematics, 11*, 23–41.

Bauersfeld, H. (1988). Interaction, construction, and knowledge: Alternative perspectives for mathematics education. In T. Cooney and D. Grouws (Eds.), *Effective mathematics teaching* (pp. 27–46). Reston, VA: National Council of Teachers of Mathematics and Lawrence Erlbaum Associates.

Bauersfeld, H. (1995). 'Language games' in the mathematics classroom: Their function and their effects. In P. Cobb and H. Bauersfeld (Eds.), *The emergence of mathematical meaning: Interaction in classroom cultures.* Hillsdale, NJ: Lawrence Erlbaum Associates.

Bauersfeld, H., Krummheuer, G., and Voigt, J. (1988). Interactional theory of learning and teaching mathematics and related microethnographical studies. In H-G Steiner and A. Vermandel (Eds.), *Foundations and methodology of the discipline of mathematics education* (pp. 174–188). Antwerp, Belgium: Proceedings of the TME Conference.

Bernstein, R. J. (1983). *Beyond objectivism and relativism: Science, hermeneutics, and praxis.* Philadelphia: University of Pennsylvania Press.

Blumer, H. (1969). *Symbolic interactionism.* Englewood Cliffs, NJ: Prentice-Hall.

Bredo, E., and McDermott, R. P. (1992). Teaching, relating, and learning. *Educational Researcher, 21*(5), 31–35.

Brown, J. S., Collins, A., and Duguid, P. (1989). Situated cognition and the culture of learning. *Educational Researcher, 18*(1), 32–42.

Carraher, T. N., Carraher, D. W., and Schliemann, A. D. (1985). Mathematics in streets and in schools. *British Journal of Developmental Psychology, 3*, 21–29.

Cobb, P. (1989). Experiential, cognitive, and anthropological perspectives in mathematics education. *For the Learning of Mathematics, 9*(2), 32–42.

Cobb, P., and Bauersfeld, H. (1995). The coordination of psychological and sociological perspectives in mathematics education. In P. Cobb and H. Bauersfeld (Eds.), *Emergence of mathematical meaning: Interaction in classroom cultures.* Hillsdale, NJ: Lawrence Erlbaum Associates.

Cobb, P., Wood, T., and Yackel, E. (1993). Discourse, mathematical thinking, and classroom practice. In N. Minick, E. Forman, and A. Stone (Eds.), *Education and mind: Institutional, social, and developmental processes* (pp. 91–119). New York: Oxford University Press.

Confrey, J. (1990). A review of the research on student conceptions in mathematics, science, and programming. In C. B. Cazden (Ed.), *Review of Research in Education* (Vol. 16, pp. 3–55). Washington, DC: American Educational Research Association.

Davydov V. V. (1988). Problems of developmental teaching (part I). *Soviet Education, 30*(8), 6–97.

Fish, S. (1989). *Doing what comes naturally.* Durham, NC: Duke University Press.

Forman, E. (1992, August). *Forms of participation in classroom practice.* Paper presented at the International Congress on Mathematical Education, Quebec City.

Geertz, C. (1983). *Local knowledge.* New York: Basic Books.

Greeno, J. G. (1991). Number sense as situated knowing in a conceptual domain. *Journal for Research in Mathematics Education,* 22, 170–218.

Hanks, W. F. (1991). Foreword. In J. Lave and E. Wenger (Eds.), *Situated learning: Legitimate peripheral participation* (pp. 13–26). Cambridge: Cambridge University Press.

Hiebert, J., and Carpenter, T. P. (1992). Learning and teaching with understanding. In D. A. Grouws (Ed.), *Handbook of research on mathematics teaching and learning* (pp. 65–98). New York: Macmillan.

Johnson, M. (1987). *The body in the mind: The bodily basis of reason and imagination.* Chicago: University of Chicago Press.

Krummheuer, G. (1992). *Lernen mit 'format': Elemente einer interaktionistischen lerntheorie.* Weinheim, Germany: Deutscher Studien Verlag.

Lave, J. (1988). *Cognition in practice: Mind, mathematics and culture in everyday life.* Cambridge: Cambridge University Press.

Lave, J., and Wenger, E. (1991). *Situated learning: Legitimate peripheral participation.* Cambridge: Cambridge University Press.

Leont'ev, A. N. (1981). The problem of activity in psychology. In J. V. Wertsch (Ed.), *The concept of activity in Soviet psychology.* Armonk, NY: Sharpe.

Mehan, H., and Wood, H. (1975). *The reality of ethnomethodology.* New York: John Wiley.

Minick, N. (1989). *L. S. Vygotsky and Soviet activity theory: Perspectives on the relationship between mind and society.* Literacies Institute, Special Monograph Series No. 1. Newton, MA: Educational Development Center, Inc.

Newman, D., Griffin, P., and Cole, M. (1989). *The construction zone: Working for cognitive change in school.* Cambridge: Cambridge University Press.

Nicholls, J. G. (1989). *The competitive ethos and democratic education.* Cambridge: Harvard University Press.

Nunes, T. (1992). Ethnomathematics and everyday cognition. In D. A. Grouws (Ed.), *Handbook of research on mathematics teaching and learning* (pp. 557–574). New York: Macmillan.

Piaget, J. (1970). *Genetic epistemology.* New York: Columbia University Press.

Piaget, J. (1980). *Adaptation and intelligence: Organic selection and phenocopy.* Chicago: University of Chicago Press.

Putnam, H. (1987). *The many faces of realism.* LaSalle, IL: Open Court.

Rogoff, B. (1990). *Apprenticeship in thinking: Cognitive development in social context.* Oxford: Oxford University Press.

Rorty, R. (1978). *Philosophy and the mirror of nature.* Princeton: Princeton University Press.

Rorty: R. (1983). Method and morality. In N. Haan, R. N. Bellah, and P. Robinson (Eds.), *Social science as moral inquiry* (pp. 155–176). New York: Columbia University Press.

Saxe, G. B. (1991). *Culture and cognitive development: Studies in mathematical understanding.* Hillsdale, NJ: Lawrence Erlbaum Associates.

Schoenfeld, A. H. (1987). What's all the fuss about metacognition? In A. H. Schoenfeld (Ed.), *Cognitive science and mathematics education* (pp. 189–216). Hillsdale, NJ: Lawrence Erlbaum Associates.

Schutz, A. (1962). *The problem of social reality.* The Hague, Holland: Martinus Nijhoff.

Scribner, S. (1984). Studying working intelligence. In B. Rogoff and J. Lave (Eds.), *Everyday cognition: Its development in social context* (pp. 9–40). Cambridge: Harvard University Press.

Sfard, A. (1991). On the dual nature of mathematical conceptions: Reflections on processes and objects as different sides of the same coin. *Educational Studies in Mathematics, 22,* 1–36.

Solomon, Y. (1989). *The practice of mathematics.* London: Routledge.

Steffe, L. P. (1996). Prospects for alternative epistemologies in education. In L. P. Steffe (Ed.), *Constructivism in education.* Hillsdale, NJ: Lawrence Erlbaum Associates.

Steffe, L. P., Cobb, P., and von Glasersfeld, E. (1988). *Construction of arithmetical meanings and strategies.* New York: Springer-Verlag.

Thompson, P. W. (1994). Images of rate and operational understanding of the fundamental theorem of calculus. *Educational Studies in Mathematics, 26,* 229–274.

van Oers, B. (1990). The development of mathematical thinking in school: A comparison of the action-psychological and the information-processing approach. *International Journal of Educational Research, 14,* 51–46.

Voigt, J. (1985). Patterns and routines in classroom interaction. *Recherches en Didactique des Mathematiques, 6,* 69–118.

Voigt, J. (1992, August). *Negotiation of mathematical meaning in classroom processes.* Paper presented at the International Congress on Mathematical Education, Quebec City.

von Glasersfeld, E. (1984). An introduction to radical constructivism. In P. Watzlawick (Ed.), *The invented reality* (pp. 17–40). New York: Norton.

von Glasersfeld, E. (1987) Learning as a constructive activity. In C. Janvier (Ed.), *Problems of representation in the teaching and learning of mathematics* (pp. 3–18). Hillsdale, NJ: Lawrence Erlbaum Associates.

von Glasersfeld, E. (1989a). Constructivism. In T. Husen and T. N. Postlethwaite (Eds.), *The international encyclopedia of education* (1st ed., supplement vol. 1, pp. 162–163). Oxford: Pergamon.

von Glasersfeld, E. (1989b). Cognition, construction of knowledge, and teaching. *Synthese, 80,* 121–140.

von Glasersfeld, E. (1992). Constructivism reconstructed: A reply to Suchting. *Science and Education, 1,* 379–384.

von Glasersfeld, E. (1996). Sensory experience, abstraction, and teaching. In L. P. Steffe (Ed.), *Constructivism in education.* Hillsdale, NJ: Lawrence Erlbaum Associates.

Vygotsky, L. S. (1960). *Razvitie vysshikh psikhicheskikh funktsii [The development of the higher mental functions].* Moscow: Akad. Ped. Nauk. RSFSR.

Vygotsky, L. S. (1978). *Mind and society: The development of higher psychological processes.* Cambridge: Harvard University Press.

Vygotsky, L. S. (1979). Consciousness as a problem in the psychology of behavior. *Soviet Psychology, 17*(4), 3–35.

SECTION 3
LEARNING AND ASSESSMENT: CURRICULUM IMPLICATIONS

10

Problem Solving as a Basis for Reform in Curriculum and Instruction: the Case of Mathematics

James Hiebert, Thomas P. Carpenter, Elizabeth Fennema, Karen Fuson, Piet Human, Hanlie Murray, Alwyn Olivier and Diana Wearne

[. . .]

The purpose of this chapter is to propose one principle for reform in curriculum and instruction. The principle is this: students should be allowed to make the subject problematic. We argue that this single principle captures what is essential for instructional practice. It enables us to make sense of the chaos, to sort out what is indispensable from what is optional. By itself, the principle does not specify curriculum nor prescribe instruction. But it does provide a compass that points classroom practice in a particular direction and that checks the alignment of its basic elements.

Allowing the subject to be problematic means allowing students to wonder why things are, to inquire, to search for solutions, and to resolve incongruities. It means that both curriculum and instruction should begin with problems, dilemmas, and questions for students. We do not use 'problematic' to mean that students should become frustrated and find the subject overly difficult. Rather, we use 'problematic' in the sense that students should be allowed and encouraged to problematize what they study, to define problems that elicit their curiosities and sense-making skills.

To develop our proposal, we focus on mathematics. Although we recognize that the subject matters (Stodolsky, 1988) and mathematics possess some unique features, we believe that the principle is relevant for all school subjects and that the issues we raise will be familiar to educators working in other disciplines.

This chapter has been edited.

To illustrate what the principle means for practice and to provide a point of reference, we first present an example from a second-grade classroom in which the development of arithmetic is treated as problem solving. We chose this example because the distinctions we will try to articulate are revealed most clearly when considering a topic that is usually treated as a routine skill. After presenting the example, we begin our analysis by reviewing briefly the history of problem solving in the curriculum. We note that the classroom episode we have just presented is at odds with most historic views of problem solving. We then re-establish the principle of problematizing the subject by building on John Dewey's notion of reflective inquiry. We argue that the benefit of this approach is that it yields deep understandings of the kinds that we value. We close by contrasting our view of problem solving with other current views on how problems should be used in teaching mathematics and by pointing to several common dichotomies that seem to collapse from this perspective.

A Classroom Example

Ms. Hudson's second-grade class is located in an urban school with a large Latino population. Prior to this lesson, in January, the students had been working on addition and subtraction problems, developing their own methods for solution. Some students had been using base-10 materials, such as sticks with 10 dots on them. This day's problem was to find the difference in the height of two children, Jorge and Paulo, who were 62 inches tall and 37 inches tall, respectively. After most of the students had worked out a solution, Ms. Hudson asked for volunteers to share their methods.

Gabriela, the first student to share, had solved the problem by counting up from 37 to 62. In the process, she counted by 1s and 10s, keeping track of her counts by drawing single dots to represent 1s and drawing sticks to represent 10s. She counted from 37 to 40, making 3 dots as she counted. Then she counted from 40 to 60 by 10s, drawing 2 sticks to show the 2 10s. Finally, she counted up to 62, making 2 more dots. She described her solution as follows:

> Gabriela: 'I said, "How much does Paulo have to grow?" so 37 plus 3 more [pointing to the 3 dots] is 38, 39, 40, and 50 [pointing to a 10 stick], 60 [pointing to another 10 stick], 61, 62 [pointing to 2 more dots]. So this is 23, 24, 25 more he has to grow.'
>
> Ms. Hudson: 'OK. Roberto?'

Roberto had first drawn a picture of Jorge and Paulo and extended a horizontal line from the top of Paulo's head across to Jorge. He had then drawn 6 10 sticks and 2 dots to represent 62. He took away 37 by first crossing out 3 sticks to take away 30. Then he put a mark on the 4th stick about three tenths of the way down and wrote a small 7 below the mark to show the 7 taken away and a 3 above the mark to show that 3 were left over. He then combined the 3 above the mark, the 2 dots, and the remaining 2 sticks to get 25. Here is what Roberto said:

> Roberto: 'I shrunk the big guy down by taking away the little guy from him [pointing to his drawing of Paulo and Jorge]. I took 3 10s from the 6 10s and 7 from this 10 [pointing to the 4th stick]. That leaves 3 and these 2 are 5 and 2 10s left is 25.'
> Ms. Hudson: 'OK. Now I am going to ask Jose how he did it.'

Jose had added up from 37 to 62 using a combination of numerals and drawings to help. He had written, in a single line, '37', then '3' (to make 40), then 2 sticks (to make 60), then '2' (to make 62). He then looked back and combined the 3, the 2 sticks, and the 2 to get 25.

> Jose: 'I did it like Gabriela, but I wrote 3 and then my 10 sticks and 2 and then added them to get 25 more the little guy needs.'

Maria was the next student to share a strategy. She had written 62 minus 37 in vertical form and used a more conventional subtraction procedure except that she first subtracted 7 from 10 (rather than 12), combined the 3 left over with the 2 to get 5, then subtracted 3 10s from the 5 remaining 10s to leave 2 10s and 5.

> Maria: 'I subtracted Paulo from Jorge like Roberto did, but I used numbers. I took one of the 10s to get enough to take away the 7, so that was 3 and 2 more was 5 1s, and there were 2 10s left, so 25.'
> Ms. Hudson: 'Can someone tell how Roberto's and Maria's methods are alike?'
> Carlos: 'They both took away the little guy.'
> Ms. Hudson: 'Anything else?'
> Jazmin: 'They both had to open a 10 because there weren't 7 1s to take away. So Roberto took his 7 from that 10 stick. He took 7 and left 3. And Maria took a 10 from the 6 10s and wrote it with the 1s and then took the 7 to leave 3.'
> Ms. Hudson: 'So they were both thinking kind of alike but wrote it in different ways?'
> Students: 'Yes.'

For the students in this class, the generation of procedures for computing with multidigit numbers was a problem-solving activity. Ms. Hudson had not demonstrated any of the methods that the students shared. The students constructed their own methods, either individually or collectively through peer interactions, using their knowledge of the base-10 number system.

What is striking about this example is not that students solved an exceptionally difficult problem nor that they displayed brilliant insights but rather that students became engaged in genuine problem solving in what is potentially the most routine of activities. These second graders worked diligently on the problem for over 10 minutes and then spent another 10 minutes presenting and discussing alternative solution methods. The students did not perceive the task as routine, and they were motivated to find and explain their alternative methods. This all happened because they were allowed to problematize what is usually taught through demonstration and repeated practice.

A Brief History of Problem Solving in the Curriculum

Most historic accounts of problem solving in school mathematics would not characterize finding the difference between 62 and 37 as a genuine problem nor would they identify the activity of the students in Ms. Hudson's class-room as an instance of problem solving. The reason is that conceptions of problem solving have been colored by a distinction between acquiring knowledge and applying it. The distinction suggests that computation pro-cedures should be acquired first and then applied to solve problems. But the distinction is more pervasive than this.

Acquisition and Application

Since the early 20th century, the mathematics curriculum has been shaped periodically by concerns about preparation for the workplace and for life outside of school (Stanic and Kilpatrick, 1988). These concerns have framed the debates about curricula around applications. The salient distinction has been between acquiring knowledge in school and applying it outside of school. Problems have been used as vehicles for practicing applications.

The 1930s and 1940s witnessed a movement to design the mathematics curriculum around real-life situations. Students were to learn the mathe-matics they needed in the context of solving problems. This would ensure that the knowledge they acquired would be useful. Opposing views argued that this 'incidental' learning was haphazard and insufficient. Important mathematics would get lost. The curriculum should rather be designed around the important ideas and skills that should be acquired (see Brownell, 1935; Reeve, 1936).

The tension between acquiring knowledge and applying it is not special to mathematics. It is at work in most disciplines that comprise the school curric-ulum. How much emphasis should be placed on acquiring the concepts and skills of the subject and how much on applying them in realistic situations?

The Focus on Application

Recent concerns about school learning have noted the wide gulf between acquiring and applying knowledge. One response has taken the form of 'problem-based learning'. A number of faculty in professional schools around the country have noted that the knowledge acquired in the class-room does not transfer well to the profession, whether it be medicine, engineering, social work, or education (Boud and Feletti, 1991a). In order to increase the usefulness of students' knowledge, some schools have adopted the model of problem-based learning or case-based instruction

(Shulman, 1992). As described by Boud and Feletti (1991b), problem-based learning 'is not simply the addition of problem-solving activities to otherwise discipline-centered curricula, but a way of conceiving of the curriculum which is centered around key problems in professional practice. Problem-based courses start with problems rather than with exposition of disciplinary knowledge' (p. 14). As was the case 50 years ago, critics claim that this approach focuses only on applications and worry that important information will get lost in the less predictable curriculum.

Mathematics education has witnessed a similar resurgence of interest in developing curricula that encourages the study of mathematics in the context of real-life problems. In contrast to the basic-skills curricula of the 1970s, with its emphasis on acquiring the mechanics of mathematics, the recent reform recommendations place a heavier emphasis on applications and connections of mathematics to the real-world (National Council of Teachers of Mathematics, 1989, 1991). Large-scale, real-life problems are proposed as appropriate contexts for learning and assessment (Burkhardt, 1981; Cognition and Technology Group at Vanderbilt, 1990; Lesh and Lamon, 1992; Romberg, 1992). Mathematics acquired in these realistic situations, proponents argue, will be perceived by students as being useful. Rather than acquiring knowledge that is isolated from real situations, students will acquire knowledge that is connected to such situations, and they will be able to apply this knowledge to a range of real-life problems. Although these approaches have been widely endorsed, we believe they do not resolve the difficulties that are inherent in the distinction between acquiring knowledge and applying it. The distinction may be somewhat blurred, but it still exists.

An Alternative View of Problems and Problem Solving

We believe that the distinction between acquiring knowledge and applying it is inappropriate for education. By making the distinction, educators have separated mathematical activity into two artificial categories and then have created equally artificial methods to bring them back together. To understand some of the philosophical roots of the distinction and to develop the alternative principle of problematizing the subject, we reconsider John Dewey's analysis and his central notion of reflective inquiry.

Revisiting the Distinction Between Acquisition and Application

The separation between acquiring knowledge and applying it builds directly from the distinction in philosophy between knowing and doing. Dewey (1929) argued that its ancient roots can be found in humans' desire for certainty. We have a long-standing belief, said Dewey, that knowing produced by reason and thought is potentially certain. Ideas can be abstracted from the particulars of experience and thereby become stable and reliable. Doing, on the other hand, is unreliable and uncertain. The outcomes are not always predictable. Doing involves interacting with the real world, and such interactions are filled with changing circumstances that we cannot control.

What is important here is that the distinction between knowing and doing has become so pervasive and so subtle that it permeates our thinking. 'We are so accustomed to the separation of knowledge from doing and making that we fail to recognize how it controls our conceptions of mind, of consciousness and of reflective inquiry' (Dewey, 1929, p. 22). Among other effects, the distinction has spawned a number of familiar dichotomies such as theory versus practice, reason versus experience, and acquiring knowledge versus applying knowledge.

Dewey's View of Problem Solving

Dewey moved beyond the pervasive, almost inescapable distinction between knowing and doing by a strikingly simple approach: he considered the methods people ordinarily use to deal with everyday problems to turn doubtful and uncertain situations into ones that are more predictable and certain. Dewey (1910, 1929, 1938) observed that thoughtful but ordinary methods of solving problems share fundamental features with the more refined methods of scientists, and the differences are in degree, not in kind. Dewey placed great faith in scientific (and ordinary) methods of solving problems. He referred to the methods by several names including the 'experimental practice of knowing' (1929) and 'reflective inquiry' (1933). He believed reflective inquiry was the key to moving beyond the distinction between knowing and doing, thereby providing a new way of viewing human behavior. More than that, he believed that the method provided a target for intelligent human behavior. To the extent that we could use the method of reflective inquiry, we would be acting intelligently. 'The value of any cognitive conclusion depends upon the *method* by which it is reached, so that the perfecting of method, the perfecting of intelligence, is the thing of supreme value' (Dewey, 1929, p. 200, emphasis in original).

The fundamental features of reflective inquiry can be stated simply: (1) problems are identified; (2) problems are studied through active engagement; (3) conclusions are reached as problems are (at least partially) resolved. It is worth elaborating briefly on each feature.

Identifying problems. The process begins with the recognition or definition of a problem. Problems are identified as such if the participant sees a quandary or feels a difficulty or doubt that needs to be resolved. 'The origin of thinking is some perplexity, confusion, or doubt. Thinking is not a case of spontaneous combustion' (Dewey, 1910, p. 12). Stated in slightly different terms, 'All reflective inquiry starts from a problematic situation' (Dewey, 1929, p. 189). The importance of this claim for Dewey lay not only in the fact that problems trigger reflective inquiry but also in the proposition that those who engage in reflective inquiry look for problems. They problematize their experiences in order to understand them more fully. This results in a radical reorientation. Familiar objects, including subject matters in school, are treated as 'challenges to thought They are *to be* known, rather than objects of knowledge. . . . [t]hey are things *to be* understood' (Dewey, 1929, p. 103, emphasis in original). 'The subject-matter which had been taken as satisfying the demands of knowledge, as the material with which to frame solutions [becomes] something which sets *problems*' (Dewey, 1929, p. 99, emphasis in original).

When we treat an object as a problem to be solved and examine it carefully, said Dewey (1929), we begin to understand it, to gain more control over it, and to use it more effectively for our advantage. The objects can be school topics, including things as ordinary as arithmetic computation procedures. As in Ms. Hudson's class, treating procedures as problems and examining them carefully affords students the chance to understand them, gain more control over them, and use them more effectively.

Searching for resolutions. Once a problem has been identified, the participant actively pursues a solution by calling up and searching out related information, formulating hypotheses, interacting with the problem, and observing the results. Several characteristics define this activity. It involves action, overt doing, that changes something about the problem and/or the situation in which the problem is embedded. Activity is central to the process. This is why Dewey (1929) claimed that, 'The experimental procedure is one that installs doing as the heart of knowing' (p. 36).

A second defining characteristic of searching for solutions 'involves willingness to endure a condition of mental unrest and disturbance' (Dewey, 1910, p. 13). It is always tempting to establish certainty too quickly by jumping to conclusions. But this undermines the process. Reflective inquiry, which Dewey (1929) equated with scientific forms of investigation, takes a much different view: 'A disciplined mind takes delight in the problematic . . . . The scientific attitude may almost be defined as that which is capable of enjoying the doubtful' (p. 228).

School instruction, said Dewey, is plagued by a push for quick answers. This short-circuits the necessary feeling of uncertainty and inhibits the search for alternative methods of solution. The result is a single, mechanically executed procedure that may yield the correct answer but shifts the attention away from the quality of methods. 'Probably the chief cause of devotion to rigidity of method is, however, that it seems to promise speedy, accurately measurable, correct results . . . . Were all instructors to realize that the quality of mental process, not the production of correct answers, is the measure of educative growth something hardly less than a revolution in teaching would be worked' (Dewey, 1926, pp. 206–207). As the excerpt from the second-grade class demonstrates, attention to method and process can be realized even in areas of the curriculum where rigidity of method and speedy answers have been the norm.

Reaching conclusions. Eventually some conclusion is reached, some resolution is achieved, some hypotheses are refined. The outcome of the process is a new situation, and perhaps a new problem, showing new relationships that are now understood. 'The outcome of the directed activity is the construction of a new empirical situation in which objects are differently related to one another, and such that the *consequences* of directed operations form the objects that have the property of being *known*' (Dewey, 1929, pp. 86–87, emphasis in original). The benefits of reflective inquiry lie not in the solutions to problems but in the new relationships that are uncovered, the new aspects of the situation that are understood more deeply. When the second graders were finding the differences in heights, they were exploring relationships within the number system, not just finding an answer. The relationships constructed are the things of primary value.

According to Dewey (1929), these relationships and understandings are what is left after the problem has been resolved. They constitute knowledge for the participant. 'Fruits remain and these fruits are the abiding advance of knowledge. . . . Knowledge is the fruit of the undertakings that transform a problematic situation into a resolved one' (pp. 192, 242–243). This does not mean, of course, that every participant will be left with the same knowledge. The nature of the knowledge will depend on the prior knowledge available to the participant when engaged in inquiry and the kind of operations that were used during investigative activity. But new understandings of some kind are the expected outcome of the process.

Moving beyond Dewey

[. . .]

As we continue our argument, we depart from Dewey, in practice if not in spirit, in two respects. We extend the range of tasks that can become problematic beyond those he cited as exemplary problem situations, and we extend the arguments that link reflective inquiry with understanding. Although Dewey's voice will still be heard in the discussion and we will show that our proposition is largely consistent with Dewey's position, we build the details of our argument from our own work and that of others.

Problematizing Mathematics and Developing Understanding

We work from an assumption that understanding is the goal of mathematics instruction. In fact, we justify the practice of problematizing the subject by claiming that it is this activity that most likely leads to the construction of understanding. To support this claim, we look at how problematizing fits within two very different views of mathematical understanding: a functional view and a structural view. These views can be seen as competing and even incompatible. The reason we include both is to show that the principle of allowing students to treat the subject problematically can be interpreted meaningfully from both perspectives. This allows us to consider students' construction of understanding from different perspectives and to uncover aspects of this process that might otherwise remain hidden.

Functional Understanding

From a functional perspective, understanding means participating in a community of people who practice mathematics (Brown *et al.*, 1989; Derry, 1992; Lave *et al.*, 1988; Lave and Wenger, 1991; Schoenfeld, 1988). Understanding is participating. 'Knowing is not the act of an outside spectator but of a participator' (Dewey, 1929, p. 196).

The functional view focuses on the activity of the classroom. Understanding is defined in terms of the ways in which students contribute to and share in the collective activity of the here and now. We argue that the key to shaping classroom activity that invites participation is to allow the subject to be problematic. We can be more specific.

The role of the teacher. The teacher bears the responsibility for developing a social community of students that problematizes mathematics and shares in searching for solutions. A critical feature of such communities is that the focus of examination and discussion be on the methods used to achieve solutions. Analyzing the adequacy of methods and searching for better ones are the activities around which teachers build the social and intellectual community of the classroom. In our example, Ms. Hudson can be seen guiding the discussion so the focus was placed on eliciting methods and analyzing their features. [. . .]

We touch on two specifics of the teacher's role: providing information and setting tasks. Dewey (1910) recognized the importance of the first issue: 'No educational question is of greater importance than how to get the most logical good out of learning through transmission from others' (p. 198). Clearly students can benefit from having access to relevant information; they would make very slow progress if they were asked to rediscover all of the information available to the teacher. On the other hand, too much information imposed with a heavy hand undermines students' inquiries. Our position is that the teacher is free, and obligated, to share relevant information with students as long as it does not prevent students from problematizing the subject.

In Dewey's time, as in ours, teachers more often erred on the side of providing too much information with too prescriptive a tone. Recall Dewey's concern with a single rigidly prescribed method. However, in an instance of history repeating itself, Dewey (1933) noted later that some teachers who were applying his ideas had the mistaken impression that they were supposed to withhold information and ideas from students and simply let them explore. There are some today who advocate such an approach. We agree with Dewey's (1933) observation: 'Provided the student is genuinely engaged upon a topic, and provided the teacher is willing to give the student a good deal of leeway as to what he assimilates and retains (not requiring rigidly that everything be grasped or reproduced), there is comparatively little danger that one who is himself enthusiastic will communicate too much concerning a topic' (p. 270).

The teacher will need to take an active role in selecting and presenting tasks. Tasks do not just appear, and it is unlikely that students spontaneously will create tasks that sustain reflective inquiry in mathematics. To select appropriate tasks, the teacher must draw on two resources: knowledge of the subject to select tasks that encourage students to wrestle with key ideas and knowledge of students' thinking to select tasks that link with students' experience and for which students can see the relevance of the ideas and skills they already possess.

It is at this point that we part company with Dewey. Although Dewey (1926) identified the same two sources of knowledge that are essential for selecting tasks and although he did not explicitly preclude the range of tasks that we endorse, he usually pointed to tasks that were drawn from students' outside-of-school experiences (Cremin, 1964; Dewey, 1915). Dewey (1933) later criticized the practice in some 'progressive' classrooms of simply importing out-of-school activities and assuming that learning would occur incidentally (see Prawat, 1995), but he continued to underscore the benefits of relatively large-scale real-life problems.

We propose that reflective inquiry and problematizing depends more on the student and the culture of the classroom than on the task. Although the content of tasks is important, the culture of the classroom will determine how tasks are treated by students. Tasks such as 62 minus 37 can trigger reflective inquiry because of the shared expectations of the teacher and students although they may look routine and are contained entirely within the domain of mathematics. Given a different culture, even large-scale real-life situations can be drained of their problematic possibilities. Tasks are inherently neither problematic nor routine. Whether they become problematic depends on how teachers and students treat them. This means that tasks of much greater variety than described by Dewey can be used by teachers to help students problematize mathematics. This is a central point of our proposal, and we will take it up again later.

The role of the students. Students share the responsibility for developing a community of learners in which they participate. We highlight two aspects of the students' role in reflective inquiry classrooms. First, students must take responsibility for sharing the results of their inquiries and for explaining and justifying their methods. This creates the openness that is essential for examining and improving the methods and for becoming full participants in the community. 'One of the most important factors in preventing an aimless and discursive recitation consists in making it necessary for every student to follow up and justify the suggestions he offers . . . . Unless the pupil is made responsible for developing on his own account the *reasonableness* of the guess he puts forth, the recitation counts for practically nothing' (Dewey, 1933, p. 271, emphasis in original).

A second responsibility for students is to recognize that learning means learning from others, taking advantage of others' ideas and the results of their investigations. This requires students to listen. We have in mind more than listening out of politeness or respect, but also listening because of a genuine interest in what the speaker has to say (Paley, 1986). In this sense, listening serves both a social and intellectual function. To become full participants in a community of peers doing mathematics, students must become good listeners.

Structural Understanding

From a structural view, understanding means representing and organizing knowledge internally in ways that highlight relationships between pieces of information (Hiebert and Carpenter, 1992). Whereas the functional view focuses on the activity of the classroom, the structural view focuses on what the students take with them from the classroom.

To deal with what knowledge is retained after classroom lessons end, we build on (1) Dewey's (1929) idea that knowledge is the fruit of activity that resolves problematic situations, (2) Brownell's (1946) observation that understanding is better viewed as a by-product of activity than as a direct target of instruction, and (3) Davis' (1992) more recent formulation of this idea as the residue that gets left behind when students solve problems. Residue provides a way of talking about the understandings that remain after an activity is over. We noted earlier that the nature of the residue will depend, in part, on the prior knowledge with which the student enters the activity. It will also depend on the nature of the problem that is being solved. We highlight three kinds of residues.

Insights into structure. Insights into the structure of the subject matter are left behind when problems involve analyzing patterns and relationships within the subject. In Ms. Hudson's class, the second graders analyzed the ways in which procedures worked and how procedures were the same and different. To do this they needed to use what they knew about the base-10 number system and relate it to using their 10 sticks, counting by 10s and 1s, regrouping 10 1s as 1 10, and so on. This kind of reflective activity is likely to yield new relationships, new insights into how the number system works. In fact, the evidence suggests that young students who are presented with just these kinds of problems and engage in just these kinds of discussions do develop deeper structural understandings of the number system than their peers who move through a more traditional skills-based curriculum (Cobb *et al.*, 1991; Hiebert and Wearne, 1996).

Strategies for solving problems. Two kinds of strategies are produced by working through problematic situations. One is the particular procedures that can be used for solving particular problems. The second is the general approaches or ways of thought that are needed to construct the procedures.

When second graders solve whole-number addition or subtraction problems, when sixth graders solve fraction multiplication problems, or when ninth graders solve algebra equations, they acquire specific procedures and techniques for solving specific problems. The procedures that get left behind depend on the kinds of problems that are solved. These procedures make up the kinds of skills that ordinarily are taught in school mathematics. The evidence suggests that students who are allowed to problematize arithmetic procedures perform just as well on routine tasks as their more traditionally taught peers (Carpenter *et al.*, 1989; Fennema *et al.*, 1996; Cobb *et al.*, 1991; Hiebert and Wearne, 1992, 1996; Kamii and Joseph, 1989). In other words, specific procedures for specific tasks constitute one kind of residue.

A second, and perhaps more important, kind of strategic residue could be called meta-strategic. By working through problematic situations, students learn how to construct strategies and how to adjust strategies to solve new kinds of problems. What gets left behind are the conceptual underpinnings and methods for actually working out new procedures when they are needed. The best evidence for this residue is the fact that students who have been encouraged to treat situations problematically and develop their own strategies can adapt them later, or invent new ones, to solve new problems (Fennema *et al.*, 1993; Fuson and Briars, 1990; Hiebert and Wearne, 1996; Kamii and Joseph, 1989; Wearne and Hiebert, 1989).

It is worth noting that when students develop methods for constructing new procedures they are integrating their conceptual knowledge with their procedural skill. This is significant because one of the most common findings in research on students' mathematics learning is that they often show a separation between conceptual and procedural knowledge (Hiebert, 1986). Given traditional instruction, students possess understandings that they do not use to inform their procedures, and they memorize and execute procedures that they do not understand. When students experience curricula that treat mathematics as problematic, this separation is infrequent (Carpenter *et al.*, 1989; Fuson and Briars, 1990; Fuson *et al.*, 1996; Hiebert and Wearne, 1992, 1996; Kamii and Joseph, 1989; Murray *et al.*, 1992). This is not surprising. Students who treat the development of procedures as problematic must rely on their conceptual understandings to drive their procedural advances. The two necessarily are linked.

Dispositions toward mathematics. What students take away from any instructional activity is only partly accounted for by cognitive descriptions (Doyle, 1988; Schoenfeld, 1985). Students also form attitudes and beliefs about the subject which, in turn, influence their orientation toward future activities. These dispositions are constructed from the way in which the subject is treated by the curriculum and the teacher, the kinds of tasks students complete, and the everyday rituals of the classroom. We believe that problematizing mathematics provides an opportunity for students to 'recognize the inventiveness of their own practice' (Lave *et al.*, 1988, p. 69) and to see mathematics as an intellectual activity in which they can participate. There is evidence that students who engage in reflective inquiry, who are allowed to treat mathematics as problematic, develop these and other positive dispositions toward mathematics (Carpenter *et al.*, 1989; Cobb *et al.*, 1991).

[. . .]

Other Views of Problem Solving in the Curriculum

Because of its multiple connections to understanding, we believe the principle of treating mathematics as problematic is the most powerful and practical way to think about problem solving. It is different than many historic views on the role of problem solving in the curriculum. It is also different than many current views. By comparing it with several popular views, we can clarify further some of the principle's distinguishing features.

Problem Solving Makes Mathematics Useful

As noted earlier, the belief that mathematics should be useful, outside of school, has a long history. The current version of this approach emphasizes the presentation of real-world problems as a major part of the curriculum (Boud and Feletti, 1991a; Cognition and Technology Group at Vanderbilt, 1990; Streefland, 1991). The logic of this approach usually runs as follows. Mathematics is useful if it helps to solve professional or everyday tasks. Students will be more likely to see appropriate applications if they spend considerable time working in applied situations and, in fact, will acquire domain-specific knowledge while doing so. Problems, then, become valued to the extent that they embed mathematics in outside-of-school contexts.

Prawat (1991) expressed concern that the emphasis on solving problems can easily become too utilitarian. When useful mathematics becomes synonymous with learning strategies for solving problems, attention shifts to procedures and away from ideas. Practical skills become overvalued and important ideas are neglected.

Our critique is somewhat different than Prawat's (1991). We believe that real-life problems provide a legitimate context for problematizing mathematics. If students are engaged in solving as reflective activity, then the concern about an overemphasis on skills disappears. Our concern rests with the narrowness of this approach. Real-life or everyday problems are one context, but only one context, for reflective inquiry.

The value of a problem depends on two things: whether students problematize the situation and whether it offers the chance of leaving behind important residue. The first depends not so much on the task as on the culture of the classroom. This issue will be revisited in the next section. The second does depend on the task. Tasks with different content are likely to leave behind different residues. But the residues identified earlier depend as much on the mathematical ideas embedded in the task as on the way it is packaged. Of course, important mathematical residues can be left by grappling with real-life problems. We argue only that the mathematical content be considered seriously when selecting tasks and that the definition of usefulness be expanded to a variety of problem situations, including those contextualized entirely within mathematics. The students in Ms. Hudson's class were gaining useful insights into the number system and developing general methods for modifying and inventing procedures, and the task appeared to be rather routine – find the difference between 62 and 37. Useful tasks come in many different packages.

Problem Solving Engages Students

A common argument for problem solving is that good problems are motivational. Intriguing or relevant problems will pique the interests of students and engage them in mathematics. There is an overlap between the advocates of this view and the previous one because it is often proposed that the problems with which students will become most easily engaged are those which are taken from their everyday lives.

Our concern with this view is that it can easily lead to the belief that the source of interest and motivation is the task. We believe that the basis for engaging a task is not the task itself but the prior knowledge of the student and the conditions under which the task is completed (Hatano, 1988). Whether students perceive a task as a problematic situation and whether they become actively involved in searching for solutions depends on the knowledge they bring to the task, the opportunities that are provided for solving it, and the values and expectations that have been established in the classroom [. . .]. If presented at an appropriate time, tasks such as the difference between 62 and 37, tasks that some teachers might see as boring and routine, can be engaged by students as genuine problems. The students in Ms. Hudson's class were intensively engaged in the task, not because they had a burning interest in how much taller Jorge was, but because the class had established a culture in which the students knew they had the freedom and responsibility to develop their own methods of solution.

Earlier we noted that this view represents a departure from Dewey. In particular, it represents a departure from his belief that outside-of-school tasks have a higher interest value for students and are more likely to be treated problematically. [. . .]

We agree that genuine thinking is too often absent from classrooms, but we believe that the source of the problem is not so much the tasks themselves as the way in which students are expected and allowed to treat them. Too often students are shown a procedure and asked to apply it in a straightforward way. They have few opportunities to treat situations of any kind problematically. Outside-of-school problems can provide contexts for important mathematical work, but the packaging of the task is not the primary determinant for engagement.

Problem Solving Is What Mathematicians Do

Some advocate problem solving in school mathematics because such activity is like the practice of mathematicians (Collins *et al.*, 1989; Lave *et al.*, 1988; Schoenfeld, 1985, 1988). Learning is treated as enculturation into a community of practice. The goal is that 'children might learn, by becoming apprentice mathematicians, to do what master mathematicians and scientists do in their everyday practice' (Lave *et al.*, 1988, p. 62).

Our perspective has much in common with cognitive apprenticeship (Brown *et al.*, 1989; Collins *et al.*, 1989; Lave *et al.*, 1988), and many examples of instruction that are used to characterize cognitive apprenticeship represent good examples of the kind of instruction we envision as well. From both perspectives, learning is embedded in activity, students engage a variety of problem situations, and artificial distinctions between acquiring knowledge and applying it are eliminated.

The two perspectives seem to be complementary rather than competing. Differences in descriptions emerge from differences in focus and emphasis. The master or expert plays a more prominent role in cognitive apprenticeship. The teaching activities of the expert – such as modeling, coaching, scaffolding, and fading – are central features of the model. In contrast, our perspective highlights the inquiry processes of students as they problematize the subject and search for solutions.

The difference in emphasis may stem from the fact that problem solving is not a central feature of classical trade apprenticeship from which the model of cognitive apprenticeship is drawn. Novice apprentices often learn the trade by observing and imitating the expert master. This requires that the techniques needed for handling each part of the task be made visible and demonstrated clearly. The master's role includes modeling, scaffolding, and so on. Apprentices monitor their progress by checking their work against the master's. The goal is usually a visible, identifiable product.

Reflective inquiry emphasizes the process of resolving problems and searching for solutions rather than manufacturing a product. Tasks are seen as problems and quandaries to be resolved rather than as skills to be mastered. Methods of solution are as much dependent on inventiveness as imitation. Feedback on the appropriateness of methods and solutions comes from the logic of the subject rather than from the master/teacher.

Focusing on the inquiry processes of students also suggests that the metaphor of children as small mathematicians can be pushed too far. Children are different than mathematicians in their experiences, immediate ambitions, cognitive processing power, representational tools, and so on. If these differences are minimized or ignored, children can be thought of as small adults and education can become a matter of training children to think and behave like older adults. Dewey (1956) cautioned against such programs because they can easily overconstrain the activities in which children engage.

From our perspective, children need not be asked to think like mathematicians but rather to think like children about problems and ideas that are mathematically fertile. Finding the difference between 62 and 37 does not contain the complexities of the problems on which mathematicians work, and the procedures developed by the second graders are not even those they are likely to use as adults. The similarities between mathematicians and children lie in the fact that they are both working on situations that they can problematize with the goal of understanding the situations and developing solution methods that make sense for them.

Implications for Classroom Practice

The Locus for Change

Treating mathematics as problematic requires changing the entire system of instruction. It is not achieved by injecting interesting problems into a curriculum that retains a distinction between acquisition and application. It is not achieved by adding problem solving into the mix of ongoing classroom activities. Rather, it is achieved by viewing the goal of instruction and the subject from a very different perspective.

Because the conditions that determine whether students will treat the subject as problematic reside in the classroom, the locus for change resides here as well. The culture of classrooms will need to change, and this kind of change begins with teachers. Many teachers, having experienced more traditional classroom cultures and more conventional approaches to problem solving during their education, will need to change their conceptions of the subject in fundamental ways. Working out new orientations to a subject and changing classroom practice are not easy things to do. But Ms. Hudson and a growing number of teachers have shown that it is possible to move toward such practice (Heaton and Lampert, 1993; Fennema *et al.*, 1992; Fennema, *et al.*, 1996; Fraivillig *et al.*, 1996; Resnick *et al.*, 1992; Schifter and Fosnot, 1993).

The Collapse of Old Dichotomies

[. . .] First, as we mentioned earlier, the choice between telling students and letting them discover is redefined. Allowing students to treat tasks as genuine problems may involve various configurations of sharing information and discovery. Teachers do not need to do only one or the other. Of course, some invention is likely to be part of the kind of problematizing and reflective inquiry that leads to understanding. As Piaget (1971) remarked, 'The essential functions of intelligence consist in understanding and in inventing. . . . It increasingly appears, in fact, that these two functions are inseparable' (pp. 27–28). But, as Dewey (1933, 1956) noted, information and direction from the teacher still play an important role.

A second issue that can be seen in a new way is the distinction between 'real-life' problems and 'school' problems. The question of which are better turns out to be irrelevant. The important questions are (1) has the student made the problem his or her own, and (2) what kind of residue is likely to remain. These are the criteria that address, respectively, whether problems are appropriate and whether they are important. Because both school and real-life problems can fit these criteria, the question of which is better is not useful. Many configurations are possible.

A third common dichotomy is between cognition and affect. Should instruction focus on the development of intellectual competence or positive attitudes? The easy answer, of course, is both. But once these are separated, there is a tendency to consider what must be done to foster each. Activities are weighed in terms of their likely contribution to one or the other. In contrast, the inquiry process that attempts to resolve problems is necessarily driven by both affect and cognition. 'This conception of the mental [treating situations as problematic] brings to unity various modes of response; emotional, volitional, and intellectual' (Dewey, 1929, p. 225). Students do not separate them. There is no need for the teacher to choose between the two.

A final dichotomy concerns the control of the curriculum. Should the curriculum begin with the child and move from the bottom up [. . .], or should it begin with the structure of the discipline and move from the top down (Davydov, 1990)? At the local classroom level, should the problems be generated by the students or presented by the teacher? Once again the notions of reflective inquiry and mathematical residue provide the relevant criteria. Reflective inquiry can occur and important residue can be left whether the problems come from the child's everyday world or from the world of mathematics, whether they are generated by the child or presented by the teacher. It is not necessary to choose one or the other.

Treating mathematics as problematic is a principle that provides a different vantage point from which to look. It resolves some old problems, creates some new challenges, and helps us see things in a different way. Having a different place to stand is a wonderful thing.

References

Boud, D., and Feletti, G. (Eds.). (1991a). *The challenge of problem-based learning.* New York: St. Martin's Press.

Boud, D., and Feletti, G. (1991b). Introduction. In D. Boud and G. Feletti (Eds.), *The challenge of problem-based learning* (pp. 13–22). New York: St. Martin's Press.

Brown, J. S., Collins, A., and Duguid, P. (1989). Situated cognition and the culture of learning. *Educational Researcher, 18*(1), 32–42.

Brownell, W. A. (1935). Psychological considerations in the learning and teaching of arithmetic. In W. D. Reeve (Ed.), *The teaching of arithmetic. Tenth yearbook of the National Council of Teachers of Mathematics* (pp. 1–31). New York: Teachers College, Columbia University.

Brownell, W. A. (1946). Introduction: Purpose and scope of the yearbook. In N. B. Henry (Ed.), *Forty-fifth yearbook of the National Society for the Study of Education: Part I. The measurement of understanding* (pp. 1–6). Chicago: University of Chicago.

Burkhardt, H. (1981). *The real world and mathematics.* London: Blackie.

Carpenter, T. P., Fennema, E., Peterson, P. L., Chiang, C.-P, and Loef, M. (1989). Using knowledge of children's mathematical thinking in classroom teaching: An experimental study. *American Educational Research Journal, 26*, 499–531.

Cobb, P., Wood, T, Yackel, E., Nicholls, J., Wheatley, G., Trigatti, B., and Perlwitz, M. (1991). Assessment of a problem-centered second-grade mathematics project. *Journal for Research in Mathematics Education, 22*, 3–29.

Cognition and Technology Group at Vanderbilt. (1990). Anchored instruction and its relationship to situated cognition. *Educational Researcher, 19*(6), 2–10.

Collins, A., Brown, J. S., and Newman, S. E. (1989). Cognitive apprenticeship: Teaching the crafts of reading, writing, and mathematics. In L. B. Resnick (Ed.), *Knowing, learning, and instruction* (pp. 453–494). Hillsdale, NJ: Erlbaum.

Cremin, L. A. (1964). *The transformation of the school: Progressivism in American education, 1876–1957.* New York: Vintage Books.

Davis, R. B. (1992). Understanding 'understanding'. *Journal of Mathematical Behavior, 11*, 225–241.

Davydov, V. V. (1990). *Types of generalization in instruction.* Reston, VA: National Council of Teachers of Mathematics.

Derry, S. J. (1992). Beyond symbolic processing: Expanding horizons for educational psychology. *Journal of Educational Psychology, 84*, 413–418.

Dewey, J. (1910). *How we think.* Boston: Heath.

Dewey, J. (1915). *Schools of tomorrow.* New York: E. P. Dutton.

Dewey, J. (1926). *Democracy and education.* New York: Macmillan.

Dewey, J. (1929). *The quest for certainty.* New York: Minton, Balch and Co.

Dewey, J. (1933). *How we think: A restatement of the relation of reflective thinking to the educative process.* Boston: Heath.

Dewey, J. (1938). *Logic: The theory of inquiry.* New York: Holt.

Dewey, J. (1956). *The child and the curriculum; The school and society.* Chicago: University of Chicago Press. (Original works published 1902 and 1915, respectively)

Doyle, W. (1988). Work in mathematics classes: The context of students' thinking during instruction. *Educational Psychologist, 23*, 167–180.

Fennema, E., Franke, M. L., Carpenter, T. P., and Carey, D. A. (1992). Learning to use children's mathematical thinking: A case study. In R. Davis and C. Maher (Eds.), *Schools, mathematics, and the world of reality* (pp. 93–112). Needham Heights, MA: Allyn and Bacon.

Fennema, E., Franke, M. L., Carpenter, T. P., and Carey, D. A. (1993). Using children's mathematical knowledge in instruction. *American Educational Research Journal, 30*, 553–583.

Fennema, E., Carpenter, T. P., Franke, M. L., Levi, L., Jacobs, V. R., and Empson, S. B. (1996). A longitudinal study of learning to use children's thinking in mathematics instruction. *Journal for Research in Mathematics Education*, Vol. 27, no. 4, pp. 403–34.

Fraivillig, J., Murphy, L., and Fuson, K. C. (1996). *Advancing children's mathematical thinking in everyday mathematics reform classrooms.* Manuscript submitted for publication.

Fuson, K. C., and Briars, D. J. (1990). Using a base-ten blocks learning/teaching approach for first- and second-grade place-value and multidigit addition and subtraction. *Journal for Research in Mathematics Education, 21,* 180–206.

Fuson, K. C., Smith, S. T., and Lo Cicero, A. (1996). *Supporting Latino first graders' ten-structured thinking in urban classrooms.* Manuscript submitted for publication.

Hatano, G. (1988). Social and motivational bases for mathematical understanding. In G. B. Saxe and M. Gearhart (Eds.), *Children's mathematics* (pp. 55–70). San Francisco, CA: Jossey-Bass.

Heaton, R. M., and Lampert, M. (1993). Learning to hear voices: Inventing a new pedagogy of teacher education. In D. K. Cohen, M. W. McLaughlin, and J. E. Talbert (Eds.), *Teaching for understanding: Challenges for policy and practice* (pp. 43–83). San Francisco, CA: Jossey-Bass.

Hiebert, J. (Ed.). (1986). *Conceptual and procedural knowledge: The case of mathematics.* Hillsdale, NJ: Erlbaum.

Hiebert, J., and Carpenter, T. P. (1992). Learning and teaching with understanding. In D. A. Grouws (Ed.), *Handbook of research on mathematics teaching and learning* (pp. 65–97). New York: Macmillan.

Hiebert, J., and Wearne, D. (1992). Links between teaching and learning place value with understanding in first grade. *Journal for Research in Mathematics Education, 23,* 98–122.

Hiebert, J., and Wearne, D. (1993). Instructional tasks, classroom discourse, and students' learning in second-grade arithmetic. *American Educational Research Journal, 30,* 393–425.

Hiebert, J., and Wearne, D. (1996). Instruction, understanding and skill in multidigit addition and subtraction. *Cognition and Instruction*, Vol. 14, no. 3, pp. 251–83.

Kamii, C., and Joseph, L. L. (1989). *Young children continue to reinvent arithmetic.* New York: Teachers College.

Lave, J. (1988). *Cognition in practice.* Cambridge, England: Cambridge University Press.

Lave, J., Smith, S., and Butler, M. (1988). Problem solving as an everyday practice. In R. I. Charles and E. A. Silver (Eds.), *The teaching and assessing of mathematical problem solving* (pp. 61–81). Reston, VA: National Council of Teachers of Mathematics.

Lave, J., and Wenger, E. (1991). *Situated learning: Legitimate peripheral participation.* Cambridge, England: Cambridge University Press.

Lesh, R., and Lamon, S. J. (Eds.). (1992). *Assessment of authentic performance in school mathematics.* Washington, DC: American Association for the Advancement of Science.

Murray, H., Olivier, A., and Human, P. (1992). The development of young students' division strategies. In W. Geeslin and K. Graham (Eds.), *Proceedings of the sixteenth PME Conference Vol. 2* (pp. 152–159). Durham, NH: University of New Hampshire.

National Council of Teachers of Mathematics. (1989). *Curriculum and evaluation standards for school mathematics.* Reston, VA: National Council of Teachers of Mathematics.

National Council of Teachers of Mathematics. (1991). *Professional standards for teaching mathematics.* Reston, VA: National Council of Teachers of Mathematics.

Paley, V. G. (1986). On listening to what the children say. *Harvard Educational Review, 56,* 122–131.

Piaget, J. (1971). *Science of education and the psychology of the child.* New York: Viking.

Prawat, R. S. (1991). The value of ideas: The immersion approach to the development of thinking. *Educational Researcher, 20*(2), 3–10.

Prawat, R. S. (1995). Misreading Dewey: Reform, projects, and the language game. *Educational Researcher, 24*(7), 13–22.

Reeve, W. D. (Ed.). (1936). *The place of mathematics in modern education. Eleventh yearbook of the National Council of Teachers of Mathematics.* New York: Teachers College.

Resnick, L. B., Bill, V., and Lesgold, S. (1992). Developing thinking abilities in arithmetic class. In A. Demetriou, M. Shayer, and A. Efklides (Eds.), *Neo-Piagetian theories of cognitive development: Implications and applications for education* (pp. 210–230). London: Routledge.

Romberg, T. A. (Ed.). (1992). *Mathematics assessment and evaluation: Imperatives for mathematics educators.* Albany, NY: State University of New York.

Schifter, D., and Fosnot, C. T. (1993). *Reconstructing mathematics education.* New York: Teachers College Press.

Schoenfeld, A. H. (1985). *Mathematical problem solving.* Orlando, FL: Academic Press.

Schoenfeld, A. H. (1988). Problem solving in context(s). In R. I. Charles and E. A. Silver (Eds.), *The teaching and assessing of mathematical problem solving* (pp. 82–92). Reston, VA: National Council of Teachers of Mathematics.

Shulman, J. H. (Ed.). (1992). *Case methods in teacher education.* New York: Teachers College.

Stanic, G. M. A., and Kilpatrick, J. (1988). Historical perspectives on problem solving in the mathematics curriculum. In R. I. Charles and E. A. Silver (Eds.), *The teaching and assessing of mathematical problem solving* (pp. 1–22). Reston, VA: National Council of Teachers of Mathematics.

Stodolsky, S. S. (1988). *The subject matters: Classroom activity in math and social studies.* Chicago: University of Chicago Press.

Streefland, L. (Ed.). (1991). *Realistic mathematics education in the primary school.* Utrecht, The Netherlands: Utrecht University Center for Science and Mathematics Education.

Wearne, D., and Hiebert, J. (1989). Cognitive changes during conceptually based instruction on decimal fractions. *Journal of Educational Psychology, 81,* 507–513.

11

Assessment Issues in a Performance-based Subject: a Case Study of Physical Education

Doune Macdonald and Ross Brooker

The educative worth of performance-oriented subjects in schools, such as art, music, drama, or physical education, has often been viewed with some suspicion. Questions surround the educative potential of their content and their worth in relation to other serious subjects such as mathematics. Based on the premise of a mind/body dichotomy, they have historically been afforded low status due to their seemingly practical nature in educational contexts which favour overtly intellectual activity (Kirk and Tinning, 1990). Criticism has also been made of the assessment procedures associated with the subjective awarding of grades for activities such as games-playing or dance performance which has further undermined their educational worth in the eyes of curriculum decision makers. Consequently, the issue of assessment has become central in any ongoing questioning about the contribution of these subjects to worthwhile school knowledge. More specifically, in a context of increased accountability how can relevant, comparable and equitable assessments of student work within and across schools be carried out in subjects which value a broad range of 'practical' performances alongside 'theoretical' knowledge?

The Assessment Context

While assessment of student performance has always been an item on the school education agenda, in recent times it has come into much sharper focus due to an increased emphasis on schools becoming more accountable for the outcomes of the education which they offer. This is occurring in a context where western governments have linked their economic futures so closely to the success of their educational enterprise that accountability has pervaded policy and practice at all levels of education. As Masters (1994) suggests 'measures of student performance are central to any consideration of effectiveness or efficiency of educational provision' (p. 2). In the Australian context, this contention has been exemplified by the prolifera-

171

tion of several sets of standards designed to measure and report student performance (e.g., national profiles). Such 'benchmarks' have been formulated with a view to promoting comparable student outcomes from schooling that contribute to a national effort for social and economic reform (Dawkins, 1988, p. 5). These developments are inextricably linked to assessment procedures and practices at the level of classrooms, schools and school systems. Even though an overemphasis on accountability may be perceived as having negative consequences for the curriculum and assessment process, it has served to remind performance-based subjects such as Physical Education that if they are to be regarded as serious (and share the attendant privileges of such a positioning) then they too must address assessment issues.

A further aspect of the context for the assessment agenda in Australian education has been the development of a social justice strategy (*Towards a Fairer Australia*, 1990) which emphasized, amongst other things, equal access to educational opportunities. This is especially significant in an economic rationalist climate where the outcomes of education are strongly linked to students' life chances. In the present social climate of limited employment opportunities for school leavers and with the demand for tertiary places running at several times the supply, competition is intense. Parents naturally feel extremely sensitive to the comparability issue and want their students to compete on an equal footing with other students from the same school and with students from other schools (Sadler, 1993. p. 4).

Embedded in these contexts is the need for assessment programmes and practices to be underpinned by fairness and equity principles, and for teacher judgements about student performance to be comparable within and across schools. A third criterion concerns the need for assessment to be a legitimate extension of the appropriate teaching and learning process for the particular subject area and consistent with the nature of knowledge for that subject. It is not the individual application of these criteria that determines trustworthy outcomes from assessment, but it is the simultaneous promotion of such criteria which becomes particularly complex in a performance-based subject which values the integration of theoretical and practical knowledge.

School-based Assessment in the Queensland Secondary Context

The responsibility for assessment in Queensland (an Australian State) senior secondary schooling is shared between the school and a central, quasi-autonomous authority – the Board of Senior Secondary School Studies (BSSSS). Curriculum and assessment policy is determined by the BSSSS but schools are responsible for adapting the subject curriculum to meet the local context and for designing and implementing an appropriate assessment programme for that curriculum which must then be accredited by the

BSSSS. This practice is referred to as school-based assessment. One of the consequences of this shared approach is that the quality of assessment across schools is variable as the BSSSS assessment policies and procedures are 'adopted unevenly' (Maxwell, 1995, p. 90). Accountability is addressed through established (by the BSSSS) moderation procedures that are designed to ensure comparability of standards of assessment in subjects across schools. Maxwell (1995) has identified the key elements that provide the form and shape of school-based assessment in the Queensland secondary context which clearly reflect tenets of authentic assessment as previously discussed. These key elements are identified below.

1. Broad framework subject syllabuses provide a common structure from which schools design their own programme of teaching and learning according to local circumstances, resources, student interests and learning styles, teacher interests and learning styles and school assessment policies (e.g., style and frequency of assessment). The syllabus is the main reference point for the moderation of standards within a subject.
2. Continuous, or progressive, assessment that is distributed throughout a programme of study for a subject rather than being administered at or near the end. This process encourages the use of a variety of assessment tasks and allows evidence of student achievement to be gathered progressively during the two years of study.
3. As part of the syllabus framework, criteria and performance standards appropriate to the subject are identified. *Criteria* are the characteristics or dimensions to be considered and *standards* are statements of the levels of quality to be achieved. Assessments of student work are made by teachers gathering evidence of performance in relation to the criteria and making judgements against the specified standards. Maxwell (1995) points out that a 'defensible judgment is one that is "reasonable" rather than one that is "correct" '(p. 94).
4. Assessment tasks, written performances, evidence of other performances and assessment results are all gathered into a portfolio of assessment materials which can be used for 'clarification and verification of the profile and assistance in determining the final level of achievement' (Maxwell, 1995, p. 95). At the end of a course of study, a student's final result for a subject is recorded in terms of one of five global Levels of Achievement (very high, high, sound, low, very low), which are labelled descriptively and defined by the syllabus standards. These are ratified by teachers through the presentation and defence of student work samples in cluster group meetings.

In the broader context of accountability, this chapter examines assessment issues which are particularly problematic in a performance-based subject in a school based assessment context, namely senior secondary physical education. We firstly address significant problems in assessment as they relate to physical education, drawing on general and physical education literature. We then analyse issues of authentic assessment, comparability of judgments and equity arising from the implementation of a trial senior physical education syllabus. Such a trial is particularly instructive for uncovering the inherent dilemmas surrounding the assessment process as it is a regulated process designed to promote discussion. We conclude that while the syllabus encouraged many of the tenets of authentic assessment, the achievement of comparable judgements and equity in assessment remain problematic issues.

Assessment in Education and Physical Education

The collection of systematic, rigorous and valid assessment information has frequently not been a priority in physical education, thereby limiting evidence of worthwhile outcomes, student effort and achievement, and, in turn, subject status (Lund, 1992; Matanin and Tannehill, 1994; O'Sulllivan 1994; Pieron, 1994; Veal, 1992). Veal (1992) spoke of 'real' and 'pretend' physical education where real physical education, albeit limited in practice in the United States (USA), focuses on student learning, active student involvement and accountability for these elements. In supporting Veal's notion of real physical education, Vickers (1992) argued for an increased emphasis on academic content knowledge linked to physical activity, in order to make physical education more academically defensible. While innovations in New Zealand and Australia which position physical education as a legitimate senior subject have been recognized (O'Sullivan, Siedentop, and Tannehill, 1994), there still remains widespread concern with respect to comparability and equity in the subject which frequently involves a diverse group of students (physically, socially, and intellectually), in differing contexts, addressing a range of content, across theory and practice. Under these circumstances, significant issues in the assessment of a performance-based subject such as authentic assessment practices, comparable judgements of student performance, and the equitable construction and application of assessment criteria and standards become problematic and therefore require scrutiny

Authentic Assessment

Moves in Britain, USA, and Australia to formalize the recording of physical education outcomes are underway with outcomes-based education underpinning the nationalization and rationalization of primary and lower secondary schooling. While it is recognized that rigorous assessment does not ensure the success of all physical education. Lund (1992) claims that the viability of physical education would dramatically improve if teachers reported students' achievement in preset instructional curriculum criteria and goals through formative and summative mechanisms. In an empirical study in the USA, Matanin and Tannehill (1994) studied physical education programmes which revealed that grades were awarded primarily for active participation, then knowledge, and finally skills. As a result, they questioned the extent to which the students were being physically *educated*.

Veal (1992) advocated authentic assessment as a way of ascertaining competence and mastery in real physical *education*. She considered authentic assessment as regular and ongoing, with connections between daily instructional tasks and assessment, focusing upon observable skills, and with a connection of skills to real-life situations (such as game situations rather than isolated skills) as learning indicators. Wiggins recommended that properly designed authentic forms of assessment should share four fundamental characteristics:

> First, they are designed to be truly representative of performance in the field . . . Second, far greater attention is paid to the teaching and learning of criteria to be used in assessment. Third, self-assessment plays a much greater role than in conventional testing. And, fourth, the students are often expected to present their work . . . to ensure that their apparent mastery is genuine (1989, p. 45)

Eisner's (1993) proposed eight criteria for creating and appraising new assessment practices in education embrace Wiggins's recommendations and further suggest that assessment tasks should:

1. Reveal how students go about solving a problem, not only the solutions they formulate (p. 226).
2. Reflect the values of the intellectual community from which the tasks are derived (p. 227).
3. Have curricular relevance, but not be limited to the curriculum as taught (p. 230).
4. Require students to display a sensitivity to configurations or wholes, not simply to discrete elements (p. 230).

It has also been pointed out that assessment should move beyond isolated snapshots of students' performances (Graue, 1993) and that the criteria for assessment be made explicit for the students in the interests of student learning equity (Gipps, 1995; Hewitson, 1988).

Yet, attempts to implement authentic assessment in physical education have generated some educational and procedural concerns. Perhaps the most pervasive concern centres on the need for teachers to shift their focus to the 'process of learning rather than focus on specific skill development' (Connell, 1989, p. 241). It follows that teachers will need to revisit their programmes and teaching approaches to position assessment as integral to the teaching-learning process and not something which is 'done' summatively at a particular time in the term as a 'bolt-on' extra (McConachie Smith, 1991, p. 13) if at all. In making this conceptual shift, teachers must also reconsider the nature of their assessment tasks and change, or at least supplement, objective tests (such as the timing of speed in athletic or swimming events) which are narrow when compared to authentic assessment guidelines, poor measures of student learning (Carroll, 1991; Matanin and Tannehill, 1994; Veal, 1992) and unjustly discriminatory.

As it is widely argued that physical activity is central to physical education (Arnold, 1988; Kirk, 1988), it follows that authentic assessment tasks should focus on physical activity. Given that there is also a body of discipline knowledge informing the study of physical activity, there have emerged issues relating to the approach to testing of what has been labelled 'theory' and 'practice'. Should they be tested separately and, if so, how and in what balance? McConachie Smith argued:

> If the focus of physical education is to remain centred on engagement in physical activity then one is selecting that knowledge and understanding which assists in the improvement of performance or contributes towards the establishment of values and the ability to make informed judgement about physical activity participation. (1991, p. 12)

On this basis, authentic assessment would attempt to integrate the learning and assessment of the practical *and* theoretical skills, knowledge and understandings (McConachie Smith, 1991; Macdonald and Brooker, in press) even though the assessment of theory is generally regarded as being the most legitimate indicator of student achievement.

Comparability of Teachers' Judgements

Recommendations for authentic assessment in physical education include the comparable judgement of students' performances against prespecified criteria for success which are shared with the students. Comparability in this context refers to whether 'the performances of all students who are awarded a particular grade in a subject area are within the range of performances associated with a designated level of achievement, of equivalent quality regardless of the school attended' (Sadler, 1993, p. 8). Criterion-referenced assessment, a process of making judgements and grading of each student's work or performance on one or more assessment criteria (Hewitson, 1988), lends itself to an authentic assessment process (Gipps, 1995). However, under school-based criterion-referenced assessment a range of threshold performance standards is specified to differentiate levels of student performances, and these must be shared across tasks, teachers and schools (Hewitson, 1988).

Implicit in questions of how defensible and comparable school-based assessments of student work can be carried out in a subject which values both theoretical and practical performance are a number of issues with respect to how judgements may be made. First is the question of whether the same criteria and standards can lend themselves to the range of learning experiences, activities, and assessment tasks which might be included in physical education. For example, can a criterion associated with student *evaluation* be equally applicable to a sociology of sport essay, to a strategic decision in games play, and to the aesthetic appreciation of a dance? Literature within physical education (e.g. Arnold, 1988; McConachie Smith, 1991) and motor learning/psychology (Abernethy *et al.*, 1994) would suggest that this is feasible and defensible on the grounds of students' parallel learning processes across cognitive and psychomotor dimensions. Second, assessment tasks that create opportunities for students to meet the stated criteria must be formulated. For this to occur teachers need a sound grasp of what the criteria mean, the students' learning processes, and purpose of the unit's content (Walters, 1991). Third, the teacher must be confident in judging the student's performance against the criteria and standards. One report on assessment practices in a Health and Physical Education Programme for senior school students suggested that, in matching students' performances to the criteria, teachers were overly generous in relation to physical skill performance causing concern about the parity of standards across the components of the subject (Allen, 1991).

Once common school-based criteria and standards for assessment have been established, authentic assessment tasks to address the criteria have been created, and students' performances have been matched to those criteria, it is then necessary to develop shared understandings of the criteria and tasks across the various sites where assessment takes place. Apart from teacher meetings where written work samples may be compared, the need has been expressed for more support for the standardization of assessment particularly in the practical domain through the production of illustrated workbooks and video tapes (Francis and Merrick, 1994; Fryer, 1986; Macdonald and Brooker, in press). Concern, however, has been expressed by teachers over the time demands of such standardization procedures (Fryer, 1986) and the effect on the individuality of school programmes can be questioned.

Equity and Assessment

In most Western contexts the outcomes of schooling are linked to a student's life chances and, therefore, the issue of equity in relation to assessment is of critical concern. In articulating the nexus between the two, Gipps and Murphy point out that:

> Assessment is intimately linked with the whole area of equality and equity, since our measure of achievement depends almost uniquely on some form of assessment; formal assessment is the 'objective' quantitative indicator used in virtually all studies of equality of educational opportunity. Assessment is therefore as important to the equity debate as equity issues are to assessment. (1994, pp. 15–16)

If students are to compete on an equal footing then assessment practices must be enacted with the concept of equity in mind. Three important issues arise in this regard: (1) the nature of the knowledge to be assessed and equated with achievement (e.g., giving students the opportunity to demonstrate what they know); (2) the appropriateness of the approach to assessment to allow for student difference (e.g., language used; administration of the test; the context in which a test takes place), and (3) the influence of cultural knowledge on the construct being assessed (Gipps, 1994; Gipps and Murphy, 1994; and after Apple, 1989). To pursue an equitable approach requires that the 'contexts and approaches of one group do not dominate' (Gipps, 1995, p. 275).

The consideration of these issues becomes especially important in a subject such as Physical Education where a greater range of student characteristics affecting assessment (by comparison with other subjects without a physical performance component) already exist. In addition to academic ability and sex differences, there are such factors as body shape, size, ethnicity, and environmental conditions outside the classroom that have implications for equitable assessment.

Stroot (1994), in her critique of physical education curricula, claims that there has been considerable concern about the domination of subject matter (and assessment) in line with masculine values such as physical strength and size, aggression, competitiveness and motor elitism. This reinforced earlier work of Dewar (1990) who argued that physical education generally privileged 'the young, the able-bodied, the lean and muscular, the middle classes, heterosexual men and white Christians' (p. 76). Clearly the differing opportunities for learning, such as may occur on the basis of this hegemony, can result in 'real differences in performance among groups' (Gipps, 1995, p. 274).

One way of ensuring greater equity in terms of the curriculum and assessment may be to involve students in the curriculum process. Spackman (1995) suggests that teachers be reminded to involve students 'in planning, performing and evaluating activity' (p. 33). It has also been suggested that equity in assessment is undermined in circumstances where 'what is valued by the test developer' is not made clear to students. Consequently it is essential for students to be given an 'explicit account of the constructs being assessed and of the criteria for assessment' (Gipps, 1995, p. 274).

Another important issue with respect to assessment and equity concerns the need for students to have sufficient assessment opportunities to perform well. The National Forum on Assessment (NFA)(1992) has pointed out that to ensure fairness students should not only have 'multiple opportunities to meet standards' (which then may raise a question about authenticity) but also be given 'information about the opportunities to meet those standards' (p. 32). This also raises questions of the nature of standards that are appropriate to assess a performance-based subject such as physical education. While Matanin and Tannehill (1994) argue that objective standards of assessment are necessary to 'enhance a student's physical well-being, motor skills, and knowledge base about physical activity' (p. 427), others would suggest that they take little account of individual differences, such as stature, and therefore are not indicative of the physical *education* process (Stroot, 1994) which in turn, links with concerns for assessment to be authentic.

Case Study of a Senior Physical Education Syllabus

The BSSSS physical education syllabus is in its formative stages within a five year trial/pilot process in a limited number of schools throughout the state. Its forerunner syllabus in health and physical education has been an extremely popular tertiary-entrance subject (fifth largest student enrolment) as is proving to be the case with the General Certificate of Secondary Education (GCSE) offerings (Carroll, 1986; Francis and Merrick, 1994). Dissatisfaction with the subject grew, however, on many fronts, including the overemphasis on written (theory) work which was most easily produced and compared in a school-based assessment process.

The data for this case was gathered by the authors as BSSSS appointed evaluators of the trial process. The 11 trial schools were those which expressed an interest to the BSSSS to join the trial process. Over the two trial years, the trial involved 27 teachers (79 per cent males) and 822 students (61 per cent males) in years 11 and 12. Qualitative data were gathered through: audiotaped interviews with key stakeholders; field notes recorded during the two to four visits to each trial school over the two year period; and at teacher meetings where the trial was discussed. All 27 trial teachers were interviewed twice for at least one hour. Ten to fifteen students per school, representing a balance of sexes and achievement levels, were also interviewed in each year of the trial. The syllabus document was also examined in terms of its: internal consistency and interpretability; relevance and meaning to teachers and students; suitability of its breadth, depth and subject matter; appropriateness of assessment requirements and standards; and the efficacy of its theoretical frameworks.

Data analysis proceeded in accordance with the questions included in the brief to evaluators as well as following a grounded approach that elicited the concerns of the stakeholders in the investigation (Cohen and Manion, 1989; Glaser and Strauss, 1967). Interview data were transcribed for analysis to determine emerging themes and issues. This was contextualized, clarified, and supplemented through reference to field notes. Given that there were several sources of qualitative data, and that each school presented its own set of data, there was opportunity to triangulate findings as a means of establishing trustworthiness. Using case data from the trial of the Queensland senior physical education syllabus, the following section explores how the syllabus trial has raised and addressed school-based assessment issues in a performance-based, tertiary-entrance subject.

Assessment in Senior Physical Education

The syllabus draws on Arnold's (1979) justification of physical education as the study of physical activity through learning *about* movement (rules, concepts, procedures), *through* movement (valued aesthetic, moral, social or health outcomes) and *in* movement (actual participation). Participation *in* movement is central to the syllabus. Learning experiences, assessment tasks, and the criteria and standards reflect this centrality. In doing so, there is an inter-relationship of conventional theory (learning *about*) and practice (learning *in*). Drawing on philosophical argument, Arnold (1988) claimed that cognitive processes or intelligent critical actions are indispensable to *knowing how* (learning *in*). Furthermore, Abernethy *et al.* (1994) from a motor learning perspective have argued that the learning processes in the *about* and *in* dimensions of learning are similar. On this basis, it is valid for the criteria for assessment (i.e., *gather* and *sort, recall, apply* and *evaluate*) of the *in* and *about* dimensions to be the same. It should be noted that the *through* dimension, primarily concerned with affective outcomes, is not, at this point, part of the assessment programme even though most students and teachers are involved in physical activity for affective reasons.

The *in* dimension focuses on four physical activities taken over the two years and is drawn by each school from categories of activities representing games (e.g., basketball), performance (e.g., athletics) and aesthetic (e.g., gymnastics) pursuits. These activities are integrated with studies *about* physical activity, which address: learning and performance of physical skills; development and significance of physical fitness: and physical activity as an institutionalized and formalized component of Australian society (BSSSS, 1992). In describing her programme, Sally stated that, 'There's nothing here that's forced . . . or unnatural' in the links between *in* and *about*. Reflecting on her unit which integrated psychology with athletics, she considered that:

> The unit on psychology . . . has been fairly influential for all their units. They started thinking more about what they are thinking about when they perform, and how that affects performance.

Authentic Assessment in Physical Education

Many of the assessment practices encouraged by the syllabus reflect the tenets of authentic assessment and they were generally well received by the trial teachers and most students. In particular, teachers and students felt that the quality of learning was enhanced by the assessment of both learning *in* and *about* being shaped by common criteria. Typical of the assessment tasks which reflect the 'real-life' (i.e., comes from conflating the assessment of theory and practice) quality of authentic assessment were: the creation and appraisal of a fitness programme related to the unit's physical activity; the keeping of a reflective journal which draws on scientific principles to analyse student's progress in the performance of a physical activity; or evaluating the participation patterns of different groups of students in a physical activity using sociological concepts. Also in line with authentic assessment was the student-centred structure of these tasks:

> Students will be writing their own reflective diary, plus they'll each have their own videotape and audiotape to encourage evaluation. I think kids . . . are going to be forced to articulate some of the things that occur naturally to them in the decisions that they make. (Graham)

Such an approach offers insights into the extent of student understanding that has occurred.

However, students' identified some concerns with respect to the tasks, such as their non-specificity size ('too big to finish in the time') and understanding of assessment processes. One student reflected:

> . . . on a test we had to do, we had to assess ourselves on our golf swing. I can't understand how a teacher can mark us for the way we assess ourselves!

This does not represent an attack on authenticity but rather a need for new assessment procedures and practices to be clearly explained to students. Teachers did, however, recognize the importance of promoting the students' understanding of the assessment programme. Simon explained that 'We're trying to talk criteria to them (the students) all the time . . . They're becoming familiar with them on their actual assessment task sheets.'

Many teachers found it difficult at first to devise assessment tasks which were authentic, particularly in terms of integrating *in* and *about*. Also, some teachers did not have sufficient grounding in literacy to be able to formulate the sophisticated tasks which were required.

> A lot of PE [physical education] teachers are doing it [teaching PE] because they like . . . the sport orientation to it. Now you've got to be at least like a junior English teacher to set up and sort of guide them [students] into writing these assignments. (Gary)

Teachers as well as students were under pressure to conform to the hegemony of accountability.

Another issue which emerged with respect to authenticity, and one that intersects with equity, was the use of objective testing in the programmes (Matanin and Tannehill, 1994). Some teachers believed that to measure speed, distance or strokes, was in line with the purpose of the activity (authentic).

> I will retain objective standards of performance in my athletics unit because if you're going to include performance sports, their basis is objective standards. This is the goal. If you want to make an Australian representative team, these are the times you have to run. So, it's the same here. I find them a source of motivation for the kids . . . but they know it's just one means of assessment. (Clive)

However, others were concerned with the equity implications of the tasks when, for example, students are set different standards for achievement based on 'norms' established for competitive sport, rather than for educative purposes.

> You get different levels of maturation; kids who are very well developed in year 12 and others who are just entering puberty . . . Why should a very small kid be disadvantaged by an objective measurement? (Gail)

In terms of authenticity, these issues attack the very core of physical education and how it should be assessed. What is the nature of physical education? Is it sport or competitive performance, or is it intelligent performance (as it is conceptualised in this syllabus) or is it something else?

Comparability in Judging Student Performance in Physical Education

The most important issue raised by the teachers with respect to the assessment of student performance concerned the setting and operationalizing of the standards against which judgements are made of individual performance and subsequent comparative judgements of performance. It was pointed out by teachers that the establishment of appropriate standards for each of the five levels of achievement was a critical task. In the context of a discussion about comparability of assessment, one teacher suggested that '(for assessment) to be valid in the eyes of the Board (of Senior Secondary School Studies) there is going to have to be a lot of work done . . . just articulating what the ideal performer at VHA (very high achievement) level does'. This raises the question of where the standards of performance should be drawn from and how they should articulate with the essence of the subject.

Establishing standards for the performance (*in*) aspect of the subject was particularly difficult and two approaches were suggested by teachers in the trial but as yet remain untested. One approach would be to establish the highest level of achievement standard (VHA) from performances by persons who undertake the activity at a club or representative level. This has the disadvantage of setting a standard out of the reach of most secondary school students. The other approach would be to establish the standards by surveying the performances of a large number of students in the school physical education context. A further concern with respect to establishing standards related to how successfully such standards could accommodate the number and diverse range of activities (e.g. rock climbing; volleyball; water polo; dance) that are available for schools for their physical education programme.

A second key issue in the establishment and application of standards, concerned the way in which teachers were to interpret fairly and accurately the criteria and standards (which is at the same time linked to equity), again particularly with respect to students' performance *in* physical activity. Their questions included, 'What is *gather* and *sort* evidence in performance?', 'How do we know a student is *evaluating* during a game?' Teachers expressed these dilemmas:

> I cannot see in the written criteria for exit how you can differentiate between gather and sort and recall in physical activity . . . I'm sure it's going on in a physical activity, but I'm wondering how a teacher can see that it is demonstrated. (Clive)

> I'm sort of grappling with that area actually. For example, you can see a person playing tennis. They can be serving, then they hit a deep shot, then they move to the net. If their opponent does a lob they know they have to get back, but if they don't get back, how can you assess this as them not having the process ability to evaluate the situation? (Alison)

While the practices of school-based assessment using pre-specified criteria and standards give focus and flexibility to the assessment programme, there were concerns with the lack of shared understanding of the syllabus' criteria and standards. Trevor suggested the importance of this shared understanding.

> At the end of the day the kids' outcomes across the state have to be comparable. And if there's not a shared understanding of what the syllabus means . . . then it's not good enough . . . I think that in a school it's essential that there be a very, very strongly shared understanding of what the syllabus means and what the work programme means.

A source of frustration for teachers surfaced during the teacher meetings which provided an opportunity for their interpretations to be clarified. It became apparent that those interpretations endorsed by the BSSSS personnel were not necessarily consistent with the syllabus document. Ron felt that 'it's a very serious problem . . . (with) things being expected that are not written in the document . . . We need some definite guidelines.'

The desirability of assessment being guided by prespecified criteria and standards of performance (Hewitson, 1988) was not questioned, but it was clear from the data presented above that the interpretation and application of the criteria and standards of performance was a significant issue for teachers. While the assessment framework was based on the assumption that the same criteria and standards could be adopted for the full range of learning experiences in the course (Arnold, 1988; McConachie Smith, 1991), the implementation of the framework was limited by a lack of clear understanding by teachers of the meaning of the criteria and standards of performance. This could be partially explained by the newness of the assessment framework, but it was also a function of the lack of clarity provided by the syllabus development process.

Throughout the syllabus trial, three approaches to gathering evidence to share judgements were explored. First, student performances were assessed by teachers against their (developing) conceptions of the criteria and standards. This was undertaken both as an individual exercise and also by teachers working collaboratively with a colleague on the one assessment task. Brett reported:

> Kim and I have seen each others' classes perform, so we've been trying to monitor comparability in that line. Also, at the end of every term, we get the two classes together to compete against each other . . . we draw parallels through the two classes.

While this was the preferred approach, in terms of gathering evidence for comparable assessments it was not without problems. It became obvious that multiple interpretations of the criteria and standards were possibly due to such factors as teacher experience, the level of teacher expertise, and teacher familiarity with the criteria and standards.

Second, in some schools, assessments were conducted by visiting experts who had specialised knowledge in the activity that was under consideration. They were typically people from sporting clubs or a teacher who coached in the area. This approach was limited by the fact that the expert was unfamiliar with the performance standards and that it separated assessment from the teaching and learning process. As one teacher put it, 'we did try this with dance . . . and there were great problems with them understanding our terminology and criteria . . . the reports that they were writing were invalid'. The major contribution of this approach was summed up by a teacher who pointed out that it 'validated the same judgments that we made'. Visitation by peers from other schools was seen as slightly more desirable because 'teachers know what they're looking for . . . they're (more likely to be) familiar with the standards and criteria'. One pragmatic shortcoming of this approach was raised by Sally in that schools 'have to find replacement teachers to cover their classes . . . who pays?' As is seemingly the case with most school education, the necessity for comparable judgements of performance is moderated by what can be afforded.

The third approach involved the use of video to record evidence of student performance. While it was perceived by teachers to have some merit there were also a number of problems which were technical, practical and conceptual in nature as the following comments from teachers indicate:

> Touch football doesn't lend itself to videoing at all. Squash does in some respects . . . something like gymnastics is perfect. It [video] is okay for drills because you have got a very small area and it's a closed skill . . . but when it comes to the decisions they [students] make on the field it is impossible to be able to pan the whole field so that I can identify one student. (Sally)

> You can't expect them to demonstrate a VHA every time they walk onto the field . . . every time you have got the camera on . . . unless you video that student every time they're on the field for the entire period they're on the field. (Brett)

> Only video the best . . . the theory being that if the best 12 performances are in line with the standards, then so will the others. (Arthur)

Inherent in the teachers' comments are a range of issues that are not easily resolved: the cost of suitable videoing equipment; the availability of additional staff to assist with the videoing of students; the intrusive nature of videoing in some activities; the limiting nature of selecting activities that lend themselves to successful videoing; the effect of the quality of video record on the assessment of the student's performance; and what is actually presented and what is actually edited. It was suggested that one approach to the issue of developing comparable assessments would be for standards tapes to be produced by the BSSSS for distribution to all schools indicating, as one teacher commented, 'This is what we expect at school standard'.

The standardization of assessment for a performance-based subject within and across sites is not easily achieved due to the broad range of variables that have to be accounted for in the assessment process. While the use of videos, workbooks (Francis and Merrick, 1994; Fryer, 1986), and visiting experts may have some merit in standardizing assessment, to implement such measures would seem to place unreasonable demands upon the time (Fryer, 1986) and level of technical expertise of teachers to bring about an acceptable result. It may well be that a more worthwhile and productive strategy would focus on developing shared understandings of the desired standards through effective staff development.

Equity and Assessment in Physical Education

While it is acknowledged that assessment is designed to discriminate between students' performances, there is a need for assessment procedures and practices in physical education to be based on principles of equity so that students are not unnecessarily disadvantaged. The difficulty in achieving such a goal is multiplied by the complexity of variables that intervene in a subject where physical performance is central to the assessment programme but is not necessarily the sole indicator of being physically educated.

Although the subject was designed to produce physically educated young people and not with students of any particular academic or physical ability in mind, its potential to provide satisfying experiences for students of different sexes, with differing goals, ethnicity, interests, body shape, and abilities was questionable. The question of fairness in student achievement was raised by both teachers and students who expressed their concern that students with certain characteristics would be advantaged in the assessment process. Strength, size, sex, and, in some cases, the intersection of those characteristics, contributed to the dominance of some groups over others (Gipps, 1995).

In one school context, the girls who had been successful in the activities chosen for the subject were described by the teacher as 'very talented physically and . . . quite strong physically'. Girls with these particular characteristics were seen as not being 'disadvantaged'. However, the statement by the teacher that 'some activities will always suit some (body shapes, sexes) rather than others', suggested that student characteristics as a determinant of success, was embedded in the physical education programme for that school. Not surprisingly, students also perceived that physical characteristics had an impact on student outcomes (Dewar, 1990; Gipps, 1995; Stroot, 1994). A female student commented that 'guys . . . they've got a better physique for athletics'. Another female student pointed out that:

> Some of us actually want to participate in sport [physical education] but don't because [we] get intimidated. The girls go in there to play and in the whole game will not get the ball . . . the guys pass it to their mates.

In commenting on the fairness of the assessment process for netball, a teacher suggested that female students should be 'judged as ladies' because 'physical strength (of males) is a definite advantage, and height'. What does being judged as a female in netball entail? Should all females be judged similarly?

A related equity issue concerns the extent to which the physical activities selected (the nature of the knowledge [Gipps and Murphy, 1994]) for the school programmes influenced the outcomes for students. More so than most school curriculum areas, physical education inherently carries influential socio-cultural baggage such as the level of opportunity for students to participate in physical activities outside of school, the preexisting skill levels of students, and student interest in particular physical activities. In the trial, schools were required to select four activities from three broad categories, and in most cases, the choice was made on the basis of staff expertise and the availability of facilities and resources, and, to a lesser degree, on student interest and expertise. This was limiting from three perspectives. First, and inevitably, the selection of activities favoured some body types (despite students' technical knowledge and skill) over others, yet the possibility of giving students individual choice (particularly in small schools) was constrained by availability of facilities and resources. A second limitation was the perceived relationship between the number of activities in a school physical education programme and the life chances of students. In a discussion about the syllabus requirements, one teacher pointed out that four activities were 'appropriate for students who are planning a career in a particular activity but not so appropriate for students interested in pursuing a range of broader (physical education-related) careers who would benefit from a broader range of activities'. A third constraint was the general rejection of physical activities from the aesthetic category (only 5 per cent contribution to programmes across trial schools) on the basis that the boys, in particular, would reject the subject if an aesthetic activity were to be included.

The criteria for assessment focused on the integration of both theoretical and practical knowledge. To do well, students had to perform equally well on both academic and physical tasks. Students were very aware, through the assessment tasks, that the subject demanded ability in both academic and physical areas. In discussions with students about the relationship between the demands of the subject and ability levels, the following comments exemplified their responses:

> Some people are really good at prac. and they'll get A pluses in prac., and they'll get C minuses in theory . . . then they'll get let down and (overall) go down to something like a C plus or something.

> A lot of guys have got a head start if they are sporting.

Similar concerns were expressed by teachers, one of whom pointed out that:

> you can have good sportsmen (*sic*) who technically achieve higher order process because they read the game and take the right options . . . (but) because they're not higher order in their assignment work . . . that's it forever. (Angela)

When asked who could do well in the subject, one student suggested that it was, 'Someone who's pretty good at sport . . . physically . . . and with a bit of a brain'. In one school context the intersection of sex, ability and success was reported by the teacher:

> I think on the whole the boys have probably had a fairly reasonable series of highs and our girls are really struggling. We don't have any really high achieving female sportspeople doing the course . . . we've got some of the best boys in the school. (Gail)

A final issue from the physical education trial related to the limited opportunities afforded students to demonstrate their best level of performance (Gipps and Murphy, 1994). Students were not afforded the opportunity to demonstrate what they could do. In commenting on the assessment of table tennis, a student pointed out that it was 'a little hard to assess how people really played because some days you might have an off day. It wasn't really that accurate to assess how you play'. However, in line with authentic assessment practices and the BSSSS's assessment processes, this concern was more cautionary than widespread. While it may be argued from the perspective of authentic assessment, that one-off opportunities to perform well are characteristic of competitive sporting events, it is a question of finding a suitable balance between fair and equitable educational assessment practices in a school context and the desire to be rigidly authentic.

Conclusion

Within the context of a competitive academic curriculum, the implementation of the physical education syllabus has provided some direction for the assessment of performance-based subjects. A strength has been its movement towards authentic assessment that: is characterized by relevant, applied and substantial tasks; is regular and ongoing; draws on a broad disciplinary base; and, is primarily student centred. However, the syllabus has been less successful at defining criteria and standards, especially standards related to physical performance, in ways that are clearly understood and shared by teachers and students across a wide range of activities. At a systemic level there appears to be the need for more support through initiatives such as the production of exemplary assessment tasks and videos depicting expected standards of performance. Also of concern were issues of equitable access, opportunity and outcomes for students of differing sexes, abilities, backgrounds, and statures. In this regard, Gipps (1995, p.

275) suggests using 'different tasks for different groups' and, while potentially more equitable, would provide an enormous challenge for human and
material resources and to the establishment of shared standards. In considering Gipps's suggestion, it is necessary to ask whether such an approach
violates the integrity of what the subject is about or can some of that
integrity be compromised to meet other educational goals for students, and
if so by how much?

While there are lessons to be learned for the assessment of performance-
based subjects from developments in physical education reported in this
chapter, it is clear that further work is required to advance the quality of
assessment in (and consequent accountability of) such performance-based
subjects. It is not sufficient to suggest that more authentic, comparable and
fair assessment can be achieved for performance-based subjects in school
education on the basis of developing conceptually strong programmes.
Implementation processes of such programmes must encourage reflection
on how and why specific content is chosen, and what standards are in line
with the educational goals of the subject.

It remains to be answered whether performance-based subjects should
reject the strictures of assessment and accountability and simply concentrate on providing students with experiences that characterise the chosen
subject area (such as the joy of movement). Yet, experience in physical
education from other countries (e.g., USA) suggests that to chart such a
course comes with costs such as loss of teacher morale, lower subject status,
less challenging learning, and diminished resources.

[. . .]

References

Abernethy, B., Burgess-Limerick, R. and Parks, S. (1994) Contrasting approaches
to the study of motor expertise. *Quest*, 46, 186–198.
Allen, R. (1991) *A survey of health and physical education exit achievements: Con-
tent, process or skill?* Initial report. Brisbane, Queensland: Board of Senior Sec-
ondary School Studies.
Arnold, P. (1979) *Meaning in movement, sport and physical education.* London:
Heinemann.
Arnold, P. (1988) *Education, movement and the curriculum.* London: Falmer.
Board of Senior Secondary School Studies (1992) *Trial senior physical education
syllabus.* Brisbane, Queensland: Board of Senior Secondary School Studies.
Carroll, B. (1986) Examinations in physical education: An analysis of trends and
development. In *Trends and developments in physical education. Proceedings of
the VIIIth commonwealth and international conference on sport, physical educa-
tion, dance, recreation and health* (pp. 233–239) London: E. and F. N. Spon.
Carroll, B. (1991) Assessment in the national curriculum: What the teacher has to
do. *British Journal of Physical Education*, 22(2), 8–10.
Cohen, L., and Manion, L. (1989) *Research methods in education.* London:
Routledge.

Connell, R. (1989) Cognitive processes and motor behaviour. In D. Sugden (Ed.), *Cognitive approaches in special education* (pp. 232–245) London: Falmer.

Dawkins, J. (1988) *Strengthening Australia's schools.* Canberra: Australian Government Publishing Service.

Dewar, A. (1990) Oppression and privilege in physical education: Struggles in the negotiation of gender in a university programme. In D. Kirk and R. Tinning (Eds.), *Physical education, curriculum and culture: Critical issues in the contemporary crisis* (pp. 67–100) Basingstoke, UK: Falmer.

Eisner, E. (1993) Reshaping assessment in education: Some criteria in search of practice. *Journal of Curriculum Studies*, 25, 219–233.

Francis, J., and Merrick, I. (1994) The future for advanced level GCE physical education and sport studies. *British Journal of Physical Education*, 25(3), 13–16.

Fryer, B. (1986) Curriculum development and assessment in physical education: a Scottish perspective. In *Trends and developments in physical education. Proceedings of the VIIIth commonwealth and international conference on sport, physical education, dance, recreation and health* (pp. 49–56) London: E. and F. N. Spon.

Gipps, C. (1994) *Beyond testing: Towards a theory of educational assessment.* London: Falmer.

Gipps, C. (1995) What do we mean by equity in relation to assessment? *Assessment in Education*, 2, 271–281.

Gipps, C., and Murphy, P. (1994) *A fair test? Assessment, achievement and equity.* Buckingham: Open University Press.

Glaser, B., and Strauss, A. (1967) *The discovery of grounded theory.* Chicago: Aldine.

Graue, M, E. (1993) Integrating theory and practice through instructional assessment. *Educational Assessment*, 1, 283–309.

Hewitson, M. (1988) The concept of performance in criterion-referenced assessment. In N. Baumgart (Ed.), *Reports and records of achievement for school leavers* (pp. 240–252) Canberra: Australian College of Education.

Kirk, D. (1988) *Physical education and curriculum study: A critical introduction.* London: Croom Helm.

Kirk, D., and Tinning, R. (1990) *Physical education, curriculum and culture: Critical issues in the contemporary crisis.* Basingstoke, UK: Falmer.

Lund, J. (1992) Assessment and accountability in secondary physical education. *Quest*, 44, 352–360.

McConachie-Smith, J. (1991) Assessment of progression in national physical education. *British Journal of Physical Education*, 22(2), 11–15.

Masters, G. (1994, March) *Setting and measuring performance standards for student achievement.* Paper presented at the Public Investment in School Education: Costs and Outcomes Conference, Canberra.

Matanin, M., and Tannehill, D. (1994) Assessment and grading in physical education. *Journal of Teaching in Physical Education*, 13, 395–405.

Maxwell, G. (1995) School-based assessment in Queensland. In C. Collins (Ed.), *Curriculum stocktake* (pp. 88–102) Canberra: Australian College of Education.

National Forum on Assessment (1992) Criteria for evaluation of student assessment systems. *Educational Measurement: Issues and Practice*, Spring, 32.

O'Sullivan, M. (1994) High school physical education teachers and their world of work: Scope and direction of the project. *Journal of Teaching in Physical Education*, 13, 324–332.

O'Sullivan, M., Siedentop, D., and Tannehill, D. (1994) Breaking out: Codependency of high school physical education. *Journal of Teaching in Physical Education*, 13, 421–428.

Pieron, M. (1994) Studying the instruction process in teaching physical education. *Sport Science Review*, 3(1), 73–82.

Sadler, D. R. (1993) *Comparability in school-based assessment in Queensland secondary schools.* Paper prepared for the Tertiary Entrance Procedures Authority, Queensland.

Spackman, L. (1995) Assessment in physical education. *British Journal of Physical Education*, 26(3), 32–34.

Stroot, S. (1994) Contemporary crisis or emerging reform? A review of secondary physical education. *Journal of Teaching in Physical Education*, 13, 333–341.

Towards a fairer Australia: Social justice and program management: A guide (1988) Canberra: Australian Government Publishing Service.

Veal, M. (1992) The role of assessment in secondary physical education: A pedagogical view. *Journal of Physical Education, Recreation and Dance*, 63(7), 88–96.

Vickers, J. (1992) While Rome burns – Meeting the challenge of the reform movement in education. *Journal of Physical Education, Recreation and Dance*, 63(7), 80–87.

Walters, D. (1991) A theoretical analysis of G.C.S.E. physical education practical assessment criteria. *British Journal of Physical Education*, 22(2), 23–26.

Wiggins, G. (1989) Teaching to the (authentic) test. *Educational Leadership*, 46(7), 41–47.

12

Outcomes, Competencies and Trainee-centred Learning: the Gap Between Rhetoric and Reality

Alison Wolf

This chapter reviews developments in the assessment of vocational qualifications during the last decade, including the relationship between assessment methods and patterns of teaching and learning. It takes as its starting point a detailed examination of reforms in the UK, which are particularly interesting because they have been so far-reaching and also so distinctive. The first section addresses the general approach of 'competence-based' qualifications, and the rationale for the inclusion of core skills (now renamed key skills) within these. Section 2 summarizes the evidence from evaluations and research projects on how far the objectives of these awards have been realized. Section 3 then discusses, more briefly, the extent to which any similar trends can be discerned in other countries, notably fellow-members of the European Union.

1 Competence-based Reforms and NVQs

Introduction

During the 1980s and early 1990s, British vocational education was subject to comprehensive reorganization and reform by central government. The underlying justification for change, and for the introduction of approved 'National' qualifications, was the perceived link between high levels of vocational training and economic growth. The proximate cause was the notion that the existing 'jungle of qualifications' reduced training levels because people did not understand what different qualifications meant and therefore did not pursue or value them. Both these arguments appealed to politicians seized with economic panic about the future of British prosperity in a 'global' economy (Wolf, 1998). What the politicians did not foresee was what emerged very early in the reform: namely, a highly distinctive approach to both pedagogy and assessment.

In the early 1980s, on the eve of reform, most 16/17 year olds either left school for the job market, or obtained apprenticeships which combined work with formal training, or enrolled for other full-time courses of a more or less vocational nature. Many of the latter were of a traditional nature, offering training of the type also associated with apprenticeship – in, for example, construction, catering, hairdressing, craft engineering. However, there was also a rapidly growing group of full-time courses which combined general educational with a more or less specific vocational content, and which also offered the possibility of progression to higher level awards of a technician nature or, in the longer term, degrees. The Diplomas offered by BTEC (the Business and Technician Education Council) in, for example, Business, Tourism, Child Care or Engineering were of this type, and formed the single largest such group.

Overlapping with this range of provision for young people, there existed a huge number of specialized vocational awards, some offered by quite large 'awarding bodies', others by tiny sector-specific ones. Some of these awards were taken predominantly by young people. For example, the very popular Nursery Nursing awards run by the NNEB provide the recognized qualification for private nannies as well as nursery workers. Others were taken by adults in particular sectors, and as such well known within that sector and virtually unheard of elsewhere.

Except in a very few cases, the process of examining and awarding these specialized vocational qualifications was unregulated by the state; although the qualifications were often delivered through state-supported institutions, especially 'Further Education Colleges'. A wide variety of assessment methods was in use; with some 'awarding bodies' using written examinations almost exclusively, others a combination of written and practical tests, and others (notably BTEC) operating entirely with teacher assessment.

All this changed when the National Council for Vocational Qualifications was established with a remit to create a complete system of nationally recognized, transparent qualifications, with hierarchical levels, into which the 'jungle' of existing awards could be organized. The National Council set itself to create criteria which any vocational award must meet if it was to be recognized as a 'National Vocational Qualification' (an NVQ). These criteria reflected, from the start, a very distinctive set of assessment principles – referred to by senior officials as the 'NVQ methodology' – which the Council was able to promote effectively through the positive incentive of government development funding, and the sanction that non-approved qualifications would be ineligible for use in government-funded training courses. It is discussed in detail in the section following.

Although the government hoped that NVQs would be taken by large numbers of people in work, they also envisaged their becoming the main alternative to academic A levels for young people. Civil servants and politicians alike persuaded themselves that young people would prefer their occupational relevance and learning style. However, by 1990, it was obvious that the large and growing majority of young people was opting for full-time study but rejecting NVQs. Those not taking the academic A levels were selecting semi-vocational awards such as the BTEC Diplomas mentioned above.

The government therefore decided to extend its reform of qualification structures by introducing a new sort of award, intended for young people in full-time post-compulsory education. Plans for a 'range of general qualifications within the NVQ framework' were announced in a White Paper of 1991; the National Council for Vocational Qualifications was charged with their development; and General National Vocational Qualifications (GNVQs) were launched in 1992. Although the government's charge to the National Council did not require a close match between the NVQ structure and the new award, the Council took the opportunity afforded by GNVQs' introduction to extend the 'NVQ methodology' (*sic*) into mainstream education, and the awards were developed with the same features.

Developing New Vocational Qualifications: the Approach of the National Council for Vocational Qualifications

The defining characteristic of NVQs and GNVQs was, from the start, a particular theory of assessment. This theory derived in part from views about *learning*; and had a major impact on both teaching/training styles and on the way in which candidates' work was both prepared and assessed.

National Vocational Qualifications (NVQs)

All NVQs must be *competence-based*. This means that they must conform to a particular model of criterion-referencing (Wolf, 1995b) which involves an emphasis on outcomes and the decoupling of assessment from particular institutions or learning programmes. Anyone who can present the relevant evidence should be able to present themselves for assessment and obtain the relevant award. Any accredited NVQ must be positioned at one of five hierarchical levels and must also be:

'based on national standards required for performance in employment . . .'

'based on assessment of the outcomes of learning, normally arrived at independently of any particular mode, duration or location of learning'

'awarded on the basis of valid and reliable assessment . . .'

'free from unnecessary barriers restricting access and progression and available to all those who are able to reach the required standard by whatever means' (NCVQ, 1995: p. 6)

The intention was that NVQs should be authentic reflections of workplace practice, but should also encapsulate a national standard, so that any employer knew exactly what a particular award-holder could do. This guarantee was seen as central to the future success of NVQs as a valuable asset in the labour market. It was argued that the competence-based approach guaranteed national standardization, because of the clarity and detail with which the outcomes were specified. This specification quite quickly took on a very tightly regulated form.

NVQs derive from and to a large extent consist of occupational *standards*, developed by bodies representing a particular industry; and which define, in outcome terms, what occupational 'competence' consists of. Each takes the form of *units*, sub-divided into elements. Each element in turn contains *performance criteria*, which define the outcomes which must be demonstrated; a *range statement* defining the range of situations in which the performance criterion must be applied; lists of *underpinning knowledge and understanding*, and lists of *evidence requirements* showing what would count as sufficient evidence of competence.

An NVQ must involve direct assessment of the outcomes specified in the occupational standards and it was argued that, using the standards, one could collect and assess evidence over time, including, especially, naturally occurring evidence in the workplace. The National Council also argued that, as a necessary corollary of the commitment to completely transparent qualifications, all NVQs must be based on exhaustive assessment. Evidence must be presented for every single performance criterion across every part of the 'range'. Otherwise, one would lose precisely the transparency and standardization which NVQs were designed to provide.

As Eraut *et al.* (1996) have pointed out in the most extensive study yet of assessment practice for NVQs, the result of this approach is that 'assessment and quality assurance is dominated by paperwork. . . . NVQs typically involve over a thousand separate assessment decisions', all of which must be documented. The first, major effect of the NVQ system was therefore to give an enormous boost to the use of portfolios. 'The need to record all these decisions, together with some indication of the evidence on which they were based, helps to explain the almost universal adoption of the portfolio system for storing assessment information.' (Eraut *et al.*, op cit: p. 8) In engineering, construction and business administration, Eraut *et al.* found no less than 95 per cent of candidates to be preparing and presenting portfolios (Eraut, op cit: p. 29).

General National Vocational Qualifications (GNVQs)
Whereas NVQs are very specific vocational awards, GNVQs (which are intended for young people) are much broader in conception, with only a dozen or so titles, compared to hundreds for NVQs. For example, NVQs in the construction sector will attest to your skills as a bricklayer, OR a carpenter OR a plasterer. A Construction GNVQ will involve you in one or two years of full-time study ABOUT the construction industry. Nonetheless the National Council determined to adopt the same competence-based approach as for NVQs. GNVQs too must be specified 'in the form of outcomes' and 'be available to all those who are able to reach the required standards by whatever means' (NCVQ, 1992). Another major innovation in GNVQs was the introduction of 'core skills' as a necessary part of any award; and these are discussed in the following section. Figure 12.1 provides an example of the GNVQ outcomes which students must achieve. At

present GNVQs are offered at level 1 (Foundation), 2 (Intermediate) and 3 (Advanced). The example here from level 3, represents a common format.

Business Planning Level 3 Element 8.2: Produce and present a business plan

---

Performance criteria
1. purposes of a business plan are explained
2. business objectives for a single product or service are identified and explained
3. marketing plan is identified
4. production plan is described
5. resource requirements and ability to meet the requirements are identified and explained
6. financial data and forecasts to support the plan are produced
7. monitoring and review procedures for plan are identified
8. business plan is presented to an audience

Range: Purposes of a business plan: to seek finance; to gain finance; to monitor performance
   Objectives: supply of goods or service; achieve sales volume; achieve sales value; achieve market share; make profit; break-even
   Marketing plan: pricing, promoting, distribution, selling, timing
   Production plan: premises, machinery, raw materials, labour
   Resource requirements: human, physical, financial
   Financial data and forecasts: time period, cash flow forecast, start-up balance sheet, projected profit and loss and balance sheet
   Monitoring and review: monthly profit and loss and balance sheet

Evidence indicators: A five-part business plan relating to a single product or service in written form with oral presentation to a simulated potential provider of finance. The five parts are objectives, marketing plan (outline only), production plan (outline only), resource requirements, financial support data. (The marketing plan referred to could also be that plan which is produced for element 8.3.) Evidence should demonstrate understanding of the implications of the range dimensions in relation to the element. The unit test will confirm the candidate's coverage of range.

Figure 12.1   *Examples of GNVQ elements*

GNVQ assessment was conceived from the start as portfolio-based. Although the National Council wanted only portfolio-based assessment, Government officials and ministers insisted on an element of external testing. Nonetheless, the external element was reduced to a series of short and simple multiple-choice 'mastery' tests covering basic factual information. Grading of GNVQs is entirely on the basis of the portfolio.

Core skills
A major innovation in GNVQs was the introduction of core skills as a necessary part of any award. The concept, in something close to the GNVQ manifestation, originated in a speech by the then Secretary of State Kenneth Baker, made to the Association of Colleges of Further & Higher Education (ACFHE) AGM on 15 February 1989. In his speech, Baker proclaimed the need 'for an initiative to promote further education' and for

a broad education post-16. He then produced a list of 'core skills', intended to clarify his proposals, arguing that

> As I see it, there are a number of skills . . . which young people and adults in future will all need. They could be expressed as a list of core skills . . . say, the following:
> – communication – written and oral. How to explain a complicated working procedure, or deal with a tricky customer.
> – numeracy. Not simply adding a column of figures, but understanding orders of magnitude.
> – personal relations – team working and leadership
> – familiarity with technology . . .
> – familiarity with systems . . .
> – familiarity with changing and social contexts . . . especially foreign language knowledge.

In late November 1989 letters to the then curriculum and examination authorities for schools asked them to advance 'core skills' in post-16 provision by incorporating them *within existing awards* and to consult with the National Council for Vocational Qualifications (NCVQ). While the school authorities eventually concluded that the incorporation of core skills into academic qualifications at 18 plus was not, in fact, feasible, NCVQ embraced them eagerly. 'NCVQ is clear that core skills must form part of general NVQs . . . (I)t is proposed that the development and assessment of core skills will be integrated in the vocational activities which make up the learning programmes for students.' (NCVQ, 1991, 5.1 & 5.4)

Five assessed core skills were proposed, but central government doubts resulted in only three, Communication, Application of Number and IT, being made compulsory. 'Working with others', and 'Improving own learning and performance', were introduced, but made optional. In practice they were virtually never assessed or recorded formally, even in the early years of GNVQs (FEDA *et al.*, 1994, 1995, 1997).

Although some of Kenneth Baker's core skills have fallen away, the final policy developed by NCVQ was nonetheless very close to his original one. First, these skills, across the board, must be integrated into learning programmes. Second, 'clearly defined levels' (Baker, 1989, par 47) are ascribed to core skills through some formal assessment process: they are assessed as level 1, 2, 3 etc. In theory, levels of core skill attainment are independent of the level of the qualification within which they are being delivered; so a student could, in principle, get a level 3 in Application of Number on the basis of work being done for a level 1 GNVQ.

The core skills specifications have been drafted and redrafted a number of times since their inception. Figure 12.2 shows the latest version of one of the Communication elements for level 2 GNVQs. As explained above, these skills are supposed to be delivered, displayed and assessed entirely within the context of the student's vocational studies.

NCVQ developers have consistently emphasized 'that the NCVQ Core Skill Units are strongly oriented towards application of skills, knowledge and understanding rather than simply 'knowledge of things' such as

---

1998

Element 2.2: Read and respond to written material

Performance Criteria
When reading and responding, you must:
1 **select and read** appropriate **materials** for a purpose
2 **extract information** from text and images
3 **collate** the necessary **information** from different sources

Skills and Knowledge
You are expected to be able to:

Select and **read** materials
- identify materials which are likely to contain the information you need for your purpose (*e.g. to obtain facts, evidence, opinions, ideas to include in written material or an oral report*)
- read different types of short documents (*e.g. business letters, memos, notices, forms, notes*) and extended documents (*e.g. reports, textbooks, articles*), including those which have images (*e.g. charts, diagrams, sketches, photographs*)
- use different reading techniques (*e.g. skimming material to gain a general idea of content, scanning material to find relevant information*)
- use sources of reference, such as a dictionary, and ask others when you are unclear about what you have read.

Extract *information*
- identify the line of reasoning and main points from text (e.g. recognize 'signal words' such as 'therefore', 'so', 'whereas', how texts are put together to compare and contrast) and interpret images
- question the relevance and accuracy of what you read
- make structured notes on the main points and ideas, with references. Collate information
- compare information taken from different sources, noting points of difference and agreement
- identify any further information you need.

Figure 12.2   *Unit from Level 2 Communications*

mathematical processes' (NCVQ, 1993a). One of the main architects of the approach explains the difference, as he sees it, between Core Skills and the external qualifications – the General Certificate of Secondary Education (GCSE) – which English pupils take at 15 plus in a wide range of academic subjects.

> English GCSE is not the same as core skills in Communication, Maths GCSE is not the same as Application of Number. The simplest way of thinking of the difference is that the core skills demand application and contextualisation; GCSE exams and coursework can, and often do, demand this; but it is not necessary (Oates, 1995, pp. 4–5 passim).

> For core skills to be accepted as legitimate by most learners in post-compulsory education they should be rooted in their vocational goals. Which means that they cannot be added on as extra 'subjects' but should arise as a natural and fully contextualised aspect of vocational learning . . . the primary responsibility for the development and assessment of the skills rests with teams of vocational teachers. (Oates and Harkin, 1995, p. 192)

The Theory of Curriculum and Learning which Underpins National Vocational Qualifications

NVQs and GNVQs have no official syllabus, being defined by their assessment requirements; but they do share an official pedagogy, albeit one which has received rather little attention. The awards are meant to reward, and in the case of GNVQ explicitly encourage, learners to 'take responsibility for their own learning': to cover material as fast as they are able or as slowly as they need, and to get credit for things they have done in the past; and not to be constrained by a schedule of external examinations. Portfolios are conceived of as 'candidate-led', since this can 'promote candidate involvement and responsibility for their own assessment' (NCVQ, 1995, p. 31).

The philosophy of learning embraced by the National Council derives largely, as do its detailed assessment requirements, from a model elaborated by its former Deputy Director, Gilbert Jessup. Jessup argued that the approach, that of an 'outcomes based' qualification system, could and should revolutionize education and training. In a passage entitled 'The Autonomous Learner' he argued that:

> The new education and training model places the learner at the centre of the system. . . . Prospective learners will be provided with far more exact information on the functions performed in occupations and professions. . . . Given open access to information and professional guidance where required, individuals will be much better placed to make realistic education and career choices. . . . Companies , like colleges and training institutions, will become centres of learning. Learning will be tailored to suit the ability and opportunities of the individual. (Jessup, 1991, pp. 115–117 passim)

Jessup was consistently critical of existing school and college-based courses. The NVQ approach 'places the learner at the centre of the system. . . . (It) will give learners a degree of control over their own learning which has not been possible with traditional courses and examinations' he argued (ibid., pp. 115–116). Central to his conception are action plans and official guidance to 'providers' of NVQs and GNVQs notes that 'individual action planning is needed . . . students should be encouraged to consider their achievements to date, interests and preferences, career aspirations and learning needs. From this starting point an action plan can be developed.' (NCVQ, 1993a)

The most visible manifestation of the philosophy of learning underpinning these qualifications are the grading criteria for GNVQs. The importance attached to action plans was noted above: in the case of GNVQs it has been simply impossible to complete the award without one. As Figure 12.3 indicates, whether or not a candidate receives a pass, merit or distinction on their award depends on the evidence they provide of planning; of ability to gather information; and of self-evaluation.

A number of Council publications have provided exemplar material showing what student work at pass, merit and distinction levels would look

	Pass	Merit	Distinction
Planning 1: Drawing up plans of action	Satisfies all evidence requirements	Candidate independently draws up plans of action for a series of discrete tasks. The plans prioritize the different tasks within the given time period.	Candidate independently draws up plans of action for complex activities. The plans prioritize the different tasks within the given time period.
Planning 2: Monitoring courses of action	Satisfies all evidence requirements	Candidate independently identifies points at which monitoring is necessary and recognizes where revisions to courses of action are necessary. Appropriate revisions to plans are made with guidance from teacher/tutor.	Candidate independently identifies points at which monitoring is necessary and recognizes where revisions to courses of action are necessary. Appropriate revisions to plans are made independently.
3. Information seeking and information handling (A): Identifying and using sources to obtain relevant information	Satisfies all evidence requirements	Candidate independently identifies, accesses and collects relevant information for a series of discrete tasks. Candidate identifies principal sources independently and additional sources are identified by the teacher/tutor.	Candidate independently identifies, accesses and collects relevant information for complex activities.
4. Information seeking and information handling (B): Establishing the validity of information	Satisfies all evidence requirements	Candidate independently identifies information which requires checking for validity. Candidate checks validity of information using given methods.	Candidate independently identifies information which requires checking for validity. Candidate independently selects and applies appropriate methods for checking validity.
5. Evaluation (A): Evaluating outcomes and alternatives	Satisfies all evidence requirements	Candidate judges outcomes against original criteria for success; identifies alternative criteria that can be applied in order to judge success of the activities.	Candidate judges outcomes against original criteria for success and identifies and applies a range of alternative criteria in order to judge success of the activities.
Evaluation (B) Justifying particular approaches to tasks/activities	Satisfies all evidence requirements	Candidate justifies approach used; indicates that alternatives were identified and considered.	Candidate justifies approach used basing justification on a detailed consideration of relevant advantages and disadvantages. Alternatives and improvements identified.

Note: The candidate must meet all the 'evidence requirements' – i.e. provide (written) evidence that they have covered all the specified outcomes – before their portfolio can be graded. The original GNVQ grading criteria made no mention of mastery of content. Grading was entirely a function of ability to plan one's work; ability to seek and handle information; and ability to evaluate approaches, outcomes and alternatives. While content mastery has now been added it remains only one among four equally weighted dimensions. In every case, the criteria are applied to the overall portfolio.

Figure 12.3 *Grading criteria for Advanced GNVQs (1994 version)*

like; and these give some indication of what the criteria mean for course delivery (NCVQ, n.d.). Comments in the text include:

> In order to show evidence towards distinction (at Intermediate level) a student must show planning skills in relation to complex activity. . . . Her diary entries . . . record her independence in organizing visits to firms and making the visits alone, providing evidence towards distinction . . . Her diary entries also show that although her plans didn't always run smoothly, she identified and overcame problems, as required for a distinction grade . . . (p. 34)

> The student quickly realised that he needed to revise his action plan, as he had not scheduled enough time . . . He consulted his tutor to find out whether his revised plan was appropriate, and therefore showed evidence towards a merit grade (Advanced: planning, criterion 2) (p. 95)

The approach to pedagogy and assessment adopted by the National Council was unique in a number of respects. Nonetheless it was also, inevitably, affected by ideas which were widespread in UK educational circles. Bates argues that the approach endorsed by NCVQ is best understood as 'the most recent British version of vocational progressivism' (Bates, 1998). In this context she identifies, particularly, GNVQs' emphasis on the 'development of individual autonomy or learner "empowerment" through the installation of pedagogic principles which transfer responsibility for learning to students themselves' (*ibid.*). To this, we would add the approach to teaching and learning embodied in the core skills requirements. The next section discusses how far these principles were realized.

2   Implementation: the UK Experience

The Impact on Learners

The intentions are clear: what about the actuality? The main source of information on GNVQ activities comes from the annual reports published by official government inspectors who observe a large number of institutions, but whose reports are both largely unquantified, and, inevitably, couched in extremely measured terms. The following quotations from inspectors' reports give some flavour of GNVQs in process, and suggest that some at least of the expected patterns of activity prevail.

> The students' coursework portfolios were reviewed by the teachers throughout the year. In most cases they were reviewed through a tutorial system: the portfolios were particularly well-managed in about one-third of the courses . . . There were several instances, however, when portfolios were poorly managed and students were given insufficient advice about what to include (or) how to improve evidence. (OFSTED, 1994, para 58)

> The majority of teaching was well planned and effective . . . A variety of learning styles were (*sic*) used. These included assignments, group work, oral presentation, simulations, case studies, practical work, independent study, role-play, educational visits and work experience. . . . Much of the work required research and the acquisition of information which was then incorporated into the assignments.

. . . both staff and students expressed concern that the emphasis on paper-based planning and recording were leading to insufficient emphasis on practical outcomes, finished work and good presentation. (FEFC, 1994, paras. 37–38)

These reports do not indicate how far GNVQs have stimulated any major departure from the teaching methods used on either the full-time vocational courses for 16–19 year olds which they displaced (and which used continuous assessment by teachers) or from academic (A level) courses for this age-group. However, some recent research does allow for direct comparisons between GNVQ and A level (academic track) classrooms, and is based on systematic classroom observation and student feedback on learning requirements (Meagher, 1997).

In the area of learning requirements, student feedback reveals some strong and clearly perceived differences. GNVQ students are considerably more likely than A level students to state that

the method of working
the precise definition of the task
the pace of work

are set by the student. However, no such differences from A level are perceived in the extent to which the work involves the application of past learning to new topics or the use of 'problem solving' activities.

Direct observation and student feedback on the frequency of activities also indicate significant but not invariable differences. Figure 12.4 summarizes the relative importance of different activities in a sample of observed A level courses (4 A level subjects: total of 40 lessons) and GNVQ courses (4 GNVQ courses: total of 42 lessons).

Activity	A level classrooms	GNVQ classrooms
Discourse	73%	38%
Note making and taking	6%	6%
Other classroom activities	18%	43%
Off task and administrative	4%	13%

Note: Discourse: includes answering and initiating curriculum questions, teacher or student led discussion, management questions. Other work: includes individual help by teacher, teacher presentation of topic, exercises from past papers, help from/to another student, use of IT.

Figure 12.4 *Percentage of class time spent on different types of activity (Meagher, 1997)*

In the A level classrooms by far the most frequent single activity was answering a curriculum question, which takes up almost half the time; with initiating a contribution only about a quarter as likely to occur. In the GNVQ classrooms, answering a curriculum question was also the single most likely event to occur; but it did so less often, taking up an average of a fifth of class time; and being helped individually by the teacher was almost as common (15 per cent) followed by work on assignments (9 per cent).

Finally, A level students were rarely observed off task (though that may include sitting passively while a few students dominate the conversation) and also rarely seen working collaboratively. GNVQ students were quite regularly seen off task, and also very likely to work collaboratively during class with one or two other students.

Some intensive case-studies by Bates (1995; 1998; Bates and Dutson, 1995) provide insights into the dynamic of GNVQ classroom practice. The classrooms Bates studied were staffed by enthusiasts for the approach, eager for individualized learning to replace the didactic methods they saw as typical of other courses. Their comments to the students emphasized that 'the agenda is yours rather than mine', and that students must take an 'adult, professional' approach. Following initial presentations on a topic, students were expected to work independently for much of the time.

Bates notes that this approach certainly required students to become responsible for planning their work to meet deadlines, and to manage it over quite long periods; though she also notes that the distinction between this and the more familiar concepts of 'homework' and 'coursework' is one of degree rather than kind. At the beginning, she found 'students spoke in terms of "liking" the extra freedom, . . . of being "treated like adults . . . and as responsible people" . . . As the first year progressed, however, attitudes became more ambivalent . . . ' (Bates, 1998)

Two problems are particularly worthy of note. The first is the heavy demand for 'evidence' imposed by GNVQ portfolio contents which, as with NVQs, must contain evidence of achieving every single outcome. As a result, 'students became *hunters and gatherers* of information . . . and estimated that 50 per cent of their GNVQ could be spent' locating and collecting information (Bates, op cit). This, indeed, was the major form their 'responsibility' took. Secondly, the main objective of the students was to obtain the qualification, not to promote a certain form of learning. 'Coping' strategies became widespread. Action plans were written after the work was completed; 'creative copying' was widespread; since getting a book from town counted for more, you did that even if it was in the school library anyhow.

An evaluation of GNVQ assessment alternatives by Broadfoot *et al.* included a survey of student opinions and yielded similar conclusions. The authors concluded that 'most students enjoyed the style of learning which the GNVQ approach encourages . . . (It) led to the development of self-discipline and self-confidence in planning and undertaking assignments . . . However the learning style and assessment system do possess possible negative consequences . . . GNVQ (is seen) as a complex system, difficult to organize and manage, and loaded with paperwork . . . Such perceived obstacles resulted in students feeling under constant pressure and could be demotivating' (Broadfoot *et al.*, 1995, p. 14).

These passages may help to explain an apparent paradox. Although the evidence from students is generally positive, GNVQs have, in practice, had an extremely high drop-out rate. Nationally, only 42 per cent of those registering in 1994 for a two-year, level 3 (Advanced GNVQ) completed their studies successfully; while for the one year Intermediate course, the comparable rate was 37 per cent in 1994–5, rising to 51 per cent in 1995–6. One important factor in explaining non-completion is the failure of many students to keep up a steady rate of portfolio completion. This varies enormously between institutions in the number of completed units which students had entered into their portfolios by halfway through the course.

There has been far more in-depth study of GNVQ processes than of those involved in NVQs. This reflects the greater importance of GNVQs in the process of selecting and sorting young people for higher education and the labour market; but also the difficulty of actually observing NVQ assessment. The ideal for the latter is that it should be integrated as far as possible with natural workplace performance. However, the extent to which this occurs varies enormously between occupational sectors.

In business administration, where the NVQs require evidence of competence in a large number of office tasks (photocopying, filing, memos, telephone skills, taking minutes etc.) the paper-based nature of the tasks makes it quite easy to carry out a normal task, and at the same time 'log' it as a piece of evidence for assessment. Business Administration candidates are correspondingly more likely than others to find the process of accumulating portfolio evidence unproblematic and even enjoyable (Crowley-Bainton and Wolf, 1994). Construction sites, in contrast, are ill-suited to training and assessment; and construction NVQs are delivered overwhelmingly through college courses and industry training workshops. The demands of NVQs have changed the nature of the training curriculum by changing the nature of the assessment. As one government report noted:

> The curricular changes brought about by NVQs have encouraged the expansion of realistic working environments in colleges. In agriculture, catering sand hairdressing, development has been concentrated more on changing management and assessment procedures. In office studies, engineering and construction, substantial changes have been necessary in accommodation and resources. (Welsh Office, 1992)

Bates' work (see especially Bates and Dutson, op cit) analyses in considerable detail the difficulty of integrating assessment into such contexts as catering, and the 'marginalisation of NVQ activity' which the demands of an actual workplace impose. In an occupational setting it is the need to get the job done which takes first place; and the idea of a 'trainee-led' or 'learner-centred' programme for the day has little force when set against operational demands.

The need to monitor and build up a portfolio covering all outcomes is the focus for most trainer-candidate discussions in NVQs. This alone implies a clear difference between NVQs and their precursor vocational awards in terms of candidates' priorities and activities. What is far from obvious is that this realizes the original objectives and philosophy of student-centred learning.

The Impact on Teachers

For staff the impact of NVQ and GNVQ requirements has been very clear: a huge increase in the time spent on assessment. Many teachers still praise the GNVQ approach to learning, but very few support its implications for staff. NVQ teaching/training staff are often reluctant to express views publicly, since many depend directly on contracts from government agencies who are funding special training schemes; but in colleges, criticisms of the assessment burden of GNVQs are echoed even more forcibly by those with NVQ responsibilities.

The GNVQ Assessment Review Project used a sample of 24 courses and course teams in 12 institutions. (FEDA *et al.*, 1994) Using teacher logs, the authors found that the average amount of time spent on assessment-related activities by each GNVQ teacher was 13 hours a week.[1] There was wide variation around this mean – from 26 hours to 5 hours a week – but this was largely explained by differences in class size. The project concluded that this enormous amount of assessment was partly a result of the particular assessment scheme adopted for GNVQs, which requires both that the student provide evidence that every component of the 'outcome' specifications has been met, and that the portfolio then be graded as completely separate exercise. However, it is also a function of the sheer volume of material generated. The student assignments used by the National Council in preparing exemplar-based guidance are typically about 100 pages in length and only partially fulfil the requirements for one GNVQ unit. (Students complete 6 for a one-year and 12 for a 2-year course.)

Inevitably, teachers have come to see this burden of assessment as not only unmanageable but also as something which has a major and negative impact on their teaching and students' learning. In 1995, a review of GNVQ assessment was set up; and work carried out for this included a comprehensive survey of schools and colleges offering GNVQs (see Figure 12.5).

	% positive	% neutral	% negative
To what extent has the current GNVQ assessment regime enhanced and/or hindered effective teaching and learning?	13.2	19.9	58.7
How appropriate are the current assessment procedures for the GNVQ?	19.9	18.9	55.3
How manageable are the assessment and recording requirements?	8.8	13.2	73.4
How effective are the current grading criteria and procedures for selecting evidence for grading?	4.9	20.2	70.8

Note: Rows do not sum to 100 per cent because of (varying) non-response rates.

Figure 12.5   *GNVQ centres' views on assessment requirements, 1995 (Source: NCVQ, 1995)*

---

[1] All teachers in the sample were teaching other courses in addition to GNVQ.

The Implementation of Core Skills

While most people in the UK would applaud any attempt to broaden the post-16 curriculum, major problems have also arisen in connection with the core skills which are a mandatory part of GNVQs. Inspectors' reports on GNVQs have been consistent in identifying major problems with core skills delivery.

As explained above, students' core skills are assessed and certified separately, but the performance is meant to be embedded in the vocational curriculum. However, as I have argued elsewhere, it is, in practice, impossible to make reliable statements about whether embedded 'core skills' are at a particular level, or equivalent to those embedded in another different context (Wolf, 1991). The emptiness of 'core skills' statements bereft of their context is best understood by illustration. Take, for example, a skill such as 'decide between alternative courses of action'. The basis for accreditation might be a decision between sending documents by mail or courier: or, equally possibly, between fitting out an office with Apple Macs or IBMs, or between reading physics or law at university.

Now suppose that you are told that someone has demonstrated their ability to 'decide between alternative courses of action' or even that they have shown it at level 3. On its own, this statement tells you virtually nothing. You need the context – was this a case of deciding how to send a letter, or selecting a large computer system? Once you know the context, the information then tells you something about the individual: but, taking it the other way round, does the general statement actually *add* anything to the context? And if it adds nothing, then why have it at all?

The superficially more concrete language of some academic 'core skills' statements do not get one much further. 'Carry out calculations correctly' using a range of techniques – percentages, ratios, etc. – is a central performance criterion in Application of Number Level 2. What does it mean? That an individual can calculate a given percentage of an integer? But can they also operate with percentages of more than 100? Can they include decimal places? Calculate percentages as part of a problem, and not just a sum? Convert percentages into decimals?

The point is not that 'core skills' do not exist: or that statements about people's ability are intrinsically meaningless. *It is rather that these skills are by definition inseparable from the contexts in which they are developed and displayed, and that they only make sense (or, rather, the same sense) to those who are alike in understanding and recognizing those contexts.*

As GNVQs have developed, more and more schools and courses are simply delivering core skills through separate lessons. (FEDA *et al.*, 1995, 1997) Many experienced vocational professionals whose own maths education ended decades before have found the task of delivering and assessing 'Application of number' through their vocational lessons impossible, and handed the task over to maths teachers: the same is even more true with Information Technology. Only 'Communication' is generally assessed in an integrated form – reflecting the large volume of paper in a typical portfolio, in which instances of the different Communication outcomes can be found.

This separate delivery is, of course, completely foreign to the spirit of GNVQ pedagogy. The fact that it has happened in spite of many GNVQ teachers' commitment to this pedagogy underlines the problems attendant on this approach.

3   European Development

This section summarizes developments in vocational assessment outside the UK, and especially the countries of the European Union, with particular reference to the use of competence-based qualifications and the idea of core skills. Increasing participation rates have been universal across the EU in the last twenty years and have been accompanied by consistent Community-wide efforts to upgrade the content of vocational courses, and in particular to increase the amount of general education provided. Three major concerns have been: to reflect the changing demands of the economy, to make movement between different tracks a practical reality, and to improve the status of vocational options. It should also be noted that, while there have been major changes in the content of vocational track curricula, there has been very little change in the structure or content of post-compulsory/upper secondary academic curricula over this period.

Competence and Validity

A quick skim of the policy literature on vocational education within the EU can give the impression that the UK's embrace of competence-based assessment reflects general trends. Certainly the *term* competence occurs frequently: especially in discussions of the need for more general skills and broad-based competencies in the workplace of the future. However, the reality is that vocational education and assessment in other EU states is virtually untouched by the notion.

The Netherlands is the only other European country to have been attracted by the notion of competence and taken some action in response. Dutch vocational education is largely school-based (like that of France, Spain, Sweden, Greece and Portugal); but with a relatively strong apprenticeship tradition. The school system itself is extremely hierarchical and structured, with divisions between programmes (and schools) starting at age 13 or 14. At that point there are no fewer than four alternatives, each with its own modal destination (university, higher vocational education, senior vocational education, apprenticeship).

Reforms implemented in autumn 1993 were intended to bring the content and delivery of both apprenticeship and senior vocational education (which is school-based) closer to the requirements of industry. As the Dutch ministry of education and science explained, the major element of the new legislation 'is the new relationship it establishes with the business world. The wishes of the business community are to be a decisive factor in shaping courses (both with regard to new courses and to changes in or abolition of existing courses)' (Netherlands Ministry of Education & Science, 1993: p. 10; Wolf, 1995c).

Rather than examination syllabuses, attainment targets are being developed by a partnership of employer organizations, trade unions, and government agencies, and defining the 'knowledge, skills and professional attitudes pupils should minimally attain' (Netherlands Ministry of Education & Science, 1993). The purpose is very similar to that behind the English reforms: to increase the validity of vocational programmes, by making them much more directly a function of industrial and commercial requirements. However, there are also major differences in delivery. For example, while NVQs are based directly and entirely on the 'standards' which industrial bodies produce, in The Netherlands, industrial targets will be translated into syllabuses by the Ministry of Education. The Dutch intended, like the British, to delegate the whole assessment process, both the devising of assessments and their marking, to those delivering the training. This policy has been abandoned.

Elsewhere, vocational assessment follows traditional lines. In school-based systems, a combination of paper-based exams and practical tests obtains. In the German-speaking countries with their strong apprenticeship traditions, assessment is practical, with strong employer involvement. But it is the responsibility of organized committees (typically based in chambers of commerce), not totally decentralized; is syllabus-based; and is neither exhaustive nor defined in outcome terms. Rather than the constant revolution of the UK's last decade, the picture in *assessment* terms is one of stability.

For example, German apprenticeships involve formal examinations: but the format of these has changed little in recent years and they are, in any case, not the key determinant of what is learned – unlike the other countries discussed here, which are far more assessment-driven. Formal testing is the responsibility of the local chambers of commerce, and of committees (drawn from local employers) who take charge of particular vocational areas. Candidates take both practical and written tests – the former often occupying the better part of a day, the latter generally multiple-choice tests bought in from one of the specialized national agencies producing such papers. The tests – particularly the practical ones – are certainly demanding, but what is interesting is the pass rate: over 90 per cent in most occupations. Obviously, firms can generally be confident of bringing their apprentices up to the given standard before they take their exams.

At the core of German apprenticeship are the long-established networks involving not only employers but over a million *Meisters*, whose qualification entitles them to train, and the training regulations, which lay down exactly what training an apprentice in a given occupation is to receive. The focus of apprenticeship reform or change in Germany is not the examinations but these regulations. When, over the last two decades, there was a move to augment development of problem-solving, analytic and evaluative skills, the focus was on the training – the inputs – rather than the assessment.

While the *Meisters* are not assessors in any formal sense, the tight networks that exist not only within a company, but across the area encompassed by a chamber of commerce, and the very intensive consultation that precedes any change, means that people know what these regulations mean. In this case, the validity of the qualifications is seen as inhering in and deriving from these processes. The stability of the German system, and its success in developing an extremely highly skilled workforce, shows that there are alternatives to the competence or outcome-based perspective which are nonetheless highly 'workplace oriented'.

The workplace as validator
The UK and its neighbours do share a desire for more valid and realistic vocational assessment. For example, the French have been very concerned to increase the validity of their vocational qualifications. They have done so in part by increasing the role of industrial consultative committees in the development of new awards, and partly by adopting a language of 'objectives' (though these are far less specific and wider-ranging than the 'performance criteria' of English standards of competence). All awards (vocational and purely academic) are governed by detailed regulations. The syllabus – the *référentiels* – is expressed in objective terms: for example, carrying out a fault diagnosis, or drawing up a cutting list. However, far more detail is given than in England about the process of delivery, so that teachers not only have far more of a conventional syllabus to work from but also clear requirements and recommendations about how much time, for example, should be spent on each area.

Equally important, however, is the introduction of direct workplace experience for school-based vocational awards. The requirement for such experience applies to every variety of baccalauréat professionnel – the vocational baccalauréat which occupies the last two years of upper secondary schooling, alongside the academic bac. général. During the two years of the 'bac pro' every student must spend 16 weeks in total (generally 8 weeks a year) in industry. These periods are governed by what is, in effect, a training contract with the host enterprise, laying out objectives. Without this workplace experience, the student cannot obtain their diploma.

However, whereas English NVQs demand extremely detailed assessment practices, and careful recording of exactly which performance criteria have been achieved, the French qualification is far less prescriptive in what it demands of the employer. The regulations state quite explicitly that the activities which young people follow can be very varied (albeit within the general area of study.) The purpose of their time in the workplace is to develop 'autonomy, a sense of responsibility, and creativity', for them to learn to work in a 'real-life situation', and to understand how enterprises operate. In some cases, work experience may be carefully structured by the school, in others rather less so.

Either way, for the purposes of passing and obtaining their bac., it remains the final examinations that matter, not how students actually perform during their work experience. And while the examinations are clearly 'vocational', in that they may contain practical tests, and mathematics or French placed in the context of the relevant vocational area, the way they are marked, and their general tenor, remains emphatically that of the *education* system.

'Core skills' and General Education

Although European countries have almost all reformed the general education components of their vocational programmes in recent years none has adopted the 'core skills' approach. Instead, we can describe the changes introduced in Finland during the 1980s as being typical of those in other EU member states. The curriculum of Finnish vocational institutions was redesigned to introduce more general education, and make the coverage of the two tracks (academic/vocational) more similar. The Finnish reforms also crystallize the limitation of this approach taken in isolation. Numminen and Virolainen (1997) explain that, while the overarching aim was to make vocational education more attractive, the broadening of the vocational curriculum was basically the only thing that happened. 'Otherwise upper secondary and vocational schools hardly came closer, and the proportion of young people entering general upper secondary schools kept increasing' (p. 98).

In countries such as Luxemburg and France, where technical/vocational courses at this level always had a very high general education loading, the changes have been relatively small; but all have been in this direction. In Luxemburg 1989 reforms delayed specialization yet further, and defined a very broad, common curriculum for all tracks: in France, recent changes have again further increased the general education demands of the lower level (level 2) vocational courses, the CAP and BEP. Assessment is by exam on a subject-by-subject basis.

The reforms currently being implemented in Spain, under LOGSE, provide for a complete restructuring of post-compulsory provision, with the creation of a technological option within the new upper secondary baccalaureate programme. This school-based route is the way into upper vocational training (Formative Cycle 3); is seen as the main route for future skilled workers and technicians; and means that the students who previously entered the older vocational options (FP2) will now in practice receive a much more general education. Again, this is delivered on a subject basis.

In Sweden, the upper secondary curriculum has undergone a particularly thorough revision and there is closer integration between vocational and academic ('study oriented') programmes than in any other member state; but even here, the main change is to increase the time spent on Swedish and Maths by vocational students, and to integrate everyone's studies in these areas into an overall upper secondary syllabus. (For example, in Maths there are five different programmes, hierarchically arranged: everyone, whether in a vocational or academic programme, covers the bottom one and different courses vary in how many of the others are taken.)

The rather conventional nature of these curriculum changes (and the largely stable curricula in academic tracks) may seem somewhat surprising given the general concern of policy-makers with curriculum reform, and the development of critical thinking, higher-level competences, and the like. At the level of policy discourse, there have certainly been very consistent concerns of this type in Europe. However, in so far as these concerns have been translated into action, it has been more through changes in the way different subjects are studied and examined than through changes in the actual subjects themselves.

Thus, for example, the concept of *Schlüsselqualifikationen* has been widely discussed in Austria and Germany in the context of the dual system. The idea is to develop and accredit 'expert know-how, social competence and self-competence' (Austrian Federal Ministry for Economic Affairs, n.d.); but the emphasis is on these as 'inputs' – i.e. on designing particular curricula in ways which will encourage students to develop and demonstrate the relevant skills in a particular occupational (or academic) context. In Sweden, there has been a growing emphasis on project work *within* the curriculum, and on issues such as environmental and international questions within the subject of Nature Studies.

No European country other than the UK allows its 16–19 year old students, whether in full or part time, academic or vocational, education, to drop explicit study of their own language, or of mathematics. Further examination of trends in mathematics teaching and assessment underlines how singular UK traditions *and* reforms have been. Even Australia, Canada and New Zealand, while continuing to follow many of the UK's educational fashions, have parted company with Britain in this respect. In the United States the pick'n'mix credit-based curriculum of high school may allow some students to complete all the required mathematics courses some time before they graduate. However, even here all but a very few students will continue with mathematics until the end or close to the end of high school – not least because of its central importance in the SATs (Scholastic Aptitude tests) which play a major role in university entrance decisions. In every single one of the dynamic countries of the Pacific Rim mathematics constitutes a major compulsory part of the academic and the technical/vocational curriculum up to university entrance level.

The general conclusion must be that the last ten years' developments in UK vocational assessment must be seen as a unique experiment. It is one which the rest of the world has often watched with interest, but without much enthusiasm. Current level of activity, involving new pilots, new syllabuses, and new assessment regimes, suggest that UK policy makers are concluding that this revolution failed.

4   Conclusion

For a decade beginning in 1985, British vocational education was the arena for a number of novel and ambitious projects relating to assessment, pedagogy and student learning. Enthusiasm for some of these ideas remains high: thus 'core skills', renamed 'key skills', were endorsed by the 1996 Dearing review, for the government, of all 16–19 qualifications; and government policy currently is to introduce them, in some form, into all upper secondary and higher education. However, in other respects, the experiments launched by the National Council for Vocational Qualifications are perceived as a failure. NCVQ itself is no more, merged, in 1997, into the Qualifications and Curriculum Authority; and reforms to GNVQs will revise the approach to grading and increase the importance of both external testing and of more conventional approaches to curriculum. Whether, in the process, the GNVQ approach to student learning will survive, or whether the UK will become more like its European neighbours, it remains too early to say.

References

Association for Colleges (1995) Submission to the Secretary of State for Education on GNVQ Assessment (London: AfC).

Austrian Federal Ministry for Economic Affairs (n.d.) *Learning for Life*, Vienna: Ministry for Economic Affairs.

Baker, Kenneth, Secretary of State for Education, speech given to the ACFHE AGM on 15 February, 1989.

Bates, I. and Dutson, J. (1995) A Bermuda Triangle? A Case Study of the Disappearance of Competence-based Vocational Training Policy in the Context of Practice, *British Journal of Education and Work* 8.2, pp. 41–59.

Bates, I. (1995) The Competence Movement: Conceptualising Recent Research, *Studies in Science Education* 25, pp. 39–68.

Bates, I. (1998) The 'Empowerment' Dimension in the GNVQ: A Critical Exploration of Discourse, Pedagogic Apparatus and School Implementation, in A.D. Edwards (ed) Special Issue of *Evaluation and Research in Education*, on Vocational Education vol 12.1.

Broadfoot, P., Goulden, D., Lines, D. and Wolf, A. (1995) *Evaluation of the Use of Set Assignments in GNVQs: a report to the Employment Department*, School of Education, University of Bristol and Institute of Education, London.

Clark, L and Wolf, A (1991) Assessment of Blue Badge Guides: Final Report to the Employment Department, London: Institute of Education.

Crowley-Bainton, T. and Wolf, A.(1994) *Access to Assessment Initiative.* Monograph, Employment Department (Research Strategy Branch).

Ellis, P. Standards and the Outcomes Approach, in Burke, J. (ed) *Outcomes, Learning and the Curriculum: Implications for NVQs, GNVQs and other qualifications.* Brighton: Falmer.

Eraut, M., Steadman, S., Trill, J. and Porkes, J. (1996). *The Assessment of NVQs.* Research Report No. 4. University of Sussex Institute of Education.

FEDA, Institute of Education and the Nuffield Foundation (1994, 1995, 1997) *The Evolution of GNVQs* (First & Second Interim and Final Reports of a National Survey). London: Further Education Development Agency.

Fiehn, J. (1996) Student Perceptions of Teaching and Learning Styles in Part One GNVQ. Paper presented to the conference 'GNVQs under Scrutiny', December 1996. London: NCVQ.

Further Education Funding Council (FEFC) (1994) *General National Vocational Qualifications and the Further Education Sector in England: Report from the Inspectorate,* Coventry: FEFC.

Further Education Funding Council (1997). *GCSEs in the Further Education Sector: National Survey Report.* Coventry: FEFC.

Goff, P. (1996) *Scrutiny Programme 1995–96: Summary of Main Findings.* London: NCVQ.

Haffenden, I. and Brown, A. (1989) Towards the Implementation of Competence Based Curricula in Colleges of FE, in Burke, J. (ed) *Competency Based Education and Training.* Brighton: Falmer.

Jessup, G. (1991) *Outcomes: NVQs and the Emerging Model of Education and Training.* Brighton: Falmer.

Meagher, N. (1997) Methods and Effectiveness in Advanced GNVQ Teaching and Learning. Unpublished report to the Qualifications and Curriculum Authority by the Department of Education, University of Newcastle upon Tyne (quoted by permission of QCA).

NCVQ (1991) *General National Vocational Qualifications: Proposals for the New Qualifications.* A Consultation Paper. London: NCVQ.

NCVQ (1992) *Proposed Criteria for General National Vocational Qualifications.* London: NCVQ.

NCVQ (1993a) *GNVQ Information Note.* London: NCVQ.

NCVQ (1993b) R & D report no 16. London: NCVQ.

NCVQ (1995) *NVQ Criteria and Guidance.* London: NCVQ.

NCVQ (n.d.) *Assessing Students' Work – GNVQ in Business.* London: NCVQ.

Netherlands Ministry of Education & Science (1993) Note contributed to the Workshop on New Trends in Training Policy, ILO, Geneva 18–20 October.

Numminen, U. and Virolainen, M. (1997) The Experimental Reform of Finnish Upper Secondary Schools, in J. Lasonen (ed) *Reforming Upper Secondary Education in Europe: The Leonardo da Vinci Project Post 16 Strategies,* University of Jyväskylä, Jyväskylä.

Nuttall, D. L. (1986). The Validity of Assessments, in Wolf, A. and Silver, R. *Work-Based Learning: Trainee Assessment by Supervisors.* R&D Report 33. Sheffield: Manpower Services Commission.

Oates, T. (1995) Core skills – 1995 and the future: an NCVQ strategy paper prepared for DfEE seminar 6.9.95.

Oates, T. and Harkin, J. (1995) From Design to Delivery: The Implementation of the NCVQ Core Skills Units, in John Burke (ed) (1995) *Outcomes, Learning and the Curriculum: Implications for NVQ's, GNVQ's and other qualifications,* London: Falmer.

OFSTED (Office for Standards in Education) (1994, 1995, 1996) *GNVQs in Schools 1993/94: Quality and Standards of General National Vocational Qualifications.* London: HMSO.

Royal Society of Arts (RSA) GNVQ *Centre Guidelines: A Guide for Centres in the Delivery of General National Vocational Qualifications.* Coventry: RSA Examination Board.

Steedman, H. and Hawkins, J. (1994) Shifting Foundations: The Impact of NVQs on Youth Training in the Building Trades. *National Institute Economic Review* 149 (August).

Welsh Office (1992) *Report by H.M. Inspectors: A Survey of National Vocational Qualification Developments in Further Education Colleges in Wales.* Cardiff: Welsh Office.

Wolf, A and Silver, R (1986) *Work-based Learning: Trainee Assessment by Supervisors.* R & D Series no. 33: Sheffield, Manpower Services Commission.

Wolf, A. (1991) Assessing Core Skills: Wisdom or Wild Goose Chase? *Cambridge Journal of Education*, 21.2.

Wolf, A. (1995a) Authentic assessments in a competitive sector, in H. Torrance (ed) *Evaluating Authentic Assessment.* Buckingham: Open University Press.

Wolf, A. (1995b) *Competence-Based Assessment.* Buckingham: Open University Press.

Wolf, A. (1995c) Vocational Qualifications in Europe: Common Assessment Themes, in L. Bash and A. Green (eds.) *Youth Education and Work: World Yearbook of Education* 1995. Kogan Page.

Wolf, A (1998: in press) Politicians and Economic Panic, *History of Education* 27.3.

13

Situated Learning and Transfer: Implications for Teaching

Hans Gruber, Lai-Chong Law, Heinz Mandl and Alexander Renkl

[. . .]

Recognition of the Problem: Lack of Transfer in Learning

The phenomenon of lacking transfer can reliably be found when subjects' problem solving behavior is analyzed. [. . .] However, learning conditions can be varied by manipulating contexts and contents of problems to be worked on, so that transferability of knowledge can be dramatically increased (Catrambone and Holyoak, 1989).

[. . .]

One central aspect of many transfer approaches is that pragmatic aspects are considered. In particular, the problem solver's goals and the situational context have to be considered. Therefore, a close conceptual connection can be found between experimental research on transfer and situated learning approaches. [. . .] Up to now, however, this connection has seldom been explicitly expressed. So to say, the spontaneous transfer from research on transfer to situated learning theory has occurred only rarely.

The low solution rates in experimental laboratories as well as in classroom instruction raise the problem of how to design learning environments so that knowledge application – in other words: transfer – becomes probable. One requirement is the analysis of problem solving processes and the identification of conditions that facilitate transfer. The problem solving processes involved in analogical reasoning are often modelled as a four-part sequence: (a) constructing mental representations of source problems and target problems; (b) selecting source problems as candidates for being transferred onto target problems; (c) performing mapping processes analyzing several components of source problems and target problems; (d) extending the mapping processes to generate solutions. The critical phases

---

This chapter has been edited.

within this model are (a) how relevant source problems can efficiently be found and (b) how relevant features can be identified that serve to trigger mapping processes in order to develop a model of the target problems.

Experimental research has identified several components that facilitate successful transfer. Gick and Holyoak (1980) found that retrieving from memory aspects relevant for drawing analogies occurred more often when hints had been given. Of the two phases of spontaneous transfer, noticing an analogy and applying the analogy in the solution process, the former one seems to be the main problem. Elucidating possibilities to transfer from source problems to target problems therefore is a central task of instruction. The situated learning approaches claim to achieve exactly this function, in the way of increasing the probability of successful transfer.

Holyoak and Koh (1987) showed that transfer could be facilitated by creating generalized rules or schemas. However, the existence of schemas alone did not produce increased transfer, but the schemas' quality was of importance. Schema quality substantially correlated with the amount of spontaneous transfer; high quality schemata which were based on the deep structure of problems instead of surface similarities increased transfer. Gick and Holyoak (1983) stimulated their subjects to induce solution schemata by (a) presenting an abstract of the source problems, (b) presenting a verbal description of the basic principle, (c) presenting a diagrammatic picture of the basic principle. In none of these conditions could transfer be increased. Only when multiple source problems were presented and additionally a solution schema was provided, could transfer be increased. Concordantly, it was found that the rate of spontaneous transfer was also increased if multiple source problems were presented without presenting a solution schema. Presumably, subjects themselves inductively constructed problem schemata which afterwards were used to solve the target problems (Catrambone and Holyoak, 1989; Gick and Holyoak, 1983, 1987). Presenting problems from multiple perspectives as well as fostering subjects' activity in constructing coherence between examples, which have proved to be crucial determinants of transfer in experimental research, are also central concepts in situated learning approaches.

Other components have been identified which are important in determining the amount of transfer. These components mainly refer to the encoding and retrieval conditions, for instance, memory organization (Bassok and Holyoak, 1989; Ross, 1989), mode of presenting information (multimodality: Gick and Holyoak, 1983; visual support: Gick, 1985), preknowledge and expertise (Chi *et al.*, 1981; Chi *et al.*, 1982; Gick and Holyoak, 1983; Novick, 1988).

Many of the components identified in experimental studies have been implemented in computer simulations. It could be shown that the same mechanisms that were used in modelling human learning could be used to account for machine learning processes as well. [. . .]

The research reported above belongs to the traditional cognitive paradigm. In this context, knowledge is regarded as an abstract entity that resides

in the heads of individuals. The problem of transfer is a problem of application of these abstract entities in situations that are different from the learning
context. The approaches reported give some explanations why relevant
knowledge is not transferred, although it is present in the mind of the problem solver or learner. A completely different view on transfer is held by the
situated cognition camp. Knowledge is not conceived as an abstract entity
that is independent of situations. On the contrary, knowledge is principally
bound to situations. The question then is how transfer can occur at all. In the
next section we provide an overview about the positions of five prominent
researchers from the situated cognition movement.

Situated Cognition and Learning: Review of Theoretical Frameworks

Transfer, being an elusive problem, has fallen in and out of the central
focus several times in the history of psychological research (Singley and
Anderson, 1989). Situated cognition, with its main focus on the interactions
between people and the historically and culturally constituted contexts in
which they are embedded, has emerged as a new school of thought in
cognitive science in recent years. This section sets out to explore the main
arguments of five representative views put forward respectively by Jean
Lave (cognitive anthropology), Barbara Rogoff (cognitive anthropology),
James Greeno (ecological psychology), Lauren Resnick (socio-cognitive
approach) and William Clancey (neuropsychology). Each of these situationists conceives situated cognition and transfer differently according to
his/her own philosophical orientation. Therefore, a spectrum of views of
transfer can be identified. Indeed, the diversifications hinge crucially on the
interpretations of specific theoretical constructs including representation,
knowledge, learning and culture.

Lave's Theory of Cognition in Practice

Based on her commitments to anthropological perspectives, neo-Marxist
social theories as well as the Frankfurt School of philosophy, Lave poses a
strong oppositional stance against the presuppositions that ground mainstream cognitive science (Pea, 1990), particularly assailing perspectives on
transfer (Lave, 1988). To take her extreme position, Lave objects (to) the
use of the term 'transfer' because it suggests that knowing is a matter of
mechanically re-applying inert concepts in different situations. Lave's arguments pertaining to transfer revolve around three central issues.

Issues pertinent to transfer
The first issue is continuity of cognitive activity across contexts which is
assumed to be a function of knowledge stored in memory and general

cognitive processes. Lave questions such an assumption and argues that person-acting, arenas, and settings appear to be implicated together in the very constitution of activity. More to the point, Lave (1988) comments that '. . . transfer is characterized as occurring across unrelated, or analogically related, or remotely related situations, but never across settings complexly interrelated in activity, personnel, time, space or their furnishings' (p. 40). By the same token, Lave strictly criticizes functional psychological theory which treats school as 'the decontextualized (and hence privileged as well as powerful) site of learning that is intended for distant and future use' (p. 9). For the sake of supporting her postulations, Lave assembles a diversity of evidence for situationally specific arithmetic practice and concludes that there appear to be qualitatively different practices of arithmetic in different settings (e.g., supermarket, grocery shops, and small stores). In short, she commends an analytic approach as the explanation of continuity of cognitive activity across contexts which is a matter of social reproduction, and thus of dialectical relations between the constitutive order (including semiotic systems, political economy and social structure) and the experienced lived-in world.

The second issue is nature of knowledge. The learning transfer research rests on the assumption of cultural uniformity which is entailed in the concept of knowledge domains whose boundaries and internal structures are presumably independent of individuals. Lave refutes such a notion which suggests that knowledge has no interactive, generative or action-motivating properties. Another problematic notion is 'knowledge-as-a-tool' which implies the dissociation between cognition and sociocultural context.

The third issue is learning process and communities of practice. To substantiate her situated view of learning by investigating apprenticeship training forms which appear in various forms in different contexts (e.g., Vai tailors, Yucatec midwives, butchers), Lave (1991) concludes that learning is not to be identified with the acquisition of structures or in gaining a discrete body of abstract knowledge, but takes place through legitimate peripheral participation in ongoing social practice (Lave and Wenger, 1991); the process of changing knowledgeable skill is subsumed in processes of changing identity in and through membership in a community of practitioners; and mastery is an organizational, relational characteristic of community of practice. Taken together, Lave advocates a move away from the learning transfer genre to a social theory by which dialectic relations among persons, their activities, and contexts are implicated in success (and failure) of portability of learned skills across situations rather than merely cognitive strategies.

Implications for schooling and instruction
Lave (1988, 1990a,b, 1991) insistently emphasizes the power of everyday practice and that processes of learning should be embedded in the communities of practice in which the centripetal participation of apprentices are the pivotal concern. Unfortunately, she has not stated explicitly how transfer of appropriated skills across contexts can be facilitated and the mechanisms

so involved have not been unambiguously specified. On the other hand, she ardently advocates cooperative learning because the sociological mechanisms so involved lead to equitable knowledge accessibility. She also remarks that analyses of learning in and out of school should be used as a basis for generating research design. More to the point, she stresses that an understanding of social organization in school should be a central theme both in curricular design and in teacher training. Nonetheless, Lave and other's (e.g., Brown *et al.*, 1991a,b) challenge the assumption that schools are privileged sites for learning is a radical one that many find disturbing and thus have dismissed it as unrealistic and therefore irrelevant to the present social conditions (e.g., Palinscar, 1989; Wineburg, 1991).

In sum, one of Lave's central achievements is recasting problem solving from 'a cognitive psychological perspective that tends to treat problems as givens, to a dialectical one that sees problem-solving activity in everyday situations as arising from conflict-generating dilemmas that require resolution' (Pea, 1990, p. 29). Moreover, critical insight can be obtained from her method of close observational research *in situ*. Her work can impose a striking urge on cognitive psychologists as well as educationalists to reconsider the orthodox explanations of cognitive processes in general and traditional ways of teaching in particular.

Rogoff's Theory of Apprenticeship in Thinking and Transfer of Learning

The central tenet of Rogoff's theory is that children's cognitive development is inseparable from the social milieu in which children learn according to a cultural curriculum; from their earliest days, they augment skills and perspectives of their society with the aid of other people. In fact, apart from the influences of her anthropological background, many of her ideas are originated from Vygotskian notion of Zone of Proximal Development which has exerted consequential influences on developmental psychology (Rogoff and Wertsch, 1984). Moreover, her theory extends one step further by including nonverbal communication as well. Guided participation is the kernel concept of Rogoff's theory. Such conception implies that both guidance and participation in culturally valued activities are essential to children's apprenticeship in thinking. Guidance is either tacit or explicit, and participation may vary in the extent to which children or care-givers are responsible for its arrangement. Underlying the processes of guided participation is inter-subjectivity: a sharing of focus and purpose between children and their more skilled partners and their challenging and exploring peers (Rogoff, 1990).

Mechanisms of transfer – bridging from known to new
Transfer of knowledge is conventionally interpreted as to hinge upon the similarities between novel and old situations that should be subjectively

recognized by an agent. However, even more important than the active role of the individual in linking contexts is the part played by other individuals and cultural scripts for problem solution in guiding the individual's application of information and skills to a new situation (Rogoff *et al.*, 1991). Children, who are supposed to play their active part, may seldom be independently responsible for discovering the connections between problems or transforming available knowledge to fit new problems (D'Andrade, 1981). The building of bridges between the known and the new is thus assumed to be predominantly supported through adult-child interactions. For instance, adults helping children to make connections may specify how the new situation resembles the old. Parallels between two situations (e.g., a laboratory task and a more familiar real-life context) are drawn or highlighted to foster the transfer of the related skills and relevant information (Rogoff, 1984). Formal instruction and informal social interaction provide the child with a model of an expert applying appropriate background information to a new problem, thereby giving the child experience in the skillful generalization of knowledge to new problems. Nevertheless, the research data regarding the enhancement of cognitive skills through guided participation are rather inconsistent (see e.g., Gardner and Rogoff, 1990; Gauvain and Rogoff, 1989). The enabling effects of guidance are age-dependent, and are related to the readiness of the expert partners to take up their leading role [. . .] as well as to the motivational problem of both partners involved in the participation (Rogoff, 1991).

In fact, as mentioned in the foregoing discussion, the claim that analogical transfer can be enhanced by giving individuals explicit hints or evoking in them a process of comparing old and new information is evident by some empirical data (see e.g., Spencer and Weisberg, 1986). These facilitation strategies are analogous to bridging instructions adopted in apprenticeship learning. Hence, in the view of guided participation, spontaneous transfer, which is regarded as one of the highest cognitive capacities, is less likely to occur. However, it has to be borne in mind that Rogoff's research focused on infancy and early childhood. The comparisons drawn with other empirical studies, for which mostly adult subjects are employed, may be inappropriate.

Implications for teaching
Rogoff regards guided participation, in which an active learner participating in culturally organized activity with a more skilled partner, as an important means to enhance transfer. Moreover, she emphatically claims that both formal instructions and informal social interactions are essential for bridging the old and novel contexts. Other crucial features of guided participation include the importance of routine activities, tacit as well as explicit communication, supportive structuring of novices' efforts, and transfer of responsibility for handling skills to novices. Furthermore, she remarks that the apprenticeship system should involve a group of peers who serve as resources for one another in exploring the new domain and helping and challenging each other.

In sum, Rogoff's notion of apprenticeship in thinking with its emphasis on the supportive role played by an expert partner offers an inspiring perspective for interpreting transfer. Her meticulous integration of ethnographic and psychological evidence with her own theoretical claims results in a thought-provoking synthesis that deserves painstaking exploration and further advancement (Valsiner, 1991). [. . .]

Situated Cognition as Perceiving Affordances: Greeno's Theory

With the term 'situativity theory', Greeno aims to promote situated cognition to a higher position in the hierarchy of concepts for studying the mind. Accordingly, situativity is assumed to be a general characteristic rather than a special kind of cognition. It refers to a point of view that cognitive activities should be understood primarily as interactions between agents and physical systems and other people (Greeno, 1992; Greeno and Moore, 1993). Greeno postulates his situativity theory mainly based on an ecological psychology perspective and applies Gibson's (1979/1986) notion of affordance to explain the mechanisms underlying situated cognition. He adapts the term affordance to refer to properties of things in the environment that are relevant to their contributions to interactions that people have with them. The issue of perceiving affordances is crucial in the theoretical view of situativity and as such depends significantly on Gibson's pivotal concept of direct perception, which implies that environmental stimuli are simply picked up instead of being conceived with the mediated symbolic representations (e.g., a chair is perceived as 'sit-on-able' and a path is perceived as 'walk-on-able'). To advance one step further, Greeno attempts to expand the explanatory function of his theory by incorporating some ideas which are rooted in Barwise's (1989) situation theory in logic such as registered state of affairs, situation types and the temporal continuity of situation. Nevertheless, his postulations reflect to some extent his roots in information processing theory.

A change in epistemological assumptions

Under the rubric of situated cognition, a radical change in epistemological assumptions is observed (Greeno, 1989). Rather than viewing knowledge as some form of 'substance' residing in the minds of individuals, it can be understood as some kind of relations between an individual and a physical and/or social situation. Based on this relational view, knowing is the ability to interact with things and other people in a situation, and learning is the improvement in that ability, i.e., getting better in participating in a situated activity. The question of transfer, then, is to understand how learning to participate in an activity in one situation can influence (positively or negatively) one's ability to participate in another activity in a different situation. The answer must lie in the nature of the situation which depends on the goals of the activity, which are important as they direct individuals' attention to the features in a situation (i.e., perceiving affordance).

Mechanisms of transfer: affordance-activity coupling and the role of action schemas

Greeno and his colleagues attempt to re-interpret the empirical findings of some traditional experiments on transfer of different natures under the framework of affordance (Greeno *et al.*, 1993, pp. 110–140). They conclude that besides perceiving affordances, the construction of schemata contributes substantially to the success of transfer. It is claimed that whether the activity can be transferred successfully when the structuring of the activity changes in certain aspect depends on which affordance the action schema has incorporated in the initial learning, and how the subject applies the schema in transfer. The schemata so involved are processes rather than data structures. However, such a differentiation is vaguely explicated. In the affordance-activity view, transfer occurs because of general properties and relations of the person's interaction with features of a situation. If the affordance changes, then transfer depends on there being a corresponding transformation in the activity. Furthermore, symbolic representations can play an important role in transfer, but they are considered as only the instrumental parts of activities rather than being fundamental or ubiquitous. In fact, Greeno appears ambivalent towards the role of symbolic representations in understanding cognition. This can be vindicated by his ascribing an encompassing definition to representations (Greeno *et al.*, 1993, p. 108). More to the point, Greeno *et al.* (1993) suggest that a hypothesis which includes symbolic cognitive representations can be adopted when there is evidence for such a representation. However, the argument then focuses on the very nature of evidence which depends critically on the problematic definition of representation.

Implications for teaching

Based on his situated view of learning, Greeno (1989) comments that much of the knowledge that students acquire in school instruction is not relational in many situations in which generative relations would be valuable. With his epistemological assumption that learning involves construction of knowledge rather than its passive acquisition Greeno (1991) suggests that learning environments should include collaborative settings where teachers act as partners, coaches as well as models, and where students can work together as well as engage in exploration of ideas. Furthermore, to enable transfer, Greeno *et al.* (1993) propose that instructions should influence the activity so that it includes attention to affordances that are invariant across changes in the situation and that will support successful interactions in situations that have been transformed.

In sum, Greeno has proposed an insightful alternative for understanding the problem of transfer under the novel perspective of his situativity theory. However, owing to the problematic characteristics inherent in the concept of affordance as illustrated by contrasting definitions [. . .], the conjectures thus derived appear controversial and the variables involved are difficult to operationalize. Besides, his stance toward the uses of symbolic representations is somehow ambivalent. Nonetheless, as Greeno says 'The shift of the level of analysis from hypothesized cognitive events to hypothesized interactive events appears to be a simple move. But the ways in which those interactive events are organized are open to empirical research' (Greeno, 1992, p. 1).

Situated Cognition as Socially Shared Cognition: Resnick's Theory

Based on the Vygotskian sociocultural approach, an evolving perspective with its principal postulation that social interactions act as constituents of cognition has been advocated by Resnick and some other theorists. The fact that human cognition is so varied and so sensitive to cultural context requires that mechanisms by which people actively shape each other's knowledge and reasoning processes are investigated (Resnick, 1991). Only by understanding the circumstances and the participants' subjective construction of the situation can a valid interpretation of the cognitive activity be established. The question 'Can a person who contemplates alone in a confined room be conceived as involving in socially shared cognition?' is aptly raised. The answer hinges on the claim that cognitive tools embody a culture's intellectual history. Not only theories, implicit or explicit, but even ways of reasoning themselves are socially determined. In the same vein, it can be argued that all mental activities, from perceptual recognition to memory to problem solving, involve either representations of other people or the use of artifacts and cultural forms that have a social history (Levine *et al.*, 1993).

Evaluating formal schooling

Resnick has performed some insightful analyses on the missing links between practical intelligence and school knowledge with some intriguing evidence in the fields of arithmetic and literacy (Resnick, 1987, 1990, 1992). Some broad claims about the privileged status of school where knowledge so acquired bears on life after school are severely challenged. Some worrisome discontinuities between learning in school and the nature of cognitive activity outside school have been identified (Resnick, 1987, p.16). Briefly said, the fact that traditional schooling focusses on individual, isolated activity, on unaided thought, on symbols correctly manipulated but divorced from experience, and on decontextualized skills, may be partly responsible for our school's difficulty of teaching processes of thinking and knowledge constructions, and for repeated failure to demonstrate transfer across situations (Resnick, 1989). In short, both the structure of the knowledge used and the social conditions of its use may be fundamentally mismatched.

Innovative cognitive strategies for transfer

To explicate the problem of transfer, self-monitoring of cognitive processes is one of the novel conjectures proposed. Indeed, the habit of imposing meaning – the tendency to elaborate and seek relationships – has been considered as one of the major factors for generalizing knowledge and skills across contexts (Resnick, 1989). Taken together, this newly formulated mental discipline theory situates learning ability in a combination of skills and disposition for elaborative and generative mental work. This emergent orientation leads to the view that cognition must interact with motivational, emotional, and social aspects of a person's life. Moreover, Resnick attempts to unite situated cognition with a genetic account in which later developing competencies in some sense depend on earlier ones. Learning is a matter of passing through successive situations in which one becomes a competent actor. Through the process of adapting concepts or ways of acting borrowed from one's past to a particular situation, a new contextualized form of competence can be created.

Implications for teaching

In view of the shortcomings identified in the venture of schooling currently practiced, a general need to redirect the focus of schooling to encompass more of the features of successful out-of-school functioning is well acknowledged. Accordingly, Resnick (1987) outlines the following implications. The foremost concern is that the treatment of the subject matter should be tailored to engage students in processes of meaningful construction and interpretation (e.g., Palinscar and Brown, 1984) that can block the symbol-detached-from-referent thinking. Alternatively, a special form of 'bridging apprenticeship' that uses simulated work environments and specially designed social interactions may be more appropriate to meet the real-life need and can bridge the gap between theoretical learning and actual practice. Furthermore, schools should make their endeavor to prepare students to be good adaptive learners, so that they can perform effectively when facing transitions and breakdowns.

In sum, Resnick has put her efforts in revealing the discontinuity and mismatch between the knowledge outside and within school, which is the core factor that accounts for failure to transfer across contexts. She directs our attention to the important role played by social interactions in shaping cognition. For the improvement of the existing educational system, she proposes that a broad cultural shift in the direction of the socially shared cognition should be involved and that learning should be enhanced through apprenticeship training.

Situated Cognition as Coordinating Without Deliberation: Clancey's Theory

To rebut against the framing assumption that all behavior can be represented as symbolic models (Vera and Simon, 1993), Clancey (1993) put forward his provocative contentions for the situated cognition approach. The skeleton of his theories, which incorporate some neuropsychological concepts and are inspired by Dewey's (1896/1981) as well as Bartlett's (1932) works (Clancey, 1992a), is the notion of ongoing coordinations between perception and action.

Neuropsychological mechanisms: perception-action coordinations

Based on his proposed 'First-person and Third-person Representation' hypothesis, Clancey (1993) points out that one can interpret knowledge and its symbolic representations as the results of a sense-making process in which an observer (third-person) describes patterns of behavior of an intelligent agent. Conversely, first-person's interpretation of a representation (e.g., reading a map or plan) is inventive, not a process of retrieving definitions or mechanically reciting meaning. Human interpretation and hence use of symbols, plans, productions, etc. are not ontologically bound; understanding and comprehending (intending, believing, etc.) are not just manipulating symbolic categories, but are ongoing relations between perceiving and acting (Clancey, 1992a, 1993). More to the point, perception and action arise together automatically and are coordinated without involving any intermediate encoding-symbol manipulation- decoding sequence, thus avoiding combinatorical search. That is, coordination and learning are possible without deliberation, which is a classification observers impose on behavior.

Clancey (1993, p. 94) interprets situated cognition based on neuropsychological mechanisms. The essence of his propositions is a dynamic and adaptive cognitive architecture which consists of modular subsystems (including social and neural processes) whose organizations emerge dialectically (i.e., they are mutually constraining and separately coherent) and the overall problem is how coordination of these subsystems is possible. To substantiate his theoretical suppositions, Clancey cites some relevant observations inferred from neuropsychological research (Roschelle and Clancey, 1992). Additionally, he adopts Edelman's (1992) neural net model to illustrate situated action view of sensorimotor coordination (see Clancey, 1993, p. 97). [. . .]

Interpretations of transfer of learning

On the basis of his situational stance, Clancey (1993) re-interprets various cognitive constructs. Particularly, the notion of externalization of knowledge and symbolic representation is controversial (see e.g. Sandberg and Wielinga, 1992) and has substantial impact on the problem of transfer. Accordingly, knowledge is a capacity to adaptively re-coordinate perceiving and acting and cannot be inventoried. It can therefore be postulated that knowledge cannot be simply transferred because it does not exist in transferable form (Clancey, 1992b). On the other hand, knowledge representations are not structures in the minds of people, but external, perceivable structures open to debate, negotiation and reinterpretation. He remarks that representing can occur within the brain, but always involves sensorimotor aspects and is interactive.

Furthermore, a situated theory of knowledge (Brown *et al.*, 1991a) challenges the widely held belief that the abstraction of knowledge from situations (i.e., representation) is the key of transferability. In the same vein, Clancey remarks that 'Transfer is possible not because the student has memorized abstractions, but because these have become ways of seeing and coordinating activity' (1992b, p. 161). While disputing the 'transfer of expertise' metaphor (i.e., pouring knowledge into the head of the student) for describing learning, Clancey claims that knowledge acquisition should be viewed as a process of creating representations, inventing language, and, in general, formulating models for the first time (Clancey, 1992a).

Implications [. . .]

[. . .]

In sum, Clancey's postulations are not easy to understand. The core concepts of his theory, for example, the issue of perception-action coupling (i.e., how perception is related to performance), are intricately defined in terms of neuropsychology. Nevertheless, his sharp criticism of symbolic processing system reminds us of the extent of the gap between neurobiology and cognitive science models, and offers a new perspective from which to re-conceptualize one of the most important as well as problematic theoretical constructs in psychology: representation.

Communalities and Differences in Situated Cognition Perspectives

Situated cognition, albeit with its origin being traced to Heideggerian and Dewey's philosophy (and to more recent Piagetian and Vygotskian sociocultural perspectives), still remains a 'loosely coupled' school of thought. Undeniably, the radical concepts put forward by some situated cognition proponents require a major shift in world view and invoke significant epistemological changes. Being a new approach, situated cognition seems to offer a promising key to unlock the shackles bound to such an age-old problem as transfer. Roughly speaking, transfer involves certain kind of interaction, be it at cognitive, social or neuropsychological level, which enhances the performance of activity in a novel situation by repeating what has been experienced. Nonetheless, the terms employed in this oversimplified definition need to be qualified and elaborated for each of the aforementioned situated cognition perspectives.

As the views are so diversified, it is extremely difficult for these researchers to reach a consensus on the nature and significance of transfer. In spite of the diversifications so addressed, all of these situationists formulate their theories with the basic assumptions that there is indivisibility between cognition and culture, with the unit of analysis that is commonly grounded on the amalgamation of person, activity and setting, and with the core supposition that knowledge is actively constructed rather than passively absorbed by an intelligent agent. [. . .]

Questions for Further Research

The situated cognition approach and its view on transfer is rather new. Thus, there are many open questions that further research has to tackle. We discuss three important issues that merit attention in the near future: Are the models of situated cognition precise enough? Do the situated cognition concepts provide predictions that depart from the traditional cognitive paradigm and that withstand empirical falsification trials? Can the theoretical and the instructional concepts of situated cognition and learning be more closely integrated?

The Lack of Precision

One of the major problems inherent in the situated cognition approaches is its seemingly inconsistency which makes it susceptible to confusing inter-pretations. However, considering the different backgrounds of individual theorists, such divergence in views is to be expected. Being a new disci-pline, situated cognition approach inevitably has some drawbacks. There is a lack of a precisely defined and testable set of concepts and mechanisms that might account for a situated cognition system's behavior. Notions such as person-acting (Lave) and affordance (Greeno) do not fit common sense thinking and depart from traditional scientific concepts in significant ways. This may be an advantage to the extent that they bear a fresh perspective on unresolved problems such as the question of transfer. The disadvantage of such new, ill-defined, and contra-intuitive concepts is that they are fuzzy and imprecise. This deficit is also related to the next issue, the missing empirical findings with respect to situated cognition.

Lacking Empirical Evidence

A very pressing problem is the empirical verifiability of the situated cogni-tion approaches. The hypothesized concepts and processes are far too loosely defined to be subjectable to confirmation or falsification through observation and experiment. Furthermore, as situated cognition theories stress the importance of contexts, experiments in the laboratory, which try to control for the context, do not seem to be the ideal way of investigation anymore. From the perspective of situated cognition, context should not be controlled or ruled out, but integrated into the theoretical framework and the respective empirical studies. Thus, new research designs have to be developed that fit the situated cognition models. In order to see whether it is reasonable to claim that situated cognition theories can best explain the problem of transfer, empirical studies are required to prove the fruitfulness of this new perspective. Further research efforts to conduct systematic empirical research and to refine theoretical framework are to be called forth.

Coherence Between Theoretical and Instructional Concepts

Up to date, the theoretical-conceptual models and the instructional approaches that are subsumed under the label of situated cognition are only loosely related. Authors from the theoretical-conceptual camp draw some instructional conclusions out of their assumptions and, vice versa, educationally oriented researchers refer to theoretical concepts of situated cognition. However, it can neither be stated that the instructional models are straightforward deductions from some basic models on situated cognition nor that the theoretical concepts of situated cognition can serve as valid basis of the educational models. On the contrary, there seems to be a contradiction between the theoretical and the instructional use of the term situated cognition or situated learning. On the one hand, the term situated is used in a descriptive way in order to characterize the nature of cognition and learning (e.g., Clancey, Greeno, Lave). This means that cognition and learning are always and under any circumstance situated. The second meaning of situatedness is a prescriptive one and it is primarily used within instructional research. It refers to learning processes in which the learner is actively involved in authentic problem solving. These two meanings of situatedness contradict each other. From the radical situated cognition point of view, there are no situated and non-situated learning environments, because cognition and learning are always anchored in situated activity. On the other hand, the claim of educational researchers that there is something that can be called non-situated learning challenges the basic assumption that learning is always situated. Unfortunately, these contradictions are often unrecognized and the term situated is used in a mindless way.

To sum up, the situated cognition perspective provides a fresh and new look upon cognitive phenomena. However, at the present stage, the theoretical conceptualizations are rather vague. Future research will show whether the situated cognition model can provide a more appropriate account of cognitive phenomena such as transfer.

Note

The original chapter includes sections on Technology-Based Approaches to situated cognition.

References

Bartlett, F. C. (1932). *Remembering – A study in experimental and social psychology.* Cambridge: Cambridge University Press.

Barwise, J. (1989). *The situation in logic.* Stanford, CA: Centre for the Study of Language and Information, Stanford University.

Bassok, M., & Holyoak, K. J. (1989). Interdomain transfer between isomorphic topics in algebra and physics. *Journal of Experimental Psychology: Learning, Memory, and Cognition, 15,* 153–166.

Brown, J. S., Collins, A., & Duguid, P. (1991a). Situated cognition and the culture of learning. In M. Yazdani & R. W. Lawler (Eds.), *Artificial Intelligence and Education (Vol. 2).* Norwood, NJ: Ablex.

Brown, J. S., Collins, A., Duguid, P. (1991b). Debating the situation: Rejoinder to Palinscar and Wineburg. In M. Yazdani & R. W. Lawler (Eds.), *Artificial Intelligence and Education (Vol. 2).* Norwood, NJ: Ablex.

Catrambone, R., & Holyoak, K. J. (1989). Overcoming contextual limitations on problem-solving transfer. *Journal of Experimental Psychology: Learning, Memory, and Cognition, 15,* 1147–1156.

Chi, M. T. H., Feltovich, P. J., & Glaser, R. (1981). Categorization and representation of physics problems by experts and novices. *Cognitive Science, 5,* 121–152.

Chi, M. T. H., Glaser, R., & Rees, E. (1982). Expertise in problem solving. In R. J. Sternberg (Ed.), *Advances in the psychology of human intelligence (Vol. 1).* Hillsdale, NJ: Erlbaum.

Clancey, W. J. (1992a). *'Situated' means coordinating without deliberation.* Paper presented at the McDonnell Foundation Conference 'The Science of Cognition', Santa Fe, New Mexico.

Clancey, W. J. (1992b). Representations of knowing: In defense of cognitive apprenticeship. *Journal of Artificial Intelligence, 3,* 139–168.

Clancey, W. J. (1993). Situated action: A neuropsychological interpretation response to Vera and Simon. *Cognitive Science, 17,* 87–116.

D'Andrade, R. G. (1981). The cultural part of cognition. *Cognitive Science, 5,* 179–195.

Dewey, J. (1896/1981). The reflex arc concept in psychology. *Psychological Review,* III: 357–370, July. Reprinted in J. J. McDermott (Ed.), *The philosophy of John Dewey.* Chicago: University of Chicago Press.

Edelman, G. M. (1992). *Bright air; brilliant fire: On the matter of the mind.* New York: Basic Books.

Gardner, W., & Rogoff, B. (1990). Children's adjustment of deliberateness of planning according to task circumstances. *Developmental Psychology, 26,* 480–487.

Gauvain, M., & Rogoff, B. (1989). Collaborative problem solving and children's planning skills. *Developmental Psychology, 25,* 139–151.

Gibson, J. J. (1979/1986). The theory of affordances. In J. J. Gibson, *The ecological approach to visual perception.* Hillsdale, NJ: Erlbaum. (Original work published in 1979.)

Gick, M. L. (1985). The effect of a diagram retrieval cue on spontaneous analogical transfer. *Canadian Journal of Psychology, 39,* 460–466.

Gick, M. L., & Holyoak, K. J. (1980). Analogical problem solving. *Cognitive Psychology, 12,* 306–355.

Gick, M. L., & Holyoak, K. J. (1983). Schema induction and analogical transfer. *Cognitive Psychology, 15,* 1–38.

Gick, M. L., & Holyoak, K. J. (1987). The cognitive basis of knowledge transfer. In S. M. Cormier & J. D. Hagman (Eds.), *Transfer of learning.* San Diego: Academic Press.

Greeno, J. G. (1989). Situations, mental models and generative knowledge. In D. Klahr & K. Kotovsky (Eds.), *Complex information processing: The impact of H.*

A. *Simon* (21st Carnegie-Mellon Symposium on Cognition). Hillsdale, NJ: Erlbaum.

Greeno, J. G. (1991). Mathematical cognition: Accomplishments and challenges in research. In R. R. Hoffman & D. S. Palermo (Eds.), *Cognition and the symbolic processes: Applied and ecological perspectives.* Hillsdale, NJ: Erlbaum.

Greeno, J. G. (1992). The situation in cognitive theory: Some methodological implications of situativity. Presented at the *American Psychological Society*, San Diego, CA.

Greeno, J. G., & Moore, J. L. (1993). Situativity and symbols: Response to Vera and Simon. *Cognitive Science, 17*, 49–59.

Greeno, J. G., Moore, J. L., & Smith, D. R. (1993). Transfer of situated learning. In D. K. Detterman & R. J. Sternberg (Eds.), *Transfer on trial: Intelligence, cognition, and instruction.* Norwood, NJ: Ablex.

Holyoak, K. J., & Koh, K. (1987). Surface and structural similarity in analogical transfer. *Memory & Cognition, 15*, 332–340.

Holyoak, K.J., & Thagard, P. R. (1989). Analogical mapping by constraint satisfaction. *Cognitive Science, 13*, 295–355.

Lave, J. (1988). *Cognition in practice: Mind, mathematics and culture in everyday life.* Cambridge: Cambridge University Press.

Lave, J. (1990a) The culture of acquisition and the practice of understanding. In J. W. Stigler, R. A. Shweder, & G. Herdt (Eds.), *Cultural psychology: Essays on comparative human development.* Cambridge: Cambridge University Press.

Lave, J. (1990b) Views of classroom: Implications for math and science learning research. In M. Gardner, J. G. Greeno, F. Reif, A. H. Schoenfeld, A. diSessa, & E. Stage (Eds.), *Toward a scientific practice of science education.* Hillsdale. NJ: Erlbaum.

Lave, J. (1991). Situating learning in communities of practice. In L. B. Resnick, J. M. Levine, & S. D. Teasley (Eds.), *Perspectives on socially shared cognition.* Washington, DC: American Psychological Association.

Lave, J., & Wenger, E (1991). Situated learning: Legitimate peripheral participation. Cambridge: Cambridge University Press.

Levine, J. M., Resnick, L. B., & Higgins, E. T. (1993). Social foundations of cognition. *Annual Review of Psychology, 44*, 585–612.

Novick, L. R. (1988). Analogical transfer, problem similarity, and expertise. *Journal of Experimental Psychology: Learning, Memory, and Cognition, 14*, 510–520.

Palinscar, A. S. (1989). Less charted waters. *Educational Researcher, 18(4)*, 5–7.

Palinscar, A. S., & Brown, A. L. (1984). Reciprocal teaching of comprehension-fostering and comprehension-monitoring activities. *Cognition and Instruction, 1*. 117–175.

Pea, R. D. (1990). Inspecting everyday mathematics: Reexamining culture-cognition relations. *Educational Researcher, 19(4)*, 28–31.

Resnick, LB. (1987). Learning in school and out. *Educational Researcher, 16(9)*, 13–20

Resnick, L. B. (1989). Introduction. In L. B. Resnick (Ed.), *Knowing, learning and instruction: Essays in honour of Robert Glaser.* Hillsdale, NJ: Erlbaum.

Resnick, L. B. (1990). Literacy in school and out. *Daedalus, Spring*, 169–185.

Resnick, L. B. (1991). Shared cognition: Thinking as social practice. In L. B. Resnick, J. M. Levine, & S. D. Teasley (Eds.), *Perspectives on socially shared cognition.* Washington, DC: American Psychological Association.

Resnick, L. B. (1992). From protoquantities to operators: Building mathematical competence on a foundation of everyday knowledge In G. Leinhardt, R. Putnam, & R. A. Hattrup (Eds.), *Analysis of arithmetic for mathematics teaching.* Hillsdale, NJ: Erlbaum.

Rogoff, B. (1984). Introduction: Thinking and learning in social context. In B. Rogoff & J. Lave (Eds.), *Everyday cognition: Its development in social context.* Cambridge, MA: Harvard University Press.

Rogoff, B. (1990). *Apprenticeship in thinking. Cognitive development in social con-text.* New York: Oxford University Press.

Rogoff, B. (1991). The joint socialization of development by young children and adults. In P. Light, S. Sheldon, & M. Woodhead (Eds.), *Learning to think: Child development in social context 2.* London: Routledge.

Rogoff, B., Gauvain, M., & Ellis, S. (1991). Development viewed in its cultural context. In P. Light, S. Sheldon, & M. Woodhead (Eds.), *Learning to think: Child development in social context 2.* London: Routledge.

Rogoff, B., & Wertsch, J. V. (1984) (Eds.). Children's learning in the 'Zone of Proximal Development'. *New Directions for Child Development, no. 23.* San Francisco: Jossey- Bass.

Roschelle, J., & Clancey, W. J. (1992). Learning as social and neural. Paper pre-sented at the *AERA Symposium: Implications of cognitive theories of how the nervous system functions for research and practice in education,* Chicago.

Ross, B. H. (1989). Distinguishing types of superficial similarities: Different effect on the access and use of earlier problems. *Journal of Experimental Psychology: Learning, Memory, and Cognition, 15,* 456–468.

Sandberg, J., & Wielinga, B. (1992). Situated cognition: A paradigm shift? *Journal of Artificial Intelligence in Education, 3,* 129–138.

Singley, M. K., & Anderson, J. R. (1989). *The transfer of cognitive skill.* Cambridge, MA: Harvard University Press.

Spencer, R. M., & Weisberg, R. W. (1986). Context-dependent effects on analogical transfer. *Memory and Cognition, 14,* 442–449.

Valsiner, J. (1991). Building theoretical bridges over a lagoon of everyday events: A Review of Apprenticeship in thinking: Cognitive development in social context by Barbara Rogoff. *Human Development, 34(5),* 307–315.

Vera, A. H., & Simon, H. A. (1993). Situated action: A symbolic interpretation. *Cognitive Science, 17,* 77–86.

Wineburg, S. S. (1991). Remembrance of theories past. In M. Yazdani & R. W. Lawler (Eds.), *Artificial Intelligence and Education (Vol. 2).* Norwood, NJ: Ablex.

14

When Is Experiential Learning not Experiential Learning?

Mike Wallace

[. . .]

Introduction

A few years ago I experienced an intensive outdoor management training course at a venue deep in the country. I was placed in a team for five and a half days, together with a colleague I had known for a couple of weeks, and six managers from different walks of life whom I had never met before. We spent packed days and evenings tackling time-limited tasks in competition with other teams. After each task there was a reflective team review. A facilitator weaned us away from our concern with our frustrations over the task to examine our feelings and our team performance. These sessions were supplemented with lectures which drew eclectically on theories and research in offering us guidance for improving our performance as managers. We also learned rudiments of a sport which was designed to be challenging for us as individuals. I learned how to do a 'ferry glide', traversing a two-person canoe up a series of rapids, and how to come down them without ending up in the drink.

Our team had been bottom of the league all week, failing dismally to achieve our tasks. Each could be solved only if we achieved synergy as a team, whether the task was a treasure hunt (we were too busy arguing about who should look for what), a simulation where we had to manoeuvre a container of nuclear fuel into safe storage (we blew up the world), or, on the penultimate evening, a short comic drama (we failed to get enough laughs).

As we were about to pack up for the night, exhausted and resigned to our failure, the final task was announced. It was to last sixteen hours and whichever team won on this occasion would be declared the course winner. Every type of task we had already undertaken was included, so I had to shoot those rapids yet again. It was a highly charged experience, and my crowning glory was to crack the code which was the key to our team's success. We won.

What did all these powerful experiences do for me as a manager back in my university workplace? The short answer is not a lot, because I was

---

This chapter has been edited.

inhibited from transferring what I learned about teamwork into my work setting. Yet the disinhibition required for me to make the most of my experience was not simply a matter of adopting a more positive attitude towards learning.

I was asked at the outset to suspend any disbelief and enter into the spirit of the course. Accordingly I took the decision to learn, and my engagement with the learning opportunity remained strong throughout. While most of the experiences cost me dear in terms of frustration, failure and, at times, fear, the strength of these emotions was far outweighed by the benefits of excitement, challenging tasks and ever tighter bonding within the team. At the low point after flunking each task, the facilitator asked participants whether they wanted to 'go for the keys' (to their car) so that they could drive off into the sunset, thereby shifting from an enhancement to a maintenance learning strategy which would be terminal as far as the course was concerned. We all admitted that the thought had crossed our minds, but nobody did it because of our strengthening motivation to 'go the extra mile' with our team mates and come out winners.

Our final triumph had left me with a feel-good factor that favoured my enduring effort to maximise the learning opportunity – but try conveying that to colleagues who don't know what you've been up to, don't share the matey feelings you have generated within your course team, and whom you are not supposed to tell about it. For the organisers had asked us not to divulge the secrets of our experience, claiming that the success of the course depended on participants being blissfully unaware about what they were in for at the start of the programme; many companies sent different managers each year, and amongst middle managers the training was surrounded in mystique which contributed to its desirability as a perk.

My transfer problem was rooted in the way the team tasks and setting were (sadly perhaps!) far removed by design from my routine managerial work and its context. Yet the course organisers had stated the assumption that we would be able to transfer what we had learned from one group, one set of tasks and one setting into another. This article of faith is open to question since it ignores the possibility noted by Eraut (1994) that additional learning is required of participants, and their workplace colleagues who have not attended an off the job course, if the desired transfer of learning into the workplace is to be made. No support was offered for transfer beyond encouraging participants to refer back to principles articulated during the course.

Significance of Different Experiences

My – contentious – answer to the riddle posed in the title of this chapter is: when experiential learning for job performance is based on 'vicarious' experience (Bailey, 1987). The further a learning experience departs from the tasks that are the object of training and the situation in which they have to be performed, the more vicarious it becomes, and the more additional learning has still to take place in the real context of these tasks.

My problem over transfer of learning from off the job course to on the job practice is, perhaps, no more than we would expect according to research in fields as diverse as cognitive psychology and the training of teachers. The latter research will be discussed later; the former has contributed to an ongoing debate over the degree to which knowledge employed in practice is situation specific, a product of the activity, context and culture in which it is developed and used.

The theory of 'situated cognition' articulated by Brown *et al.* (1989) was based on research into how people go about learning when free to do so in their own way. They argued that knowledge required for action is intricately linked to the context in which it is learned. A new context implies new learning in which old cognitive schemata become modified. On this account, I had more to learn and the conditions were not favourable for my induction, since the culture of the course which I had absorbed was anathema to the culture of the workplace. Others have argued that there are generic skills which can be transferred to different situations but their application entails picking up detailed contextual knowledge (Perkins and Salomon, 1989) – in other words, transfer entails additional, context-specific learning.

Present definitions of experiential learning appear to cover too much ground. Wutzdorff (1994, p.2), for example, argues that diverse approaches to experiential learning share common assumptions:

> this commitment to experiential learning is grounded in a philosophy that engages the learner actively in whatever is being learned. It is a philosophy that asserts that the development of knowledge and the acquisition of skills belong as partners in education, where each can transform the other. Therefore experiential learning necessarily goes beyond reading and listening as the primary routes to effective learning.
>
> By directly engaging the learner in what is being studied, experiential learning then also re-shapes the teacher-learner relationship. Often this change means that the teacher steps out of the role of authority figure and possessor of knowledge and moves into a facilitator role. Experience itself becomes the teacher. The emphasis then is placed on the reflective process, where teachers and peers join the learner in making meaning out of whatever has been experienced.

The emphasis is on active engagement of learners, the primacy of their learning experience, facilitation (as opposed to transmitting knowledge), and making sense of experience through reflective dialogue between facilitator and learner. However, no distinction is made between different kinds of experience and the degree to which they relate to the context in which the learning is designed to be used.

Although the learning experience I went through was real enough – both demanding and exciting – and I certainly learned a great deal, it was not the same experience as learning to do my job more effectively. The training achieved all that it could do: provide me with generic principles which I had yet to learn how to put into practice at work.

In recent years, the popularity and diversity of activities labelled as experiential learning have increased dramatically within the realms of initial and in-service teacher training (the latter including management training for senior staff). It is striking how many of these activities are based on vicarious experiences such as role-play exercises and simulation games; but where the aim is to improve job performance, any old experience will surely not do. The purposes of this chapter are therefore twofold: to question some of the theoretical underpinnings of the experiential learning movement; and to make a case for liberating learners from the transfer problem associated with vicarious training experiences by focusing learning support for beginning teachers, experienced teachers and senior managers firmly on the real job in its real setting. The remaining sections will explore the theoretical base of experiential learning; consider evidence which points to the importance of learning support in the context of use; and employ a model developed in the light of this evidence to consider how to make the most of experiential learning within training design.

Conceptions of Experiential Learning

Two of the most influential accounts of learning through experience will be examined. Advocates of training methods based on participants' experience (e.g. Dennison and Kirk, 1990; Hobbs, 1992), including outdoor management training (e.g. Beeby and Rathborn, 1983; Bank 1985), have made widespread reference to the theory of experiential learning put forward by Kolb (1984). The process of learning is conceived as a four-stage cycle (see Figure 14.1). Immersion in immediate concrete experience is viewed as the basis for observation and reflection. Observations are assimilated into an idea, image or theory from which implications for future action may be derived. These implications, hunches or hypotheses then guide planning and implementation of experimental action to create new experiences. Learners require the skills of learning how to learn in this way: the ability to immerse themselves openly in new experiences (CE), to reflect on these experiences (RO), to integrate observations into more abstract conceptual schemes or theories (AC), and to use these theories to guide decision-making and experimental action to solve problems (AE), leading to new concrete experiences.

Different learning situations foster different skills. An affective environment highlights experiencing of concrete events; a symbolic environment emphasises abstract conceptualisation; a perceptual environment encourages observation; and a behavioural environment stresses taking experimental action. Tasks within my experience of management training provided a range of environments which fostered most experiential learning skills. The

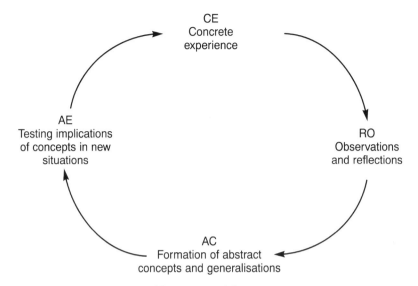

Figure 14.1   *Kolb's experiential learning model*

simulation exercise, for example, provided affective, perceptual and behavioural elements of a learning environment. It was strong on concrete
experience, the opportunity to observe the consequences of our actions, and
repeated chances (until we dropped the container of nuclear fuel) to experiment with new ways of solving the problem which the team had been set.
While it was weak on abstract conceptualisation, the lecture sessions provided a complementary symbolic environment where we were presented
with a range of concepts which we could apply to our more active tasks.

Kolb's research into how far the cycle was reflected in individuals' learning behaviour revealed wide variation, commonly being biased towards
one or more elements. He claims that individuals' preferred learning styles
become more effective the more they reflect the complete cycle. My management training experience quickly revealed such differences in behaviour: some team members were keen to leap before they looked,
moving into action almost as soon as the task had been set (a bias towards
active experimentation and concrete experience). Others wanted to look
before they leaped, taking more time to explore the parameters of the
problem and to employ problem-solving strategies in coming up with a plan
of campaign (a bias towards reflective observation and abstract conceptualisation). In my team, some arguments arose because each type of
learner could see the negative consequences of the other's approach: concrete experience junkies wondered if the abstract conceptualisers would
ever let them get started, while the latter despaired of the way the former
wasted time rushing down blind alleys because they had not thought
through the problem.

So far so good, but does the theory go far enough? It certainly captures
aspects of learning experience and points to practical implications, includ-

ing the desirability of maximising the opportunity of any experience to support learning and the need to diagnose the bias in individuals' learning styles and foster balanced learning habits.

However, there remains an important gap in the argument. Any experience may indeed offer potential for learning, but Kolb does not address the transferability of what has been learned from one experience into another. The theory explains how learning through a particular experience takes place. I certainly learned from the treasure hunt how to work with my team of that week in doing treasure hunts. The point of the exercise, however, was not to train me as a treasure seeker, but as a member and leader of a different workplace team with very different tasks. The trainers assumed that I could automatically transfer this learning. It follows from Kolb's theory that a second set of experiential learning cycles would be required for the additional learning in my everyday environment that was necessary for the course to impact on my job performance.

While the theory holds good as far as it goes, lack of attention to the new learning that performance of tasks in each new setting entails appears ironically to have allowed many trainers, in the name of experiential learning, to assume that the vicarious experience of off the job training is sufficient preparation for the real experience of the job itself. The more vicarious the experiential learning experience, the more additional learning is required for transfer into the context of use and the greater the need for learning support with transfer. Conversely, the closer the experiential learning experience becomes to the context of use, the less additional learning is required and the easier transfer becomes.

Kolb himself has endorsed a wide range of activities as offering experiential learning, including case studies, computer simulations, the use of video, theatrical techniques, internships (which approximate to teaching practice in initial training), management role-play exercises, and even educational travel (see Lewis, 1986). According to his theory, each lies within the parameters of experiential learning. All experiences are real in the sense that they engage participants in cycles of action and reflection and draw on their past experiences but, where the aim is to train for performance elsewhere, a training experience which is divorced from the job can never be more than a valuable supplement to the vital experience of learning to do the real thing.

An alternative conceptualisation, compatible with the theory of experiential learning, is the notion of the 'reflective practitioner' developed by Schon (1983, 1987). He notes how individuals display competence in the uncertain, unique and complex situations of practice, yet their awareness of how they perform their tasks so skilfully is limited. In taking action they employ knowledge which is primarily tacit and intuitive. Most action is routine but when confronted with problems, they respond in one of two ways. They may either stand back and reflect on their action or 'reflect in action', a largely intuitive process of questioning tacit assumptions that failed to lead to the anticipated results. Such assumptions might include needlessly inhibiting implicit

theories about themselves as learners [. . .]. They then employ other knowledge in experimenting to solve the problem. The theory helps to explain
how Kolb's experiential learning cycle may operate, suggesting that intuitive
reflection in action may take place continually during concrete experience as
well as the reflection on that action entailed in standing back and observing,
conceptualising and planning experimental action.

Yet Schon also stops short of distinguishing between preparatory and
real job experiences. He suggests that initial training for professionals
should include a 'practicum' where problematic situations are tackled [. . .].
Students are encouraged by a coach to think and talk as they work, so
developing their capacity to reflect in action:

> A practicum is a setting designed for the task of learning a practice. In a context
> that approximates a practice world, students learn by doing, although their doing
> usually falls short of real-world work. They learn by undertaking projects that
> simulate and simplify practice; or they take on real-world projects under close
> supervision. The practicum is a virtual world, relatively free of the pressures,
> distractions, and risks of the real one, to which, nevertheless, it refers. It stands in
> an intermediate space between the practice world, the 'lay' world of ordinary life,
> and the esoteric world of the academy.
>
> (Schon, 1987, p. 37)

The 'virtual world' of the practicum is related to the real work situation,
but offers students the opportunity to practise their performance without
having to cope with the full complexity and risks of the job. A practicum
may be designed to approximate more closely to the job situation over time
as students gain in confidence and competence but, even in such a case, it
still offers a qualitatively different experience from the actual job where
mistakes really matter. The question remains over how students learn to
become competent job performers once they emerge from the protected
world of the practicum to undertake 'real-world work' without further
support. Schon's version of a practicum offers a vicarious experience in
that it is designed to simulate the job situation, leaving the beginning
professional with the additional learning task of building on what has been
learned in the practicum in order to become a competent practitioner.

[. . .] Evidence from extensive research and professional experience indicates that the effectiveness of off the job training can be greatly enhanced if
support is given for the integration of what has been learned into job
performance. This is arguably the most important – yet so often neglected –
component of training design.

Training for Transfer of Learning Between Experiences

[. . .] Joyce and Showers (1988) carried out a rigorous study of in-service
training for teachers that suggests how transfer of learning may be promoted. The focus of the training was complex teaching methods, such as

enabling pupils to enhance their critical thinking skills. The researchers identified different components of training and their combinations which led to different outcomes for trainees. [. . .]

A combination of all five training components favours effective integration of new skills or the refinement of existing ones within trainees' repertoire. Presentation of the theory or rationale for a new teaching method raises trainees' awareness and an additional demonstration of the method in use, by such means as a video, gives them the more detailed understanding necessary to perform the skills involved. Opportunities to practise the method in the training setting, possibly through a simulation, enhance skill performance in the training situation itself. Yet there is little transfer of what has been learned into trainees' practice as teachers. The skills may be employed mechanically but are unlikely to be deployed creatively and appropriately. Skills are soon lost as few trainees practise them regularly without provision of further support. When opportunities for constructive, factual feedback are given on trainees' performance while practising the method in the training session there is generally some transfer: new skills are often eventually used in the classroom, they are deployed appropriately for the situation at hand and they are integrated with the existing repertoire.

The additional training component of on the job coaching by colleagues who have also received training is particularly powerful in promoting transfer. Coaching implies that teachers observe each other in the classroom and give mutual feedback to see how far the skills are being practised; they examine how far the use of the teaching strategy is appropriate; and they participate in collaborative problem-solving and action-planning sessions.

The combination of didactic and practical training activities that Joyce and Showers demonstrated to promote the learning of complex teaching skills is congruent with Kolb's experiential learning model. Presentation of theory and demonstration of good teaching according to this rationale give a basis for initial conceptualising and observation while practice, feedback and coaching provide opportunities for experimentation, con-crete experience and reflective observation, using the concepts of the theory. The five components together require at least two experiential learning cycles: one for presentation of theory, demonstration, practice and feedback in the training setting; the other for practice feedback and coaching in the job. Both contexts require reflection in action (as trainees practise off the job or attempt to implement new teaching strategies on the job) and reflection on action (prompted by presentation of theory and demonstration off the job, and provision of feedback and coaching on the job).

[. . .] My experience of management training was entirely off the job, consisting mainly of practice and feedback (in a team with most of whose members I would never have to work again), together with some presenta-tion of theory but little demonstration of good teamwork practice.

Learning and Learning Support for Job Performance

[. . .]

Learning for performance of management tasks (and, by extrapolation, teaching tasks) is conceived as a series of stages, linked to the contribution various forms of learning support can make to the transition from one stage to the next. The key stages of learning and the sequence in which they may occur are summarised on the left-hand side of Figure 14.2. The diagram indicates that the starting point for learning, consistent with experiential learning theories, is the concrete experience of learners' existing performance. A challenge to performance may be followed by several possibilities. Learning may entail some or all of the intermediate stages which lie between the original challenge and development of the ability to integrate new information and skills into skilful performance of teaching and management tasks in the job.

I will take the example of teachers who are required to implement curriculum changes entailed in central government reforms. The challenge to existing performance may be stimulated by official documents or accounts in the media, signalling the required changes. Teachers' awareness may increase further as they are forced to compare their educational beliefs and values with those underpinning the reforms in thinking through how they may respond in a way that they can justify. Greater awareness may lead to the development of a rationale for changes to be made in teachers' existing performance of tasks associated with particular curriculum areas. More specific, practical ideas on how to make changes, by, for example, redesigning curriculum activities and reorganising resources, may follow from the rationale for change. These ideas may lead to practice in making changes by guiding actions to change, resource, teach and assess the curriculum. Improvement in job performance may result from gradual integration of these experimental actions into teachers' approach to the tasks of curriculum development and implementation.

Critical awareness relating to educational and managerial beliefs and values and having a rationale are not a necessary part of job performance itself. The only necessity is to have the know-how to do the job; developing critical awareness and a rationale are not essential for action (hence the bypass arrows in the diagram). In the example, it is plausible for teachers to proceed from a challenge to their existing performance either to the rationale for changes in the curriculum or direct to practical ideas on how to go about making them. Reflection may be confined to monitoring learning how to implement the new practical ideas. Even so, it is surely desirable that teachers are encouraged to consider why they are doing things so that the performance of teaching and management tasks is both informed rather than critically unreflective and justified rather than perceived as merely technical. Raising awareness and justifying action, together with a rationale for change, may be necessary for making informed and justifiable judgements about changes in task performance.

Stages in
learning process

Components of
learning support

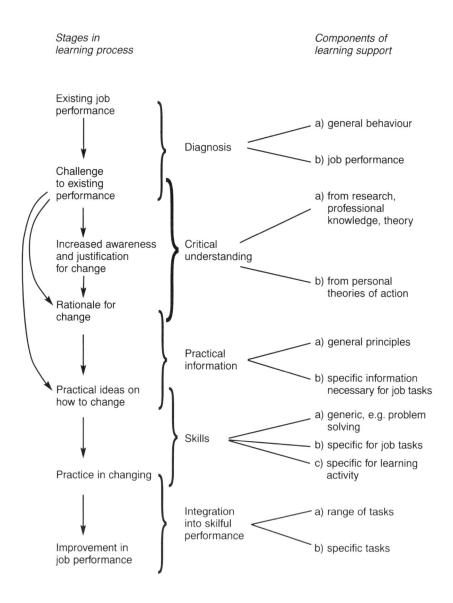

Figure 14.2   *Linking the learning process with learning support*

Similarly, teachers may conceivably have implicit theories about themselves as learners that are entirely supportive of their engagement in learning. Awareness raising is not a necessary condition for performance. Yet it

is important for learning support to facilitate bringing these theories to the surface, since many learners are likely to hold ones that are unnecessarily self-inhibiting. If you don't look you won't find out.

The sequence of stages in the model of learning may be matched with different components of learning support which activities within a training programme may offer. Transition between each stage and the next may be promoted by one, or for most intermediate stages two, components of learning support. These components are subdivided to highlight variation in the type of support they provide.

Some form of diagnosis helps individuals or groups to bring present behaviour into question and identify a need for change. The focus may vary widely from their general behaviour as adults both inside and outside work to very specific aspects of their job performance. This challenge to existing performance may lead to the attempt to develop awareness and to justify proposed changes according to educational and managerial beliefs and values. The development of critical understanding about the job and its wider context is brought about by exploring the beliefs and values that inform learners' actions in the job. Since this process is essentially cognitive, learners may explore the perspective through which they interpret their performance by drawing on a range of concepts and ways of interpreting practical experience. These concepts and perspectives may be more or less abstract and more or less directly linked to the job. They inform the choice of actions and therefore are reflected in but are not a necessary component of job performance itself.

Critical understanding may be promoted by exploring concepts and perspectives from two main sources which are not completely distinct. One source is research, professional knowledge and theory, the stuff of books and educational courses, which constitute a distillation of practical experience interpreted through various concepts. Promoting critical understanding from this source is a powerful means of encouraging learners to question the assumptions of which, as Schon argues, they may otherwise remain largely unaware. The second source is practitioners' personal theories of action, the interpretation of their experience of the performance in question and of being a learner which may, of course, embody concepts and generalisations drawn from research, professional knowledge and theory, often unrigorously.

However, a limitation of reliance on practitioners' personal theories lies in the probability that they may share unquestioned assumptions which go unchallenged. Experiential learning as widely practised makes strong use of personal theories of action but very limited use of sources of abstract conceptualisation originating outside learners' experience, which could profitably embrace considerations to do with their approach to learning.

Increased awareness and the attempt to justify a change in performance leads to the development of a more specific rationale, usually embodying concepts within a perspective reflecting a particular set of educational and managerial beliefs and values. Equally, as discussed earlier, it is possible that a challenge to existing performance may lead directly to a rationale from within the learners existing theory of action or from the perspective offered by a trainer, without a major effort to increase awareness and justify the change through development of critical understanding.

A rationale informing the change to be made links with more specific practical ideas on how to bring about this change in performance. Alternatively, the challenge to existing performance may lead directly to provision of practical ideas which guide the performance. Moving from a rationale for action to specific ideas on the steps to take in making a change may be promoted by the provision of practical information which varies in scope from general principles to detailed, specific information necessary for job tasks.

The transition from thinking about action to practice in making a change in performance, whether in a training institution or in the job, is promoted through support with the learning of skills. The degree of specificity of these skills varies from the generic, especially approaches to problem solving, to those that are specific for job tasks. Additionally, support may be given with developing skills which are specific for the learning activity such as study skills, and those that assist more generically with learning to learn, like using intuition to solve problems.

Finally, support may be given for the process of integration of what has been learned into a skilful performance within the job context. The focus of this support varies from the general, covering the approach to a broad range of tasks, to the particular, referring to specific tasks embodied in the job. [. . .]

Conclusion: Reality Check

The design of training programmes entails selection of learning support activities from a range of possibilities, each of which promotes the transition between particular stages of the learning process. The model encourages designers to ensure that learning support activities cover the transition between all the different stages of learning implied by the aims of the programme. [. . .] In designing training programmes for job performance, the key to successful use of activities which focus on participants' experience is to ensure that support is included for the key transition to improved performance in the job.

Some of the power of the more vicarious experiential learning activities lies in their very unreality. Outdoor experiences can be highly stimulating simply because participants are freed from their everyday world of office or classroom work and are given completely fresh challenges to meet. Simulations can provide a safe environment for modelling aspects of the job situation where risks can be taken without fear of real consequences, and processes that take months in real time can be compressed into minutes or hours. Activities based on vicarious experience clearly have a rightful place in trainers' learning support repertoire, but pride of place must be given to the more mundane but potentially more powerful activities which focus on participants' normal job experience.

So as to make the most of the range of activities which have been given the experiential learning label, it is essential to consider, first, what a programme is intended to achieve. Where anticipated outcomes are diffuse, as in personal development programmes which feature outdoor adventure activities, there is no specific performance target. By contrast, a key aim in training for job performance is to enhance that performance in some way. Second, the various stages in the learning process that participants will have to go through in order to achieve the programme aims should be identified. Third, activities (whether carrying the experiential label or not) should be selected that are likely to facilitate the transition between these stages of learning. Especially important for training programmes is the reality check: ensuring that the final transition into skilful performance in the job is covered! Fourth, consideration should be given to how effective learning strategies may be fostered through these chosen activities.

It seems clear that, in the design of effective training programmes, vicarious experiential learning activities are a more or less valuable luxury; real experiential learning activities which get to the heart of enhancing job performance are not. [. . .]

Note

Some tables and references from the original have been omitted.

References

Bailey, A. (1987) *Support for School Management*, London: Croom Helm.

Bank, J. (1985) *Outdoor Development for Managers*, Aldershot: Gower.

Beeby, M. and Rathborn, S. (1983) 'Development training – using the outdoors in management development'. In *Management Education and Development*, Vol. 14, No. 3, 170–81.

Brown, J. S., Collins, A. and Duguid, R. (1989) 'Situated cognition and the culture of learning'. In *Educational Researcher*, Vol. 18, No. 1, 32–42.

Dennison, B. and Kirk, R. (1990) *Do, Review, Learn, Apply: A Simple Guide to Experiential Learning*, Oxford: Blackwell.

Eraut, M. (1994) *Developing Professional Knowledge and Competence*, London: Falmer Press.

Hobbs, T. (ed.) (1992) *Experiential Training: Practical Guidelines*, London: Tavistock/Routledge.

Joyce, B. and Showers, B. (1988) *Student Achievement through Staff Development*, London: Longman.

Kolb, D. (1984) *Experiential Learning*, London: Prentice Hall.

Lewis, L. (ed.) (1986) *Experiential and Simulation Techniques for Teaching Adults*, London: Jossey-Bass.

Perkins, D. and Salomon, G. (1989) 'Are cognitive skills context-bound?'. In *Educational Researcher*, Vol. 18, No. 1, 16–25.

Schon, D. (1983) *The Reflective Practitioner*, New York: Basic Books.

Schon, D. (1987) *Educating the Reflective Practitioner*, London: Jossey-Bass.

Wutzdorff, A. (1994) Foreword, in M. Keeton (ed.) *Perspectives on Experiential Learning: Prelude to a Global Conversation about Learning*, Chicago: International Experiential Learning Conference Committee.

SECTION 4
LEARNING AND ASSESSMENT
PROCESSES

15

Design of MIST – a System to Help Students Develop Metacognition

Sadhana Puntambekar and Benedict du Boulay

[. . .]

Interest in metacognition in computer-based systems has been relatively recent. As expressed by Dillenbourg, the process of becoming aware of one's own knowledge or one's own cognitive processes, i.e., the reflection process, is a topic of growing interest among researchers on metacognition and among Educational Computing Systems (ECS)[1]. Attempts to help students reflect on and regulate their learning with the help of computer systems have mainly taken three forms: 1) manipulating the interface, 2) collaboration, and 3) reflection – each of these being used as a means to foster understanding. TAPS, Teaching Arithmetic Problem Solving[2–4] and TiPs[5] are designed to help students solve arithmetic word problems. TAPS provides users with a graphical interface with tools for constructing problem trees. Students' problem solving routines are made explicit by constructing such trees and their understanding of the concept is fostered by graphical reification. This enables students to see their solutions so that they are then open to manipulations and discussions. STUDY is designed to promote in learners both a knowledge about the content and knowledge about the cognitive strategies[6]. The system consists of an interface with menus that help students to set goals, choose study methods, etc. The idea is that directing one's own learning will lead to greater participation on the part of the learner thus resulting in enhanced understanding and also better memory. Students can thus take

This chapter has been edited.

an increased initiative in learning. Winne explains the role of STUDY as a means to examine how learners exercise and develop self-regulation in the absence of scaffolding that might be provided by teachers, peers, or advanced technologies[7].

Metacognition in ITSs has taken another interesting form. This is based on the Vygotskian concept that understanding one's own learning is enhanced by interaction with others during learning. There is evidence in the psychological literature that learning with a peer helps one to understand one's own learning. The social context thus supports the individual's learning[8]. Chan and Baskin in their 'Integration Kid' put forth the notion of a computer based learning companion who learns alongside the student[9]. There is thus a trilateral relationship between the teacher, the student, and the companion. The teacher's role is mainly to monitor the situation, i.e., to generate problems, explain with examples, offer comments, and intervene only when the student and the companion both fail to solve the problem. The student and the companion take turns in solving the problems – so that while one is solving, the other is watching, offering suggestions only when needed. Another attempt to have a computer based co-learner is by Dillenbourg who introduces a machine based co-learner[10]. This is based on the concept that mutual regulation leads to an internalization of regulation skills – i.e., it leads to self-regulation.

Collins and Brown suggest the use of reflection to help students develop metacognitive strategies[11]. Students can be shown performance of an expert to enable them to reflect and find their own mistakes. Records of the student's own performance may also help in self-monitoring. In Algebraland and Geometry Tutor, students are shown problem-spaces, i.e., abstractions of the problem solving process. Students are shown the states in the problem solving process that they reached and how they reached them. For example, in Algebraland the program forms a tree of the various steps that the student performs in order to solve the problem. However, as Dillenbourg describes, 'the availability of reflection tools does not guarantee that users do indeed reflect on their learning experiences. We can only claim that the learners reflect if they perform some activities on the representation of their problem solving'[1]. Although the systems mentioned above do recognize the importance of metacognition, they do not explicitly help students to learn about the process involved in learning. It is important that students should be helped to concentrate on their learning, so that they understand the activities they are engaging in, and use this increased understanding across different tasks. Thus, instead of simply making reflection tools available, 'or designing systems that compensate for metacognitive deficiencies by becoming increasingly directive', it is crucial that 'we develop systems that support the learner's metacognitive activities (or, even better, that develop their metacognitive skills)'[1].

This chapter describes MIST (Metacognition In Studying from Texts), a system that deals explicitly with helping students develop metacognition. [. . .]

Design of MIST

Theoretical Framework

During the last decade and a half, there has been an increasing realization of the fact that in order for students to become effective learners, they should be *aware* of the process of learning and take *control* of their learning[12]. Metacognition, or learning 'how to learn', is now recognized as a vital aspect of learning. Metacognition refers to one's knowledge concerning one's cognitive processes and products or anything related to them . . . metacognition refers, among other things, to the active monitoring and consequent regulation and orchestration of these processes in relation to the cognitive objects or data on which they bear, usually in service of some concrete goal or objective[13]. Brown recognizes two important aspects of metacognition – knowledge about cognition and regulation of cognition[12]. The first, *awareness* or knowledge about cognition, is the knowledge learners have about their own cognitive resources, themselves as learners and about the learning tasks. The second, *control* or regulation of cognition, consists of active regulation skills such as goal setting, planning one's next move, checking, evaluating, and modifying. Brown emphasizes that the goal of instruction should be to enhance students' conceptual understanding of the processes that they employ during learning, to help them to monitor and regulate these processes, thereby producing more insightful and intentional learners[14]. According to Brown, a great deal of academic learning, though not everyday learning is active, strategic, self-conscious, self-motivated, and purposeful. Hence learners operate best when they have insight into their own strengths and weaknesses and access to their own repertoires of strategies for learning[15].

The research described here concentrates on metacognition in one important area of learning, that of studying from texts for reasons given below. Studying from texts is a complex process. According to Fischer and Mandl, the requirements demanded of a learner while studying from texts are quite severe[16]. This is because the major goals of learning from texts are to work out the core information contained in the texts, to reduce it to its main ideas, to comprehend it, and to integrate it with the learners' existing body of prior knowledge. In addition to this, learners should be able to retrieve the knowledge quickly and without effort at the right time and place. It is thus a very demanding task and it is not surprising therefore, that so many high school, college, and even university students report learning difficulties.

Early work on metacognition has been in the area of studying from texts and Brown, Bransford, Ferrera, and Campione's tetrahedral model for studying from texts (adapted from Jenkins' model) has been the main theoretical basis of this research[17]. This model describes learning from texts as an interaction of four factors – text, task, skills, and the learner herself. According to Brown, Armbruster, and Baker, learners can be made aware of such features of the text as text difficulty, relative importance of the various propositions in a text, and the inherent structure of the text[18]. Students are faced with different types of tasks in an academic setting and it is thus important for them to consider the task, i.e., the purpose for which they are reading a particular text, and allocate resources accordingly. Thus, a student reading to find specific information would have a different strategy for learning than one who is reading to get all the details. In addition to the text and task, the learner herself is an important factor affecting metacognition. The learner's own past knowledge, strengths and weaknesses, skills, etc. is an important aspect of learning. Activation of prior knowledge helps to improve learning by helping the learner associate the present learning with something she/he already knows. The final factor that contributes to metacognition is the knowledge about study strategies. In order that students use the strategies that they learn during training, students should also be told about when and why a particular skill should be used in addition to knowledge about how to apply a skill.

Main Features of MIST

Process based interface

The main focus in the design of MIST has been to understand what students actually do during learning from texts and to provide methods to help them become more self-aware while they are engaged in the activity. Thus the processes or activities of the learner have been more important than the product or performance measure which is a result of that doing. According to Brown, in order to train students to think about what they are doing, they should be taught to ask themselves 1) Stop and think, 2) Do I know what to do, 3) Is there anything more I need to know before I begin, and 4) Is there anything that I already know that will help me[19]. Students can be taught to think by making them interrogate themselves. However, students need to be prompted in order that they remember to interrogate themselves. Hence it is important to have an on-line monitor that keeps track of the students' processes. What is required is a mechanism for 'eliciting' self-awareness and -control. This can be achieved by manipulating the students' learning environment in a way that gradually 'engineers' the development of metacognition. Students should therefore be prompted in such a way that they will be forced to stop and think and regulation will 'evolve' as a result of the interaction. [. . .]

MIST's interface and interactions with the students are based on the processes that a student might engage in during learning. Such an interface is based on the assumption that 'making covert, abstract processes visible, public, and manipulable, would serve as a necessary catalyst for reflective metacognitive activity'[4]. Thus the interface is based on the activities that the students would undertake during learning and students can choose from a range of activities. To build a system that will help students to learn effective strategies in the context of their academic goals was one of the prime concerns of this research. Researchers such as Derry and Murphy[20], Duffy and Roehler[21], and Garner[22] emphasize that in order for students to use the skills with understanding and also subsequently to use the skills in novel learning situations, it is important that students be taught the skills in context. Psychologists have differentiated between embedded and detached training. By embedded is meant that students are taught the skills within their current academic context. A detached approach is that in which strategies are not clearly related to such a context. It is generally believed that students should be taught skills within a meaningful context.

[. . .] MIST was designed in such a way that students can come to it with any text from which they wish to learn and use it as an 'advisor' to help them learn 'how to learn'. One of the greatest advantages of this system is that, since the system depends on, and is seen (by the students) to depend on the students' judgment about the type of text, choice of skill, about what to do next, at every point in the process of learning, the system induces the student to think and then proceed. Thus, in a way, the system allows the metacognitive knowledge to evolve as a result of experiences that the student acquires during learning. If the students' judgment of text is wrong and hence the resulting choice of skill is wrong, the student will realize this on her own with the system helping her to think about alternative ways. This kind of interaction will thus be helpful in developing the thinking skills that will assist the learners to monitor the process of learning. Another major advantage of this system is its applicability. It can be applied to any text which the student brings and this increases the possibility that the student will relate the knowledge gained by the interaction to real life learning. Relating knowledge of strategies to their current academic goals will increase the possibility that students will generalize the skills to learning beyond the training situation.

It may be noted that although MIST does not have any specific knowledge about the texts that students wish to study from, it nevertheless has knowledge about the types of activities that students might engage in during learning from texts. Thus, interactions with students are based on the activities that students undertake during learning rather than on the subject domain that they are learning. It may therefore be said that MIST has knowledge about metacognition (control and regulation of cognition) rather than the specific subject domain, as explained in the next section. The system's interface is based on the metaknowledge about the process of studying from texts, the activities that students undertake during learning. The first part of the system helps students become aware of the various cognitive skills that can be used, where, when, and how they should be used, and how they should pay attention to the different types of tasks and texts and activate any prior knowledge that they may have. In the second part of the system, students can choose options relating to planning, text processing or reading, and memory enhancing (organizing information). Students can engage in specific planning and monitoring activities. For example, students can plan and set goals, activate prior knowledge, set study time and plan the methods or skills that they will use. During text processing, students can engage in activities such as selecting main ideas, reviewing, and summarizing. They can engage in various organizing skills such as making trees, tables, nets, and also predict the types of questions that can be asked. By choosing the options, students are asking themselves questions which make them think about the activity of learning. Because it has knowledge about metacognition and not the specific subject domain, rather than providing feedback at the domain level, intervention by the system is at the meta level and is intended to help students think about what they are doing and why they are doing it.

MIST has been built as a two part system based on the two aspects of metacognition-awareness and control[12] [. . .] In order for a system to help students learn about learning or studying from texts, the first thing is to make students aware of the various factors affecting regulation, i.e., knowledge about the task, text, learner, and study strategies. Awareness training being the first prerequisite of metacognition, the system's first important task is to impart knowledge regarding the different factors affecting metacognition. The first part of MIST is a non-interactive browser which helps students become aware of the four factors affecting metacognition in studying from texts. The browser is simply a network of screens implemented in Supercard. It has buttons for navigation but does not react to the student as an individual. There are three major topics in the Browser: 1) planning, 2) general skills, and 3) specific skills. Under planning is included knowledge about features of the text, the types of tasks (purpose of studying), and activating one's prior knowledge. Students are given information about the types of tasks that they could face (for example, studying for a gist or studying for details) and are also informed about the different nature of these tasks. They are informed about aspects of the text and are made aware of the fact that they should pay attention to the typographical cues of the text. They are also informed about how certain skills are more appropriate to certain texts – for example if the text compares attributes of different objects, then drawing a two-dimensional table would be an appropriate skill. [. . .]

The Browser also advises students to think actively about any prior knowledge that they may have about the text. General skills include skills such as skimming, finding main ideas, and underlining that can be applied to any text. Specific skills are more specialized skills such as making trees, semantic nets, writing a paraphrase, and making tables. Each skill is presented with examples. There are 'example' cards attached to each skill which provide students with examples for the skill. The example cards also show the text that the skill has been applied to. Students can thus read about the different skills and the examples of that skill.

The interactive part of the system consists of a network of cards that are driven by the students' responses. The cards are grouped into three main topics – planning, reading, and post reading. During each of the stages the students choose options depending on the activities that they want to engage in. In the planning and the reading stages, the students' interaction is limited to clicking on the various activities on the screen. Students take turns to click on the options. Each student in the pair gets her own set of cards which are color coded for that student. However, during the post reading stage, students can work together on the computer screen to make trees, tables, nets, and outlines. The drawing tools provided by MIST are designed to help students draw lines, rectangles, circles, and write words or phrases. Students can also move the figures drawn by them or get rid of them. [. . .] Apart from trying to make the invisible processes 'visible,' MIST also attempts to structure the students' learning by helping them proceed through the stages and provides feedback based on their activities. During the planning stage, MIST offers students menus to:

- set a goal or purpose
- classify the text according to its features
- allocate study time based on the text and task
- think about and decide what methods will be appropriate for the current purpose
- think about any prior knowledge about the text

By setting goals, thinking about the text and activating any prior knowledge, students are helped to become active participants in the learning. They are forced to think about what they want to do and how they want to do it. The two students take turns to choose the options during the planning stage. While one of them is making the choices, the other student is asked to observe. During the reading stage, students can choose from options such as:

- Read text
- Identify important points
- Summarize
- Review text

During this stage students actually read the text, find main ideas, review text, reread, etc. The work is done outside the computer and the system helps the students to work together by keeping a record of their choices and initiating interactions between them. The post reading stage offers students tools to construct trees, maps, nets, etc. Students can:

- Write a paraphrase/outline[23]
- Make two dimensional tables[24]
- Make trees/spider diagrams (used by many school students)
- Make semantic nets[25]
- Predict questions[8]

These activities are aimed at helping the students to organize their knowledge and are based on research on learning strategies as indicated above. Students can choose from the different skills and they can work together to make the trees, nets, etc. on the computer screen. When students choose a particular skill, a 'floating palette' window with tools appears along with another window with a blank card where the students can draw. During this stage, students work together with one of them in charge of the mouse. After they have finished with a skill such as drawing a tree or a table, they are asked whether they think they have used the appropriate skill and whether they have included all the main points. This is to encourage them to think about what they have done and to give them an opportunity to change it if they wish. The figures drawn by each student are written in a file. Another option provided by the system in the post reading stage is 'predict questions'. Students can predict the questions that may be asked in a test. Predicting questions is done in two stages. First of all, they think about the *types* of questions – for example, they can predict whether they will be asked to write a short answer, a comparison, critique, or any other type. They then proceed to write the specific questions that may be asked. This is in some ways similar to the predicting in reciprocal teaching[8]. However, students using MIST also have the chance to think about the types of questions thus forcing them to think hard about the content of the text. Once again, the types of questions are recorded and the questions that students write down are written to a file. During this stage, students can also choose the 'Revise' option to revise from their notes or from the textbook itself.

Collaboration

Another important feature of MIST is that students learn in pairs with support from the system. The importance of the social context in supporting an individual's understanding of her own learning (i.e., metacognition) was emphasized by Brown and Palincsar[8]. In recent years there has been a considerable rise in interest among designers of computer systems in exploring computer support for collaborative learning. There have been different levels and ways of using computers for collaboration. [. . .] Consequently there are systems that support human-computer collaboration[9, 10], and systems that support human-human collaboration with a computer[26]. Implicit in the numerous attempts at computer supported collaborative learning is the notion of providing more opportunities for reflection and understanding while learning. One of the main aims of the research described here has been to explore, in a more direct way, the use of collaboration to foster metacognitive understanding among pairs of students interacting with the computer system. MIST is built in such a way that students learn together, with the system providing support, until they acquire proficiency and become independent learners. Both the students interact with the menus on the screen. They learn together, cooperating with and helping each other. The system intervenes in such a way that the interest and motivation of each of them is maintained while helping them learn self-regulation skills. MIST's inability to comment on the specifics of the text is thus to a large extent compensated by having students interact with it in pairs. Student can help each other in choosing options such as classifying the text, choosing and applying skills. Thus, in a way, by helping each other they also help the system. In most collaborative learning situations, with or without the computer, students are just asked to learn together. It is considered natural for the more able students to help the less able. The guidelines that initiate the social interaction are not very specific. The spontaneous social process is allowed to take over. Although this is the most natural way in which students can learn together, Teasley and Roschelle point out that 'the process of collaborative learning is not homogeneous or predictable, and does not occur necessarily by putting students together . . . collaboration does not happen because students are co-present'[27].

MIST keeps a record of the activities undertaken by both the learners (though it has no independent means of checking that what has been chosen is actually carried out) and uses this as a basis to *initiate* interaction between the learners by asking them specifically to help each other. Depending upon the progress of the learners it advises either one to help the other. As indicated earlier, having students learn together does not necessarily result in them collaborating with each other. Slavin explains the 'free rider' effect in which some of the group members do all or most of the work while the others go for a free ride[28]. There is always the fear that the more able or dominant members will override the less able in social learning situations. MIST tries to reduce this problem by providing explicit instructions about how the students should help each other. More specifically, it instructs the students to either *clarify* or *explain* what they understand by the options on the screen. As has been emphasized by Guzdial, Konneman, Walton, Hohmann, and Soloway, self-explanations help students to understand the process[29]. MIST encourages the students to explain to each other during learning. For example, if both the participants S1 and S2 have finished with planning then MIST evaluates their performance. If evaluation indicates that S1 has chosen more planning activities and has shown more metacognitive understanding and S2 has not (and vice versa) then after first allowing S2 to read S1's performance summary it asks S2 to clarify what she thinks about the options presented on the screen. If S2 asks for help, then MIST asks S1 to explain first. In this way the system initiates social interactions between the pairs of learners. In the empirical work conducted, friendship pairs were used as the basis of pairing as described in the next section.

Reflection
At the end of each stage, MIST displays a summary of the students' performance (the choices that they made during learning) and asks them to check whether they want to choose any more options or change any of the options that they have already chosen. At the beginning of every session (after the first session), students are asked to recall what activities they have already engaged in. A summary of the students' choices from all the

former sessions is then presented and students are encouraged to think about their learning activities.

Apart from these, students can also review their progress during the sessions as described below. MIST allows the student to review her own progress by choosing the review progress option. At any time during learning, students can ask for a summary of their metacognitive performance. When this option is chosen, the summary is presented along with helpful questions. The system tells students about the learning activities that they chose. It then questions them to help them think whether the activities have been appropriate. Students are then advised to think about what they want to do next. If a student does not ask for a summary for a considerable period of time, the system will automatically present a summary and question the student about it. Reflection is thus combined with the more active strategy of questioning. MIST tries to encourage students to think about what they have been doing and what they want to do, thereby helping them to think about the process of learning. Apart from reviewing their own progress which can be undertaken while students are engaged in any of the stages of learning, MIST also offers the students a chance to review each other's progress. This is provided at the end of every stage before the system itself evaluates the students' performance. The system provides the student with a summary of their partner's performance and asks them to comment on it. It then provides its own evaluation of the summary. Students can thus think about the processes used by their partner. Commenting on these should help them both understand the activities better. It is, however, not possible for the system to evaluate what they say to each other, but students can compare their own evaluations with those of the system's.

[. . .]

Conclusion

MIST is one of the first attempts at building a system totally based on the processes or the learning activities of students and not on the subject domain that they are learning. It dealt explicitly with helping students learn 'how to learn'. Feedback in MIST is based on the learning activities of students, i.e., on the processes that they used. The system is designed to help students develop a systematic approach to learning from texts and supports a range of planning and monitoring activities. As it is based explicitly on the activities that students may use, the system externalizes the processes that would otherwise have been covert. By providing menus based on the process, the processes that would otherwise have been tacit are made visible so that they could be open for instruction. An important aspect of MIST is that the system did not have any subject domain representation and helped students to concentrate on the process by enabling them to study from texts that were relevant to their academic goals. In an evaluation of MIST, it was found that on the whole, the low ability students had a lot of difficulty understanding the planning options. They needed more explanation in understanding the options as well as applying them to different tasks. It was therefore concluded that the interface should be more interactive and low ability students should be helped to think about the planning options, possibly with the help of questioning about each of their choices. Another aspect that was found was that the high ability students used the interface more 'actively' – i.e., they used the planning options to elicit prior knowledge, they were more attentive toward features of the text such as diagrams, and they engaged in active self-testing and also tested each other. Students of low ability, on the other hand, used the options more rigidly and provided answers in monosyllables most of the time. These important differences could be used to improve instruction in metacognition by provoking more instances of active learning in lower ability students. Students of high ability discussed their learning extensively during the training. On the contrary, low ability students did not converse very much. Thus the system was more successful in provoking conversations and interactions in the high ability students than in the low ability ones. This aspect is important to bear in mind while designing interventions. It may be that if the low ability students had more time with the system they would have been more active learners. MIST used collaboration and reflection to facilitate learning. It was found that high ability pairs engaged in more conversation and used more self and other testing. Low ability pairs, on the other hand, did not comment much on the performance of their peers. These findings could be used to build systems that help in collaboration by providing explicit instructions about how the students should interact with each other. Similarly, more opportunities for peer review should be provided. Based on these findings MIST could be improved so that it will be beneficial to low ability students as well.

Notes

1. Ability was judged by teacher ratings and scores on the Learning and Study Strategy Inventory (LASSI).
2. Abridged, this excerpt focuses on the design of MIST. The original article included an empirical evaluation of the system.

Acknowledgments

We thank A. Hopkins and the students of St. Bedes school in Redhill for their cooperation in carrying out the empirical work.

References

1. P. Dillenbourg, The Computer as a Constructorium: Tools for Observing One's Own Learning, in *Knowledge Negotiation*, R. Moyse and M. T. Elsom-Cook (eds.), Academic Press, London, 1992.
2. S. J. Derry and L. W. Hawkes, Local Cognitive Modelling of Problem Solving Behavior: An Application of Fuzzy Theory, in *Computers as Cognitive Tools*, S. P. Lajoie and S. J. Derry (eds.), Erlbaum, Hillsdale, New Jersey, 1993.
3. S. Derry, K. Tookey, and B. Roth, The Effect of Collaborative Interaction and Computer Tool Use on the Problem-Solving Processes of Lower Ability Students, *AERA Presentation*, Atlanta, Georgia, 1993.
4. S. Derry, K. Tookey, and A. Chiffy, *A Microanalysis of Pair Problem Solving with and without a Computer Tool*, paper presented at the Annual Meeting of the American Educational Research Association, New Orleans, Louisiana, 1994.
5. K. R. Tookey and S. Derry, *Arithmetic Schema and Strategy Instruction: A Study of Two Problem Solving Training Approaches*, presented at the annual meeting of the American Educational Research Association, San Francisco, California, 1996.
6. P. H. Winne, *The Study System*, personal communication, 1991.
7. P. H. Winne, Inherent Details in Self-Regulated Learning, *Educational Psychologist*, 30, pp. 173–187, 1995.
8. A. L. Browne and A. S. Palincsar, Reciprocal Teaching of Comprehension Strategies: A Natural History of One Program for Enhancing Learning, in *Intelligence and Exceptionality: New Directions for Theory, Assessment, and Instructional Practice*, J. D. Day and J. G. Borkowski (eds.), Ablex, Norwood, New Jersey, 1978.
9. T. Chan and A. Baskin, *Studying with the Prince*, in proceedings of the conference on Intelligent Tutoring Systems, Montreal, Canada, 1988.
10. P. Dillenbourg, *Human-Computer Collaborative Learning*, unpublished doctoral dissertation, University of Lancaster, 1991.
11. A. Collins and J. Brown, The Computer as a Tool for Learning through Reflection, in *Learning Issues for Intelligent Tutoring Systems*, H. Mandl and A. Lesgold (eds.), Springer-Verlag, New York, 1988.
12. A. L. Brown, Metacognition: The Development of Selective Attention Strategies for Learning from Texts, in *Directions in Reading: Research and Instruction*, M. Kamil (ed.), The National Reading Conference, Washington, D.C., 1981.
13. J. Flavell, Metacognitive Aspects of Problem Solving, in *The Nature of Intelligence*, L. Resnick (ed.), Erlbaum, Hillsdale, New Jersey, 1976.
14. A. L. Brown, Motivation to Learn and Understand: On Taking Charge of One's Own Learning, *Cognition and Instruction*, 5(4), pp. 311–322, 1988.
15. A. L. Brown, The Advancement of Learning, *Educational Researcher*, 23(8), pp. 4–12, 1994.
16. P. M. Fischer and H. Mandl. Learner, Text Variables, and the Control of Text Comprehension and Recall, in *Learning and Comprehension of Texts*, H. Mandl, N. Stein, and T. Trabasso (eds.), Erlbaum, Hillsdale, New Jersey, 1984.
17. A. L. Brown, J. Bransford, R. Ferrera, and J. Campione, Learning, Remembering and Understanding, in *Handbook of Child Psychology* (4th Edition), Cognitive Development, Vol. 3, J. H. Flavell and E. M. Markman (eds.), Wiley, New York, 1983.
18. A. L. Brown, B. B. Armbruster, and L. Baker, The Role of Metacognition in Reading and Studying, in *Reading Comprehension: From Research to Practice*, J. Orasanu (ed.), Erlbaum, Hillsdale, New Jersey, 1985.
19. A. L. Brown, Knowing When, Where and How to Remember: A Problem of Metacognition, in *Advances in Instructional Psychology*, R. Glaser (ed.), Erlbaum, Hillsdale, New Jersey, 1978.

20. S. Derry and D. Murphy, Designing Systems that Train Learning Ability: From Theory to Practice, *Review of Educational Research*, 56(1), pp. 1–39, 1986.
21. G. G. Duffy and L. R. Roehler, Teaching Reading Skills as Strategies, *Reading Teacher*, 41, pp. 414–418, 1987.
22. R. Garner, *Metacognition and Reading Comprehension*, Ablex, Norwood, New Jersey, 1987.
23. B. Taylor and R. Beach, The Effects of Text Structure Instruction on Middle Grade Students' Comprehension and Production of Expository Text, *Reading Research Quarterly*, 19, pp. 134–146, 1984.
24. B. Jones, M. Amiran, and M. Katims, Teaching Cognitive Strategies and Text Structures within Language Arts Programs, in *Thinking and Learning Skills, Vol. 1, Relating Instruction to Research*, J. Segal, S. Chipman, and R. Glaser (eds.), Erlbaum, Hillsdale, New Jersey, 1985.
25. D. Dansereau, Learning Strategy Research, in *Thinking and Learning Skills, Volume 1, Relating Instruction to Research*, J. W. Segal, S. F. Chipman, and R. Glaser (eds.), Erlbaum, Hillsdale, New Jersey, 1985.
26. C. O'Malley, Designing Computer Systems to Support Peer Learning, *European Journal of Psychology of Education*, 7(4), pp. 339–352, 1992.
27. S. D. Teasley and J. Roschelle, Constructing a Joint Problem Space: The Computer as a Tool for Sharing Knowledge, in *Computers as Cognitive Tools*, S. P. Lajoie and S. J. Derry (eds.), Erlbaum, Hillsdale, New Jersey, 1993.
28. R. E. Slavin, *Cooperative Learning: Theory Research and Practice*, Prentice-Hall, Englewood Cliffs, New Jersey, 1991.
29. M. Guzdial, M. Konneman, C. Walton, L. Hohmann, and E. Soloway, Layering Scaffolding and CAD on an Integrated Workbench: An Effective Design Approach for Project-Based Learning Support, *Interactive Learning Environments*, in press.

16

Supporting Collaborative Learning: a Gender Dimension

Patricia Murphy[1]

Introduction

A range of theoretical views including constructivist, social constructivist and socio-cultural views of learning all place emphasis on the role of classroom discourse in students' learning. As part of this emphasis collaboration between peers involving 'collective reflection', a construct defined by Cobb and colleagues (1997) as 'the joint or communal activity of making what was previously done in action an object of reflection' (p. 1258) has also been identified as a valuable learning mechanism. In the chapter a socio-cultural view of learning is advanced which recognizes that both the process and the products of learning are social. The social and cultural bases of students' experiences situate them in different ways in relation to activities. Consequently gender is a significant dimension in any analysis of classroom discourse practices. The discourse students engage in during collaborative action progresses thinking and is central to the process of knowledge construction as it is the means by which ideas are shared and assessed, feedback is received and interpreted and joint decisions taken.

Discourse in science and Design and Technology (D&T) activity goes beyond talk to include the interactions with the physical context which includes the tools – actual and representational – of the domain and the objects and materials available in the activity. The discourse is influenced by these various sources of feedback available to students. Different representations, e.g. graphical, verbal and physical, each provide different opportunities and support for collaboration between students. This chapter explores the opportunities for teacher-supported collaboration between students afforded by the investigative context of science and the problem-solving context of Design and Technology (D&T). The impact of gendered learning outside of school on students' engagement in collaborative setting is also considered. The emphasis in the chapter is on the role of planning in learning, how collaboration plays a critical and explicit part in it, and how girls and boys differ in their approach to it. Planning is seen as a dynamic process, not merely of reaching goals through carrying out planned actions, but one of forming goals which may emerge or be modified during the course of an activity (Leont'ev, 1981).

258

Background

It is important to maintain a distinction between the notions of learning to collaborate versus learning through collaboration. Collaboration skills are essential for cognitive development through collaboration so the two notions are necessarily linked. There is, however, limited appreciation that specific skills for collaboration need to be fostered *in the context of activity*. Fostering learning through collaboration requires continuous teacher support which also presumes that teachers are aware of what support is needed and what the barriers to collaboration may be. It also requires teachers to pay attention to the nature of the task that evolves between groups of students. Here a task is seen as a 'strategic fiction' that emerges through interaction (Newman *et al.*, 1989). Any task situation is inherently dialectical hence the individuals who collaborate will have a major influence on what is perceived to be the group task.

Rogoff (1990) has argued that interaction with more skilled others assists children in their development by guiding their participation in activities, helping them adapt their understanding to new situations, structuring their problem solving attempts, and motivating them to take responsibility for managing problem solving (p. 191).

> Participation involves creative efforts to understand and contribute to social activity, which by its very nature involves bridging between several ways of understanding a situation
>
> (Rogoff, 1995, p. 153)

Participants have to amend their perspectives to reach an understanding of others in a joint activity. A first stage in collaboration is the identification and sharing of common reference points and models. Hence, the shared thought process is the critical element in collaboration (Azmitia, 1988). Rogoff's recent review of research (1997) shows that adults and peers are not necessarily in positions of authority and equal status respectively; other factors apart from age are also relevant, for example relative expertise, social status within a group, or interest in controlling the activity. She concludes that

> children's participation in sociocultural activities is complexly and multidimensionally structured, with important contributions from individuals, their social partners of varying status and expertise, and of the cultural/historical activities in which they participate and which they contribute to shaping further
>
> (Rogoff, 1997, p. 40)

Truly collaborative interactions between students involve examination of the strengths and weakness of multiple ideas considered from multiple perspectives. Learning occurs as each group member's perspective is analysed, inferior ideas are rejected and superior views proposed and accepted (Kruger, 1993). Collaborative learning therefore, relies on students engaging with each other's thinking. In order to collaborate, students have to be able to share what they consider salient. To achieve this, they need to perceive a common goal in activities. This is a crucial feature of the '*share-ability*' of tasks.

Establishing collaborative learning situations that allow multiple view-points to be posed and considered depends in part on fostering autonomy in learning (Murphy and Spence, 1996). One reason for this is that students engage in more open, extended discussion and exploration of alternative meanings when allowed to construct and reformulate tasks for themselves. It is in the reformulation of tasks that students' alternative perceptions of purpose and salience are evidenced. It is also the process by which students become emotionally and intellectually committed and hence, engaged in tasks, the meaning of which they have established for themselves (Lave, 1992). Research into gender differences in performance has highlighted how gendered learning influences students' engagement in tasks and the sense they make of them.

The different socialization processes experienced by girls and boys from birth have been well documented (Wilder, 1996). Parental and societal expectations influence the activities, pastimes and interests that young children pursue. Consequently from an early age there is evidence of a divergence in children's interests and associated achievements, a divergence that continues with age (see Murphy and Elwood, 1998). The Browne and Ross (1991) study of pre-school children identified the different activities that girls and boys choose to engage with. Girls' activities were labelled as *creative*, boys' as *constructional* (p. 42). Furthermore, pupils continued to make these gendered choices in school even when ostensibly engaging in the same activity, i.e. playing with construction kits. In a study by Murphy (1997) attention was drawn to gender differences in pre-school children's role play. Girls' roles were related to family and mothering, boys' to super heroes and authority figures. It was noted that the roles and activities that children engaged with focused their attention on different aspects of their environment so that from a very early age children are paying attention to different details and developing different views of salience.

The research of the national surveys of the Assessment of Performance Unit (APU) in science and Design and Technology in the UK established that when asked to observe phenomena or respond to activities girls as a group and boys as a group paid attention to different details given the same circumstances. Girls more than boys in science took note of colours, sounds, smells and textures. Boys, on the other hand, took note of structural details. In D&T girls again focused on aesthetic variables and em-pathized with users' needs. Boys more than girls focused on manufacturing issues (Kimbell *et al.*, 1991). Given these differences it is to be expected that in learning situations where the locus of control resides with the students, as in collaborative situations, then their different commitments will influence the tasks they perceive and the value they accord them.

Children's gendered role play not only engages them with the environment in different ways but also provides different opportunities for developing language. The kind and amount of talk varies with the role children typically engage in. A mother-child discussion, typical of girls' play, is very different to that of an exchange in typical boys' play between, for example a Power Ranger, a once fashionable superhero, and a 'bad guy'. Research into pre-school children's talk has revealed significant gender differences in girls' and boys' style of communication (Thompson, 1994). These differences in communication have been shown to continue through schooling and are found in students' written as well as oral communication. Girls' tendency to work collaboratively and in discussion with others was also noted in the UK surveys of Design and Technology (Kimbell *et al.*, 1991, p. 126). Girls were observed displaying 'an ability to take on a wide range of issues in discussion' and acting as facilitators to the boys' ideas 'being able to give them lots of support and to point out the strengths and weaknesses of their ideas'.

Earlier it has been argued that discourse practices include far more than talk nevertheless effective classroom talk is an essential component of collective reflection. There is much research into the nature of effective classroom talk. Mercer (1995, p. 98) summarizes the kind of effective classroom talk in relation to collaboration. He describes it as talk in which partners *share information* and *plan* together, *presenting ideas explicitly* and clearly enough to engage in *joint reasoning, evaluation* and *decision making*. The students may *evaluate* proposed ideas or possible courses of action, *challenging* each other and *offering alternatives*, or make *requests for clarification*. These communication activities are inherent in Mercer's analytic category of *exploratory talk*, in which partners engage critically but constructively; their reasoning is explicit and interactive and knowledge is made publicly accountable (Mercer, 1995, p. 104). Elaborating briefly, *exploratory talk* visibly aims to achieve 'consensus' – shared reference in the terms used in the chapter – through both conflict and the open sharing of ideas; it's ground rules require that the views of all participants are considered, that proposals are explicitly stated and evaluated, and that explicit agreement precedes decisions and action.

Planning in science and D&T also takes place through writing, sketching and action. Talking about the outcomes of these is part of the dynamic process of collaborative planning. In Design and Technology in both primary and secondary schools it is common for students to work on individual products albeit organized in groups around tables. This emphasis on individual products limits the potential for collaboration. Collaborative activity ought, properly to be embedded in situations where students work towards shared goals. Nevertheless the potential of D&T as an environment for collaborative problem solving is considerable (Hennessy and Murphy, in press). Science in primary schools in contrast is typically organized in groups where students work on shared activities. For example children as a group will through work on a topic such as 'water' formulate an investigation that they want to pursue. As a group they then plan and enact a procedural strategy until they achieve a solution that as a group they accept. The extent to which this organization leads to collaboration has been questioned by research (Galton and Williamson, 1992).

The Data

This chapter draws on case study data from primary science classrooms and D&T workshops to consider girls' and boys' views of, and approaches to, working together. In making reference to girls and boys as groups it is assumed that the differences observed will vary within groups. This assumption acknowledges both the diversity of individuals and the concept of 'agency' in any learning situation.

The data come from two case study projects in England. The first case study looked at Problem Solving in Design and Technology Education (UK Economic and Social Research Council Grant Number R000 234458). In this project all the technological activities during a term's D&T project undertaken by groups of students in eight classrooms were captured using video- and audio-recording. The students were between 11–14 years of age. The second project examined teachers' approaches to investigative science in primary classrooms and the circumstances that support or inhibit collaboration. Again, target groups of students were audio- and video-recorded in four classrooms over several months as they undertook their normal work in science. The children in this project were 8–10 years of age. Further evidence about students' views of group work were obtained by questionnaires. These were administered to the classes of the target students but also more widely to cover primary children aged from 6–12 years old. Five cases are considered from across the projects.

Girls Collaborating – Boys Working Alone

Collaboration Unplanned

The first scenario is taken from a case study of 12–13 year olds who were designing a moisture detector. The target students included two boys, Peter and Simon, and two girls, Anna and Nancy. The project was a typical D&T one involving the students in making a product of their own over a period of many weeks. The teacher posed the problem to the class *to find a way of using [the] circuit (the moisture sensor) in a useful and meaningful way*. The contexts of use were defined by the functions selected by the teacher. These included a pot plant moisture sensor, a washing line rain alarm, and a bath water level alarm. The teacher provided students at various points with information worksheets to support their thinking. He also provided demonstrations of drawing techniques and cutting techniques to support students as they designed and made a container for their circuit *appropriate to its use*. In both worksheets and the demonstrations the teacher focused on a box-shaped container with straight lines. The only creative challenge he included was to show the class how to draw a box with a sloping front. The focus on box shapes conflicted with the teacher's own instructions to students that their designs be meaningful in the context of use.

The designing activity began with the two boys Peter and Simon on a bench with one other boy, the two target girls were seated at an adjacent table with one other girl. The boys worked in silence and alone drawing their designs. The girls, Anna and Nancy, on the other hand, sat close to each other and began by talking together. The design Peter chose was determined by the teacher's non-verbal cues. Hence Peter produced a box shape with a sloping front within the time and resource constraints of the workshop. He worked independently throughout and was praised for his behaviour and product by the teacher even though it did not meet the criterion of 'meaningfulness'. Simon tried to do an interesting design but one that bore no relationship to the function of the moisture detector and one that remained a box shape with straight edges albeit a hexagonal shape. Simon was uncertain how to produce a hexagonal design but felt unable to either approach his peers or his teacher for help. His diffidence reflected his view that it was inappropriate to be seen to be seeking help. He sought support from his peers in preference to the teacher and he did so when they had completed their own tasks. Consequently Simon spent a lot of time inactive and waiting.

The girls' immediate response to the requirement for their design to be meaningful was to identify a 'client' for their product. Anna was designing a bath alarm for her grandmother, Nancy a rain detector for a washing line for her mother. The different agendas of girls and boys in D&T given the same activity has been established by other research (Harding, 1996). Although the girls were designing different products they had sufficient shared understanding of what a meaningful design meant that they were able to collaborate in the early stages of the project. In their talk at the beginning of the session they brainstormed various interpretations of 'meaningfulness' appropriate to the context of use. Anna suggested designing a package in the shape of a bottle of shampoo for her bath alarm and began to sketch her ideas for the others to consider.

Nancy: That looks quite good actually. What about something in the bath? Something to do with water.
Other girl: Yeah.
Nancy: Cause it can go in the sink as well as in the bath. You could do it in the shape of a soap, you could have it in the shape of a sponge, or in the shape of a bubble, the shape of a, no not a tap.
Other girl: A drop thing.
Nancy: Teardrop.
Other girl: A drop of water.

Here the girls are offering alternatives and elaborating each other's ideas. Nancy began to sketch the teardrop idea to make it explicit for Anna. Presenting ideas explicitly was a characteristic of effective discourse identified by Mercer referred to earlier. The girls used the tools of the domain here even though no guidance was given to them by the teacher to do so. The girls' ability to make explicit their ideas enabled Anna to reflect on the potential of the design ideas offered, i.e. to engage in joint reasoning and evaluation. For example she rejected Nancy's suggestion of a toothbrush shaped package visualizing the circuit and its function within the whole design with the words 'don't you think it'll be a fat toothbrush?' The need for authenticity in their designs was another hallmark of the girls' approaches that we observed across the eight case studies. Again this reflects their commitment to the social context in which their problems are embedded. Boys' problems are more likely to be embedded in the 'school' context as in Peter and Simon's case. This embedding is not something that students or teachers are conscious of.

The girls as a group, albeit self-formed, decided on the 'teardrop' idea for Anna's design. Nancy, thinking ahead, identified a possible problem in relation to the design that is how such a shape could be made to stand given its curved end.

Nancy: Yeah but how are you gonna stand it up? It won't stand up will it?
Anna: Yeah but I'll have a suction pad on the back, you know one of those things?
Nancy: Yeah, I know.
Anna: Those suctions.
Nancy: Yeah, you can get them on a thing, yeah.
Other girl: Yeah, on a tile. A bit of a tile.
Anna: No, not on a tile because . . . it would stick onto the bath. It will.
Nancy: Whereabouts in the bath? Have you got any things like that?
Anna: On the side of the bath. It will, you've got [here she begins to sketch] there right? And you stick onto there, and then you ?? Yeah.

She sketched out an idea for a suction pad which she offered to Nancy for consideration. Nancy approved this resolution of the problem. As Anna proceeded to draw her design idea she became concerned about how her teardrop package would open to allow for changing the battery. Nancy keeping abreast with Anna's dilemmas while continuing with her own design once again considered her design ideas.

Anna: I'm just trying to work out where it will drop out. [i.e. the battery]
Nancy: How can the top open and then . . . on a hinge type of? How do you do this?
Anna: A piece of paper. [i.e. to draw on]. Anna sketches her idea.
Nancy: Oh it is like that.
Anna: . . . the top together with the bottom.
        . . . a handle. You could have a handle stuck onto the side and then [sketches again] like that.

It was through an interaction of talk and sketching that Anna and Nancy formulated and made explicit their ideas to each other. As part of this process they were not only developing their individual skills of self-regulation but by monitoring each other's thinking they were engaged in thinking strategically for each other. Anna reciprocated with support for Nancy who opted for a 'sock shaped' package for her washing line rain alarm. The girls continued to collaborate and develop shared solutions to emergent problems as they modelled their individual designs. However as the problems that emerged became too great for their cognitive resources they had to seek help from the teacher. The help the teacher gave was to identify the problems he perceived for himself and to offer the girls solutions. As the problem was not shared with the girls their participation was affected as it placed them in the role of instruction-followers. Consequently their collaboration broke down as neither had a common reference point within the locus of their control. The teacher's approach reflected his lack of awareness of the role of collaboration and autonomy in learning. The consequences for the girls was that they finished their projects in isolation and the learning opportunities available to them were restricted. Indeed neither ended up with a functioning device.

Collaboration Planned and not Supported

In the second scenario we turn to the primary science project. The first excerpt is from a case study of 8–9 year olds. The teacher was interested in fostering collaborative learning but had until recently organized the children to work in pairs. The activity reported was the fourth task in a series planned by the teacher to promote children's understanding of scientific procedures. The task – to investigate how a cotton reel tank moved (see Figure 16.1) and the factors affecting this movement – was selected to: (i) further develop the children's procedural knowledge of how to investigate variable effects, and to (ii) provide opportunities for the children 'to talk about what they had done, how they had done it, and how they'd achieved success, in a way that other people would understand.' To foster collaboration the teacher wanted a task that would provide opportunities for the children to 'get used to the idea of talking about what they had done'. This comment revealed that the teacher appreciated the role of talk in learning but did not necessarily have the pedagogic strategies to support it.

This activity and its organization was more like a typical D&T activity than a science one. The activity set by the teacher was to 'think about what works and doesn't work' [to make the tank move]. The children had explored the movement of the tank prior to this and had identified reasons why their tank did or did not move in a straight line. For example, one reason was that the elastic band was too thick, another that it was too small. The target students were seated around a table, two boys and three girls. The children did not discuss their task in the first instance. Instead they started to make their tanks. The initial task being to get the tank to move.

Five minutes into the task the individual girls began to talk out loud their decisions about what factors to investigate.

> Karen: I'm going to try one thing at a time. I'm going to try the elastic band.
> Alison: I'm going to try the stick too short then too long.

Only the girls at this point talked about the variables they were going to change. They did so as an exchange of information rather than an attempt to share thinking.

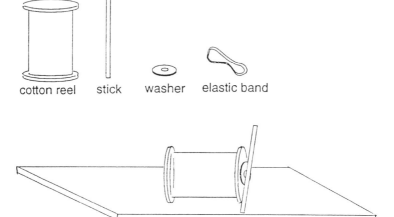

cotton reel   stick   washer   elastic band

[The stick on the side of the reel is attached to a rubber band and acts like a propeller when wound a number of times.]

Figure 16.1   *Cotton reel tank*

Karen to Violet: I think it's the stick, it's too long.
Karen: I'm going to try a really thick band.
Violet: I'm going to try a small stick.

The boys were working independently and in silence. After a while the three girls shared their observations of each other's tanks.

Alison: [commenting on Violet's tank] It goes like Karen's and mine. Look.
Violet: I need a longer stick.
Alison: It doesn't matter, it's still the same, it's not like that, it works.
Karen: [disagreeing with Alison] You need a longer stick.

Violet remade her tank with a longer stick. The girls then decided to establish a joint task to race the tanks.

Karen: Stop – we'll have a race.
Violet: Wind it up eight times.
Karen: Eight . . . no more than ten or it won't work.

After several races, the following discussion occurred between the girls.

Violet: A small elastic band doesn't work.
Karen: No, just about average.
Violet: Yes, average, not too fat and not too thin.
Alison: And the stick can't be too long.
Karen: And winding about four times, oh no ten.
Alison: And the washer is good [between the reel and the stick – see Figure 16. 1].

The final and shared task for the girls was to determine the optimum conditions for consistent movement forward of the tank in a straight line. This shared task was not supported by the teacher who through inexperience provided no strategic guidance to the children. Nor did the individualized product help support a collaborative situation, rather it was the girls' learned style of communication to talk, listen and help each other that made it possible for a shared task and a solution to emerge. The boys on the other hand continued to work independently and in silence.

Students' Collaborating

Collaboration Planned and Supported

The second excerpt from the primary science project involved a mixed group of three children. Collaboration occurred between these children in spite of their reluctance to work in mixed gender groupings. It was a common finding that students whilst liking group work more than the other ways of working, preferred same-gender groupings. If mixed-gender groupings were necessary, it was important to have equal numbers of girls and boys. Billy commented 'You need another boy if you work with girls to make it fair.' Rachel, the girl said 'I enjoy working with girls and I don't like working with boys. I don't mind a mixture if there was the same amount of girls and boys. If not, the right idea might not win if there's a vote.' Seth, the third member of the group, confirmed this common view that girls and boys think differently: 'Girls can like be a pain and really get on your nerves. Girls have different ideas, different designs, stuff like that.'

In the excerpt the students were engaged in a science activity to find out the best medium for filtering water. The task was a true group one and the teacher expected the students to collaborate to decide what they were trying to find out, what procedures to undertake to find this out, what variables to control and what to measure. They also had to predict an outcome and explain it. The final decisions they had to agree on were what equipment to use and how to record and communicate their findings. The children aged 9–10 years were used to working in groups and were expected to listen to each other and exchange views. These expectations were understood and accepted by the children.

Rachel: He [the teacher] wants you to listen to other people's ideas and I have started doing that now. Discuss which is the best idea.

Billy: He puts people together he thinks will work, who have the same ideas. Trouble is we get new ideas once we start. He wants us to discuss what we should do, then come up with a final result of what to do.

Students were provided with four materials to test; gravel, sand, peat, and soil, to see which *one* [our emphasis] would clean the best or as one of the target students said, 'We were trying to clean dirty water and seeing what would be the most effective way.' Students were given plastic cups to put the filtering medium in and were expected to make holes in the base of it. (This had already been demonstrated.)

The children in their initial planning decided to use five holes per pot, the same amount of each filtering media and the same amount of pond water. With this much agreed including their common goal, the children went off to collect equipment. They did not allocate tasks, they assumed them and let each other know by talking out loud about what they would do, for example, Rachel commented as she left the group to collect cups 'We need cups don't we?'

The teacher observing the group from across the classroom reacted to the children's activity, i.e. moving from planning to doing, and returned to the group to monitor progress.

Teacher: Have you formulated a hypothesis or a prediction of which one will be best?
Seth: Yes, we thought gravel.

The teacher confirmed that this was the view of the other two group members and then left. The children started to carry out their investigation and to monitor each other's decisions.

Rachel: So you are going to start making the holes then?
Billy: Five holes.
Seth: Okay, we want five holes.

Rachel went to get the water. In her absence the boys, who found making the holes difficult, altered the decision.

Seth: [who is making the holes] After a couple of years we should have five holes!
Billy: Why don't we just make it three holes?
Rachel: returns to the group.
Seth: Rachel, we're only having three holes. OK? Because they're big holes.
Rachel: OK.

The children were negotiating changes in decisions and offered explicit explanations for them. The children worked closely together, each contributed to the activity and continually monitored procedures and shared observations. The teacher monitored the activity by observing from afar and asking questions periodically. This meant he could keep abreast of the students' thinking and provide appropriate support when necessary. The teacher's questioning technique also placed the decision-making in the children's control. Furthermore, by repeating children's comments he gave them value.

Teacher: What's happened?
Seth: The sand's all come through with the water.
Teacher: What's actually in the jar?
Seth: Sand and water.
Rachel: Sand.
Teacher: Is that telling you that the sand is filtering out the dirt or not?
Seth: No – the water's got dirtier – it's dirtier than when it started.
Billy: The peat's gone down with it – but the gravel
Rachel: The gravel hasn't.
Teacher: Is that telling you that the gravel is better than the . . .?

Billy: Yea, yea.
Teacher: Is it?
Billy: No – no, it doesn't really.
Teacher: Why has the sand and peat gone down through it and the gravel hasn't?
Seth: Because [the holes] are too big.
Rachel: The gravel's hard and it won't fit through the holes.
Teacher: Listen to what she's saying.
Rachel: Because the holes are too big and we've made the holes like that.
Teacher: So what do you think you could do?
Rachel: Make the holes smaller.

The teacher's questioning enables the students to make explicit their thinking and reflect on it and plan.

In the final excerpts we return to the D&T context and a teacher who valued students working together on a shared product. The two excerpts come from different classrooms but with the same teacher. The teacher's style of supporting students' collaboration was very similar to the previous teacher.

In the first excerpt two girls aged 11–12 years were designing and making a collection box for a charity of their choice. The students' design had to produce an interesting effect when money went into the box to encourage donations. The girls Katie and Tania wanted to design a woodpecker effect to collect money for the Royal Society for the Protection of Birds.

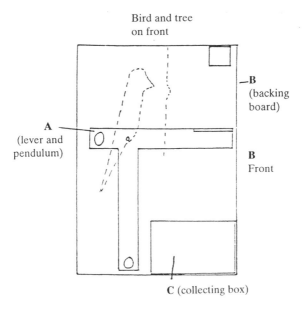

Figure 16.2 Katie's and Tania's collection box
The greater the donation the larger the 'peck' of the woodpecker.

The girls decided to work together, other students chose to work alone. They worked alongside each other on different parts of the design and kept track of each other's activity. For example when all of the components were ready for assembly Katie focused on the relationship between the position of the lever and the location of the bird in the design for the front of their board see Figure 16.2(A). Tania concerned herself with the position of the lever in relation to the coin collecting box, i.e. would the money be delivered into the box, if the lever was in another position? The following exchange showed their different concerns.

> Katie: I think that the next step is to work out where we're going to put this, because if I put this here [putting the lever mechanism on the marked position on the board], then the bird is going to be really high up so I think we need it about there, don't we? [putting the mechanism lower]
>
> Tania: Yeah, but when that [she moves the lever with a tilting action] comes past down there that's going to have to go over the side. If it's here [she moves the lever to the top of the board and tilts it], it's only going to have to go like that.
>
> Katie: No but the coin's going to be there [she tips the lever] so it is going to go like that.
>
> Tania: [doubtfully] Yeah.

Katie moved the lever further down the board and tilted it to try the effect at that point.

> Katie: It'll be the same [i.e. the amount of tilt would not alter].

Tania did not immediately accept Katie's view of her, i.e. Tania's, problem, consequently she tried out the new position for herself. She used the heaviest coin as this would produce the greatest movement to judge whether the coin would drop into the box and only then accepted the new position of the mechanism.

In other situations the girls shared the same task. For example, they worked together to make the plastic coin collection box see Figure 16.2(C). Tania began the task and Katie finished it. The girls' approach was to move between co-operation with different tasks and collaboration in shared tasks. The girls moved between co-operation and collaboration throughout the project. D&T projects unlike school science investigations take many weeks to complete. Therefore it is easy for a collaborative situation to break down. The girls' commitment to working together, their understanding of each other's different skills and abilities (Tania labelled herself as the more practical of the two, Katie she described as the thinker), their use of language and interaction with their physical model to make explicit their thinking all helped to maintain an effective collaborative relationship.

This was not the case in the final excerpt taken from a class of 12–13 year olds working with the same teacher. In this case study the project was to design an aid for a disabled child and was a group activity. The target students were two boys, David and Mark. The basic requirements for collaboration were present in the nature of the activity – a shared product and the teacher's support for the students' autonomy. Furthermore, the teacher encouraged a wide range of representations to help the students make their thinking explicit. As he put it 'a sketch is worth a thousand words'. In the initial design stage the boys collaborated to select the aid they wanted to make.

The aid the two boys decided on was an eye-tracking device for a little boy in a nearby nursery. The child tracks a ball as it moves through a tube.

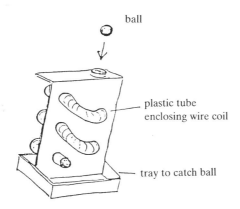

Figure 16.3   *The eye-tracking device of Mark and David*

This interaction shows how the students used talk, action and sketching to communicate and develop their ideas together. What emerged from the case study was the importance of considering these sources of interaction as interdependent.

Mark and David experiment with the plastic tube, see Figure 16.3.

Mark: It's not going to work when it's flat so we've got to raise it.

The boys drop the ball down the tube.

Mark: The problem we would have . . . is drilling the holes in the board.

Mark directed David as they together held the tube up in various positions and dropped the ball through it to assess its path. After a couple of experiments:

Mark: It must be at a degree angle, going steadily down all the time [Mark gestures by holding tube at an angle]. . . . 'cause as soon as it goes flat, it'll stop.

Mark: So we'll have to drill holes in the exact right place 'cause once we've drilled them, we can't then change them.

David: Right.

Mark: So that will be quite difficult. Let's go and write that down.

Mark and David returned to the workbench, still holding the tube. Mark warned about the way they must make the base and the supports, pointing out again that if they made a mistake they would not be able to re-drill the holes. Mark asked David to write down what he had said. The role that Mark placed David in, i.e. as his scribe, was a feature of their relationship that had significance later.

Mark dictates: We'd need it be going a slight degree down. As soon as it goes straight, it's not going to work.

Mark fetched the tube.

Mark: . . . because, as soon as it goes straight, the ball is going to stop. So when we're drilling the holes into the baseboard, we'd have to get them in exactly the right place.

Mark:	New paragraph. The other thing is the support onto the sides of the upright board because any of the little children . . .
Mark:	The reason we'd have to do that is because any of the little children, being as they are, could quite easily come along and knock it over. If they were to, they could quite easily snap the upright board off the base board. So we'll have to figure something out.
Mark:	Rather than just a board like that, you could make it more of a whole box. So if on the middle, you could come more into the back, from the top there, you could come straight down and then it would be more of a box there, which would be more supportive than just a normal board, yeah?
David:	Yeah.
Mark:	What it needs is . . . something . . .
David:	Well we could make one of those little where it hits the micro-switch somewhere on its way down and plays a tune [gesturing in a zigzag motion in the air as he speaks].
Mark:	Right, so if we were to have sort of, like have, a box . . . [Mark draws on their sheet of paper].
David:	The ball would already have to be in circuit, wouldn't it?
Mark:	Yeah. The ball would have to be on the top, there, and then it would come down. It could fall down to about there [indicating with pencil], hit the microswitch which would then set off the tune, yeah?

In the first part of the dialogue the boys relied on interaction with objects to plan by thinking through and clarifying their ideas. In the latter part of the interaction the boys were thinking through the design of the base in relation to the context of use for the device. The base needed to be stable because of the client (a young child). At this point the boys talked and sketched together as they elaborated a shared idea. The encouragement of the use of the 'sketching' and 'scribbling' allowed the students to create a shared 'mind's eye picture' of their intended design.

This collaboration was not, however, sustained between the boys. When they moved to the making of the device the difference in the boys' views of each other's practical competence became obvious. An example of this was when the boys had to chisel the wood. Neither boys had prior experience of using a chisel. David picked up the chisel first and commented 'Oh, I've never worked with one of these before'. Mark then remarked 'You'll make a horrible mess'. He then took the chisel away from David. David made no complaint but tried once more to express his wish to use the chisel, 'I'll try'. Mark ignored this and continued with the chiselling. Again, David did not complain. There were many instances like this. David would try to take part in an activity by physically placing himself in a position to do so. Each time he would be physically blocked by Mark. It was notable that the boys communicated using their bodies and did not attempt to negotiate through talk. It appeared that David lacked the skills to express his intentions or his feelings either to Mark or to the teacher. Mark allowed David the role of helpmate, but not of apprentice. Consequently he increasingly issued instructions rather than engaged in dialogue about the design and the many problems that emerged in relation to it. This meant that the opportunity for collective reflection was no longer possible and David's participation was marginalized.

The teacher was knowledgeable about how to support the students' learning in D&T but less knowledgeable about how to foster skills needed for collaboration. The essential link between these two aspects was notable in this case. Mark's view of his superior status and David's lack of awareness of how to assert himself made continuing collaboration impossible.

Discussion

Several studies have found that girls' and boys' goals for learning differ in both science and technology. As mentioned they differ in how they conceive of the problem. Student entries to a UK national design competition showed that for boys the problems were to do with the device or product and were generally technical. For girls working on similar products the problem was to do with the context of use of the product (Grant and Harding, 1987). The APU survey also found this.

> Girls appeared to work fundamentally from human needs dealing predominantly with issues. They were often cautious in their entry to a situation, wanting to know how, why and whom it was for. While studying and designing the minutiae they were constantly seeking to keep the implications of the whole in view and for some this complexity became intolerable to the point where they capitulated. Boys, on the other hand, seemed able, not only to start into the activity without knowing much, but were prepared to work on specific parts of it without considering the whole . . . possibly to lose sight of it altogether.
>
> (Kimbell *et al.*, 1991, p. 120)

Girls' preferred approach has been described as being concerned 'to really understand the task' (Kimbell *et al.*, 1991, p. 123) or to understand as much as possible, whereas the boys' approach has been described as valuing the accumulation of knowledge (Burns and Bird, 1987). These different approaches suggest a potential problem for boys and girls collaborating together. However, the approaches are complementary if brought together to achieve common goals. To help in this there is a need for teachers to provide strategic guidance about tasks so that girls are supported in tackling complexity in learning situations and boys are helped to perceive it and then deal with it. There is in addition a need for teachers and students alike to see the strengths in different ways of working and not misinterpret approaches and so constrain learning.

For example a need to seek understanding of the task by consulting peers and teachers can be interpreted as showing diffidence and lack of confidence in one's abilities. These behaviours are often taken by teachers to be indicators of girls' lower ability compared with boys. Whereas boys' preference for working alone is often interpreted in the opposite way, independence in learning being equated with high ability and achievement.

Research which has examined student learning suggests that the following characteristics underpin successful collaboration – verbally explicit planning, negotiation about alternatives, equitable involvement in shared decision making and the use of talk to reconcile conflict (Barbieri and Light, 1992; Light *et al.*, 1994). The evidence presented here demonstrates that girls more than boys typically choose to work in ways that reflect some of the characteristics of successful collaboration. The argument advanced in the chapter is that in so doing girls are drawing on ways of communicating fostered outside of school as a consequence of gendered socialization processes (Wilder, 1996) and developed further in school. Furthermore, this way of working is adopted by students irrespective of teachers' understanding of the role of collaboration in learning or of any explicit support for it. Rather it is the case that collaboration between girls breaks down as a consequence of the lack of strategic support provided by teachers. Boys, on the other hand, rarely choose to work collaboratively, again reflecting ways of communicating fostered outside of school. Nor is boys' independent working seen as problematic either by boys or by teachers. Indeed during the course of compulsory schooling and beyond independence in working and communication become associated with ability and intellectual *'flair'* (Murphy and Elwood, 1998). This perspective however increasingly conflicts with current understanding about the social nature of knowledge construction. An emphasis on independent work runs counter to understanding about the role of peer-peer and peer-expert interactions and participation in communal activity and learning (Rogoff, 1990; Lave and Wenger, 1991).

Implications

An emphasis on collaborative learning and the pedagogy to support it has emerged as research into human learning and its social nature has progressed. Present and past pedagogy has been described by Harding (1996) as a pedagogy for 'boys'. In the future pedagogy will need to change if skills of collaboration as well as collaboration for learning are to be fostered in classrooms and workshops. Something which is advocated by a wide range of agencies outside schools and emerging in debates about 'core skills' for employment etc. In order for this to happen in ways described in this chapter girls' approaches and ways of communicating will need to be valued at all phases of education rather than dismissed as indicators of 'helplessness', 'timidity' and 'mediocrity of mind'. Similarly boys' tendency to work independently needs explicit review and reflection so that it is clear to both boys and girls alike the advantages and disadvantages of different approaches. In particular boys need to be aware of the limitations gendered learning places on their potential to hear and benefit from others creative thinking. These changes can only come about if teachers are aware of the cognitive and affective benefits of collaborative learning and are supported in developing the necessary pedagogic strategies. These include knowing how to:

- maintain students' autonomy while monitoring task progress and group interactions;
- teach and support a range of communication skills;
- use a range of representations as tools for making thinking explicit;
- ascertain students' prior understandings;
- elicit different views of salience (see Murphy and Elwood, 1998 for further discussion of this in relation to the primary science case referred to);
- analyse activities so that learning goals are supported by the format and embedding features of the task (Tolmie *et al.*, 1993).

Note

1. This paper is based upon the work of two project teams which include Bob McCormick, Sara Hennessy, Marian Davidson, Eileen Scanlon, Barbara Hodgson and Liz Whitelegg, based at the Open University and Kim Issroff at University College, London.

References

Azmitia, M. (1988) Peer interaction and problem solving: when are two heads better than one?, *Child Development*, 59, 87–96.

Barbieri, M. S. and Light, P. H. (1992) Interaction, gender, and performance on a computer-based problem solving task, *Learning and Instruction*, 2, 199–213.

Browne, N. and Ross, C. (1991) Girls' stuff, boys' stuff: young children talking and playing. In Browne, N.(ed) *Science and Technology in the Early Years*, Milton Keynes, Open University Press.

Burns, J. and Bird, L. (1987) Girls' co-operation and boys' isolation in achieving and understanding in chemistry. *Contributions to the Fourth GASAT Conference Vol. 2*, Ann Arbor, Michigan, USA, pp. 16–25.

Cobb, P., Boufi, A., McClain, K. & Whitenack, J. (1997) Reflective discourse and collective reflection, *Journal for Research in Mathematics Education*, 28(3) 258–277.

Galton, M. and Williamson, J. (1992) *Group Work in the Primary Classroom*, Routledge, London.

Grant, M. and Harding, J. (1987) Changing the polarity, *International Journal of Science Education*, 9(3) pp. 335–42.

Harding, J. (1996) Girls' achievement in science and technology', in Murphy, P. and Gipps, C. (eds) *Equity in the Classroom: Towards Effective Pedagogy for Girls and Boys*, London Falmer/UNESCO.

Hennessey, S. and Murphy, P. (in press) The potential for collaborative problem solving in Design and Technology, *International Journal of Technology and Design Education*.

Kimbell, R., Stables, K., Wheller, T., Wosniak, A. and Kelly, V. (1991) *The Assessment of Performance in Design and Technology*, London, School Examinations and Assessment Authority.

Kruger, A. C. (1993) Peer collaboration: conflict, co-operation or both?, *Social Development*, 2(3) 165–182.

Lave, J. (1992) Word problems: a microcosm of theories of learning, in Light, P. and Butterworth, G. (eds) *Context and Cognition: Ways of Learning and Knowing* (pp. 74–92) Harvester Wheatsheaf, London.

Lave, J. and Wenger, E. (1991) *Situated learning: Legitimate peripheral participation*. Cambridge, Cambridge University Press.

Leont'ev, A. N. (1981) The problem of activity in psychology, in Wertsch, J. V. (ed) *The Concept of Activity in Soviet Psychology* (pp. 37–71) Sharpe, Armonk, N. W.

Light, P., Littleton, K., Messer, D. and Joiner, R. (1994) Social and communicative processes in computer-based problem solving. *European Journal of Psychology of Education*, IX, 1, 93–109.

Mercer, N. (1995) *The Guided Construction of Knowledge: Talk Amongst Teachers and Learners*, Multilingual Matters, Clevedon.

Murphy, P. (1997) Gender differences – message for science learning, in Burgen, A. (ed) *Growing Up with Science*, Cambridge, Jessica Kingsley.

Murphy, P. and Spence, M. (1996) Investigative science in the primary classroom – a case of ritual learning?, European Congress on Educational Research, September 25–28, Seville, Spain.

Murphy, P. and Elwood, J. (1998) Gendered experience, choices and achievement exploring the links, *International Journal of Inclusive Education*, Vol. 2, no. 2, pp. 95–118.

Newman, D., Griffin, P. and Cole, M. (1989) *The Construction Zone: Working for Cognitive Change in School*, Cambridge, Cambridge University Press.

Rogoff, B. (1990) *Apprenticeship in Thinking: Cognitive Development in Social Context*, Oxford University Press, New York.

Rogoff, B. (1995) Observing sociocultural activity on three planes: participatory appropriation, guided participation, and apprenticeship', in Wertsch, J. V., Del Rio, P. and Alvarez, A. (eds) *Sociocultural Studies of Mind*, Cambridge University Press.

Rogoff. B. (1997) Cognition as a collaborative process, in Duhn, D. and Siegler, B., *Handbook of Child Psychology*, John Wiley & Sons, New York.

Thompson, R. B. (1994) Gender differences in communicative style: possible consequences for their learning process, in Foot, H., Howe, C., Anderson, A., Tolmie, A. and Warden, A. (eds) *Group Tutoring*, Southampton, Computational Mechanics Publications.

Tolmie, A., Howe, C., Mackenzie, M. and Green, K. (1993) Task design as an influence on dialogue and learning: primary school group work with object flotation, *Social Development*, 2(3) 183.201.

Wilder, G. Z. (1996) Antecedents of gender differences in the supplement to Willingham, W., Cole, N. (1996) *Gender and Fair Assessment*, Princeton, New Jersey, Educational Testing Services.

17

The Validity and Reliability of Assessments and Self-assessments of Work-based Learning

Yves Benett

[. . .]

Introduction

Higher education institutions have [. . .] been reminded that work-based learning is not new (Duckenfield, 1992); for example, it forms part of the professional development of trainee teachers and social workers, and is a component of sandwich degree courses. However, what is contentious is the idea that work-based learning is 'valid' and may be accredited within academic programmes of study. Thus, although at the University of Huddersfield (Benett *et al.*, 1989) we have developed appropriate procedures for assessing the supervised work experience of undergraduates when they are placed in industry and business, a question which continues to be asked is 'to what extent are such assessments valid and reliable?'
[. . .]

Some Concepts of 'Validity'

[. . .] 'Validity' contains two distinct components, the intention of the assessor and the nature of what is to be assessed (Bateson, 1984). A number of implications flow from this definition of 'validity' and from some concepts of 'validity' (such as face validity, content validity, predictive validity, criterion-related validity and construct validity) which have been described in the relevant literature. These implications are discussed below in connection with the assessment of learners at the workplace.

This chapter has been edited.

Face Validity

To take first the concept of 'face validity' (Nunnally, 1967; Cohen and Manion, 1980), in so far as students' assessments of work-based learning are intended to indicate their performance at the workplace and are based on practical projects (which are set by employers themselves and are undertaken at the workplace itself), these assessments are grounded in the reality of the workplace with its own rules, norms, expectations and prohibitions. Common sense dictates that, on the face of things, one would be justified to claim face validity for these assessments.

Content Validity

On the other hand, any claim to 'content validity' may be questionable for, within the meaning of the term, validity requires sampling adequately from the 'domain of content', that is, from all the relevant tasks that could in theory be assigned to students at the workplace. This is clearly problematical, since the domain may not be clearly delineated (such may be its size and complexity) and is 'infinite' (McGrath, 1970); and the sample of tasks on which assessments are based may not always be sufficiently representative of the domain. However, in practice, one may claim that assessments at the workplace have content validity if multiple sources of evidence of learning are used as a basis for assessment (and self-assessment), since they would allow a broad range of key issues to be addressed.

Predictive Validity

The notion of 'predictive validity' (for the assessments of work-based learning) is conceptually simple and appealing. The procedure for determining it is, in principle, straight-forward enough; it consists of studying the extent to which these assessments (whether made by students or by others) predict accurately the performance of students in their subsequent, professional careers. [. . .]

Criterion-related Validity (also Called 'Concurrent Validity')

This notion of validity requires that, in addition to the assessments of work-based learning which are made by workplace supervisors, there should be independent assessments that are based on similar tasks and that are used as the criteria for making judgements about performance at the workplace. Thus, independent assessments may be made by external 'verifiers' given that the concept of 'verification' seems now well established (Gealy *et al.*, 1991).

However, this notion of validity may well throw into doubt the validity of students' own assessments of their work-based learning. This is because, as explained above, this particular notion of validity entails comparing students' own assessments of their performance in a particular task at the workplace with the assessment which is (a) made by an assessor (normally the student's workplace supervisor) with 'expert' knowledge of working in the same occupational area, and (b) based on the expert's direct observation of the student's performance (on the same or similar task). The expert's assessment thus serves as a criterion (against which to judge the worth of students' self-assessments) and the validity of the students' self-assessments are questionable if their assessments do not approximate the expert's assessments.

However, there are several issues here and they need to be disentangled. To begin with, the assumption is that 'experts' assessments are themselves valid in that their specialist, practical and experiential knowledge, acquired over a period of time and through 'real', practical experience at the workplace, legitimises their claims to having the necessary expertise. The assumption is most probably justifiable for, as practitioners, they would have acquired a considerable repertoire of reasons for their actions and decisions at the workplace. Their own 'practitioner theory' (Usher and Bryant, 1987) would have been the product of 'situational thinking', and may have entailed, in addition, borrowing concepts and model constructs from 'formal theory' (that is, theory which is generated through conceptual representations of an abstract kind usually associated with academic studies). They would also claim to have internalised the standards of performance required of practitioners at the workplace. Moreover, these same standards would have provided them with a frame of reference for assessing students' performance at the workplace.

The point here is that, arguably, in so far as the criteria which underpin the establishment of these standards have been clearly identified, made explicit and agreed with a body of qualified and experienced practitioners (after free and open discussion), such criteria, and the standards which are derived from them, may be described as 'objective' though not absolute (Benett, 1986). Furthermore, these standards are independent of any learning programmes and project work that students may undertake (Mansfield, 1991). Consequently, the validity of students' self-assessments of their performance at the workplace depends on whether students have internalised these standards (and the underpinning values) and are able to assess their performance against these 'objective' criteria and standards.

However, the matter is further complicated because although standards of performance at work may be 'objectively' set, an element of subjectivity (and hence of likely bias) may creep into the assessment of performance, even if unwittingly. For the 'private variables' (Galtung, 1967) that characterise individuals (such as their thoughts, feelings, intentions, personalities and so on) and that make up a large part of their 'psychological environ-ment' may well bias their assessments of their own performance. Certainly, students have their own conceptualisation of supervised work experience and their conceptualisation imposes a structure on their experience and on how they make sense of it (Wellington, 1986). The difficulty is that these 'private variables' are inaccessible except, perhaps, through verbal interac-tion with others. Consequently, it is important that students interact genu-inely with their workplace supervisors and disclose to them their thoughts, feelings and intentions about their work. Such interactions will help work-place supervisors to 'verify' that the students' self-assessments meet the necessary criteria. Indeed, it is through such interactions that the students' self-assessments are likely to approximate the workplace supervisors' as-sessments. However, account must be taken of the fact that the workplace supervisors, too, may be similarly biased in their assessments; their ego-defensiveness and their stereotyping of students' characteristics, motiva-tion and role have been reported (Ashworth and Saxton, 1988).

It should be pointed out that such bias as there may be on the part of either workplace supervisors or students constitutes a threat to what is known as 'internal validity' (Kerlinger, 1975) – to use the language of experimental research; that is, such bias raises questions about the extent to which assessments of students' performance at the workplace are 'real' and it clouds certainty about the relationship between work-based learning and *performance* at the workplace.

Construct Validity

Another consideration when looking at the issue of validity when assessing work-based learning is the emphasis put on the assessment of 'compet-ence'. The claim is made that competence is a hypothetical construct (Mitchell and Cuthbert, 1989) of what individuals are theoretically able to do and this ability is judged by the performance of what they actually do in particular circumstances. Now, the validity of a construct may be studied by looking at the tissue of relationships between the construct under study and other theoretical constructs (Cronbach and Meehl, 1955); if that particular construct shows the relationships which are theoretically predicted for it, one may claim 'construct validity' for it. It follows from this line of reason-ing that the 'validity' of the construct 'competence' at the workplace could be determined by examining its predicted relationships with other relevant constructs. 'Knowledge' of theory is such a relevant construct; this is be-cause there is conceptual evidence that 'competence' is a 'factorially com-plex construct' (Guildford and Fruchter, 1975), that is, it comprises a number of factors and one of these is the theoretical knowledge which underpins performance at the workplace (Wolf, 1990). All of this adds up to a suggestion that the relationship between assessments of work-based learning (including self-assessments) and assessments of college-based learning (in the theoretical components of courses) should be investigated empirically; evidence of convergence between these assessments would support the claim of 'construct validity' for the former, although divergence would also be enlightening. Indeed, the whole issue of the inter-penetration of theory and practice in vocational education should be explored (Usher and Bryant, 1987; Benett *et al.*, 1989).

However, there is yet another tantalising question to be addressed. For, given that statements of competence are generalisations (based on assessments of performance in a sample of tasks), to what extent can these generalisations be justified and hence 'external validity' (Kerlinger, 1975) be claimed for these assessments? The answer to this question may well lie in recent formulations about the collection and analysis of qualitative data in the social sciences (Ritchie and Sykes, 1986). These formulations would take us back to the fundamental point that an essential component of the validity of assessments is the assessor's intention; this would suggest that assessors should be very clear about their intentions when assessing students at the workplace, and should identify the boundaries and limitations of the interpretations they make of assessments at the workplace.

Validity of the Learning Process

The discussion so far has centred on the validity of assessments at the workplace and hence on what it is that is being assessed. If one unpacks what is being assessed at the workplace, one finds that it includes components such as practical skills, the application of theoretical knowledge, competence, attitudes, personal development and experience (Mathews, 1987; Mitchell and Cuthbert, 1989; FEU, 1986). However, one important consideration about this set of components is that the assessment of 'experience', in particular, is problematic since 'mere activity' at the workplace does not constitute experience (Dewey, 1916). Also, a clear distinction must be made between 'experience' as such, that is, living through the events and through the stimulations, interactions, activities and responses within these events (Steinmaker and Bell, 1979), and what is actually learned through that experience. Indeed, according to Evans (1988), unless the learning derived from that experience can be identified, there is no learning to assess; a mere description of the experience is not enough, however important to the individual that experience may have been.

It also emerges from the relevant literature that, from the perspective of learning through experience, learning is not to be conceived in terms of its outcome (which implies, usually, how much has been learned, how well it has been learned and what grade or mark it merits). Instead, learning is to be conceived as a continuous process which is grounded in experience. Consequently, the proposition in the present chapter is that when considering the validity of assessments of work-based learning, one must consider not only the assessment of learning outcomes but also the assessment of the learning process and *its* validity. It is, therefore convenient at this point to turn to the work of Kolb (1984) because of his many insights into the nature of the learning process.

According to Kolb, the learning process involves 'adapting' to one's environment by accommodating ideas, assimilating experience, reflecting and acting. The process is described as a four-stage cycle. At each stage in the cycle there is a different mode of adaptation to the environment and the four modes of adaptation involve, respectively:

(a) Concrete experience;
(b) Reflective observation;
(c) Abstract conceptualisation; and
(d) Active experimentation.

From this perspective, when assessing work-based learning an appropriate evaluative stance is to ask whether the learning process is valid in the sense that it enables the learner to experience at the workplace the four adaptive modes identified in the learning cycle – on the assumption, of course, that this theory of experiential learning has a valid basis.

In addition, this stance requires an assessor (and self-assessor) to ensure that the learning process incorporates an explanation of how, at each stage in the learning cycle, the learning activities relate to this theoretical framework.

However, another consideration is the fact that the learning process which is set in train during a particular learning episode at the workplace depends on a number of factors, and, in particular, on:

(a) The orientation of the workplace itself (as a learning environment) towards each of the four adaptive modes in the learning cycle (Kolb, 1984);
(b) The personal approach of the individual to learning (Marton and Saljo, 1984).

To take the workplace (as a learning environment) first, it may emphasise in its orientation some, but not all, of the adaptive learning modes already mentioned; for example, it may provide experience of concrete, 'real-life' problems, but not promote 'reflection'. One must, in this case, question the validity of the learning process for what is at issue here is 'systematic reflection'; and this is a matter of discerning the relation between what one tries to do and what happens in consequence. It also implies pausing and, as it were, glancing backward on one's action (Dewey, 1938; Schutz, 1967; Boud *et al.*, 1985). The methods adopted for such structured reflection include, for example, the use of diaries, self-development journals, peer appraisal and structured discussions. These methods involve, among other things, obtaining full accounts of what has taken place, evaluating events, categorising and analysing experiences and drawing out lessons for the future. Such reflection serves to consolidate, to interpret and pattern, to develop concepts and theories (Stanton, 1984) and to carry forward what is learned from one's actions (Freire, 1972). Consequently, establishing the validity of an assessment (and self-assessment) of learning at the workplace must entail evaluating the extent to which systematic reflection of this kind is part-and-parcel of the learning process.

Turning next to an individual's personal approach to learning; unfortunately, it seems that firm evidence of how students go about their learning at the workplace is hard to come by. However, one may speculate that the finding that, in educational settings generally, students display basically three different approaches to learning is of relevance to learning at the workplace; these approaches have been described respectively as 'deep', 'surface' and 'strategic' (or 'achieving') (Marton and Saljo, 1984; Richardson *et al.*, 1987; Biggs, 1990).

A 'deep' approach consists of searching for basic underlying meanings and structural interrelationships, and leads to 'superior performance' (Eley, 1992). A learner adopting this approach tends to relate the task in hand to what is already known, to read widely, to discuss with others, to find the task as personally involving and to find learning emotionally satisfying (Biggs, 1990). Such learners want examinations that demonstrate their own thinking and tutors who encourage group discussions and interaction with their ideas (Entwistle, 1991).

A 'surface' approach consists of learning in order to satisfy imposed assessment requirements and in treating such a task as an external imposition. The student who adopts this approach tends to see learning as a means to an end (such as obtaining a job), to focus on the concrete aspects of the task and to see the components of the task as unrelated to each other and to other tasks. Such learners want examination questions which can be answered solely from their notes, tutors who can tell them what to put in their notes and courses which indicate exactly what books to read.

In the 'strategic' (or 'achieving') approach, seemingly the learners' intentions are to obtain the highest possible assessment grades by the systematic management of their time, effort and study conditions, by being alert to cues about the marking schemes being used and by manipulating the assessment system to their own advantage. The learners who adopts this approach concentrates on 'what counts'.

It should be noted that these approaches to learning are general tendencies only and that they may be 'strongly affected' by teaching methods and assessment schemes (Entwistle, 1990). Thus, a 'deep' approach may be attributed to being given 'freedom in learning' whilst a 'surface' approach may be attributed to teaching which fosters dependency through 'spoon feeding'. However, Williams (1992) has a point when he states that there has not been much research on how to promote a 'deep' approach to learning; and more recently, Saljo and Wyndham (1990) have concluded that successful learning is a function of the extent to which students feel concerned about the tasks given to them.

If one moves away from these broad generalisations, however, and asks how *individual* learners proceed when they start on a particular task at the workplace, the answer is that it depends on yet more factors, such as:

(a) Their perceptions of:
    (i)   what the demands of the task are;
    (ii) what the assessment requirements are;
    (iii) what is expected of them.
(b) Their idiosyncratic reactions to the learning environment at the workplace.

Moreover, an unresolved question is what constitutes an appropriate learning environment at the workplace. What can be said is that, in general, an environment that promotes effective learning is likely to be less teacher-centred and to provide more opportunities for student research and discussion (Burns *et al.*, 1991).

[. . .]

Concepts of Reliability

In the context of work-based learning, reliability refers to the consistency with which an assessment of performance at the workplace is made. As Anastasi (1976) explains, in classical test theory, reliability refers to the consistency of marks obtained by the same individuals, when re-examined with the same test, on different occasions, or with different sets of equivalent test items, or under other variable assessment conditions. Thus, in the context of work-based learning, reliability is linked up with the extent to which a method of assessing performance is robust enough to resist variations in making the assessment (such as variations in tasks, and in time).

Variations in Tasks

Taking variations in tasks first, the paradox is that not to vary the tasks that are set to individual learners would be irresponsible and would be to the detriment of their vocational education generally (particularly if their placement is over a long period, as it would be for an attachment on a sandwich course). Also, even if it were possible to restrict learners' activities to repeatable tasks (for assessment purposes), the increase in the reliability of the assessment which would result from such an approach would need to be balanced against the loss of 'content validity'; this is because the sample of tasks (from the domain of content) on which the assessment would be based would be much reduced in size. In any case, in practice, students on higher education courses (and often working on complex projects) are unlikely to be assessed at the workplace on repetitive tasks and on tasks for which it is relatively easy to specify, and apply, consistent standards (EDUCA, 1988). The inference is that in these circumstances it may be difficult to ascertain the reliability of the assessments.

However, close study of this issue indicates that to claim reliability for a particular assessment of performance at the workplace may, nevertheless, be justified on one condition; this is that the assessment is based on a set of tasks which, although not identical, are nonetheless consistent with respect to the key features of interest as far as the assessment process is concerned. Put differently, if there is a certain amount of commonality in the variety of tasks assessed (such as a common theme, purpose, theory or procedure), the common factor which runs through these diverse tasks is likely to bring about some convergence, and hence some consistency in the assessments.

The implication is that in order for assessors (including self-assessors) to claim that their assessments are reliable, they would need to attend carefully to the selection and design of the tasks that constitute the basis for their assessments – as, indeed, lecturers in higher education would when designing examination questions and/or college-based assignments. [. . .]

Variations in Time

The reliability of assessments at the workplace in terms of their consistency over time is also problematic. In this method of determining reliability, the assessor is required to repeat the process of assessing an individual student on the same task (or on a similar task) to ascertain that, in spite of the passage of time, the assessment remains the same. This notion of reliability seems to assume that the student's world is unchanging and that the assessment can be replicated. However, it is difficult to see how, in practice, an assessor (including a self-assessor) can ensure that the same aspects of the same task can be assessed on different occasions in the workplace. Moreover, because one expects students to develop in competence during their placements, it is precisely change (in the appropriate direction) rather than consistency that one is looking for in monitoring students' development.

The notion of reliability as consistency also implies eliciting consistent assessment data at a specific point in time; for example, different assessors may be able to assess an individual student within the same short period of time and agree among themselves on a particular assessment. In the case of work-based learning, the assessment might be made at the workplace itself (by such people as workplace supervisors, visiting tutors, external examiners and, indeed, the learners themselves) or at college, for example, at the presentation of a work-based project report to a panel of assessors. The advantage of such procedures is that with the minimum length of time between making different assessments there is less likelihood of variations in learning and assessment conditions. However, a consensus among assessors may simply reflect the fact that they have similar standards in relation to the work being assessed, rather than that the work is objectively of a certain standard (Jarvis, 1983).

Comparability

The assessment (including self-assessment) of work-based learning, often raises the question of 'comparability'; in essence, the question is whether standards of students' performance are consistent from placement to placement and from year to year (and are, therefore, comparable). The question takes one back to the cardinal principle of reliability (in terms of consistency), as explained earlier, and in this matter the role of the external examiners and of validating bodies [. . .] in maintaining standards is crucial. For even though the problems involved in trying to achieve comparability of standards are recognised to be notorious (Lindop, 1985), one may claim (with the CNAA, 1991; 1992) that a group of academic peers (course tutors and external examiners) is able to make impartial judgments on the comparability of standards. [. . .]

But while the stance taken by examining and validating bodies about the comparability of course standards in general is unambiguous at the level of institutions and of employment-based learning centres, the comparability of assessments (and self-assessments) of work-based learning is openly admitted to be plagued with problems. Nevertheless, the speculation in this chapter is that, in principle, it should be possible to develop procedures for comparing students' assessments and self-assessments from placement to placement and from year to year. To do this, one would need (for a particular occupational area) to identify a representative sample of standards with their 'elements of competence' and their associated performance criteria clearly stated (Mansfield, 1991). Comparisons could then be made from year to year on the basis of the standards achieved. The point here is that a representative sample of standards is likely to capture the essential aspects of the hypothetical construct labelled 'competence'. The reason is that competence is assumed to be the common factor – that underpins performance in the range of tasks to which each standard is intended to apply.

Conclusion

Seemingly, there has been considerable reluctance in the past to move towards a formal assessment of work-based learning which would stand up to close scrutiny (Benett *et al.*, 1989). The assumption in this chapter is that this reluctance is partly due to the conceived difficulties of achieving valid, reliable and comparable assessments, given the complex interactions of human, social, technical and practical processes at the workplace. The variability of students' placements in industry, commerce and the public sector, the differing quality of learning opportunities and the diverse approaches to the supervision of students are some of the hindrances to the assessment of learning at the workplace.

This chapter takes the view that in order to alleviate this problem of reluctance (towards assessing work-based learning formally) one must unpack the meanings of terms such as validity, reliability and comparability in the context of the assessment of work-based learning. This point is specially relevant since, in higher education, there is 'confusion about recent developments' (Otter, 1992), particularly about the assessment of competence. Also, there is a trend in higher education towards: (a) specifying learning outcomes (Otter, 1992) – as against starting course objectives; (b) profiling students' achievements – even though the very possession of a profile may be used as evidence of specific weaknesses against individual students (CNAA, 1991); and (c) self-assessments, (Department of Employment, 1990) – even if self-assessment tools may well benefit the more 'confident' students at the expense of the 'less self-assured' (CNAA, 1992).

Clarifying the meanings of the terms validity, reliability and comparability is relevant for yet another reason. This is that there is probably a question in some teachers' minds about the extent to which the concepts of validity, reliability and comparability are applicable in the context of assessments at the workplace; the argument being that each placement at work is unique and that assessments at the workplace are based on projects which vary from placement to placement.

[. . .]

While it is difficult to tease out the delicate and interrelated issues of validity, reliability and comparability in connection with assessments at the workplace, the plain conclusion is that performance standards at the workplace (and, indeed, course standards in general) are not absolute (Benett, 1986); they are established, maintained and improved through negotiation coupled with 'professional pragmatism' (Browne, 1984). However, at the level of institutions and of employment-based learning centres, it is possible to determine whether assessments (and self-assessments) of work-based learning are valid, reliable and comparable. The suggestion is that course executives, in collaboration with employers, should ensure that: (a) the learning process and the procedures for the assessment (and self-assessment) of work-based learning are well-documented and made public; (b) the most appropriate sets of tasks in which to assess competences are identified; and (c) biases (personal, professional and theoretical) are discussed with employers, other course staff and students alike.

References

Anastasi, P. (1976) *Psychological Testing* (London, Collier Macmillan).
Ashworth, P. and Saxton, J. (1988) Experiential learning during sandwich degree placements and the question of assessment. Sheffield Polytechnic. Unpublished.

Bateson, N. (1984) *Data Construction in Social Surveys* (London, Allen and Unwin).

Benett, Y. (1986) *A Fragmented View?* (London, FEU).

Benett, Y., Lee, B. and Jackson, J. (1989) The development of placement and assessment procedures in supervised work experience, *Project Report No. 31* (London, CNAA).

Biggs, J. (1990) Teaching for desired learning outcomes, in: Entwistle, N. (Ed.) *Handbook of Educational Ideas and Practices*, Ch. 6.2 (London, Routledge).

Boud., Keogh, R. and Walker, D. (1985) *Reflection: turning experience into learning* (London, Kogan Page).

Browne, S. (1984) NAB and quality in higher education, *Higher Education Review*, 17(1), pp. 45–50.

Burns, J., Clift, J. and Duncan, J. (1991) Understanding of understanding: implications for learning and teaching, *British Journal of Educational Psychology*, 61(3), pp. 276–290.

CNAA (1991) *Development of Placement and Assessment Procedures in Supervised Work Experience* (London, CNAA).

CNAA (1992) Profiling in higher education, *Project Report No. 35* (London, CNAA).

Cohen, L. and Manion, L. (1980) *Research Methods in Education* (London, Croom Helm).

Cronbach, L. and Meehl, P. (1955) Construct validity of psychological tests, *Psychological Bulletin*, 52, pp. 177–193.

Department of Employment (1990) *The Skills Link. Higher Education Developments* (Sheffield, Employment Department Group).

Dewey, J. (1916) *Democracy and Education* (New York, Macmillan).

Dewey, J. (1938) *Experience and Education* (New York, NY, Collier Macmillan).

Duckenfield, M. (1992) *Learning Through Work* (Sheffield, Employment Department, Higher Education Branch).

EDUCA (1988) Assessment; the next decade, *Flavour of the Month*, May, pp. 8–10 (Guildford, Guildford Educational Services).

Eley, M. (1992) Differential adoption of study approaches within individual students, *Higher Education*, 23, pp. 231–254.

Entwistle, N. J. (1990) Changing conceptions of learning and teaching, in: Entwistle, N. (ed.). *Handbook of Educational Ideas and Practices*, Ch. 6 (London, Routledge).

Entwistle, N. J. (1991) Student failure: disintegrated patterns of study strategies and perceptions of the learning environment, *Higher Education*, 21, pp. 249–261.

Evans, N. (1988) The assessment of prior experiential learning, *Publication No. 17* (London, CNAA).

Feu (1986) *Assessment, Quality and Competence* (London, FEU).

Freire, P. (1972) *Pedagogy of the Oppressed* (London, Sheed and Ward).

Galtung, J. (1967) *Theory and Methods of Social Research* (London, Allen and Unwin).

Gealy, N., Johnson, C., Miller, C. and Mitchell, L. (1991) Designing assessment systems for National Certificates, in: Fennell, E. (Ed.) *Development of Assessable Standards for National Certification* (Sheffield, Employment Department Group).

Guildford, J. and Fruchter B. (1975) *Fundamental Statistics in Psychology and Education* (New York, NY, McGraw-Hill).

Jarvis, P. (1983) *Professional Education* (London, Croom Helm).

Kerlinger, F. (1975) *Foundations of Behavioural Research* (London, Holt, Rinehart and Winston).

Kolb, D. (1984) *Experiential Learning* (Englewood Cliffs, NJ, Prentice Hall).

Lindop, N. (1985) *Academic Validation in Public Sector Higher Education* (London, HMSO).

Mansfield, R. (1991) Deriving standards of competence, in: Fennell, E. (Ed.) *Development of Assessable Standards for National Certification* (Sheffield, Employment Department Group).

Marton, F. and Saljo, R. (1984) Approaches to learning, in: Marton, F. *et al.* (Eds). *The Experience of Learning* (Edinburgh, Scottish Academic Press).

Mathews, D. (1987) Assessment in the workplace – news from a faraway land of which we know little, *Coombe Lodge Report*, 19(7), pp. 419–33 (Blagdon, FESC).

McGrath, J. (1970) *Research Methods and Designs for Education* (Pennsylvania International Textbook Company).

Mitchell, L. and Cuthbert T. (1989) *Insufficient Evidence? The Final Report of the Competency Testing Project* (Glasgow, SCOTVEC).

Nunnaly, J. (1967) *Psychometric Theory* (New York, NY, McGraw-Hill).

Otter, S. (1992) *Learning Outcomes in Higher Education* (London, UDACE/FEU).

Richardson, J., Eysenck, M. and Piper, D. (Eds) (1987) *Student Learning: research in education and cognitive psychology* (Milton Keynes, Open University Press).

Richie, J. and Sykes, W. (1986) *Advanced Workshop in Applied Qualitative Research* (London, Social and Community Planning Research).

Saljo, R. and Wyndham, J. (1990) Problem solving and academic performance and reasoning. A study of Joint Cognitive Activity in the formal setting, *British Journal of Educational Psychology*, 60(3), pp. 245–255.

Schutz, A. (1967) *The Phenomenology of the Social World* (Evanston, IL, Northwestern University Press).

Stanton, G. (1984) A profile of personal qualities, in: *Profiles in Action* (Blagdon, FESC).

Steinmaker, N. and Bell, M. (1979) *The Experiential Taxonomy; A New Approach to Teaching and Learning* (London, Academic Press).

Usher, R. and Bryant, I. (1987) Re-examining the theory-practice relationship in continuing professional education, *Studies in Higher Education*, 12(2), pp. 201–212.

Wellington, J. (1986) Determining a core curriculum: the limitations of transcendental deductions, in: Taylor, P. (Ed.) *Recent Developments in Curriculum Studies* (Slough, NFER-Nelson).

Williams, E. (1992) Student attitudes towards approaches to learning and assessment, *Assessment and Evaluation in Higher Education*, 17(1), pp. 45–58.

Wolf, A. (1990) Unwrapping knowledge and understanding from standards of competence, in: Black, H. and Wolf, A. (Eds) *Knowledge and Competence* (Sheffield, Employment Department Group).

18

Cultural Bridging and Children's Learning

Kathy Stredder with case study material by Karen Emmott and Chris Carpenter

Introduction

Cultural bridging creates a curriculum where children's cultural knowledge is explicitly acknowledged and becomes a source for their own, and others', learning. In this chapter we consider two teachers' strategies for implementing cultural bridging within multi-ethnic classrooms. They developed their strategies for the purpose of improving learning and raising achievement. Although the chapter refers specifically to minority ethnic cultures, cultural bridging can be applied to other cultural groupings.

There are three kinds of cultural bridges exemplified in the case studies below. The first of these is in the teachers' choice and use of knowledge about minority cultures. Both Karen and Chris chose to cover key concepts by incorporating examples from Asian cultures. Although these examples extended the 'content' of the mandatory curriculum, their main purpose was to facilitate learning by creating opportunities for participation, interaction and cognitive challenge. In other words, learning the concepts rather than the detail of the chosen examples was the aim.

Cultural bridges can also be introduced through task-setting which allows children to draw on their cultural experiences. This might involve doing home or community based 'research'. It might take the form of working collaboratively with other children on activities drawing on their personal experiences. In the two case studies below, tasks of these kind supplement the introduction of examples from minority cultures and show how children's understanding was deepened.

Learning is also about children's feelings about themselves and others. Of particular importance is a child's identity and how this affects their interaction with others. A third kind of cultural bridge encourages children to acknowledge different languages, religious practices, and cultural traditions in their social interactions and activities in the classroom. As the case studies below show, these cultural bridges break down personal and cultural barriers, and create an environment in which all children can develop confidence and pride.

The two case studies below are of curriculum developments designed and implemented by Karen Emmott (from Leicester) and Chris Carpenter (from Bradford) on an Open University course 'Achievement and the Multiethnic School' (The Open University, 1994). The case studies illustrate the effects of their cultural bridging strategies on children's learning.

Case Study 1

Karen Emmott developed the religious education curriculum for a Year 6 class (which included equal numbers of Moslem and non-Moslem children) exploring the concept of pilgrimage. She chose the pilgrimage of the Moslems, Hajj, as a focus. She didn't know what the Moslem children knew about Hajj, so she decided that the introduction to the topic deserved both some discussion and input, to help her assess what the children knew, and also begin a process by which she framed the concepts. She went on to give the children a variety of opportunities to explore the key stages of Hajj and its key rituals. They did this through performance, written work, and art and design work.

Her presentation spanned six lessons and included the following:

- Lessons 1 and 2 – introduced the concept of pilgrimage by discussing the differences between journey and pilgrimage; cross-cultural references to Christian, Hindu and Moslem pilgrimages, followed by a video on Hajj;
- Lesson 3 – focused on Hajj, with activities aimed at covering why Moslem people make Hajj, their religious observances, and the spiritual significance and emotional experience of Hajj;
- Lesson 4 – dramatized Hajj by developing a role play based on a boy making his pilgrimage to Mecca, exploring the meaning of the rituals, and an understanding of the spiritual dimensions of Hajj;
- Lessons 5 and 6 – project work including choice of writing or art and design work, around Hajj and Islamic art and the Arabic language.

Sessions 1 and 2

In Karen's first session the children brainstormed their ideas about journeys. She found that none was familiar with the term pilgrimage, and only one Moslem child knew where Mecca was. In the second session the video on Hajj was shown, and the children were asked to fill in a worksheet on the video. Later evaluation by the children showed that this activity was the least well liked because of the inaccessibility of the video.

Nevertheless the discussion below took place after the video on Hajj was shown in the second session. It involved six children, three of whom were Moslem and bilingual. Several of the six children experienced learning difficulties. The dialogue demonstrates how the focus on Hajj allowed the minority ethnic group children to participate fully by drawing on their family experiences, and how it offered all the children a way to explore pilgrimage in terms of sacrifice, spirituality, penance and ritual.

Emma: If I was a Moslem, going on Hajj would be really important because I'd see the places Mohammed had been to. It would be a hard journey though, because it's so hot, but it has to be hard otherwise you wouldn't feel you were doing something important.

Dobir: My uncle went on Hajj last year and he said it was really good. He said lots of people were crying as they walked around the Ka'aba because they were close to the house that God lives in and it was a really strong thing.

Ryan: It was good about those people walking to Arafat 'coz it makes it really hard for them so God will forgive them for their sins. I wouldn't like to pray all day in a desert – no way

Naomi: It's funny about them wearing special clothes, because it's like when my granddad goes to the temple and he has to wear a shawl when he prays. Some different people have to take off their shoes when they pray to God as well, don't they?

Wesley: Miss, what the Ka'aba made of?

Toslima: I know. It's made of bricks and it's covered in a black and gold cloth. You can't see it on the video, but there's a door and my uncle says only special people like the King can go inside. There's a magic window as well as that you can see out of when you go inside.
(Ruzina disputes this.)
It's true – you can see it on the calendar picture. All the pictures have it. My mum says if you haven't got any sins and you go inside, you can look through the window and go straight to God when you die.

Teacher: Water is important in lots of pilgrimages. Moslems on Hajj drank at the spring that Allah had created to save Hagar and her son. When I went to Lourdes I drank from the spring where the Virgin Mary is supposed to have shown herself. The water is supposed to help cure you.

The discussion begins with the children reflecting on the experience of the journey Moslems have when they travel to Mecca, but it develops into a detailed discussion of rituals and religious beliefs. In a short period of time (less than two sessions), these six children appear to have begun to discern the main features of Hajj, and in so doing, the concept of pilgrimage. Furthermore, each child makes a meaningful contribution.

Dobir and Toslima, both Moslems, were able to act as information-givers and experts. Dobir gave 'inside' knowledge – 'lots of people were crying . . .' – and verified it with reference to his uncle's Hajj. Toslima's more complex knowledge of Hajj motivated her to respond to Wesley's question before the teacher could. 'You can't see it . . . but there's a door . . . only . . . people like the King can go inside.' Her response to Ruzina, It's true . . .' conveyed the confidence she felt.

In contrast to Dobir and Toslima, Emma, Ryan, Naomi and Wesley asked questions or were reflexive in their comments. Their lack of direct experience meant that they were trying to make sense of Hajj, and for Emma and Ryan it was the suffering which was uppermost in their minds.

Putting themselves in the place of Moslems on a journey to Mecca required them to empathize. Through their empathy they were also grappling with the notions of sacrifice and penance.

Below are Karen's reflections on the way that cultural bridging affected the children's learning during the first two sessions. She emphasizes the way in which the bridging helped her to assess the children, instil confidence, and create a context for discussion and engagement, particularly on the part of the Moslem children.

I found the opening sessions interesting in several ways. Firstly the sessions reflected the fact that many of our children have a very low level of general knowledge and awareness of world issues. It was clear that most children were tackling the concept of a pilgrimage for the first time and were tentatively exploring the ideas of common cross-cultural rituals such as prayer and penance. Some of the Moslem children's ideas about Hajj were based on half truths or were less than accurate. I found that children from all ethnic groups therefore found the first sessions useful to discover and/or clarify facts about religious journey and specifically Hajj.

Secondly it was interesting to see the way in which the cultures were being bridged within the classroom, albeit very tentatively. The Moslem children were quite shy at first in offering their comments to the class, preferring to discuss things individually with a trusted teacher, often *sotto voce*. By the end of the video session, however, several of the Bangladeshi children were spontaneously offering information to the class and querying other children on their comments. Their confidence in a safe classroom atmosphere seemed to have grown. The atmosphere also encouraged the class teacher, a practising Catholic, to talk about her visit to Lourdes and linked what she had done with some of the rituals of Hajj. I was interested to see that the cultural bridging was happening in both directions.

Most interesting, though, was the reaction engendered in the more informal atmosphere outside the classroom. I found that during playground duty I was surrounded with Bangladeshi children . . . wanting to talk about Hajj. Sometimes comments spilled over into other lessons . . . Toslima brought a calendar with pictures of Mecca. . . . the Moslem children had been discussing the project between themselves and at home . . . the children displayed a growing confidence in their own ability and status.

Sessions 3 and 4

In sessions 3 and 4, Karen capitalized on the children's engagement and interest. She set tasks ('differentiated materials allowed for picture ordering, sentence matching, assisted and free writing' which the children could choose from), and organized a drama session which required them to rehearse, contextualize and deepen their learning about the Hajj. These language-based activities focused specifically on the rituals of Hajj, emphasizing the purpose of the pilgrims' journey to Mecca, the nature of their prayers and penance at the Ka'aba (God's house), and the rituals surrounding the local geography and celebrations back home.

What is unusual about each of the sessions 3 and 4 is the lead role that the Moslem children played in extending the class's understanding of Hajj. At the end of session 3, Toslima, Ruzina and Nasima took the initiative and asked if they could show the class how they pray, and so after their dinner break, they 'washed, dressed in burquas and recited their morning prayers in Arabic, with a commentary in English provided by one of the other Bangladeshi children. Their prayers were watched . . . respectfully . . . and encouraged many questions about Islamic ritual . . .'

In session 4, the drama lesson, the children were asked to reveal the contents of the imaginary suitcase they had packed to take with them on Hajj. The Moslem children showed their detailed knowledge of Islamic religious requirements. 'The non-Moslem children . . . (had) clothes, toiletries, toys . . . (while) the Moslem children filled it with the Koran, tasbih (prayer beads), ihram (ritual dress for men) or burquas, and gool (home made Bangladeshi toothpaste.)' The Moslem children explained the religious purpose of each Islamic item in their suitcases.

In Karen's account of the drama session, she points out the responses of the Bangladeshi girls. She describes how the drama teacher, Richard, remarked that he had never seen the girls so involved, as usually they were fairly reserved in his drama session. Richard's observation and Karen's comment, that the girls 'capitalized on their cultural advantages and enjoy(ed) playing a leading informative role', has additional resonance when this activity of preparing and packing for a journey is viewed as the kind of gendered role they might associate with female members of their families. In other words, the coincidence of cultural and gendered experience, played out collaboratively, allowed the girls to participate and respond at a level associated with the most successful children.

Sessions 5 and 6

The final sessions (5 and 6) were spent on children doing follow-up and supplementary 'project' work. This was intended to give the children a tangible outcome and an expression of their learning. To ensure the children's sense of achievement, she gave them a choice of 'projects' to do, which were in themselves differentiated, and so would meet the different needs of the children in the class.

They wrote in Arabic by consulting the Arabic speakers, and they studied photographs of mosques from around the world to see how Islamic design and calligraphy had been incorporated. Karen judged that 'the work on Arabic extended the children's appreciation of language diversity' and 'many children were being introduced to new concepts of design . . . perhaps appreciating non-Western art for the first time.'

The more advanced children did independent research and produced some accurate and informative factual writing. One such piece is set out below. It shows a good grasp of the stages of the pilgrimage, and the rituals, of Hajj.

The Hajj
Once a year Moslems all over the world do certain things to worship Allah their God. Around two million Moslems attend each year to the Hajj. The Moslems

travel to a place called Mecca which is in Saudi Arabia. Now the pilgrims get dressed outside the Mosque. The reason why the pilgrims dress the same is because they are all equal against Allah. They walk around the Ka'aba seven times because Abraham walked around the Ka'aba seven times after he built it. After, they walk between the hills of Safa and Harwa seven times because Abraham's wife ran between the hills seven times, and after the seventh time she prayed to Allah and he made a spring for her and her baby to drink.

The pilgrims get ready for a long sweaty journey to the Mount of Mercy. The pilgrims get ready for the hard part of the Hajj because you have to pray for six hours. The pilgrims go to these three stone pillars that represent the devil and throw stones at them. All the pilgrims go back to Mecca and they all rush to try and kiss a stone which Abraham built the Ka'aba on. When he wanted to build the Ka'aba higher Allah made the stone go higher but hardly anyone can kiss it.

This child's essay shows a good understanding of Hajj. It has coherence, clarity and detail (it carefully explains the links between the history and rituals of Moslems' pilgrimage to Mecca); and it gives an expression of feeling about Hajj (it talks about being 'equal', 'the long sweaty journey', the 'hard part'). It is obvious that the child feels in command of the knowledge, and is not simply copying out something written by others.

The essay below takes a different approach to looking at Hajj, and is an even clearer demonstration of the child's ownership of their topic of study.

Hajj and Home
After the pilgrims celebrate going on the Hajj, they celebrate by decorating their homes. On the outside of the pilgrim's house it will have a picture of the Ka'aba and other scenes from the Hajj, including their journey to Mecca and Arabic calligraphy from the Qur'an. They used to have camels on the walls as a main method of transport, but nowadays it is common to see a jumbo jet, train, coach or car depicted on the wall of the house. The pilgrims do not use pictures of animals or people, since this is forbidden in Islam.

The piece is compelling because its combines a personal account with knowledge of Hajj and changing cultural practices.

The children with learning difficulties also showed an understanding of Hajj. Although many of them did not choose to write, their project work was a combination of drawings of the religious symbols of Hajj and Islam, writing in Arabic and English, and artwork based on Islamic design.

Below is Karen's written evaluation of her curriculum strategy. She highlights the way in which the cultural bridging offered all the children a range of learning experiences which were beneficial. She also points out that her own, and the class teacher's, relationships with the children had developed in a positive way.

On the whole I was very pleased with the outcome of the project. I felt that all the objectives . . . had been met in varying degrees, but without a doubt the most exciting outcome was the cultural bridging that had occurred. The Moslem children had worked enthusiastically and responded . . . by sharing their knowledge and culture without embarrassment. Their self esteem had obviously grown and, having started quiet and shy, many ended up as 'resident experts' on the topic. The non-Moslem children had shown respect for the skills of the Moslem children and some had spontaneously asked for help from them. Several of the children had created links with their home by bringing in artefacts and talking to family about the project.

The development in teaching relationships had been a two-way affair. I had learned a lot from the children about their culture and skills and they had learned that I was open and sympathetic about their values and religion. The class teacher commented that she had learned a lot about Islam: 'I suppose I was quite ignorant before'. Richard commented on how surprised he was by the level of involvement in the drama – he had seen a different side to several of the children.

It was clear to me that the achievement of many of the children had been raised. The more able children had taken the opportunity to do some independent research and had produced some accurate and informative factual writing. The special needs children had all been involved in the project and had retained, to varying degrees an understanding of the topic. . . . More importantly the Moslem children had felt a sense of achievement because they knew a lot about the topic already and were able to use their skills to produce work of a high quality.

The results of a survey at the end of the project were very interesting, and confirmed many of the premises about access, choice and classroom organization on which I had based this project. The most popular area was the project-work, because of the element of choice. The children said they liked it 'because we get to choose what we want to do'; and 'it was fun and I found out a lot'.

Survey of Year 6 Class Studying the Topic of Pilgrimage

Eighteen children (3/4 of the class) returned the questionnaires. The results are as follows:

1. Which lesson did you enjoy the most?

video	1
picture work	4
drama	5
project work	8

2. Which lesson did you do your best work in?

video	1
picture work	5
drama	5
project work	7

3. What helped you to do good work?

you understood what you had to do	17
the work was at the right level for you	15
you had a choice of work	15
you were interested in the work	14
you were praised by the teacher or friends	10
there was a relaxed feeling in the classroom	10
people didn't muck around	9
your friends helped you	9
the books/worksheets were easy to understand	9
the teacher helped you	8

4. Which lesson did you not do good work in?

video	6
picture work	5
drama	3
project work	4

Karen also identified a number of areas of concern. She referred to the fact that the Bangladeshi children did not write in Bengali, although she didn't know why. On reflection she wrote, 'Perhaps they did not feel the need to. Whilst offering opportunities for celebrating cultural differences, we must also recognize that we stereotype children if we expect them to behave in a certain way.'

Her overall conclusion, however, was that her strategy had confirmed the importance of a culturally responsive curriculum in the role of raising achievement. 'It was clear that the buzz and enthusiasm in the classroom had been in response to a topic area which recognized, respected and capitalized upon cultural values and skills.'

Case Study 2

Chris Carpenter developed a geography curriculum strategy with a Year 7 class, focusing on the concept of settlement. As a language support teacher Chris partnered a class teacher in a middle school of 500 pupils of which 96 per cent were of Asian origin. He chose to teach about the social, economic and political factors affecting migration as a way of exploring the geographical concept of 'settlement'.

Chris's work spanned six sessions:

- Session 1 – (to a sub-group of the whole class) introduced concepts of migration and settlement, and involved pupils in relating these to their own families' experiences of resettlement in Britain. Focused on push/pull factors motivating migration, especially the political and economic conditions in the Indian subcontinent after Indian independence.
- Session 2 – discussion (in sub-group) of the notion of partition, and its effects on migration followed by group reading of a personal account of a boy's experience of migrating to Britain. Pupils were asked to find out about their family's first migrant (pioneer settler) to Britain.
- Session 3 – pupils (from sub-group) reported on their family's pioneer settler; followed by teacher input to whole class on 'push' factors (population increase, underemployment, poverty and family competition drawing on Islamic Britain (Lewis, 1994)); and on patterns of migration ('chain migration' – the chain being made up of pioneers, unskilled male workers, wives and children, then the British born). Sub-group draw up questionnaire on migratory experiences in the family to be presented to whole class in session 4.

- Session 4 – presentation by sub-group to whole class on 'push/pull' factors, including reports on their reading about Indian sub-continent partition and on Yasmin's personal account of migration, followed by small group activities exploring aspects of the migration topic. Questionnaires were taken by the whole class.
- Session 5 – pupils from sub-group draw up bar graphs and pie charts representing family land ownership, wealth in home country, language spoken, home regions, year of arrival, family's first migrant; followed by class discussion of this data to uncover further factors affecting migration.
- Session 6 – whole class invited to write a newspaper article about a pioneer settler, or about a pioneer settler's reflections on their first days in Britain. Pupils' personal (family) stories used as a basis for this.

Throughout the six sessions, Chris worked with a group of seven mixed ability children while his partner teacher took the remainder of the class. Chris's intention was to prepare his small group to lead a presentation on migration in sessions 4 and 5 to the whole class. He also wanted to strengthen the relationships between the seven children. The children in the small group had different languages and cultures (Bangla and Gujarati) and included the only two Sikh children in the class. By giving them a shared experience, he hoped to develop their confidence and group skills as well as their understanding of the topic.

Sessions 1 and 2

From the beginning Chris's overarching aim was to make explicit the links between settlement, migration and the children's family experiences of resettlement in Britain. The personal introductions which the seven children undertook in pairs was the starting point for actively involving the children. Most of them had never had a one-to-one conversation with each other. Chris comments,

> Talking in pairs was a good start, with most talking with somebody they had never had a real one-to-one conversation with. Two boys didn't know that Shahida spoke Bangla, and nobody knew that Fazeela's family had come from East Africa, yet these children have been in the same class group for at least two years.'

Not only did this help the children break down social and cultural barriers, but it also clarified a relevant geographical starting point and context for each of them. (One came from Kenya, two from Panjab (India), one from Panjab (Pakistan), two from Azad (Kashmir), and one from Sylhet, Bangladesh.)

Because some of the children in the sub-group were not advanced in their reading and writing of English, it was difficult for them to read academic geography texts. Chris responded to this by carefully selecting and restricting their assigned reading. Below are some notes which one of the pupils did at home in preparation for his presentation to the group. The pupil shows a grasp of the social and political effects of partition as well as empathy for the victims.

> When Kashmir was split in two the line was drawn through people's houses. Eventually the people did move out of the way but an even bigger problem was that Kashmir's leader was a Hindu.
>
> A lot of people were trying to get a new place to live because their houses and farms were crashed down. A lot of people got killed in this partition. There were soldiers and tanks wandering around destroying houses and farms. (The pupil also drew a map showing 'the partition of Kashmir').

Chris's overall comment on the pupils' work on partition in sessions 1 and 2 was:

> I think the subject of partition in 1947 was well received because it's something the pupils have heard about, but never really been clear about, the cause and effect, and they were therefore interested to learn of a historical event which is very relevant to them in their understanding of their own cultural background.

Sessions 3 and 4

In session 3, the sub-group analysed their findings about their families' pioneer settlers using the four 'push' factors described in Islamic Britain (Lewis, 1994): population increase, underemployment, poverty, and family competition. On the basis of their families' experiences they challenged some of Lewis's conclusions. For example, Chris reported that the children were critical of the Lewis's assertion that poverty was a factor that pushed people to migrate. While they acknowledged that most migrant Pakistanis were poor in comparison with their British counterparts, they argued that it was not the poorest people in Pakistan who emigrated. On the contrary, it was usually those who were well enough off to organize and support their migration who left.

The children were also able to expand on the 'underemployment' factor. They referred in particular to those people in Pakistan who had worked for the British civil service, and armed services, who were retired after Independence, and had few job prospects. These were an important group of people who experienced underemployment as a push factor.

In the same session there was a class discussion of the 'four phase pattern of migration' (pioneers, unskilled male workers, then wives and children, and finally the British born). The children quickly took on board this tool for analysing migration because it corresponded with what they had found out from their families. They also criticized the gendered assumption that the first phases of migrants were male. Although the children agreed that it was probably right that it was the men who had migrated first, they also registered that there was something 'unfair' about this. This led to one of the children admitting that her grandmother had been the first in her family to migrate, although she had come with her son.

In session 4 the subgroup presented the work they had done on partition, pioneer settlers, push/pull factors, and the questionnaire. Chris's aim, for 'the pupils in the sub-group to (have) recognition for the work they had done' was achieved. 'Certainly the apparent confidence that they displayed in reading, explaining, and helping to organize discussion groups showed a level of involvement and understanding that hitherto hadn't been seen in those pupils in geography.'

Session 5

In session 5 Chris gave the sub-group further opportunities to apply and develop their knowledge about migration. They collated the data on pioneer settlers from the whole class, and prepared graphs on the following:

What relation was the pioneer settler
Year of arrival
Home region
Language spoken
Wealth in home country
Family land ownership

From this information they speculated further on the causes of migration. For example they wondered why more of their families had migrated in the years of 1970/71 than in any other years; they asked why so many of them had a family connection with the army; and they noticed that they were mostly second generation settlers. This led the class to deduce the following:

i) 'Why were there more arrivals in 1970/71?' Probably due to the Immigration Act of 1971 which restricted immigration further with the introduction of sponsor letters.
ii) 'Why do so many pupils have a family connection with the army?' As grandfathers and fathers retired from the army there was often not enough land for them to settle on, yet they did have a retirement cheque that helped towards a ticket to Britain. Also after the Commonwealth Immigrants Act of 1962 when a voucher system (classifying as A, V or C according to, promise of a job, skilled, or unskilled) was introduced, preference was given to ex-servicemen (Lewis, 1994). And in Shaista's case her grandfather had received a letter from the Queen asking him to come and work in the Bradford textile mills in 1970.
iii) 'If most of us have a grandfather or great-grandfather who first came here, how many of us have parents born in this country? or were born here ourselves?' This was discussed with a show of hands that indicated nearly all parents were born outside Britain and had entered as teenagers (as in the chain migration pattern). Only four out of the 32 pupils in the class were born outside Britain, making 87.5 per cent second generation settlers. This figure correlates with the national statistics for the period 1988–90 that shows 87 per cent of Pakistanis, and 61 per cent of Bangladeshis under 16 years of age were born in Britain (Jones, T., 1993.) The class thought this figure had probably increased by now and it would be interesting to survey a larger sample like all the school.

The children's conclusions again showed that they had internalized information about push/pull factors, and chain migration, and were able to analyse their families' experiences. One of Chris's original aims, that the children should be comfortable with examining their own backgrounds, was also met. Chris wrote 'Hearing the pupils ask questions about themselves and their families in an analytical way was very encouraging, and showed their progress towards understanding and feeling comfortable with (discussing) their own identities.'

The development of the children's work over the five sessions suggests that children had had a stimulating and effective learning experience. Their involvement in conceptualising and analysing migration offered them a way of seeing their experiences in relation to established knowledge which in turn legitimated those experiences. The children were also able to see how their family histories and personal experiences were affected by key social changes, and political and economic factors.

Session 6

The short essays below were written as the final piece of work for this topic. (The children had a choice of writing about a pioneer settler, or writing from the perspective of a pioneer settler who reflects on their early days in Britain.) The essays all show how they have been influenced by the learning done in class. They relate to the 'push' and/or 'pull' factors which motivated migration. The more sophisticated essays include details about arrangements affecting immigration to Great Britain, as well as the kinds of treatment 'pioneer settlers' received.

All of these essays were written in class in session 6. The coherence and focus of each of the pieces suggests that the children had a good understanding of what they had studied. (Below the essays are comments made by Chris when he evaluated the success of his curriculum strategy.)

Memories by Yousaf
I settled in Britain in 1984 in December with my family, and granddad. They came because there wasn't enough rain, and sunshine. They were given a passport, visa, and a sponsor letter, from a very rich man from Britain. We needed a job in Britain, and money. They didn't used to have jobs in Pakistan. When I came to Britain and I got out of the plane, and I looked out of the window and saw lots of white people, they were talking in a different language which I couldn't understand. Few weeks later I went to college and passed my GCSE, then I went to University. In 1990 I got a good job at Bradford.

Memories by Kapil
I remember that I came to Britain in 1968. It was very different from India. The people were different, and also spoke a different sort of English.

I came about three years after my brother came. It was 1971 when the new law was passed. So people had to bring a visa, and have a sponsor.

There was a lot more jobs for people to do. That is the main reason I came.

Comments by Chris on Yousaf and Kapil – 'Yousaf and Kapil clearly showed they had learnt a lot of the content of the topic. I think Yousaf is projecting himself into the role and showing his aspirations when he ends with ' . . . pass my GCSE . . . went to University . . . got a good job.' Kapil had appeared self-conscious of his Sikh Indian background, which put him in a minority group, and was very reluctant to make comments openly in class until he had been asked to report back on the partition of India alongside his Muslim workmate. Hopefully he will continue to participate in class discussion on this topic with slightly raised self esteem . . .'

Old Memories by Shokat

My Granddad lived in Pakistan Azadkashmire district Mirpur. He was a medium wealthy person. He owned some land. He speaks Punjabi. In Pakistan he had a job of making jumpers. In 1961 he decided to come to Britain and intended to do textile work (making jumpers). When he came to Britain he was taken to court. He had to describe himself and tell the job he did in Pakistan. The judge said 'you'll have to make jumpers here as well. You are going to work in Bradford where the mill is'.

My Granddad stayed with his wife's brother. In Pakistan he worked in the army and fought for England in the second world war afterwards. Afterwards when he got some money he kept sending it to his family in Pakistan and then he called his family over bit by bit. First came his wife then his elder son, then his other son and then his other son and by this time his sons had their own houses.

The Memories by Shazad

When my dad came to Britain he found everything strange. He did not know about electricity, gas, oil, the cold weather, the white people. He found the new technology strange. When he first came the carpets were strange to him. In 1962 when my dad wrote an application for a job the manager was surprised that a person who had just come from Pakistan could write English neatly. He told my dad to write out the letter again. When my dad wrote the letter the manager was very pleased and my dad got the job. My dad was very happy when he got the job. My dad was staying with my aunty's son and when he went back to Peterborough to tell him the good news, they were very happy. My dad then brought my family here. My dad was very happy when we all learned English quickly. We were quite rich because my Granddad (great) was a teacher.

Comments by Chris on Shokat and Shazad – 'Shokat and Shazad gained more (than Yousaf and Kapil) from this approach, showing understanding of the ordeals their elders went through on arrival in Britain e.g. facing the patronizing bureaucracy of an immigration course, and the racist stereotyping attitudes of employers.'

Chris's written evaluation refers to both the children's progress and his own. With regard to the children generally, his view was that their motivation and involvement had increased and their responses to tasks became 'more active' thus making achievement more possible.

For himself, leading discussions and encouraging and guiding their investigations on this topic meant that 'I . . . had to learn new content and increase my background knowledge of the topic. This has been valuable to me by improving my understanding of the pupils' heritage, something that is often required, and increases the teachers' ability to communicate with pupils in a meaningful and collaborative way.'

Chris goes on to write that 'working in this way goes beyond making content more interesting and accessible, in that it also contributes to a subtle shift in pupils' attitudes to learning.' He concludes by commenting 'real achievement can only occur in an environment which allows for this kind of collaboration, [and] implies that I have to be prepared to learn more with the pupils, and always look for opportunities in which I can create such an environment . . .'

These statements set out a view of learning which give emphasis to the way pupils relate to each and the teacher, through the use of their personal knowledge and identity, and the extent to which the teacher's approach allows the children to play a key role in evolving the knowledge that is learned.

Conclusions

These written accounts of curriculum enactment cannot begin to convey to us the totality of what was going on in the classrooms, or with the children. Nevertheless Karen and Chris had a remit to develop their teaching and analyse the children's learning outcomes, and so their case studies provide us with some concrete evidence of cultural bridging and its effects.

One of the most exciting and convincing outcomes of their teaching is the evidence of pupils' internalizing new knowledge. Whereas at the outset of Karen's topic, none of the children knew about pilgrimages, by the end not only did they understand that a pilgrimage involved a journey, and that Hajj was the Moslem's pilgrimage, but they had also begun to process the ideas of ritual and penance.

In a similar way Chris suggested that, although some of his pupils had heard family accounts of migration, they did not have a geographical knowledge of this. As a result of their guided reading, home research, and group analysis, however, they learned that migration was a function of push/pull factors, and that these factors were subject to geographical, historical and culturally specific conditions. Their writing demonstrated a good grasp of the topic.

The evidence of the case studies is that this knowledge-processing was in part the result of children's expressions of cultural experiences and differences. Individual children had a stake in their learning because it was linked to what was personal and meaningful. As they shared their knowledge they were able to extend and develop their understanding and what they knew. Karen's class did this by recreating Hajj through discussion, the Moslem children's prayer demonstration, the dramatized Hajj, and the individual writing and project work. Chris's group did this by doing home research, reading, analysing data collaboratively, and writing biographical accounts. In all of these learning activities the children were assembling and applying their knowledge, and accessing new knowledge through interactions with each other, their teachers, and other resources. Their personal stories, however, were always at the heart of their learning.

Both Karen and Chris also describe the success of cultural bridging in terms of pupil involvement, enthusiasm and openness about themselves and their identities. This effect is evidenced from the moment they introduce cultural explicitness as a feature of the learning situation. In Karen's classroom both the majority and minority ethnic group children demonstrated this in their discussion of Hajj in session 2, and in the excitement it generated outside the classroom. Chris's group of seven pupils experienced this immediately when they introduced themselves to each other in terms of their language background and family's geographical origins. The pupils' written accounts (which include experiences of racial prejudice) also exemplify the positive effect of cultural bridging.

Finally, both teachers acknowledged the positive effects that cultural bridging had on them. Karen described the development of teaching relationships as a two-way affair which allowed her to learn about the children's cultures. Chris referred to his own learning about pupils' heritages and the way this contributed to his ability to communicate and collaborate with pupils.

In the everyday world of the classroom, teachers have to use their professional knowledge to make judgements about children's learning. This requires knowing as much as possible about every individual child, their previous curriculum experiences, and information about their progress, attainment, and needs. In the multi-ethnic classroom the presence of cultural differences can also affect the learning situation. Teachers cannot be expected to know all about children's cultural backgrounds (although they can sometimes be helped by referring to their school's ethnic records if these exist); nor is it necessary. It is the children who can be seen as the knowledge-bearers and it is cultural bridging which taps this knowledge and brings a new and exciting dimension to the classroom.

References

Carpenter, C. (1996) Extending the Geography Curriculum, (assessed project work for the OU course, Achievement and the Multi-ethnic School, E632)

Emmott, K. (1996) Action-research project aimed at raising achievement in the multi-ethnic school, (assessed project work for the OU course, Achievement and the Multi-ethnic School, E632)

Jones, T. (1993) *Britain's Ethnic Minorities*, Policy Studies Institute, London.

Lewis, P. (1994) *Islamic Britain*, I. B. Tauris and Co. Ltd.

Open University (1994) Achievement and the Multi-ethnic School (E/E632) including:
Achievement in the Multi-ethnic School, Book One, prepared by Kathy Stredder.
Curriculum Planning and Development, Book Two, prepared by Kathy Stredder with material by Tricia Patterson.
Managing Social Relations, Book Three, prepared by Kathy Stredder.
Involving Parents and the Community, Book Four, prepared by John Gabriel.

19

Anyone for Tennis? Social Class Differences in Children's Responses to National Curriculum Mathematics Testing

Barry Cooper and Máiréad Dunne

[. . .]

Introduction

This chapter reports some aspects of work funded by the ESRC which has as its focus children's interpretations of and performance on the national tests of mathematics for 11 and 14 year-olds in English schools.[1] The project has collected data via tests and interviews from children in three primary and three secondary schools. This chapter will draw on the data from primary schools to demonstrate why certain realistic mathematics test items might be associated with the under-estimation of children's actually existing capacities in mathematics and, furthermore, that the degree of such under-estimation varies by social class. The work of Bernstein and Bourdieu is drawn upon to offer an explanation for the tendency of the competence/performance gap to vary by class. Although the focus of the chapter is on class differences, some data will be provided on associated gender differences. [. . .]

The Policy Background

There is no space here to provide more than a sketch of the policy background within which this work has proceeded ([. . .] Cooper, 1994a and 1994b). However, there are several key points to note. The 1988 Education Act introduced both a national curriculum and associated national assessment of children at the end of Key Stages, including Key Stage 2 at age 11.

This chapter has been edited.

There was considerable debate and conflict around this time and subsequently about the nature of both the curriculum and the form of its assessment. This debate resulted in the initial proposals for assessment mainly by teachers in their classrooms being replaced by a stress on testing via group paper and pencil tests (DES, 1988; Brown, 1992). While there has been a restatement more recently on the importance of teacher assessment (Dearing, 1993), England now has an institutionalised pattern of annual national testing of children at ages 7, 11, 14, and 16. The first national league tables for 11 year olds were published in early 1997.

There is one other key point which must be made. Mathematics – though it clearly has a central core concerning number, space, measure, etc. – is like other school subjects, not fixed and unchanging. As a result of periodic renegotiations of what counts as school mathematics the cognitive demands made on children change over time (Cooper, 1983, 1985a and b; 1994a). In England in recent years such a renegotiation has led to an apparent weakening of the boundary between everyday knowledge and esoteric mathematical knowledge both in the curriculum and in its assessment (Cockcroft, 1982; Cooper, 1994a). While in the 1960s and early 1970s the preferred version of school mathematics tended to favour 'abstract' algebraic approaches (though, at the same time, dominant versions of school mathematics also incorporated newer applications of mathematics), the dominant orthodoxy since the time of the Cockcroft report of 1982 has favoured the teaching and learning of mathematics within 'realistic' settings (Cockcroft, 1982; Dowling, 1991; Boaler, 1993). This preference within the world of mathematics educators was reflected in the early versions of the national tests, as we shall see below. It has been argued that test items contextualising mathematical operations within 'realistic' settings might be expected to cause particular problems of interpretation for working class students [. . .]. It is this possibility that we intend to explore here.

The project

The project is combining quantitative and qualitative approaches. A key feature of the work is the use of sociological ideas concerning the cultural nature of cognition to make theoretical sense of children's responses to assessment contexts and items (Bernstein, 1996; Lave, 1988; Wertsch *et al.*, 1995). The project is collecting a variety of forms of data from three primary schools (10–11 year-olds) and three secondary schools (13–14 year-olds).[2] In early 1996 tests were constructed, using previous National Curriculum tests as an item bank. The tests were designed to include a variety of item types, contextualisations and topic areas. All of the primary students took the same test while the secondary school students were allocated tests tiered by 'ability' as judged by their teachers.[3] These tests were administered to some 140 primary and some 450 secondary school students in

February 1996. Subsequent to this, all of the primary school children and some 100 of the secondary school children worked through the test for a second time in the context of an individual interview with one or other of the researchers. In May 1996 all 590 children participated in the statutory National Tests in mathematics and we have also collected the marked scripts from this exercise (two papers per child. In addition we have collected other data from these schools: background information on the students (parental occupations, measured 'ability', gender) and teachers' assessments of children's level of mathematical understanding. This chapter will use the data from primary students(10–11 years of age).

Class Culture Cognition and Testing

The idea that children (and adults) experience difficulty in understanding and meeting the demands of formal educational tasks – and that these difficulties are not randomly distributed across the social structure is hardly a recent one (Mercer and Edwards, 1987; Holland, 1981). Neither is it an idea particular to sociologists (e.g. Cole *et al.*, 1971; Cole, 1996). However, it is sociologists who have been mainly associated with particular versions of the claim in the post-war period (Bernstein, 1990 and 1996; Bourdieu, 1977 and 1986). Early versions of Bernstein's thesis of a cultural discontinuity between the (lower working class) home and the school attracted considerable critical debate, with the claim being made by various critics that his thesis was flawed by an attachment to a 'deficit' model of the working class child and family. Bernstein has, of course employed considerable energy in attempting to answer these critics (Bernstein, 1990, 1996) and, perhaps more importantly, has revised his ideas substantially over a period of almost forty years. The resulting theoretical account (Bernstein, 1996) seems primarily to be a relational account of cultural differences and their consequences within organised educational systems akin to that Bourdieu has developed over a similar period. While there are important differences between the two (especially with respect to their use of the concept of rules: Bourdieu, 1990a and b), both are arguing that subordinate groups within society lack access, relatively speaking, to the cultural resources which schools demand of children and which, in their nature, reflect the ways of life of dominant social groups. Bernstein captures this via his concept of code: Bourdieu via his concept of habitus. While, notwithstanding their expressed intentions, it may in both cases be possible to detect a residual tendency for 'academic', 'abstract' forms of thought to be favoured over alternatives (e.g. Bourdieu and Wacquant, 1992: 83–89) this is hardly the central thrust of their relational sociologies of education and culture. To the extent such a 'preference' remains visible in their work it probably reflects the partial dependence of both thinkers on Durkheim's analyses of the relation of cognition to the form of the division of labour in society and an associated realist claim that 'minds' and mental processes do differ across social orders characterised by qualitatively different decrees of complexity of the division of labour. The debate on the latter claim continues, closely connected with debates about the effects of literacy and methods of testing human capacities (e.g. Spradley, 1972; Keddie, 1973; Gould, 1984; Street, 1984; Lave, 1988; Nunes *et al.*, 1993; De Abreu, 1995; Cole, 1996).

We will show here that working and intermediate class children seem to be more predisposed than service class children, at age 11, to employ *initially* their everyday knowledge in answering mathematics test items and that this can lead to the under-estimation of their actual capacities with respect to the demands of the school discipline of mathematics as it is currently defined. We will therefore be using the idea of cultural difference in a critical examination of the differential validity of these tests.

Before presenting our account, a few comments on social class are in order. There has long been, and still is a vigorous debate about whether and how to use this concept in social and educational research (e.g. Crompton, 1993; Apple, 1995). We are currently employing the class scheme developed by Goldthorpe and others (e.g. Erikson and Goldthorpe, 1993) and, in particular, are coding children's social backgrounds in terms of a 'dominance' model as set out by these authors (Erikson and Goldthorpe 1993: 238). We have data, inevitably of variable quality, on the current or most recent occupation of the parents/guardians of the children in our sample. We suspect that a proportion of our classifications will contain error. It is also the case that there is, at best, a simplification of social reality involved in attempting to characterise a child's familial context of socialisation by a measure taken at a point in time. As Featherman *et al.* (1988) have shown, there is considerable occupational movement amongst parents of young children and much of it is across the class boundaries described by Goldthorpe. It is also likely that, to some extent, the 'effects' of class which we discuss in this chapter are 'effects' of parents' educational careers, linked to their own origin and destination class, i.e. of the distribution, in Bourdieu's (1994) terms, of educational capital (*'capital scolaire'*). Partly as a result of Featherman's findings and partly as a result of our sample size, we have chosen to employ in the body of the chapter a three category version of the class scheme, with the original 11 categories being collapsed into groupings previously described by Goldthorpe and his co-workers as the service class, the intermediate class and the working class see appendix 1 for descriptions of the groupings).

Some Illustrations

It is often argued that what characterises formal educational knowledge above all else is its disconnectedness from everyday life and concerns

(Neisser, 1976; Mercer and Edwards, 1987). Sociologically speaking, this description might be improved by a reference to whose concerns the knowledge is disconnected from (Young, 1971). Since it is often argued in educational circles that there has been a move since the 1960s – at least until recently – to introduce applications of a 'relevant' nature into curriculum areas like mathematics, it might be useful to begin with a brief illustration of the ways in which 'realistic' test items still demand a 'disconnected' response from children in spite of their surface appearance. Consider the item in Figure 19.1, drawn from the 1992 tests for 14 year-olds.

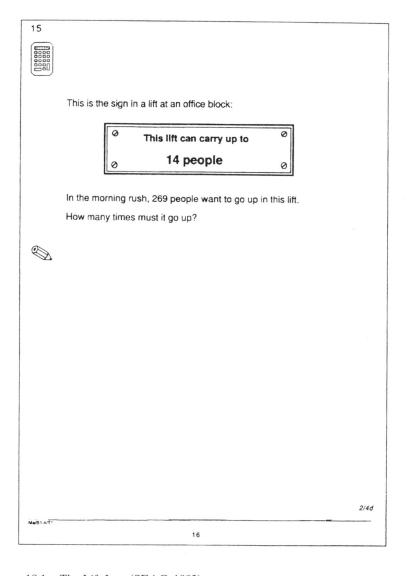

Figure 19.1   *The Lift Item* (SEAC, 1992)

This item is one of a type much discussed in mathematical educational circles. The 'correct' answer is 20 times. The key point is that the child's answer must not be fractional. The lift can not go up (and down) 19.2 times. The child is required therefore to introduce a 'realistic' consideration into his or her response. In fact the child must manage much more than this. He or she must introduce only a small dose of realism – just about enough. The child must not reflect that the lift might not always be full or that some people might get fed up and use the stairs or that some people require more than the average space – e.g. for a wheelchair. Such considerations – 'too much realism' – will lead to a problem without a single answer, and no mark will be gained. [. . .] Children's and schools' interests now hinge on managing these complexities in a legitimate manner.

Various writers have employed the notion of educational ground rules to capture what is demanded of children in these cases (Mercer and Edwards, 1987). There is clearly some affinity between this concept and those of recognition and realisation rules as recently employed by Bernstein (Bernstein, 1996; Cooper, 1996; 1998). However, it can be seen that it would be quite difficult – if not impossible – to write a set of rules which would enable the child to respond as required to the lift question. Certainly, the rule in the sense of a mandated instruction to employ 'realistic' considerations would not do, since 'how much' realism is required remains a discretionary issue. It is this problem that has led to a range of attacks on the use of rules to model human activities (Taylor, 1993) and, in particular, has led Bourdieu to reject a rule-based account of cultural competence. His concept of habitus aims to capture the idea of a durable socialised predisposition without reducing behaviour to strict rule-following (Bourdieu, 1990a and 1990b). Bourdieu sometimes describes what habitus captures as 'a feel for the game' and we can see that this describes fairly well what is required by the lift problem and others like it (for a qualitative comparison across a range of test items of two children who differ markedly in their 'feel for the game' see Cooper, 1996, 1998).

Before moving to a more in-depth discussion of two items, drawing on the responses of more than 100 children, we want to give one more illustration of what the 'feel for the game' can require of children taking the national tests. Consider Figure 19.2, which bases mathematics on shopping – a fairly common 'relevant' topic for children.

This problem, for those socialised into 'esoteric' mathematics, reduces to the solution of the pair of simultaneous linear equations set out below (in pence).

$$C + P = 90$$
$$2C + P = 145$$

One way of solving the problem – legitimately from the point of view of the marking scheme – would be to see this embedded structure and apply whatever technique has been taught for solving such equations. Alternatively, the embedded equations might be solved in a more 'intuitive'

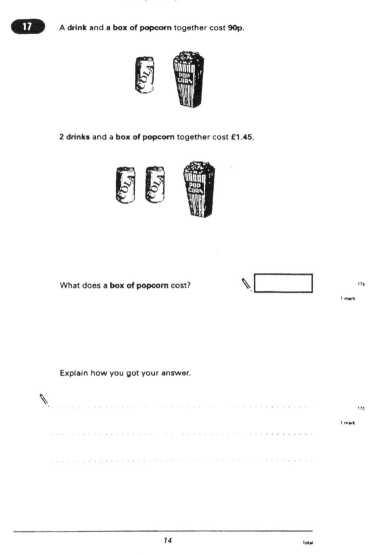

17 A drink and a box of popcorn together cost **90p**.

2 drinks and a box of popcorn together cost **£1.45**.

What does a **box of popcorn** cost?

17a

1 mark

Explain how you got your answer.

17b

1 mark

14

Total

Figure 19.2   *The Shopping Items* (SCAA, 1996)

manner. However, what the child *must* not do (note the 'rule'-like formulation!) is to read the item as an invitation to draw on what they know about and from shopping contexts. Here is an example of what can happen if the child makes this 'mistake':

Example 1
Working class girl (written response from national test in May 1996):
I said to myself that in a sweetshop a can of coke is normally 40p so I thought of a number and the number was 50p so I add 40p and 50p and it equalled 90p.

This response, instead of recognising the hidden structure of the problem – the pair of simultaneous equations, uses just the first 'equation' plus knowledge of the price of cola gained from *shopping in everyday life* to generate a solution. In some respects this solution, which includes correctly worked arithmetic, is efficient – if one is rushing through a timed test – but it is, nevertheless, 'incorrect' given the total information available and the context of a school mathematics test. We are left not knowing whether the child has the 'competence' required to solve the pair of equations taken together. What is it that the child has 'failed' to do? Has she failed to read the whole question? Or to solve the equations? Or to bracket out her everyday knowledge? It may be that, in Bourdieu's terms, this child lacks the required 'feel for the game'. (To answer this we would need to examine her responses across a range of items.)

Notwithstanding the problems of 'rule' on the side of the child – the acquirer of educational knowledge – Bernstein's use of 'rule' does seem to capture a key feature of the power relations this child finds herself in. Those defining the test items, and in particular, what counts as acceptable answers are indeed setting out a series of 'rules' at least in the sense of regulations. Bernstein's use of the concepts '*recognition and realisation rules*' brings this out. His usage of these concepts can only be grasped within the overall structure of his account of educational codes, based in his account of classification and framing. A brief summary follows.

In his constantly developing general theory of pedagogic codes Bernstein, on the one hand, describes the organisation of educational knowledge on the side of the pedagogic transmitter in terms of particular values of *classification* and *framing* (translating power and control relations) and, on the other hand, describes the learner, i.e. the acquirer, in terms of access to *recognition* and *realisation rules* (Bernstein, 1996). Very briefly, and crudely, classification refers to the degree of insulation between categories – discourses, practices, agents, etc. Framing refers to the balance of control over pedagogic communication in local interactional contexts. 'Classification refers to *what*, framing refers to *how* meanings are to be put together, the forms by which they are to be made public, and the nature of the social relationships that go with it' (Bernstein, 1996: 27). Recognition rules. 'at the level of the acquirer', are the means by 'which individuals are able to recognise the speciality of the context that they are in' (31). Realisation rules allow the production of 'legitimate text'. 'The recognition rule, essentially enables appropriate realisations to be put together. The realisation rule determines how we put meanings together and how we make them public' (32). These rules are potentially independent of one another, e.g. 'many children of the marginal classes may indeed have a recognition rule, that is, they can recognise the power relations in which they are involved, and their position in them, but they may not possess the realisation rule. If they do not possess the realisation rule, they cannot then speak the expected legitimate text (32).'

It is also the case that a child may have access to the realisation rule, but not the recognition rule which allows it to become operative, as we shall see later in the discussion of the tennis item (Figure 19.4). In the case of the child's response to the shopping item above she may have in fact been able to undertake the required arithmetic/algebra. We don't know, since she was not in the test situation, given a second chance to respond to the item as a pair of simultaneous equations modelling an entirely imaginary situation.

What we will do in the remainder of the chapter is describe in some detail the patterns of response to two 'realistic' test items by social class, showing that there does seem to be a stronger predisposition among working and intermediate class than service class 11 year-olds to draw 'inappropriately' on their everyday knowledge in the context of mathematics testing. In the second case we will demonstrate that this leads to an under-estimation of what children are actually able to do and hence raises potential equity issues with respect to these tests. The first item concerns an imaginary traffic survey (Figure 19.3); the second an imagined tennis competition (Figure 19.4).

The Traffic Item: the Production of False Positives?

This item (Figure 19.3) can be criticised severely on 'mathematical' grounds (Cooper, 1997). Here, however, our concern is with children's responses to it. The marking scheme asymmetrically allowed a mark for 'likely' or 'very likely' in the case of the car, and for 'unlikely' in the case of the lorry.[4] In the test of which it was a part, there was little apparent sign of any strong social class patterning to the marks awarded (see Table 19.1).

Table 19.1 *Marks obtained on the traffic item in the February 1996 test by class and sex*

(2 marks available)	Female		Male		Total	
	Mean	Count	Mean	Count	Mean	Count
Service class	1.08	26	1.09	34	1.08	60
Intermediate class	0.85	13	1.12	17	1.00	30
Working class	1.15	13	0.90	20	1.00	33
Total	1.04	52	1.04	71	1.04	123

What the test results cannot tell us, however, is anything about the children's response strategy and, in particular, whether they utilised the given data or drew on ther everyday knowledge (presumably an 'incorrect' response from the perspective of an examiner, though method was not addressed in the marking scheme). In the context of the interview we can address this issue. Children were asked, after they had circled two choices why they had chosen these. Two examples follow:

The children in Year 6 conduct a traffic survey outside the school for 1 hour.

Type	Number that passed in one hour
car	75
bus	8
lorry	13
van	26

When waiting outside the school they try to decide on the likelihood that a **lorry** will go by in the next minute.

> Put a ring round how likely it is that a **lorry** will go by in the next minute.
>
> **certain   very likely   likely   unlikely   impossible**

They also try to decide on the likelihood that a **car** will go by in the next minute.

> Put a ring round how likely it is that a **car** will go by in the next minute.
>
> **certain   very likely   likely   unlikely   impossible**

Figure 19.3   *The Traffic Item* (SEAC, 1993)

Transcript 1
A working class girl – response 'esoteric'.
M: I don't like this one.
BC: Don't you? Why don't you like it?
M: I don't know, I just don't like it – too hard for me. (She laughs.)
(She circles *likely* for lorry – no mark, *very likely* for car – one mark.)
BC: Okay, how did you decide on those two?
M: That one, you look at that, and there was only thirteen that went past in an hour, so it was not pretty like- (sic), it might have happened but it wasn't that likely it would happen, and the car, because there's seventy five went past in an hour, it's very likely but you can't be certain.
BC: Right, why can't you be certain?
M: Just in – don't know – you just can't be certain.

BC: You can't be certain. OK. I thought you – why didn't you like that one then? You seemed to do it quite quickly.
M: Yeah, but, I don't like trying to figure which one's which.
BC: Well it's fine. OK, number fourteen next.

Transcript 2
A working class boy – response 'realistic'.
(He circles *unlikely* for lorry – one mark, *very likely* for car – one mark.)
BC: Now how did you decide on those two?
Ra: Cos, because the lorry, there's not as many lorries around as there is cars.
BC: What were you thinking of, whereabouts?
Ra: Outside of school, more parents would come to like collect a child in a car than they would in a lorry.
BC: That's true, right, OK, did you look at these numbers at all here? Did you read that part?
Ra: No.
BC: OK so you did the question without looking at that part?
Ra: Yep.
BC: Right, why do you think you didn't bother to read that then, because you knew already?
Ra: Yep.

We have coded each of the children's responses to our request to explain why they choose what they chose for lorry and car (taken together) according to whether they employed the given data or their everyday knowledge of vehicles and roads. Table 19.2 shows the social class distribution of responses on a three category scale. It can be seen that working class children are almost twice as likely as service class children to refer only to their everyday knowledge in answering our enquiry (and, we might assume. the original question itself). The parallel Table 19.3, on the other hand shows less sign of any simple gender effect, with similar percentages of boys and girls using only everyday knowledge – though the fact that girls are twice as likely to use both given and everyday data may deserve further study.

Table 19.4 draws on the interview data to show the relationship between class, response strategy and mark achieved for the question in the interview context. It is not easy to see any strong relation here between class and success – though there was a relation between class and strategy (Table 19.2). Why? Possibly because the design of this particular question allowed an 'inappropriate' 'everyday' response – one which ignored the given data in some cases completely – to gain marks. Had the item employed given data that conflicted with what children have experienced in their everyday lives rather than paralleled it, then we might have seen a clear relation with class. It is worth stressing this point – the associations reported here result from, amongst other unexamined factors, the relation between what children bring to the context as a result of their academic and general socialisation (in and out of school) and the particular nature of the items. The lack of an association between class, response style and mark here can be seen as a possible example of how a really existing predisposition of a person may or may not, depending on context, lead to 'predicted' associations in a data set. The distribution of the required 'recognition rule', i.e. seems to be

Table 19.2 *Distribution of response strategies by class (traffic item – interview context)*

	Uses given data alone	Uses everyday knowledge and given data	Uses everyday knowledge alone	Totals
Service class	38	10	11	59
Percentage	64.4	16.9	18.6	
Intermediate class	16	10	4	30
Percentage	53.3	33.3	13.3	
Working class	16	6	10	32
Percentage	50.0	18.8	31.3	
Totals	70	26	25	121
Percentage	57.9	21.5	20.7	

Table 19.3 *Distribution of response strategies by sex (traffic item – interview context)*

	Uses given data alone	Uses everyday knowledge and given data	Uses everyday knowledge alone	Totals
Girls	26	16	10	52
Percentage	50.0	30.8	19.2	
Boys	44	11	16	71
Percentage	62.0	15.5	22.5	
Totals	70	27	26	123
Percentage	56.9	22.0	21.1	

Table 19.4 *Mean marks obtained on the traffic item (interview by class and response strategy*

(2 marks available) (n in brackets)	Uses given data alone	Uses everyday knowledge and given data	Uses everyday knowledge alone	Totals
Service class	1.21(38)	1.20(10)	0.91(11)	1.15 (59)
Intermediate class	0.88(16)	1.40(10)	1.50 (4)	1.13 (30)
Working class	1.25(16)	0.83 (6)	1.10(10)	1.13 (32)
Totals	1.14(70)	1.19(26)	1.08(25)	1.14(121)

related to social class leading to working class children being more likely to 'misrecognise' the demands of the problem background (Table 19.2) However, coupled with the choice of given data by the test designers, this results in an item which does not measure validly whether children can produce the required probabilistic reasoning about the given data.

In the case of the traffic item therefore, we have a clear case of a question which seems to generate 'false positives' in assessment terms (Wood and Power, 1987). Children are being awarded marks for 'non-mathematical' behaviour – as judged by 'esoteric' criteria. However, in the light of the findings discussed in the next section concerning the tennis problem (Figure 19.4), it will be seen that the children who used their

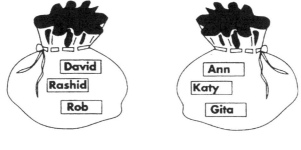

Organising a competition

David and Gitas's group organise a mixed doubles tennis competition. They need to pair a boy with a girl.

They put the three boys' names into one bag and all the three girls' names into another bag.

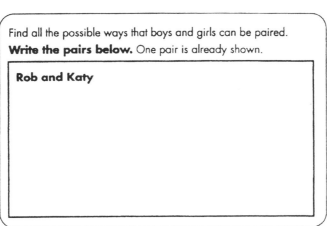

Find all the possible ways that boys and girls can be paired.
Write the pairs below. One pair is already shown.

Rob and Katy

Figure 19.4   *The Tennis Item* (SEAC, 1993)

everyday experience to decide on likelihoods perhaps could have used the given knowledge to the same end – had they been asked to do so more explicitly.

The Tennis Item: the Production of False Negatives?

The tennis item (Figure 19.4) is intended to be difficult, being judged by the test designers to be suitable only for higher attaining children.[5] Why, however, should it be difficult? [. . .]

In the terms used by Bernstein, this item seems likely to be a candidate for confusion about what is relevant knowledge to bring to bear. What might be 'appropriate' in the context of real sports competitions is not 'appropriate' or 'legitimate' in the context of a mathematics test. There is a potentially confusing boundary to negotiate.

That children find this a difficult boundary can be illustrated by the fact that several children took the apparent national origins of the competitors into account in making their decisions (see transcripts 3–5). Two of these children initially produced three pairs, and one did so after some elaboration by the interviewer of the test item's demands.

Transcript 3: girl, service class
MD: Have you finished? OK, explain to me how you worked that out then.
Child: Well, Rob and Katy they're like normal names, and they'll be OK together, and *they* sound like different country names.
MD: What Rashid and Gita?
Child: Yeah, and so, they would be quite happy as a pair because they come from a different country and they've got those names and just put them together.

Transcript 4: boy, intermediate class
Child: Done.
MD: OK, so how did you work that out?
Child: Well, Rob and Ann's sound like not really, um, (*indecipherable phrase, possibly* 'brother and sister'), so I'll come back to them. Rashid and Gita are like, sort of the same names from a different country.
MD: Mm.
Child: So it might be them two pairs, and Rob and Ann.
MD: David and Ann do you mean?
Child: I mean David and Ann.
MD: OK, so you worked it out because of where the country, is that what you're saying?
Child: Yeah.

Transcript 5: boy, working class
MD: OK, what have you done then – Rashid and Ann.
Child: Rashid and Gita, sound like different country names so that it wouldn't exactly be fair if Rashid and Gita got together, because you've got to give them a chance to meet other people.

Clearly, from the perspective of esoteric mathematics the children's national origin is not a relevant consideration, though it might well be in the everyday life of school children. What does the full data set suggest about children's reading of this question? In fact, in the February 1996 test, 28 of the 125 children produced three pairs as their answer rather than the required nine, suggesting that for these children everyday concerns *may* have dominated esoteric ones. How did success on this item relate to class and gender?

Tables 19.6 and 19.7 show that, in both the test and the interview the working class children do considerably less well on this item, for which one mark was available, than the service class children. The boys do slightly less well as a group than the girls in the test but the difference disappears in the interview. We will concentrate on class in this rest of this section.

In this case, unlike the traffic item, since we do have relevant written text available to us, we have coded the written text produced in the interview setting – as opposed to the children's verbal responses to our questions. The marking scheme allows a mark only for nine distinct pairs. Children therefore respond 'appropriately' to this item by setting out nine pairs. If they do so, it is possible to code the nine pairs as 'esoteric' or 'realistic' by reference to the way they have been grouped. Here is what we would term an 'esoteric' set:

Rob & Katy
Rob & Ann
Rob & Gita

Rashid & Katy
Rashid & Ann
Rashid & Gita

David & Katy
David & Ann
David & Gita

Here, by contrast, is a 'realistic' set:

Rob & Katy
David & Gita
Rashid & Ann

David & Ann
Rashid & Katy
Rob & Gita

David & Katy
Rashi & Gita
Rob & Ann

Table 19.5   *Mean marks obtained on the traffic item (interview) by sex and response strategy*

(2 marks available) (n in brackets)	Uses given data alone	Uses everyday knowledge and given data	Uses everyday knowledge alone	Totals
Girls	0.96(26)	1.38(16)	1.00(10)	1.10 (52)
Boys	1.25(44)	1.00(11)	1.06(16)	1.17 (71)
Totals	1.14(70)	1.22(27)	1.04(26)	1.14(123)

Table 19.6   *Mean marks achieved on tennis item in the February 1996 test context*

(2 marks available)	Female		Male		Total	
	Mean	Count	Mean	Count	Mean	Count
Service class	.62	26	.56	34	.58	60
Intermediate class	.54	13	.41	17	.47	30
Working class	.38	13	.40	20	.39	33
Total	.54	52	.48	71	.50	123

Table 19.7　*Marks achieved on tennis item in the interview context – initial response*

(2 marks available)	Female		Male		Total	
	Mean	Count	Mean	Count	Mean	Count
Service class	.81	26	.85	34	.83	60
Intermediate class	.77	13	.82	17	.80	30
Working class	.69	13	.60	20	.64	33
Total	.77	52	.77	71	.77	123

In the second case the pairs, taken in groups of three at a time, might engage in games of tennis – hence our coding of the set as 'realistic'. In the first case, each group of three could not, given the repeated use of one child's name. In most cases where children produced three pairs, in both the test and the interview, they were a 'realistic' three, using each child just once. Now it might be argued that the second nine above is a 'better' response than the first as far as tennis is concerned but it is arguably not from the point of view of 'esoteric' mathematics. The first set of pairs, from the latter point of view, is more 'abstract', more obviously 'mathematical' in its 'systematicity'. What about response style in this case? Table 19.8 shows response style is strongly related to class.

Table 19.8　*Response strategy on the tennis item (interview) by class*

	'Esoteric' pairings	Other (typically mixed)	'Realistic' pairings	Totals
Service class	47	4	8	59
Percentage	79.7	6.8	13.6	
Intermediate class	20	2	8	31
Percentage	66.7	6.7	26.7	
Working class	14	5	12	31
Percentage	45.2	16.1	38.7	
Totals	81	11	28	120
Percentage	67.5	9.2	23.3	

Table 19.9　*Mean mark obtained on the tennis item (interview) by class and response strategy (counts as above table)*

	'Esoteric' pairings	Other (typically mixed)	'Realistic' pairings	Totals
Service class	1.00	.75	.00	.85
Intermediate class	1.00	1.00	.25	.80
Working class	1.00	.80	.25	.68
Totals	1.00	.82	.18	.79

Table 19.9 breaks down the marks achieved in the interview by social class and response style. Given the apparent relation between response style and mark, it becomes particularly important to look in more detail at what happened when, in the interview, the children were given a second

chance to try to find all the possible pairs. Given the apparent tendency for working class children to choose an 'inappropriate' self-defeating strategy in their initial response it becomes a critical question whether they might have produced the nine pairs had they not 'chosen' this initial response style. In other words, is there some sense in which they might be able, in some cases, to do the mathematics 'pure and simple', given a minor cue that they have 'misrecognised' the context? Now, in fact, the cue was merely the request, once they had clearly finished writing some number of pairs fewer than nine, to consider whether they had obtained all the pairs. One example of what happened in a number of cases follows. The child here is a girl from the intermediate class grouping.

Transcript 6: girl, intermediate class

She writes the three pairs thus:

Rob and Katy
Rashid and Gita
David and Ann

MD: Done that one?
E: Yeah.
MD: OK, so tell me how you worked that one out.
E: I put those two names and – so I did those two there can and I did those.
MD: David and Ann, Rashid and Gita, OK.
E: Mm.
MD: OK, see where it says there find all the possible ways that girls and boys can be paired, do you think you've found all the possible ways?
E: No.
MD: You could find some more?
E: Yeah.
MD: OK, let me just do that, so I'll know where you stopped for the beginning. OK, go on then.
(She works at the problem. silently.)
(She adds six pairs to give:)

Rob and Katy	*Katy and David*
Rashid and Gita	*Ann and Rob*
David and Ann	*Ann and Rashid*

Gita and David
Gita and Rob
Katy and Rashid

MD: OK, so have you finished that one now?
E: Mm.
MD: And you think you've got all of them?
E: Yeah.
MD: OK, do you know? – when you first did it you stopped, after three, why did you stop after three?
E: I don't know.
MD: You don't know but why didn't you continue?
E: I didn't think that you were supposed to.
MD: OK, that's a good reason, but why didn't you think you were supposed to?
(The interview continues with the child not being able to give a reason.)

She initially produced three pairs but then obtained nine pairs when encourage to reflect on whether this was enough. She did not think she was 'supposed to' do nine – a rather rule-like formulation. How common was this type of response? [. . .] Some 10 per cent of the sample under discussion here fell into this trap of initially producing a 'realistic' three pairs and yet recovered fully from this 'inappropriate' response when offered a chance to reconsider. Furthermore, children from intermediate and working social class backgrounds were over-represented amongst this group and children from service class backgrounds under-represented, as Table 19.10 shows. Notwithstanding the small numbers involved, this result seems to suggest that differentiated responses to items of this particular type may have some important consequences in producing class-related patterns of success and failure in national testing. There is also a slight tendency for girls to be over-represented amongst this group (Table 19.11) and for the children to have lower than average 'ability' scores.

Table 19.10   *Class distribution of 3 followed by 9 children compared to sample in general*

	Service class (%)	Intermediate class (%)	Working class (%)	n (with class data)
The 12 cases	25.0	41.7	33.3	12
In whole sample	48.8	24.4	26.8	123

Table 19.11   *Sex distribution of 3 followed by 9 children compared to sample in general*

	Girls (%)	Boys (%)	n
The 12 cases	58.3	41.7	12
In whole sample	43.2	56.8	125

We can see that in the case of this question a child's apparent *response style* can lead to his or her 'mathematical' competence being under-estimated because of the way in which he or she 'chose' to read the question. These 12 cases, some 10 per cent of the total, are arguably all 'false negatives' on first response – given that the children *could* do what was required when cued to reconsider what they had written.[6] Their *performance* has not reflected their *mathematical competence* at least in the sense of the capacity to produce nine pairs from two groups of three items and this seems to be related to the children's capacity to recognise correctly or not the demands of the context. In the light of Holland's (1951) work with Bernstein on children's preferred classifying strategies it seems that the over-representation of working class children amongst these false negatives is something we might have expected.

The Traffic and Tennis Items Compared

What can we learn from a comparison of the children's responses to these two items, one multiple choice and one open-ended'? The threats to valid and 'fair' assessment of 'competence' inherent in both types of question can be noted. In the case of the traffic item the children, because of its multiple choice nature, could obtain marks by 'inappropriately' employing their everyday knowledge. The nature of the response mode hides this from the assessor. This validity problem could have been avoided by making the given data less typical of everyday settings known to the children, i.e. by introducing 'realistic'/'esoteric' dissonance. However, had this been done, we perhaps would have found the second problem coming to the fore – the equity problem that we found in the case of the tennis item. On such a revised traffic item, working class children might have tended to have lost marks not because they could not reason probabilistically but because they referred more to everyday knowledge than their service class companions. We saw, in the case of the tennis item, that children who had the 'mathematical competence' did not always demonstrate it, without the elaboration of their response induced by the interviewer, and that this behaviour was apparently related to the social class distribution of recognition rules.

Conclusion

This chapter has concentrated on just two test items. In a parallel recent paper, we have reported a statistical analysis, by class and gender, of children's degrees of success on two broad classes of test items, termed by us 'esoteric' and 'realistic'. The 'realistic' items embed mathematical operations within contexts containing people and/or non-mathematical everyday objects while the 'esoteric' do not. All of the items discussed here would be coded as 'realistic'. [. . .] We have found a greater difference between service and working class mean performances for the category of 'realistic' than for the category of 'esoteric' items (Cooper *et al.*, 1997). The current chapter shows that part of an explanation of this general finding might be found in social class differences in the interpretation of the demands of 'realistic' questions, with working class children being more likely to draw 'inappropriately' on their everyday knowledge when responding to items. This relative failure (and it is relative, not absolute) to recognise the strongly classified nature of school mathematics in the face of surface appearances which suggest the relevance of everyday knowledge may be an aspect of the overall sociocultural predispositions discussed by Bourdieu and Bernstein. The realised meaning of the items seems to vary with social class, with the resulting negative effects on performance leading to the under-estimation of the actual competence of more working than service class children.

What Bourdieu has argued concerning 'popular' classes' responses to 'art' works seems to capture something of the features of some children's responses to the two items discussed here. He has written, in *Distinction*:

> When faced with legitimate works of art, people most lacking the specific competence apply to them the perceptual schemes of their own ethos, the very ones which structure their everyday perception of everyday existence. These schemes, giving rise to products of an unwilled, unselfconscious systematicity, are opposed to the more or less fully stated principles of an aesthetic. The result is a systematic 'reduction' of the things of art to the things of life, a bracketing of form in favour of 'human' content, which is barbarism par excellence from the standpoint of the pure aesthetic. Everything takes place as if the emphasis on form could only be achieved by means of neutralisation of any kind of affective or ethical interest in the object of representation which accompanies . . . mastery of the means of grasping the distinctive properties which this particular form takes on in its relations with other forms (i.e. through reference to the universe of works of art and its history). (Bourdieu,1986: 44)

Furthermore, he clearly sees the explanation for the differences in response as grounded in different material conditions of life.

> The aesthetic disposition which tends to bracket off the nature and function of the object represented and to exclude any 'naive' reaction – horror at the horrible, desire for the desirable, pious reverence for the sacred – along with all purely ethical responses, in order to concentrate solely upon the mode of representation, the style, perceived and appreciated by comparison with other styles, is one dimension of a total relation to the world and to others, a life-style, in which the effects of particular conditions of existence are expressed in a 'misrecognizable' form. These conditions of existence, which are the precondition for all learning of legitimate culture, whether implicit and diffuse, as domestic cultural training generally is, or explicit and specific, as in scholastic training, are characterised by the suspension and removal of economic necessity and by objective and subjective distance from practical urgencies, which is the basis of objective and subjective distance from groups subjected to those determinisms. (Bourdieu, 1986: 54)

These remarks, especially in their references to the concern with abstract form as opposed to human content which he sees as characteristic of dominant class responses, seem to capture equally something of the differences between children who do and do not employ the resource of their everyday knowledge in their test responses. These patterns of response do seem to be related in our data to social class background. However, we have not presented here an analysis which would justify the claim that the patterns of response result from predispositions to act in similar ways across a wide range of test items (though the findings in Cooper *et al.*, 1997, would lend some support to such a claim). The full examination of that claim will require further work.

There are a number of reasons why such work is important. First of all, it is clearly a contribution to the general study of the relations between sociocultural background and cognitive processes and products. Secondly, it has important policy implications for those in education, especially for those concerned with equity issues in testing. Mathematics is one of the key areas of study within formal educational institutions. Because of this children's success or failure in mathematics is a key factor in the determination of their subsequent life chances. In particular, as the climate of opinion seems to move in favour of greater selection at the end of primary schooling (see, e.g., Hutton, 1995: 311), the Key Stage 2 tests may well become one element of a process of selection for secondary school. More generally, researchers in the field of assessment in both the UK and the USA are increasingly concerned about the implications for equality of opportunity of recent changes in forms of assessment (Gipps and Murphy, 1994; Darling-Hammond, 1994; Baker and O'Neil, 1994). What the evidence in this chapter suggests, especially if taken together with the results reported in Cooper *et al.* (1997), is that the current attempt by mathematics educators to maintain a concern with 'relevance' in the context of the national curriculum and its testing may have unintended – and perverse – consequences for another set of concerns they may well share – those concerning equal opportunities issues (e.g. Secada *et al.*, 1995).

Appendix 1: Occupational Groupings

(combined from Goldthorpe and Heath, 1992 and Erikson and Goldthorpe, 1993)

1. Service class, higher grade: higher grade professionals, administrators and officials; managers in large industrial establishments; large proprietors.
2. Service class, lower grade: lower grade professionals, administrators and officials; higher grade technicians; managers in small industrial establishments; supervisors of non-manual employees.
3. Routine non-manual employees.
4. Personal service workers.
5. Small proprietors with employees.
6. Small proprietors without employees.
7. Farmers and smallholders.
8. Foremen and technicians.
9. Skilled manual workers.
10. Semi- and unskilled manual workers.
11. Agricultural workers.

We have collapsed 1 and 2 into a service class, 3–8 into an intermediate class, and 9–11 into a working class. [. . .]

Acknowledgements

We would like to thank all the teachers and children in the six schools for putting up with our constant demands over most of a year; Beryl Clough,

Hayley Kirby and Julia Martin-Woodbridge for their work in transcribing interviews so patiently, and the Economic and Social Research Council for funding this work. We would also like to thank Nicola Rodgers for her part in data collection, and various of our colleagues at Sussex and Stephanie Cant for their comments on drafts of papers.

[A table and references have been omitted from the original].

Notes

1. Economic and Social Research Council Project (R000235863): Mathematics Assessment at Key Stages Two and Three: Pupils' Interpretation and Performance (1995–97).
2. The schools have been selected to cover the range of social class positions of students in the English state school sector.
3. We have done this, in the case of secondary schools, in order to replicate the official practice.
4. The Statement of Attainment being assessed is (supposedly): *Use appropriate language to justify decisions when placing events in order of 'likelihood'.*
5. The Statement of Attainment for this item is: *Identify all the outcomes of combining two independent events.* The (very!) esoteric mathematical 'equivalent of the tennis item is: Find the *Cartesian product* of the sets (a, b, c) and (d, e, f).
6. From an assessment point of view, when the context was manipulated to allow them to produce their 'best' response.

References

Apple, M. (1995) 'Education, culture and class power: Basil Bernstein and the neo-Marxist sociology of education', in Sadovnik, A. (ed.) *Knowledge and Pedagogy: the Sociology of Basil Bernstein*, Ablex, Norwood, New Jersey, pp. 59–82.

Baker, E. L. and O'Neill, H. F. (1994) 'Performance assessment and equity: a view from the USA', *Assessment in Education*, 1, 1, pp. 11–26.

Bernstein, B. (1990) *The Structuring of Pedagogic Discourse*, London, Routledge.

Bernstein, B. (1996) *Pedagogy, Symbolic Control and Identity: Theory Research, Critique*, Taylor and Francis, London.

Boaler, J. (1993) 'The role of contexts in the mathematics classroom: do they make mathematics more "real"?' *For the Learning of Mathematics*, 13, 2, pp. 12–17.

Bourdieu, P. (1986) *Distinction: A social critique of the judgement of taste*, Routledge and Kegan Paul, London.

Bourdieu, P. (1990a) *In Other Words*, Cambridge, Polity Press.

Bourdieu, P. (1990b)*The Logic of Practice*, Oxford, Blackwell.

Bourdieu, P. (1994) *Raisons Practiques: sur la théorie de l'action*, Paris, Seuil.

Bourdieu, P. and Passeron, J-C. (1977) *Reproduction in Education, Society and Culture*, London, Sage.

Bourdieu, P. and Wacquant, L. J. D. (1992) *An Introduction to Reflexive Sociology*, Chicago, University of Chicago Press.

Brown, M. (1992) 'Elaborate nonsense? The muddled tale of Standard Assessment Tasks at Key Stage 3', in Gipps, C. (ed.) *Development Assessment for the National Curriculum*, London, Kogan Page and London University Institute of Education, pp. 6–19.

Cockroft, W. H. (1982) *Mathematics Counts*, London, HMSO.

Cole, M. (1996) *Cultural Psychology*, Cambridge Massachusetts, Belknap/Harvard University Press.

Cole, M., Gay, J., Glick, J. A. and Sharp, D. W. (1971) *The Cultural Context of Learning and Thinking*, London, Tavistock/Methuen.

Cooper , B. (1983) 'On explaining change in school subjects', *British Journal of Sociology of Education*, 4(3), pp. 207–222.

Cooper, B. (1985a) *Renegotiating Secondary School Mathematics*, Basingstoke, Falmer Press.

Cooper, B. (1985b) 'Secondary school mathematics since 1950: reconstructing differentiation', in Goodson, I. F. (ed.) *Social Histories of the Secondary Curriculum*, Barcombe, Falmer.

Cooper, B. (1994a) 'Secondary mathematics education in England: recent changes and their historical context', in Selinger, M. (ed.) *Teaching Mathematics*, London, Routledge, pp. 5–26.

Cooper, B. (1994b) 'Authentic testing in mathematics? The boundary between everyday and mathematical knowledge in National Curriculum testing in English schools', in *Assessment in Education: Principles, Policy and Practice*, 1, 2, pp. 143–166.

Cooper, B. (1996) 'Using Data from Clinical Interviews To Explore Students' Understanding of Mathematics Test Items: Relating Bernstein and Bourdieu on Culture to Questions of Fairness in Testing', paper presented at the Annual Meeting of the *American Educational Research Association*, New York, April, 1996.

Cooper, B. (1997) 'Assessing National Curriculum Mathematics in England: Exploring children's interpretation of Key Stage 2 tests in clinical interviews', *Educational Studies in Mathematics*.

Cooper, B. (1998) 'Using Bernstein and Bourdieu to understand children's difficulties with 'realistic' mathematics testing: an explanatory study', in *International Journal of Qualitative Studies in Education*.

Cooper, B., Dunne, M. and Rodgers, N. (1997) 'Social class, gender, item type and performance in national tests of primary school mathematics: some research evidence from England', paper presented at the Annual Meeting of the *American Educational Research Association*, Chicago, March, 1997.

Crompton, R. (1993) *Class and Stratification*, Cambridge, Polity Press.

Darling-Hammond, L. (1994) 'Performance-based assessment and educational equity', *Harvard Educational Review*, 64, 1, pp. 5–30.

De Abreu, G. (1995) 'Understanding how children experience the relationship between home and school mathematics', *Mind, Culture and Activity*, 2, 2, pp. 119–142.

Dearing, R. (1993) *The National Curriculum and its Assessment: Final Report*, London, SCAA.

Department of Education and Science (1988) *Task Group on Assessment and Testing: A Report*, London, DES/WO.

Dowling, P. 'A touch of class: ability, social class and intertext in SMP 11–16', in Pimm, D. and Love, E. (eds.) *Teaching and Learning School Mathematics*, London, Hodder and Stoughton.

Erikson, R. and Goldthorpe, J. H. (1993) *The Constant Flux: A Study of Class Mobility in Industrial Societies*, Oxford, Clarendon.

Featherman, D. L., Spenner, K. I. and Tsunematsu, N. (1988) 'Class and the socialisation of children: constancy, change or irrelevance?' in Hetherington, E. M., Lerner, R. M. and Perlmutter, M. *Child Development* in *Life-Span Perspective*, Hillsdale, New Jersey, Lawrence Erlbaum.

Gipps, C. and Murphy, P. (1994) *A Fair Test? Assessment, Achievement and Equity*, Buckingham, Open University Press.

Goldthorpe, J. and Heath, A. (1992) 'Revised class schema 1992', working paper 13, Nuffield College Oxford.

Gould, S. J. (1984) *The Mismeasure of Man*, Harmondsworth, Penguin.

Holland, J. (1981) 'Social class and changes in orientation to meaning', in *Sociology*, 15, 1, pp.1–18.

Hutton, W. (1995) *The State We're In*, London, Jonathan Cape.

Keddie, N. (ed.) (1973) *Tinker, Tailor – The Myth of Cultural Deprivation*, Harmondsworth, Penguin.

Lave, J. (1988) *Cognition in Practice: Mind, Mathematics and Culture in Everyday Life*, Cambridge, Cambridge University Press.

Mercer, N. and Edwards, D. (1987) *Common Knowledge: The Development of Understanding in the Classroom*, London, Methuen.

Morais, A., Fontinhas, F. and Neves, I. (1992) 'Recognition and realisation rules in acquiring school science: the contribution of pedagogy and social background of students', *British Journal of Sociology of Education*, 13, 2, pp. 247–270.

Neisser, U. (1976) 'General, academic and artificial intelligence', in Resnick, L. B. *The Nature of Intelligence*, Hillsdale, New Jersey, Lawrence Earlbaum.

Nunes, T., Schliemann, A. D. and Carraher, D. W. (1993) *Street Mathematics and School Mathematics*, Cambridge, Cambridge University Press.

SCAA – Schools Curriculum and Assessment Authority (1995) *Mathematics Tests Key Stage 2 1995*, London, Department for Education.

SCAA – Schools Curriculum and Assessment Authority (1996) *Key Stage 2 Tests 1996*, London, Department for Education and Employment.

SEAC (1992) *Mathematics Tests, 1992, Key Stage 3*, SEAC/University of London.

SEAC (1993) *Pilot Standard Tests: Key Stage 2: Mathematics*, SEAC/University of Leeds.

Secada, W. G., Fennema, E. and Adajian, L. B. (eds,) (1995) *New Directions for Equity in Mathematics Education*, Cambridge, Cambridge University Press..

Spradley, J. (1972) *Culture and Cognition: Rules, Maps and Plans*, San Francisco, Chandler Publishing.

Street, B, (1984) *Literacy in Theory and Practice*, Cambridge, Cambridge University Press.

Taylor, C. (1993) 'To follow a rule . . .' in Calhoun, C., Limpuma, E. and Postone, M. (eds.) *Bourdieu: Critical Perspectives*, Cambridge, Polity.

Wertsch, J. V. *et al.* (1995) *Sociocultural Theories of Mind*, Cambridge, Cambridge University Press.

Wood, R. and Power, C. (1987) 'Aspects of the competence-performance distinction: educational, psychological and measurement issues', in *Journal of Curriculum Studies*, 19, 5, pp. 409–424.

Young, M. F. D. (1971) 'Curricula as socially organised knowledge', in Young, M. F. D. (ed.) *Knowledge and Control*, London, Collier-Macmillan.

20

Securing Conceptual Development in Workplaces

Stephen Billett and Judy Rose

[. . .]

Introduction

This chapter reports an investigation which examined the use of three instructional strategies which aimed to secure the development of conceptual knowledge in workplace settings. The purpose of the research was to build upon previous work which concluded that everyday participation in work practice provides opportunities for individuals to access and secure vocational knowledge (Billett, 1992, 1993, 1994). The development of procedural knowledge (that is, means of securing goals) was apparent in this work, whereas the development of some forms of conceptual knowledge (understanding) was consistently reported as being limited. The hidden or opaque nature of conceptual knowledge was proposed as a basis for the limited development. Importantly, vocational activities are expected to rely more on this type of conceptual knowledge with the advent of new technologies and more complex forms of work practice (Berryman, 1993). Hence, vocational learners will need to be able to secure the conceptual knowledge associated with their vocational practice. [. . .]

The socio-cultural consructivist literature holds that knowledge is socially mediated. In particular, close social mediation or proximal guidance is likely to provide an expedient means for learners to access and construct conceptual knowledge in workplace settings. In these settings, the most likely prospect for achieving this goal is through the guided assistance of a more 'expert other' (supervisor or senior staff member) using strategies that will make what is hidden accessible and also embedding conceptual knowledge in social practice. Consequently, the aim of the empirical work referred to in this chapter is to investigate the efficacy of instructional strategies which can enhance the potency of guidance afforded by expert others during everyday participation in work practice. The strategies

This chapter has been edited.

selection takes into account the need for close social mediation in authentic circumstances, rather than through disembedded training activities, such as might occur in the classroom or training centre. The strategies selected for this inquiry were: (i) questioning dialogues, (ii) analogies and (iii) diagrams. The question which guides this investigation is: 'In what ways does the use of instructional strategies assist with changes to the learners' conceptual knowledge?' The settings used to appraise the strategies are small hospitality businesses – restaurants, which were selected as part of a larger inquiry into the nature of knowledge and learning in small hospitality businesses (see Stevenson, 1996).

[. . .]

Conceptual Knowledge

Cognitive psychology is concerned with how knowledge is acquired and deployed by individuals to perform activities. Within this discipline, two types of knowledge are commonly referred to as being represented in memory. These are: (i) conceptual knowledge and (ii) procedural knowledge, respectively referred to as knowing 'that' and knowing 'how' (Anderson, 1982). Whereas procedures provide the means to secure goals and sub-goals, concepts provide a conceptual basis to guide the goal-directed activity of problem-solving (thinking and acting) as well as goals for performance. Problem-solving, both the routine or non-routine type, is central to cognitive theory being the basis for performance and also the means to secure cognitive development. Routine problem-solving occurs hundreds of times each day and requires only the re-deployment of existing cognitive structures (propositional and procedural knowledge) in resolving problems previously encountered. Non-routine problem-solving requires cognitive structures to be transformed and extended when dealing with novel circumstances. In addition to securing routine and non-routine goals, problem-solving is held to be associated with cognitive change or development (Anderson, 1993; Shuell, 1990). Whereas non-routine problem-solving is generative of cognitive development through the creation and re-organisation of existing cognitive structures, non-routine problem-solving incrementally and, over time, reinforces and strengthens that knowledge and its associations (Billett, 1995).

Consequently; both conceptual and procedural knowledge are used in everyday vocational practice to organise activities and secure workplace goals. For example, before a waiter sets a restaurant table, concepts about the sorts of things that should be placed on the table are recalled from memory before the task begins. Moreover, concepts are likely to be called upon to determine whether the completed task has been accomplished to a level of satisfaction, determined by the particular restaurant. In this way, the goals 'for doing' are also concepts. However, the table is set through the deployment of procedures. Procedures secure goals that concepts provide. Hence, there is a close and interdependent relationship between concepts and procedures. The development of conceptual knowledge in the workplace is the focus of this paper as those forms of conceptual knowledge which are hidden have demonstrably been difficult for individuals to construct through engagement in everyday workplace activity (Billett, 1995).

Conceptual knowledge is differentiated by levels of increasing complexity or depth (Evans, 1991; Greeno, 1989). These levels range from simple factual knowledge (for example, names of food items) through to deeper or more complex levels of conceptual knowledge (such as principled understanding about the blending of flavours or thickening of sauces). Significantly, depth of understanding includes the strength of relationships or association amongst concepts (Groen and Patel, 1988; Novak, 1990), thereby emphasising the interconnectedness of conceptual knowledge as a basis for deep understanding (Prawat, 1989). That is, rich associations are the basis for robust and hence transferable conceptual knowledge. Depth of understanding is held to be limitless, when considered in relational terms to other cognitive structures. As conceptual linkages and associations are only limited by individuals' constructions, rather than some objective notion of objectivity, they can be said to be limitless in terms of depth.

So as discussed above, conceptual knowledge is significant as it permits the formulation of goals and assists with the deployment of procedures to secure workplace performance. Novel workplace tasks require the individual to go beyond the surface features of a problem in order to access its deep features (Chi *et al.*, 1981; Gott, 1989). Therefore, a deep level of conceptual knowledge offers a mechanism for the abstraction of principles and concepts, facilitating the resolution of novel problem-solving, such as the transfer of knowledge across situations and circumstances (Pea, 1987; Royer, 1979). Experts require deep conceptual knowledge, within a domain (such as food service, cooking and hairdressing). It also provides a basis for determining what is salient or trivial in problem situations, thus aiding their resolution. This facility determines whether a problem is viewed as worth solving and, if so, with what degree of finesse. For example, expert waiters may not deem it worth challenging troublesome or overly demanding customers, instead humouring them. In this way, experts' knowledge is organised around important principles ((propositions) which guide activities. This organisation of knowledge permits experts to analyse problems and offer more effective solutions than novices could achieve. Hence, a goal for vocational education is to secure these forms of knowledge.

Further to what has been advanced above, associations between conceptual structures determine the time taken to retrieve information from memory (Collins and Quillian, 1969). Associations which lead to indexations are held to have a number of qualities (Anderson, 1982). Firstly, if a fact is frequently encountered with a concept it becomes associated with that concept. For example, client satisfaction might become associated with prompt service at lunchtime and a more relaxed service in the evening. Secondly, the more frequently encountered a fact about a concept, the more strongly the fact becomes associated with the concept and the quicker they are likely to be verified or recalled. Therefore, frequent engagement in situations where lunch-time service needs to be prompt in contrast to service in the evening being more relaxed in order to secure customer satisfaction, may strengthen these associations. Thirdly, verifying facts that are not directly associated with a concept takes longer (for example, a solo client in the evening – do they want to linger or require prompt service?). So, as well as associations formed through frequency of encounter, there is also a need to extend those associations to accommodate what for one setting might be atypical, as with the solo evening diner.

Hence, the more richly associated conceptual networks are, the greater likelihood of recall. Indexation (how individuals link stimuli to facilitate recall) is influenced by the associations that are provided by participation in everyday activity within a physical and social environment which is authentic in terms of the knowledge's deployment. [. . .]

Learning as a Constructive Process

Individuals construct knowledge from the circumstances in which they encounter it This construction is viewed as an ongoing interpretative process and is reinforced by other ongoing and validating experiences (von Glasersfeld, 1987). For example, consider how learners might construct an understanding of client service from working in either an international standard hotel or in the local pub. Therefore, rather than being the objective learning of knowledge, it is interpretively constructed through individuals' meaning structures which determine what sense they make of particular experiences. Consider also if the service offered equates to what the learner believes 'good' service is all about (for example, is it indulgent or what is expected?) for their personal history or ontogeny (Scribner, 1985). Individuals make sense of knowledge in an interpretative and constructive way, rather than internalising externally derived knowledge. Therefore, the appropriation of knowledge is not just the internalisation of externally derived stimuli, but rather the individual's construction of those stimuli (Rogoff, 1995) Hence, it is the learner that determines what knowledge is constructed based on the interpretation of the circumstances they experience. Therefore, the construction of knowledge is mediated by social circumstances, both those in the immediate social circumstances in which knowledge is accessed and those which comprise the individual's ontogeny. [. . .] Hence, it is claimed that the direct teaching of conceptual knowledge is likely to have limited success because individuals construct knowledge through 'creation and interpretation', reciprocal processes of human interaction (Pea, 1993)

'Meaning negotiation' and 'appropriation' are two processes proposed by Pea (1993) as being integral to the constructive process. In an analogous view, Newman, Griffin and Cole (1989) contend that individuals' interpretative construction of knowledge is initially idiosyncratic; however, through social mediation, the construction becomes more congruent and communicable. It is, in part, the close guidance, which Vygotsky (1987) refers to as proximal guidance, that presents a pervasive form of social mediation, which at its most effective can engage the learner in joint problem-solving with the learner being provided with the opportunity to take a key role in the activity when the task permits. It is the individual's construction of knowledge which is progressively realised through these successive turns and actions. Through this process, the individual's knowledge becomes more congruent and communicable. Thus, as Vygotsky would argue, individuals collaboratively construct a common grounding of beliefs, meanings and understandings that they share in activity (Pea, 1993). Through this process of meaning negotiation, individuals appropriate understanding. Although more distal forms of guidance such as observing and listening, provide guidance, they may not be able to provide access to conceptual knowledge which is opaque or hidden. However, it is held that the close guidance of a more 'expert other' (teacher, co-worker, supervisor) can assist with making accessible knowledge which is remote and can also assist the individual's construction of this knowledge being coherent and communicable within a community of practice.

Developing Conceptual Knowledge

Previous workplace learning studies have indicated that, through modelling, guidance, observation and imitation, many procedures and concepts are learnt through participation in everyday work practice. This is because many aspects of the procedures are observable as is the product (Billett, 1992, 1993, 1994). However, increasingly, aspects of vocational practice are becoming opaque and disembedded from practice (Berryman, 1993; Martin and Scribner; 1991). So while there is an enhanced need for learners to access these forms of knowledge, this access may well require the use of particular instructional interventions, as the knowledge may not be readily accessible. [. . .] The selected strategies were: (i) questioning dialogues, (ii) analogies, and (iii) diagrams. These three strategies employ a common process of getting the 'learner' to provide the responses rather than the 'expert other', who acts solely as a guide. Moreover, having provided a response, the learner is then asked to clarify and explore the limits of their propositional base.

This has the effect of getting the learner to 'do the work' and construct knowledge with the 'expert other' assisting the shaping of that knowledge. [. . .]

Questioning Dialogues

Questioning dialogues comprise three phases with the learner being pressed by the 'expert other' into providing an explanation, clarification of the explanation and a response to probing questions about issues that arise from their clarification. The process is as follows:

- the learner constructs an explanation in their own words (explanation);
- clarifying that explanation (clarification); and
- exploring possible contradiction in initial conceptions (probe).

The three stages of questioning dialogues are depicted in Figure 20.1.

explanation →	clarification →	probe

Figure 20.1   *Questioning Dialogue: Stages*

Analogies

Analogies are used to assist understanding by using a situation or circumstance that occurs outside of the restaurant as a basis for illustrating something that happens in the restaurant. This permits something which is understood outside of the workplace to be used to illuminate something within it – hence moving from the known to the unknown. This approach simply utilises the learners' existing knowledge to develop new knowledge. The proposed process is to use an analogy, indicate the similarities between the analogy and what it is describing and then also indicate the differences. The process for using analogies is as follows:

- analogy (busy service time is like rush hour)
- similarity (so it's very busy and the demand is very high – maximise trips to kitchen, do those things you can beforehand); and
- difference (you have to stay calm and keep it all flowing).

The analogy process is depicted in Figure 20.2

'Expert other' presents the analogy →	describes the similarities and differences

Figure 20.2   *Analogy Process*

Diagrams

Diagrams are used to access knowledge which is difficult to secure in the workplace. The same approach of explanation, clarification and probing is used in this strategy. Again, the learner is pressed to engage in this activity with the 'expert other' providing guidance The process is as follows:

- draw it (explanation);
- why? (clarification); and
- what if? (probe)

This process is depicted in Figure 20.3.

| explanation → | clarification → | probe |

Figure 20.3   *Diagrams: Stages*

It is the three aforementioned strategies which were appraised in the empirical work which is discussed in the next section.

Method

The research method involved determining areas of conceptual knowledge that may be difficult to access through engagement in everyday work practice, identifying strategies likely to assist with accessing and developing that knowledge, trialling those strategies over a three-month period, and determining the degree of cognitive change which occurs during that period and which strategies played a role in that development. The area of small hospitality business was selected as part of a larger study. The methodology involved seven phases, as follows:

Phase 1:   Identify areas of understanding for small hospitality businesses;
Phase 2:   Secure sites;
Phase 3:   Select appropriate strategies;
Phase 4:   Train the supervisors in strategy use;
Phase 5:   Pre and post-test the subjects (trainees) at sites;
Phase 6:   Monitor use of strategies over three-month period; and
Phase 7:   Analyse data.

In the next section these phases are described.

Phase 1: Identify Areas of Understanding for Small Hospitality Businesses

An initial sub-investigation, using interviews and observations, was conducted at one small business hospitality site to identify concepts that underpinned the skills of an effective food service worker. In addition, this activity also sought to delineate those concepts which were difficult to acquire through everyday participation. From the data, two areas were identified to be the focus of conceptual development: work practice and customer service. These areas became the focus for the investigation at the three sites. To supplement the data gathered in this phase, syllabus documents from a food service course (ACTRAC, 1995) were examined to secure concepts associated with the two key areas. Subsequently these concepts were included in pre and post-test concept map exercises as a means of assessing cognitive change.

Phase 2: Secure Sites

An exhaustive search and interludes of negotiation and reassurance resulted in the securing of three small business hospitality sites. These sites comprised cafes and restaurants. Reluctance to participate in the research activity was an impediment. For some small businesses, reluctance was associated with cost and disruption to work. Despite offers to remunerate workers for their time and negotiated times when interviews would occur, there was a marked reluctance to participate. Ten subjects participated in the study. They were food service assistants guided by more 'expert others' (supervisors) who trialled the strategies with the subjects. Of the 10 subjects, three did not complete the three-month period of the investigation at the setting. So, the overall number of sites was less than intended and the number of subjects at those sites was also reduced, despite strenuous and accommodatory efforts on the part of the researchers.

Phase 3: Select Appropriate Strategies

A literature review identified instructional strategies that were likely to generate conceptual change. The most useful sources were science and maths education which yielded a number of useful approaches to encouraging conceptual change (for example, LeFevre, Greenham and Waheed, 1993; Pea, 1993; Smith, Theron and Anderson, 1993). These approaches provided a basis for considering selection as well as identifying potential strategies. As stated previously the key criteria for strategy selection were associated with (i) a focus on generating conceptual change in subjects, and (ii) their utility for application in workplaces as part of everyday work practice. Ultimately, it was Pea's (1993) contribution that provided the theoretical and practical platform and strategy selection appropriate for this study. The three strategies identified in this review are those described previously. The identified strategies are sympathetic to current theorising about the constructive nature of knowledge acquisition and the role of social mediation in that construction.

Phase 4: Train the Supervisor in Strategy Use

The use of strategies by 'expert others' (supervisors) to enhance the proximal guidance provided to the subjects (food service assistants) is central to the study. Hence, it was necessary to prepare the supervisors for their role. This preparation took the form of a half-day training session, during which the supervisors were informed of the aims of the study and its significance. Next, they were introduced to the three strategies and were able to observe and participate in these strategies being modelled. Supervisors were also supplied with a resource booklet which detailed the strategies and their use. Following this, they 'brainstormed' situations where these strategies might be usefully applied in their practice. As part of the support and guidance provided by the researchers, arrangements were also made by the research assistants to maintain contact and monitor the supervisors' use of the strategies.

Phase 5: Pre and Post-Test the Subjects (Trainees) at Sites

To identify conceptual change over the three-month period, a process of pre and post-testing was adopted, employing concept maps which used two identical set of concepts. The two sets of concepts related to the areas of customer service and work practice. Approximately 22 concepts were used for each area of occupational activity. Concept-mapping involves the use of words in the form of labels (propositions) which subjects arrange to portray their ideational structures and propositional linkages (Novak and Musonda, 1991; [. . .]). In appraising the use of concept maps, Novak (1990) emphasises the uniqueness of individuals' experiences leading to unique sets of propositions, with all concepts being to some extent idiosyncratic. However, Novak also argues that if, in a given culture, there is sufficient commonality in experience, individuals will share sufficient common meanings for concepts and therefore can communicate ideas to one another using language and other symbols. For these reasons, this method of inquiry is appropriate in eliciting data about changes in conceptual knowledge over the three-month period.

Concept maps permitted each subject to depict their conceptual organisation in customer service and work practice. The subjects were asked to place pre-prepared adhesive labels, with concepts printed on them, onto pieces of A3 paper and then make linkages amongst the concepts to indicate the interconnectedness of their conceptual base. From these originals, copies of maps were generated, using a graphics program. This process was undertaken as the strategy use was commencing at the sites and then after a three-month period as a post-test measure. In addition, the subjects and supervisors were interviewed about their perceptions of the efficacy of the strategies and the frequency with which they were used in the workplace (daily-weekly-monthly).

Phase 6: Monitor Use of Strategies

Throughout the three-month period, contact was maintained with the sites by telephone. [. . .]

Phase 7: Analyse Data

The procedures for the analysis of the data on concept maps and strategy use were undertaken as follows.

Concept maps

The concept maps were analysed to identify organisational hierarchy and interlinkages. In addition, measures about the inclusiveness of the maps, the number of linkages and isolated concepts were included. The concept maps were analysed through an examination of the organisational structure of the subjects' representation of their conceptual knowledge of the area of food service (customer service/work practice). To do this, each concept label was allocated a number and an array of these numbers was generated using tables which provided an account of the hierarchical organisation of the concepts. This depiction was undertaken for each concept map. In addition, the number of concepts included in the maps was counted as was the quantum of links amongst concepts and the number of isolated concepts, that is, those left outside of the conceptual structures. This process was undertaken for both the subjects' pre and post-test concept maps. Comparisons were then made between the pre and post-test maps. It was anticipated that if conceptual development had occurred:

i   the hierarchical arrangements were likely to become more organised (possibly around salient concepts);
ii   the number of concepts used in the maps would increase,
iii the linkages amongst concepts would increase; and
iv   the number of concepts isolated from the conceptual structure would decrease.

These would be indicative of the strengthening of conceptual structures through organisation and interlinkages. The comparison between the pre and post-concept maps are aggregated in Table 20.1.

Strategy use

The data on frequency of strategy use were collated [. . .] used to indicate the claims of how the strategies were used by the supervisors and also the perceptions of the subjects on frequency and utility. Moreover; data were gathered about why particular strategies were favoured by particular supervisors. Whereas the former analysis was used to determine the degree of conceptual change that had occurred over the three-month period, the second analysis contributed to a further deliberation associated with

Table 20.1 *Changes in organisational, hierarchical, inclusion, linkages and isolation in subjects' conceptual structures (Billet and Rose, 1996)*

subjects	Concept Maps (difference pre & post-test)		Inclusion Of Concepts (difference pre & post-test)		Linkages Amongst Concepts (difference pre & post-test)		Isolated Concepts (difference pre & post-test)	
	work practice	custom service	work practice	custom service	work practice	custom service	work practice	custom service
B2 (novice	improved hierarchy & organisation	improved organisation	+2	+8	+1	0	0	0
B3 (exp novice)	improved interlinks & organisation	improved interlinks & organisation	+1	+4	+18	+5	0	0
B4 (novice	no discernible improvement	improved organisation under key concepts	0	+3	n/a	+3	0	0
M1 (novice)	improved organisation of concepts	more detail incorporated into procedure	0	−1	+1	−1	0	−1
W1 (novice)	no discernible improvement	more associations in conceptual structure	0	0	n/a	n/a	0	+16
W3 (novice 12mth)	improvement in hierarchy & organisation	improved organisation of procedure	+1	0	+9	−2	+9	0
W4 (novice 6 mth)	improved organisation	improved organisation & hierarchy	+1	+3	+7	+10	+5	+2

making deductions about the linkages between strategy use and evidence of conceptual change.

Analyses of Findings

[. . .] As only seven subjects completed both the pre- and post-testing phases of the investigation and engaged in the final interviews, the strength of the study's findings is limited. [. . .]

Over the three-month period, there is evidence that the subjects' organisation of conceptual knowledge became more interlinked, inclusive and hierarchically organised. The question which remains most elusive is the degree to which the use of the three strategies contributed to this change. What is advanced below is that there is some evidence which links the development of conceptual knowledge to frequency of strategy use. Moreover, strategy preference (for example, analogies easier to use, or questioning dialogues useful but more difficult to use) by supervisors and subjects varied, influencing the nature of the activities experienced by the subjects.

Concept Maps

The pre and post-testing activities provided data through the subjects constructing two concept maps in each phase (Table 20.1). The data were analysed in terms of the (i) organisational and hierarchical changes occurring over the three-month period between the pre and post-testing; (ii) inclusion of concepts in the concept maps, (iii) quantum of linkages in the maps; and (iv) number of concepts isolated in terms of organisational structure. The data depicted in Table 20.1, moving from the lefthand side, refer initially to subjects and then, in the next two columns, to differences in the organisational structure within the concept maps, when comparing the pre and post-tests of the customer service and work practice concept maps. [. . .] From the descriptive measures adopted [. . .] there is evidence that between the pre and post-tests there have been changes to the subjects' conceptual structures. Given that these changes reflected increased organisational and hierarchical structures, it is postulated that the development in terms of increases in linkages and organisation could be associated with conceptual change.

The degree of change was not uniform. In the next two columns of Table 20.1, the differences between the numbers of concepts actually used in the concept maps between the pre and post-tests are reported. Overall, there is a positive increase in inclusion. This is reported more in setting B by B2 and B3. One subject, M1, had one less concept included in her customer service concept map. However, the inclusion of concepts between the pre and post-tests increased. The only exception was subject W1, whose participation in the concept maps was reported as being so conducted with a degree of disinterest and lack of engagement that the value of any judgements about differences between pre and post-tests is suspect. The other subject who appeared to make limited change was Ml. As discussed below, there are doubts about whether the strategies were ever used in this setting. Thus quite unintentionally, M1 could be viewed as a comparative sample, albeit of one.

The next two columns report changes in the quantum of linkages within the pre and post-test concept maps. There are quite significant increases in the quantum of linkages reported, particularly at settings B and W. The increase is stronger for work practice than customer service. It was anticipated that concepts associated with work practice would be more hidden or remote than customer service, with the latter being more deeply embedded in daily discourse and everyday work activities. In the final column of Table 20.1, the decrease in the number of isolated concepts is reported with most of the subjects who were in a position to increase the integration of their concepts achieving that, with the exception of M1. Although the most noticeable increase was from W1, this needs to be treated with caution, given the limited linkages made in the pre-test map. Overall, experienced novices (B3/W3/W4) appeared to realise greater change than their more novice counterparts. Furthermore, the development in settings B and W seems to be more marked than from setting M.

Strategy Use

[. . .] At setting W, all strategies were reported being used at least weekly by the supervisor. A preference for the use of analogies was confirmed by the subjects at W. At setting B, questioning dialogues were favoured by the supervisor, diagrams not used and analogies used infrequently. However; there were differences between the perceptions of the supervisor and those of the subjects about strategy use. Of the experienced novices whose conceptual structures had apparently experienced substantial change, B3 claimed to be unaware of strategy use. At setting M, although it was claimed that the three strategies were used daily, there was evidence to suggest this was not the case, because, amongst other issues, the supervisor was often absent. It was concluded that at this site there had been no systematic attempt to use the strategies.

So, in summary, at setting W there was a preference for analogies, at setting B for questioning dialogues and at setting M there was evidence that the strategies had not been used. Data on strategy use appeared to indicate that the determinants were: (i) ease of use by supervisor (ability to be able to use strategy),and (ii) ability to integrate strategy use into daily activities.

Integrating the Findings

Overall, there was evidence of development of conceptual knowledge with the exception of M1. However, there is no direct evidence for correlation between specific strategy use and conceptual change. Closer analysis of the data presented in Table 20.1, to identify relationships between the different patterns of development reported at each site and the different usage at these sites, indicates that it is possible to postulate further tentative findings. At both settings B and W, there is an increased reported linkage between concepts associated with work practice. As stated above, the concepts about work practice were included to provide a set of concepts which were likely to be more opaque than those associated with customer service. There is some patterning, which suggests that increases in linkages amongst these more opaque concepts occurred in those settings where the strategies where utilised. More specifically, given the different use of strategies in settings B and M there is some evidence of different areas of development that the strategies might be more effective in developing different forms of conceptual knowledge. For example, at W, where analogies were used extensively, the number of isolated concepts was reduced. Conversely at B, where questioning dialogues were used, the inclusion of concepts associated with customer service increased more than at W. These findings suggest tentative linkages between particular strategy use and the types of conceptual change that occur as a result of those changes. All of these claims would need to be tested further.

Conclusion

The change of subjects' conceptual knowledge through accessing particular strategies used within proximal guidance has been examined in this study. Overall, there was evidence of conceptual development among the subjects. In the setting where the proximal guidance and strategy use was the weakest, there was the lowest indication of conceptual change. In the other settings, there were different patterns of changes evident in the data and there were reported different strategy uses. Strategy use was associated with individual preference and utility in everyday practice. Yet the study's findings are limited by the reduced numbers of settings and subjects. Also, it seems that the use of diagrams was not conducive for use in this occupational context.

The findings support views about the importance of proximal guidance in the construction of knowledge and they support views which suggest that strategy use may well enhance the development of conceptual knowledge that is opaque or hidden. The findings provide indications that the methodology has promise for further use and refinement. Further work is warranted to extend the approach taken in this study to examine how proximal guidance can be used to make conceptual knowledge which is hidden more accessible. There is also the basis for these strategies to be used in everyday social practice, given the preference and preparation of the users. In addition, the use of strategies provides consideration of a self-regulated tool for use by teachers and students alike in educational settings to access and develop conceptual knowledge. [. . .]

Note

This article is a shortened version of the chapter 'Developing conceptual knowledge in the workplace' in Stevenson, J.C. (ed.) (1996). *Learning in the workplace: hospitality and tourism.* Brisbane: Centre for Skill Formation Research and Development, Griffith University.

References

Australian Committee on Training Curriculum (ACTRAC) (1995) *Restaurant Service BFB 3.*

Anderson, J.R. (1982) Acquisition of cognitive skill, *Psychological Review*, 89(4), pp. 369–406.

Anderson, J.R. (1993) Problem solving and learning, *American Psychologist*, 48(1), pp. 35–44.

Berryman, S. (1993) Learning for the workplace, *Review of Research in Education*, pp. 343–401.

Billett, S. (1992) Authenticating learning – learning in the workplace. Paper presented at the 1992 AARE and NZARE Joint Conference 'Educational research: discipline and diversity', Deakin University, Geelong, 22–26 November.

Billett, S. (1993) Authenticity and a culture of practice, *Australian and New Zealand Journal of Vocational Education and Research*, 2(1), pp. 1–29.

Billett, S. (1994) Situated learning – a workplace experience, *Australian Journal of Adult and Community Education*, 34(2), pp. 112–130.

Billett, S.R. (1995) Structuring knowledge through authentic activities. Unpublished PhD thesis. Faculty of Education, Griffith University, Nathan, Queensland.

Chi, M.T.H., Feltovich, P.J. and Glaser R. (1981) Categorisation and representation of physics problems by experts and novices, *Cognitive Science*, 5, pp. 121–152.

Collins, A.M. and Quillian, M.R. (1969) Retrieval time from semantic memory and language comprehension, *Journal of Verbal Learning and Verbal Behaviour*, 8, pp. 240–247.

Evans, G. (1991) Lesson cognitive demands and student processing in upper secondary mathematics, in Evans, G. (ed.), *Learning and Teaching Cognitive Skills* Melbourne Australian Council for Educational Research.

Gott, S. (1989) Apprenticeship instruction for real-world tasks: the co-ordination of procedures, mental models and strategies, in Rothhopf; E.Z. (ed.) *Review of Research in Education* Washington, DC, American Educational Research Association.

Greeno, J.G. (1989) Situations, mental models and generative knowledge, in Klahr, D. and Kotovsky, K. (ed.), *Complex Information Processing: the Impact of Herbert A. Simon.* Hillsdale, New Jersey: Erlbaum Associates.

Groen, G.J. and Patel, P. (1988) The relationship between comprehension and reasoning in medical expertise, in Chi, M.T.H., Glaser, R. and Farr, R., *The Nature of Expertise*, New York: Erlbaum Associates.

LeFevre, J-A., Greenham, S.L. and Waheed, N. (1993) The development of procedural and conceptual knowledge in computational estimation, *Cognition and Instruction*, 11(2), pp. 95–132.

Newman, D., Griffin, P. and Cole, M. (1989) *The Construction Zone: Working for Cognitive Change in Schools.* Cambridge, Cambridge University Press.

Novak, J.D. Concept maps and vee diagrams: two metacognitive tools to facilitate meaningful learning, *Instructional Science*, 19, pp. 29–52.

Novak, J.D. and Musconda, D. (1991) A twelve-year longitudinal study of science concept learning, *American Educational Research Journal*, 28(1), pp. 117–153.

Pea, R. D. (1987) Socialising the knowledge transfer problem, *International Journal of Educational Research*, 11(6), pp. 639–663.

Pea, R. D. (1993) Learning scientific concepts through material and social activities: conversational analysis meets conceptual change, *Educational Psychologist*, 28(3), pp. 177–265.

Prawat, R. S. (1989) Promoting access to knowledge, strategy and dispositions in students: a research synthesis, *Review of Educational Research*, 59(1), pp. 1–41.

Rogoff, B. (1995) Observing sociocultural activity on three planes: participatory appropriation, guided participation, apprenticeship, in Wertsch, J.W., Alvarez, A. and Del Rio, P. (eds.) *Sociocultural Studies of Mind*, Cambridge, Cambridge University Press, pp. 139–164.

Royer, J. M. (1979) Theories of the transfer of learning, *Educational Psychologist*, 14, pp. 53–69.

Scribner, S. (1985) Vygotsky's use of history, in Wertsch, J.V. (ed.). *Culture, Communication and Cognition: Vygotskian Perspectives* Cambridge, Cambridge University Press, pp. 119–145.

Shuell, T. J. (1990) Phases of meaningful learning, *Review of Educational Research*, 60(4), pp. 531–547,

Smith, E.L., Theron, D. and Anderson, C.W (1993) Teaching strategies associated with conceptual change learning in science. *Journal of Research in Science Teaching*, 30(2), pp. 11–126.

Stevenson, J.C. (ed.) (1996) *Learning in the Workplace: Hospitality and Tourism*, Nathan, Queensland, Centre for Skill Formation Research and Development, Griffith University.

von Glasersfeld, E. (1987) Learning as a constructive activity, in Janvier, C. (ed.). *Problems of Representation in the Teaching and Learning of Mathematics.* Hillsdale, NJ, Lawrence Erlbaum.

Vygotsky, L.S. (1987) *Thought and Language* (ed. Kouzulin, A.), Massachusetts, The MIT Press.

Index

abstract entities, transfer of learning 215–16
abstract representations 86
accountability, assessment, Queensland 173
acquisition, problem solving 154, 155–6
activity, mathematical learning 136–7
Adam
  arbitrary demands 10–12
  deficit approach 7–10
  degradation approach 12–19
  social organization of learning 6–7
adults, cognitive development 77–9
affordance-activity view 220–1
Algebraland 246
analogies
  conceptual knowledge 334
  transfer of learning 215
application, problem solving 154–5, 155–6
apprenticeship 83–4
  cognitive development 73
  distinguished from situated learning 84–6
  Germany 207–8
  model of assessment 90–1
  Rogoff's theory 218–20
appropriation, knowledge construction 333
arbitrary demand, learning disabled 10–12
art works, class responses to 324
artificial intelligence, cognition 30
artistic education 109
ARTS PROPEL 108–13
assessment
  alternative approach
    features of 100–3
    objections to 114–15
    sources for 93–100
  contrasting models of 90–1

  in education and physical education 174–9
  musical performance 51
  Project Spectrum 103–8
  shortcomings of 119
  student performance, Australia 172
  systems of 132
  vocational qualifications 191–211
  see also formative assessment; school-based assessment; summative assessment; testing; workplace assessment
Assessment of Performance Unit (APU), gender research 260
associations, conceptual knowledge 331–2
attribution error, musical assessments 51–2
Australia
  standards for student performance 171–2
  see also Queensland
Austria, Schlüsselqualifikationen 210
authentic assessment 174–6, 180–2
Autonomous Learner, The 198

Bauersfeld 138
behaviourism, learning 120
beliefs, and achievement 46–7
Bernstein, B.
  concept of rules 310, 312–13, 315–16
  theory of cultural discontinuity 307
Binet, Alfred, formal testing 91–3
biological theory, of the mind 58–68
Board of Senior Secondary School Studies (BSSSS) 172–3, 179
body
  situated cognition 36–8
  symbol processing 29–31
body-parts counting system 143–4
bootstrapping process 65